SACRAMENTO PUBLIC LIBRARY

a 3 3029 00529 3949

CEN 895.13 H874
1
Huang, Joe   Heroes and villains
C. Hurst, 1973.
3 3029 00529 3949

D0016539

895.13
H874

Huang   1500
    Heroes and villains
in Communist China
                c.1   76

CENTRAL

SACRAMENTO CITY-COUNTY LIBRARY
SACRAMENTO, CALIFORNIA

HEROES AND VILLAINS
IN
COMMUNIST CHINA

HEROES AND VILLAINS IN COMMUNIST CHINA

*The Contemporary Chinese Novel
as a Reflection of Life*

by

JOE C. HUANG

PICA PRESS
New York

Published in the United States of America in 1973 by
PICA PRESS
Distributed by Universe Books
381 Park Avenue South
New York, N.Y. 10016

© 1973 by Joe C. Huang

*All rights reserved. No part of this publication may be
reproduced, stored in a retrieval system, or transmitted,
in any form or by any means, electronic, mechanical, photocopying,
recording, or otherwise, without the prior permission of the
publishers.*

Library of Congress Catalog Card Number: 73-78947
ISBN 0-87663-710-1

Printed in Great Britain

CENTRAL

C. /

CONTENTS

FOREWORD

In the summer of 1967 I spent three months in the Harvard-Yenching Library of Harvard University. Without any specific plan I browsed through documents, newspapers, and journals. It proved to be a frustrating experience; my patience ran out after a few weeks of reading articles loaded with Communist jargon. Then I turned to fiction and was quickly intrigued by the quality of some novels published in the post-Great Leap period. I was particularly impressed by Liu Ch'ing's *The Builders*, which portrays life in the countryside under the socialist system with great lucidity. The novel tells us more about the changing behavior patterns of the peasants, as well as the party policy of launching mutual-aid teams, than any other source.

I returned the following summer with the specific project of analysing four major novels. In each case the author planned to write a multi-volume work of over a million words, but for one reason or another was unable to complete it. Such an ambitious plan suggests that the authors are serious writers, for they would not have undertaken works of an intricate nature, had their goal been merely to fulfill a propaganda assignment. That they were never able to continue their projects indicates a discrepancy between their private observation as novelists and the official demand for novels as a means of reshaping the people's attitudes. The comments on these works over a certain period, ranging from enthusiastic commendation to outright denunciation, point to a similar incongruity between the novelists' vision and the evaluation of their works by party theoreticians according to ideological criteria.

Since novels reflect social realities at given times and under given conditions, the structure, order and conditions in society and interpersonal relations may be inferred. It is possible to reconstruct life in China by focusing on the conduct of characters depicted by novelists. The reconstructed behavior patterns can be further verified against the comments made by literary critics and party theoreticians. Using this method, I discussed four models: heroes, villains, men in the middle, and cadres.

The grant I received in the spring of 1971 from the Joint Committee on Contemporary China of the Social Science Research Council allowed me to continue my research at the East Asian Research Center of Harvard University for a whole year. Since by that time portions of the manuscript had been made public,[1] I decided to change the format of my project from an analysis of characters to a broad study of the Communist system in operation.

It was a spur-of-the-moment decision that had brought me to the Center to study the novels written by authors in mainland China. If on that May morning in 1950 during the Nationalist evacuation of the Choushan archipelago I had chosen to stay behind, I might have written one of the novels myself. It had been my ambition to be a novelist when I was an undergraduate at Taiwan University. As a poor student of literature on an inadequate grant, I had to earn my way through college by selling stories, essays and short novels to newspapers and magazines in Taipei. If my memory is correct, I managed to have something like half a million words published.

The conditions under which I wrote resemble to some extent those under which the novels I studied were written. In both Nationalist and Communist China, I think, a novelist can choose simply not to write at all. If he has to write for one reason or another, he must meet the ideological criteria, pro-Communist in Peking and anti-Communist in Taipei. In all fairness, I must add that in Taipei one can escape into a world of unreality. One can write fiction of the Mandarin Duck and Butterfly School and produce stories of a melodramatic, sentimental nature for quick sale. Although no pre-publication censorship exists, editors will simply reject any serious work which may be construed as contradictory to the regime's anti-Communist policy. Thus political control works in a more subtle way; in order to sell a manuscript to publications, mostly financed or operated by the Kuomintang, one must assume an anti-Communist stance.

There are other forces working to create an anti-Communist climate. When I was in Taipei all works by left-wing authors or by those living in China were prohibited. Russian novels in Chinese translation, including works by classical masters like Tolstoy and Turgenev, were all forbidden. I remember once buying a copy of Webster's *New World Dictionary* at the bookstore of Taiwan University. The salesman would not sell it to me until all the entries about Chinese Communist leaders were blacked out. Whenever a picture of Mao Tse-tung or Chou En-lai appeared on the cover of *Life* or *Newsweek*, it would be stamped *fei* (bandit) by the censorship agency.

---

[1] Joe C. Huang, 'Villains, Victims and Morals in Contemporary Chinese Literature', *The China Quarterly*, No. 46, April/June 1971; and 'Fictional Heroes as Positive Models in Rebuilding Chinese Political Culture', delivered at the 1971 Annual Meeting of the American Political Science Association.

Under this extensive political control, people in Taiwan are thoroughly conditioned to seeing the Chinese Communist revolution as nothing but a successful rebellion against the legitimate rule of the Kuomintang. Works about life in mainland China invariably portray the Communists as ruthless and cold-blooded. One of my favorite themes then was treating Communism as against human nature. In 1957 I remember participating in a literary contest sponsored by the Department of General Political Works of the Ministry of Defense and won the first prize, with a handsome cash award, of the *san-wen* (prose fiction) genre. It was such an easy job to jerk the tears of readers, mostly mainlanders, by appealing to their nostalgia for the motherland to which they were unable to return because of the Communist control. *Motherland* (*Tsu-kuo*) was in fact the title of my 30,000-word work.

Since I came to the United States in 1958, I have been able to study material of Chinese Communist origin. A different cultural environment is conducive to forming a detached attitude, and access to a variety of sources further liberalizes one's outlook. My graduate training as a political scientist prompted me to look upon the Chinese Communist revolution from a new perspective. Finally, my teaching experience at Tougaloo College, a black school surrounded by a white community in Mississippi, led me to revise my views on human nature and revolution still further. I eventually came to realize how simplistic an approach it was to treat the Chinese Communist revolution as contrary to human nature.

In spite of the naive anti-Communist bias of my early work, it is still useful as a source for understanding the social and political reality in Taiwan, whatever its literary merit. By the same token, I am convinced that we can learn a great deal about life in China by exploring Communist novels.

Although I never lived under Communism, I spent my first twenty years on the mainland. Brought up in the countryside, I remember vividly the life-style of Chinese peasants. As a little boy, I often spent days in the houses of my peasant relatives on occasions such as weddings and funerals. Whether they lived in a thatched hut or a small tiled house, it was always dark inside, with rakes, hoes and sickles scattered around. In the front courtyard, fenced in with bamboo sticks, we children vied for space with chickens and ducks. At nightfall neighbors usually came round, and sat talking about planting, livestock, weather, rent and taxes, in the dim light of an oil lamp. As I read Liu Ch'ing's *The Builders* and Hao Jan's *Bright Sunny Days*, I would compare their narratives with my own boyhood impressions, and wonder how I would have told those stories. Inevitably my sympathy goes out to those Chinese authors who have been in trouble because their novels were found incompatible with or detrimental to the goals of the Communist Party.

While the impossibility of checking the accuracy of descriptions in novels is quite obvious, I can, for comparison, refer to the hundreds or thousands of classical novels, novels of the May 4th vintage, popular stories, story-tellers' tales, folk songs, vernacular plays and Peking operas I have read, heard and seen. If my Chinese background makes me sensitive to the nuances of character and the implications of plot development, it may also hamper my objectivity of an analyst. A rigorous analytical framework is therefore crucial, not only to state the methodology and aims of this study, but to guide myself through the research endeavor.

An Analytical Framework

The use of novels as a source of information for understanding Communist China is a hazardous business. While there have been exhaustive efforts to dig into voluminous newspaper stories, Party resolutions, and official documents, and even photographs, punctuation, and syntax considered significant, there has been no serious attempt to give an analytical interpretation of Chinese Communist novels. It appears that China scholars have demurred from using this source on account of its questionable validity. But content analysis of Communist novels can be rewarding if we define our objective precisely.

It is, therefore, appropriate to state at the very beginning what we shall look for in the stories told by Chinese Communist novelists. We shall not try to see Chinese society *per se*, for it is much larger and more complex than what is reflected in the novels. We shall limit ourselves to the exploration of the operation of the Communist system, and since the system operates in the context of Chinese society, we shall try to see how the society reacts and responds to the system. Chinese Communist novels without exception focus on certain phases, aspects, and periods in the course of the revolution. Not a single novel dwells on the private world of an individual. This tradition antedates the Communist literary policy and can be traced to the protest novels of the late Ch'ing period and the mainstream of the new literature of the May 4th Movement. Long before Mao Tse-tung's 'Yenan Forum Talks', novelists and artists had conceived of their role as painters of life in the context of great social and political changes. Literature used as a means of moral teaching has an even more venerable tradition, attributable to Confucius.[2] Further politicization of literature and art

---

[2] For discussion of popular heroes as exemplars of moral principles, see Hellmut Wilhelm, 'From Myth to Myth: The Case of Yüeh Fei's Biography', in Arthur F.

under the Communist system allows us to treat Chinese novels both as literature of human drama and literature of socio-political development. In fact, one cannot discuss Chinese Communist literature without discussing politics and one cannot use novels as a source of socio-political information without touching upon their literary merits. If we accept this premise, it is then possible to reconstruct the revolutionary process through the eyes of novelists. The problem seems to be to distinguish the empirical from the normative component, or more plainly, to distinguish reality from propaganda. It is a totally legitimate question, but unfortunately there can be no answer. A fundamental limitation in the study of China is the impossibility of verification. Which is the more reliable source, short of a direct survey: official documents, newspaper reports, interviews with refugees and defectors, or first-hand eye-witness reports? Would one source be just as plausible or as biased as another? Would a double-check improve accuracy or compound misunderstanding?

Perhaps we do not have to face this complex problem. Novels, though based on real events, must be treated as fiction; plots should never be mistaken for actual occurrences. In order to appreciate how novels can be used as a source for understanding Communist China, we must stress the distinction between the real and the factual. A story may not be factual but can be real. What makes it real is its artistic quality. Here we are confronted with another problem: whether Chinese novels can be viewed as art. There is no denying the element of propaganda in Chinese literature. But the definition of propaganda by the Chinese is remarkably different from what we understand by the term. The Chinese term *hsüan-ch'uan* suggests publicizing and spreading, closer to the Western term mass communication. What has not been seen and accepted is that Chinese Communist literature can also be art. A serious Chinese Communist novelist performs a dual role, as artist as well as propagandist.[3] An astonishingly simple distinction can be drawn between art and propaganda: art moves people while propaganda does not. A Chinese novel moves the reader not because of its propaganda message but because of its artistic presentation of reality through the novelist's private vision. While he has to comply with political reality, he also wants to create. This urge to create forces him to work by

Wright and Denis Twitchett, ed., *Confucian Personalities* (Stanford University Press, 1962), pp. 146–61, Robert Ruhlmann, 'Traditional Heroes in Chinese Popular Fiction', in Arthur F. Wright, ed., *The Confucian Persuasion* (Stanford University Press, 1960), pp. 141–76; and Yuji Muramatsu, 'Some Themes in Chinese Rebel Ideologies', *ibid.*, pp. 241–67.
[3] This point was conceded by T. A. Hsia, a prominent but anti-Communist scholar. See 'Heroes and Hero-Worship in Chinese Communist Fiction', *The China Quarterly*, No. 13, January/March 1963, pp. 114–16.

the observation, absorption and distillation of complex human affairs, which he translates into coherent, logical stories. Even if he is always conscious of ideology, his creative drive often carries him beyond ideological boundaries.

Furthermore, even if fiction is controlled by ideology, such control has its limitations. First of all, stories can be persuasive only when characters are drawn from real life and scenes are recreated from actual events. Many Communist novelists claim that their stories are either founded on data they have gathered or based on personal experience. In that case, social environment asserts itself, however subtly, in the behavior of the characters. There is always something real in fiction — the spirit of a particular age, the mood of a particular situation, the personality of a character, and the logical sequence of events. It is possible, for example, to know America through Mark Twain, Herman Melville and William Faulkner instead of William James, Charles Beard and Charles E. Merriam.

The question of artistic quality in novels leads us to the problem of the criteria used for their selection. Since the establishment of the regime in 1949, until the disruption of normal creative activities in the Cultural Revolution in 1966, the number of novels and novelettes published is unbelievably small, a total of some 120 or an average of seven to eight titles a year.[4] Very few novels have been given serious, analytical treatment in the Western press. A number of the best-known titles, frequency cited or briefly discussed in distinguished but general works[5] about literary trends in Communist China, are included in the

---

[4] My count is partially based on the information supplied in *Wen-i pao*, including (1) Feng Mu and Huang Chao-yen, 'Hsin shih-tai sheng-huo ti hua-chüan — Lioh t'an shih-nien-lai ch'ang-p'ien hsiao-shuo ti feng-shou' (A Panorama of Life in the New Era — A Brief Discussion of the Rich Harvest in Novel Writing in the Last Ten Years), *Wen-i pao*, No. 19/20, 1959, in which the authors compiled a list of 61 titles; (2) Staff Reporter, 'I-chiu-liu-i nien ch'ang-p'ien hsiao-shuo yin-hsiang chi' (Impressions of Novels Published in 1961), *Wen-i pao*, No. 2, 1962, which lists 12 titles; (3) Staff Reporter, 'I-chiu-liu-erh nien ch'ang-p'ien chung-p'ien hsiao-shuo hsün-li' (A Review of Novels and Novelettes Published in 1962), *Wen-i pao*, No. 1, 1963, which counts 21 titles; and (4) Yen Li, 'I-chiu-liu-san nien ti ch'ang-p'ien chung-p'ien hsiao-shuo' (Novels and Novelettes of 1963), *Wen-i pao*, No. 1, 1964, which also lists 21 titles. No such information is available for 1959–60 and after 1963. Among the lists are quite a few overlapping titles which were first reported for their completion of serialization in periodicals and then mentioned again as in book form.

[5] For instance, D. W. Fokkema, *Literary Doctrine in China and Soviet Influence, 1956–1960* (The Hague: Mouton and Co., 1965); Merle Goldman, *Literary Dissent in Communist China* (Harvard University Press, 1967); C. T. Hsia, *A History of Modern Chinese Fiction, 1917–1957* (Yale University Press, 1961); and Tsi-an Hsia, *The Gate of Darkness, Studies of the Leftist Literary Movement in China* (University of Washington Press, 1968).

present study. In addition, several articles dealing with Communist novels are also used for reference.[6] The major source remains Communist journals such as *Wen-i pao* (*Literary Gazette*) and *Wen-hsüeh p'ing-lun* (*Literary Criticism*) where criticisms of recently published novels frequently appeared. Discriminating critics like the critic Mao Tun and the party theoretician Chou Yang evaluated novels primarily on their literary merits.[7] Novels of a purely propagandist nature were largely ignored in their broad assessment of literary achievement.

A definite relationship exists between the quality of a novel and its circulation; invariably, better written novels have a much larger circulation. Although circulation statistics are incomplete, the number of copies printed is stated on the front or back page of each novel. From time to time, reporters and critics also supply circulation figures in their articles. Finally, a few surveys of peasants' reading habits give us a general idea of the popularity of certain novels.

Now we come to my central theme, which is, essentially, to reconstruct the operation of the Communist system under various circumstances, more or less in chronological sequence. The victory of the Chinese Communist revolution is indisputable. In the first two-thirds of this volume, we shall try to examine how the victory was achieved. In the last third, we shall focus on the goals of the socialist revolution and their implementation. All the novels selected are grouped according to their main theme, such as the underground struggle in 'white' areas, guerrilla warfare, and land reform. An effort will be made to trace the course of the revolution from its beginning through various stages to the 1960s. Under each theme, we shall identify Communist goals, analyze the obstacles encountered, and discuss the strategies and tactics employed to overcome them. The specific details described in the novels are fictional, but they can be treated as illustrations of the operation of the system.

One fundamental difference between the Chinese Communist

---

[6] The special issue on Chinese Communist literature, *The China Quarterly*, No. 13, January/March 1963; D. W. Fokkema, 'Chinese Criticism of Humanism: Campaign against the Intellectuals, 1964–65', *The China Quarterly*, April/June 1966, and 'Chinese Literature under the Cultural Revolution', *Literature East and West*, December 1969; C. T. Hsia, 'Literature and Art under Mao Tse-tung', in Frank N. Trager and William Henderson, ed., *Communist China, 1949–69: A Twenty-Year Appraisal* (New York University Press, 1970).

[7] For instance, Chou Yang, 'Wo kuo she-hui-chu-i wen-hsüeh i-shu ti tao-lu' (The Path of Socialist Literature and Art in Our Country), *Wen-i pao*, No. 13/14, 1960, pp. 6–31, and Mao Tun, 'Fan-ying she-hui-chu-i yo-chin ti shih-tai, t'ui-tung she-hui-chu-i ti yo-chin' (Reflect the Age of the Socialist Leap Forward, Promote the Leap Forward of the Socialist Age!), *Jen-min wen-hsüeh*, August 1960, pp. 8–36.

revolution and other revolutionary movements in China is the Communist attempt to reorganize the basis of society as well as to reshape people's conduct. The revolution aimed to seize political power as well as to restructure Chinese society. The two goals are inter-related. Without a change in the social structure the Communist revolution would have no operational basis; without revolutionary struggle no social changes could be effected.

Thus from the very beginning of the armed struggle, the Chinese Communist Party tried to redefine social mores and conventions and to introduce political norms and beliefs. Unless people have developed a faith in a new political system, they will not fight for the destruction of the old order. Revolution also requires personal sacrifice. Unless people believe in the cause of the revolution, they cannot be expected to risk their lives in the struggle.

Therefore, in order to understand the innate strength of the Communist system, we have to study the conduct of the revolutionaries. The characterization of heroes and cadres epitomizes normative values the system attempts to create and conventional values it has retained and refined. Although villains are intended to serve as negative models, there is more leeway in their characterization.[8] Since the negative characters tend to be based on the personal observations of the artist, they are a more reliable guide in reconstructing Chinese behavior patterns. Finally, there is the middle character, symbol of ambiguity. He is usually politically uncommitted and has both positive and negative traits for potential change in either direction. The development of the middle character often signifies the metamorphosis of Chinese society as well as the reaction of the masses toward the changing social milieu. The interaction of the four types of character — heroes, cadres, villains, and men in the middle — forms the human drama at any particular stage of the revolution.

The characterization of heroes and cadres is, no doubt, more or less ideologically oriented. The importance of ideology in the success of the Chinese Communist revolution has been generally accepted, as many fat volumes have been written on this subject. But the study of ideology, through the collected works of Mao Tse-tung, resolutions of the Party, and pronouncements of the regime, seems inadequate. Ideology, particularly the efficacy of ideology, cannot be understood by textual

---

[8] Liang Pin, for instance, pointed out, 'The negative characters can be drawn vividly, for the author can paint their face any way he wants.' See 'Man-t'an *Hung-ch'i p'u ti* ch'uang-tso' (Some General Observations on the Creation of *Keep the Red Flag Flying*), *Jen-min wen-hsüeh*, June 1959, p. 23. The same experience was shared by Ou-yang Shan; he complained that 'the positive characters are wooden; only spies are interesting.' Ou-yang Shan's view was disclosed in a wall newspaper written by the Kwangtung chapter of the Chinese Writers Association, according to *Hsing-tao jih-pao* (Hongkong), October 13, 1966.

research. An intellectual exercise of this kind may help clarify the meaning of particular speeches and expressions but does not illuminate the powerful impact of ideology on human behavior as well as on social change. The function of ideology can best be seen in the interaction of the four types of character at particular stages of the revolution. When ideology is translated into the behavior patterns of heroes and cadres who influence other characters, we see the operation of the Communist system.

Once a novelist observes an event and tries to portray it in a creative work, he is governed by the logic of the event. His characterization of a hero or cadre is conditioned by the event he depicts. While the hero's conduct may show the correct ideological orientation during the course of the story, it may be found incompatible with the ideological demands of the period when the novel is in circulation. In other words, ideological criteria may change with time. The behavior of a guerrilla, for instance, may be ideologically appropriate at the time of guerrilla operations, but may be found wanting as a positive model in the age of socialism. Or a novelist may be carried away by his creative drive to portray a hero whose conduct is incompatible with ideological criteria. Or he may deliberately create a hero whose maverick behavior violates ideological standards. All these possibilities open up a second dimension in our study in terms of conflict between the private observation of the artist and the official assessment of party theoreticians.

The conflict between creative writers and party theoreticians deserves no less rigorous analytical treatment. The very existence of the conflict between novelists and critics, both dedicated Communists, shows that life is far more complicated than ideology prescribes. The conflict is an important aspect in our study of the operation of the Communist system. The counter-ideology element in novels appears as a result of natural forces in Chinese culture, which cannot be controlled by ideology, rather than through a deliberate decision by the author. A study of this conflict will show the contradiction between art and ideology as well as the perpetual strain and tension between reality and ideology.

The interaction between the three entities — life, art and ideology — forms the focus of this study. The novels to be discussed tell the story of the Communist revolution at various stages as seen through the eyes of the novelists and told in a number of episodes. By a careful selection of episodes and quotations, we try to retell the stories in a coherent, systematic manner and place them in perspective so that the reconstruction approximates to the reality. As a secondary theme, we shall treat commentaries in the Chinese press as evidence to reinforce our thesis. If a conflict develops between the artistic work and ideological appraisal of the work, an analysis of this conflict will further illuminate the operation of the system and help define the reality more sharply.

ACKNOWLEDGEMENTS

In the preparation of this volume, I received help, encouragement and counsel from Professor Ezra F. Vogel, associate director of the East Asian Research Center, Harvard University. From the start of my research, Ezra has given me his generous support. He arranged for the facilities at the Center to be made available to me. As he is equally at home in Chinese, he read several of the novels himself and discussed their content with me. I am deeply indebted to Ezra without whose assistance and advice this book could not have been written.

At the Center I was privileged to sit in the seminar 'Chinese Social History through Popular Literature' offered jointly by Professors Patrick D. Hanan, Benjamin I. Schwartz, Ezra F. Vogel, Ying-shih Yü, and Alexander B. Woodside. It was attended by an approximately equal number of visiting faculty members and a dozen graduate students. Because of the diversity of academic backgrounds of the seminar participants, discussions were always rich and lively. The perspectives and insights of the participants about Chinese literature and society were of great value to me.

Professors John K. Fairbank, Roy M. Hofheinz, and Merle Goldman read portions of the first draft and offered helpful criticism. At an earlier stage I discussed the project with Professors C. T. Hsia of Columbia University and James W. Loewen, my former colleague at Tougaloo College, and received valuable suggestions. In the process of writing and revising the manuscript, I had many opportunities to exchange views about the latest developments in China with my good friends Ross G. Terrill, Bernie M. Frolic and Paul Pickowicz who have recently returned from trips to China. Although many people, mentioned and unmentioned, have contributed ideas, I am solely responsible for the views and interpretations expressed in this book.

My effort in writing this volume was partially inspired by the writings of the late Professor T. A. Hsia. I fondly remember the many hours I spent talking with him when I was a student at Taiwan University some twenty years ago. Nevertheless, for those who are familiar with Professor Hsia's works, it is clear that my assessment of Chinese Communist novels differs significantly from his.

xvii

The research for this book was assisted by a grant awarded by the Joint Committee on Contemporary China of the Social Science Research Council and the American Council of Learned Societies. Finally, I would like to extend my appreciation to Dr. Eugene Wu and the staff for all the conveniences allowed me in using the Harvard-Yenching Library.

J. C. H.

Westboro, Massachusetts
August 1972

1

THE FORMATIVE YEARS–THE CITY

Before the Long Marchers reached the remote, barren city of Yenan, the Chinese Communists had spent a decade in fruitless urban struggle. The period from 1921 to 1932[1] is marked by frustrations, setbacks and debacles in the history of the Communist urban revolution. From the literary point of view the era offers ample opportunities for stories of heroic martyrdom and revolutionary saga. Literature is by nature and tradition a medium uniquely fit for singing the swan song of fallen heroes. When literature becomes institutionalized to serve the interests of the masses and to articulate the policies of the government, it loses that element of pathos. It then begins to perform the same kind of function as government papers, expounding programs and seeking public support for them. Only by identifying with the weak and the oppressed can a novelist appeal to the latent yet potentially explosive power of his readers' psyche and evoke their sympathy and compassion.

Tragedies abounded in those early years when workers on strike, patriotic students, idealistic professors, and liberated women fought with their bare hands against warlords' soldiers and foreign police. But Chinese Communist novelists tell us almost nothing about the urban movement. Chinese cities, the hotbed of revolution, witnessed the marches, protests and demonstrations of a restive generation. In Peking the May 4th movement took place in 1919 and fomented the growth of Communism. In Shanghai the Chinese Communist Party was born in 1921 and the tragic slaughter of workers on strike occurred in 1925. In Canton workers suffered the agony of the Canton-Hongkong Strike and the Shakee Massacre in 1925 and experienced the uncertainty of a brief Communist uprising in 1927. These are merely a few of the best known revolutionary outbursts, all short-lived, spectacular yet ephemeral. These events, rich, colorful and exciting, are all there for literary

[1] In 1932 the Politburo of the Chinese Communist Party was moved from Shanghai to Kiangsi, and the party-led urban struggle virtually came to a complete halt. See 'Appendix: Resolutions on Certain Questions in the History of Our Party' (adopted on April 20, 1945 by the Enlarged Seventh Plenary Session of the Sixth Central Committee of the Communist Party of China), *Selected Works of Mao Tse-tung*, Vol. III (Peking: Foreign Languages Press, 1965), p. 200.

exploration, but they lie wasted, unnoticed under the heavy dust of history.

Very few Chinese novelists have undertaken to elucidate the failure in the Communist urban struggle. Ideological restrictions are a factor, although a description of the failure of the urban movement would support Mao Tse-tung's theory of peasant revolution and reinforce his repudiation of the 'erroneous lines' of Ch'en Tu-hsiu, Li Li-san, and Wang Ming. Apart from ideological considerations, most Communist authors who have been cut off from an urban environment for more than two decades are unable to tackle the complex problems of urban life. Ou-yang Shan's *Three Family Lane* and its sequel *Bitter Struggle*,[2] one of the only two novels which describe cities during the formative years of the Communist movement, will be analysed here. The other novel, *Seeds of Flame* by Ai Ming-chih, will be discussed in a later chapter, when we consider the role of workers in the Communist revolution.

Ou-yang Shan is by no means a first-rate artist; his characterization lacks depth and his story is a conglomeration of random events. Although his novel is peopled with working-class characters against a city background, he shows a lack of knowledge of the life of workers and offers few clues to the failure of Communist urban strategy. But the work unexpectedly contains some very intriguing elements. The author starts by describing the dreams of a revolutionary generation; he ends with their absorption into the existing system. In his efforts to stick to the reality of the 20s, he turns a revolutionary hero into a petty bourgeois romantic and a Communist underground worker into an inscrutable mystery. At the same time, a number of villains are presented as anti-heroes. Finally, his attempt to show inter-class relations is in effect a repudiation of the party view of class antagonism

---

[2] Ou-yang Shan's *San chia hsiang* (*Three Family Lane*) (Peking: Writers' Publishing House, 1960) is the first of a five-volume novel under the general title of 'A Generation of Noble Spirits'. Two instalments, covering the first fifteen chapters, appear in *Chinese Literature*, Nos. 5 and 6, 1961, pp. 2–71 and 3–68. *K'u tou* (*Bitter Struggle*) (Canton: People Publishing House, 1962) is the second volume. According to the cover blurb of *Three Family Lane*, the other three volumes will be *Chuang-yen yü wu-ch'ih* (*Dignity and Shame*), *Tao Yenan ch'ü* (*Go to Yenan*), and *Ta-ti hui ch'un* (*Spring Returns to Great Earth*). According to a Kwangtung Writers Association *ta-tzu-pao* (wall newspaper) of early October, 1966, the title of Volume III has been changed to *Liu-an hua-ming* (*Willows Dark, Flowers Bright*), see *Hsing-tao jih-pao*, October 13, 1966.

Another *ta-tzu-pao* by Ou-yang Yen-hsin, the author's son, discloses that Ou-yang Shan has finished the third volume and half the fourth volume, and that the first two novels have sold over a million copies. See *Hsing-tao jih-pao*, October 12, 1966. The author has requested limited circulation of *Willows Dark, Flowers Bright* within the Party without success, according to a Kwangtung Writers Association *ta-tzu-pao*, quoted in *Hsing-tao jih-pao*, November 27, 1966.

in pre-Communist China. Although his novel was denounced in 1964 and again during the frantic drive of the Red Guards in the Cultural Revolution, we have no reason to doubt his dedication to the Communist cause. This inconsistency will be explained in our discussion of the Ou-yang Shan affair.

The story of *Three Family Lane* and *Bitter Struggle* centers around the families of the comprador-capitalist Chen Wan-li, the landlord-bureaucrat Ho Ying-yuan, and the blacksmith Chou T'ieh in Three Family Lane. Chen's wife and Chou's wife are sisters; Ho's eldest son later marries Chen's second daughter. The young people of the three families are schoolmates and sworn brothers. Although Ou-yang Shan implicitly suggests that *Three Family Lane* is a contemporary version of *Dream of the Red Chamber*,[3] the novel comes nowhere near the sophistication of the classical masterpiece, with its exquisite description of landscape, penetrating characterization, and intricate plot. But the triangular love-affair between the hero Chou Ping and his cousins is not unlike that between Chia Pao-yu and his two cousins, Black Jade and Precious Clasp. This blatant imitation will provide the key to understanding the author's motives and the political dimension of the novel.

The Fading Dream of a Revolutionary Generation

A seemingly trivial episode symbolizes the reactions of the younger generation of Chinese to the plight of their country. It happens in peaceful Three Family Lane, one summer night in 1921. It is now two years since the May 4th movement. About the same time, some 700 miles north in Shanghai, a number of revolutionary leaders are forming the Chinese Communist Party. That evening, a group of seven or eight young people in exuberant mood fill the quiet lane with their noisy chatter and gay laughter. The eldest of them is twenty-one-year-old Li Ming-kuei, son of a prominent landlord in a nearby county, the only person unrelated to the three families. He is talking to Chang Tzu-hao, another landlord's son, husband of the eldest Chen daughter. Walking beside them is Shou-jen, eldest son of the landlord Ho. A few paces behind are Wen-hsiung, the only son of the comprador Chen, and Chuan, the only daughter of the blacksmith Chou. As liberated young people of the May 4th Movement, they walk boldly arm-in-arm as

[3] Ou-yang Shan, 'T'an *San chia hsiang*' (Talks About *Three Family Lane*), *Yang-ch'eng wan-pao*, December 5, 1959. Chao-yen also points out that *Three Family Lane* reminds him of *Dream of the Red Chamber* in his 'Ke-ming ch'un-chiu ti hsü-ch'ü — hsi tu *San chia hsiang*' (Prelude to a Revolutionary Epic — After Happily Reading *Three Family Lane*), *Wen-i pao*, No. 2, 1960.

though announcing to the world that they are in love. Deliberately lagging behind is another pair of lovers, Wen-t'i, Wen-hsiung's younger sister, and Yung, Chuan's second brother. More reserved, they express their intimacy by occasionally squeezing each other's hands and rubbing shoulders.

The group has just returned from a farewell party for the graduating class at the high school. The five men are now graduates, but the two girls, in their white blouses and black skirts, have yet to complete their education. Standing in front of their houses, the young people in jubilant mood are unwilling to bid each other good-night. Now that textbooks and examinations are a thing of the past, the young men, though still in their spotless white uniform, already sense the pleasure of setting off to conquer the world. In a flamboyant tone, Li Ming-kuei declares that it must be their common resolve to save China. This pronouncement meets with the approval of all the young people, who share a feeling of inexhaustible energy and boundless ambition. Chang Tzu-hao chimes in, pointing out the failure of any positive achievement since the overthrow of the monarchy ten years earlier. Ho Shou-jen pinpoints the corruption of officials as the root of the country's weaknesses. Stepping forward to face the group, now sitting in twos and threes on the stone seats, Chou Yung talks about the Civil War then going on between warlords, the looting by the soldiers, the suffering of the people, and the bankruptcy of Confucian conventions. No sooner has the applause died down than Wen-hsiung declares that with their talents, youth and vigor, they are the new masters of the whole of Canton, the whole of China, and perhaps even of the world.

The conversation soon warms up and turns to the question of how their dear motherland can be saved. The young men are so excited that they loosen their collars and eagerly proffer solutions. Li Ming-kuei stresses the need to destroy the old — the old government, the old society, the old home, even the old individual — in order to build the new. This radical, nihilist view evokes little enthusiasm. Chang Tzu-hao, more practical, proposes support for President Sun Yat-sen, and the unification of China by military force. Considering warlords too powerful to defeat, Ho Shou-jen suggests that their knowledge should be enlisted to serve the state — even the generals would appreciate their talents. Chen Wen-hsiung concedes the importance of these ideas, but regards industry and commerce as the foundation for rebuilding China. All these views are disputed by Chou Yung, who contends that organizing trade unions is the most urgent task.

There are now heated disagreements and arguments. The evening is saved by a suggestion from slim, good-natured Chou Chuan. Saying all the proposals are valuable and important, she suggests that they do something to mark this unforgettable evening. This helps to soothe the men's ruffled feelings and reconcile them. Someone suggests the formation of a permanent study society; another proposes the unbreakable tie of sworn brotherhood, binding them to help each other in their future careers. Finally, the idea of taking an oath is accepted, and one by one they raise their right hands and read aloud the pledge:

> 'We pledge ourselves to help each other in future, to devote our lives to making our motherland rich and strong. We shall never falter in this, as Heaven is our witness!'[4]

This incident, and the written pact which follows, is by no means superfluous narrative. It is typical of the young students whose innocent minds, uncorrupted as yet by material pursuits, longed for opportunities to play a role in the salvation of China, in the aftermath of the May 4th Movement. Although Canton, far away from Peking, did not respond enthusiastically to the student demonstration, the workers' strike and other events in the summer of 1919, it had now been reached by the revolutionary tide, already receding in northern cities. With Peking becoming the prey of warlords, Canton, the cross-roads of international commerce, became the cradle of revolutionary forces. Since 1917 the provisional government headed by Sun Yat-sen had been the center of gravity for many an idealistic young man. Very soon the united front between the Kuomintang and the Communists was to usher in a period of cultural bloom which, though transient, posed a challenge to the old conventions.

'Cultural renaissance', a slogan coined by Hu Shih and Ch'en Tu-hsiu in 1917, now finds a new social laboratory in Canton. Epitomizing this radical challenge to the Confucian tradition is a vernacular stage play *The Bride of Chiao Chung-ching.*[5] It is the story of a young litteratus who is torn between his filial duty to an unreasonable, domineering mother and his immeasurable love for his beautiful, frail wife. When the convention of matriarchal authority forces a divorce between the young couple, their suicides symbolize the triumph of love as well as a protest against arranged marriage. This Chinese version of Romeo and Juliet, which seems as mild as it is sentimental today, made many weep in the revolutionary '20s. When the play is performed in a high school in Canton, the attendance by the old and the young, compradors' daughters and factory workers, signals another social change in terms of equality between the sexes as well as between classes.

Changes occur not only in styles, fashions and literary expression but also in social customs. In *Three Family Lane*, the marriage between

---

[4] *Three Family Lane*, p. 73, *Chinese Literature*, No. 5, 1961, p. 71.
[5] The Chinese title of the play is *K'ung-ch'üeh tung-nan fei*, literally, *The Peacock Flies Southeast*. The vernacular play is derived from an old long poem of unknown authorship.

Chen Wen-hsiung and Chou Chuan, given an important place in the story, has many meanings. The marriage between a comprador's son and a blacksmith's daughter defies the ideological notion of class antagonism. Then, as first cousins, they contravene the social taboo on marriage between close relatives. Finally, the happy dénouement for this pair of modern lovers almost vindicates the tragic protest of Chiao Chung-ching and his pretty wife. The wedding ceremony is held in a luxurious restaurant. Instead of the traditional bridal chair, the bride rides in a car, decorated with red silk ribbons, accompanied by a band. The bridegroom wears a black tailcoat, top hat and white gloves. They exchange compliments in English, to the envy of the fasionable guests. The trend towards Westernization since the days of Li Hung-chang is clearly reflected in this 'civilized' wedding.

The spirit of the May 4th Movement, however, finds its true expression in the union between Chou Yung and Chen Wen-t'i, brother and sister of this fashionable pair. Although the wealthy comprador Chen approves of Chuan's marriage into his family, he is strongly against his daughter's becoming the daughter-in-law of a blacksmith. For the liberated young couple, his opposition is not an insurmountable obstacle. A more worldly problem is Yung's inability to afford a stylish wedding.[6] In the end, without the blessing of the parents on either side, he and Wen-t'i simply decide to take a honeymoon trip to Shanghai. As true rebels of the new era, with love as their best pledge, they find no need for ritual, witnesses, and wedding cake.

But the bold talk and brave deeds of this group of young people soon turn out to be mere frivolities of youth. When they are confronted with the realities of life, they quickly capitulate to the seduction of material gain. It is essentially young men like these who lead the Communist revolution in a different social milieu, but Canton seems to be a hostile environment for revolutionary leaders. At first most of them, including Li Ming-kuei, Ho Hsiu-jen and Chen Wen-hsiung, joined the Canton-Hongkong Strike Committee, but before long they secretly try to sabotage the strike. Li Ming-kuei, a self-styled nihilist, soon becomes a cadre in the Kwangtung Kuomintang headquarters. Ho Hsiu-jen, after graduating from the university, is appointed section head in the Bureau of Education of the Canton Municipal Government, and is later promoted to Director of Education in the Nanhai County Government. Chen Wen-hsiung's contribution in the 'settlement' of the strike is duly recognized and rewarded when he is promoted to be assistant manager of a foreign trade firm. His talent as a shrewd businessman helps him to win rapid success, and a few years later he

---

[6] According to the Chinese custom, the male side is responsible for the wedding arrangements.

becomes the manager of a trade company. The most successful of the group, however, is Chang Tzu-hao. After his graduation with the second batch of cadets from the Whampao Military Academy, he is quickly promoted to be commander of a company, then of a battalion, and finally of a regiment. After Chiang Kai-shek's Northern Expeditionary Army takes over Shanghai, he is appointed magistrate of Chapai district in the city.

The only person who fails to get anywhere is Chou Yung, the blacksmith's son. After his brief elopement with Chen Wen-t'i, they soon squander their limited means and perhaps uncertain love. Unable to afford an apartment, they live with their respective parents. Since Yung is the only person to stand by the striking workers through thick and thin, he loses his job as a primary school teacher. Under pressure from both her own father and the Ho family, Wen-t'i soon marries Ho Hsiu-jen. Although Chou Yung seems to have become a Communist, most of the time he is a wanted man on the run. Throughout *Three Family Lane* and *Bitter Struggle* he makes no contribution to the Communist revolution.

In his description of this new generation of the May 4th vintage, the author makes a mild indictment of the young people who betrayed their pledge to save China. It is equally clear where his sympathy lies. Nevertheless, his indictment is unconvincing, since these young men never meant to be Communists, and have entertained different conceptions of the salvation of China. They could argue that what they are doing is for the good of China. To unbiased readers, these young men are pursuing perfectly legitimate personal goals. The non-Communist interpretation would simply be that an urban environment is not conducive to the cultivation of Communists. Unlike China's countryside, where the class system is more rigid and society adamant against change, coastal cities like Canton readily respond to new ideas, adjust to new trends, and absorb talented young people. The Chinese Communist revolution aims to overthrow the established order, but cities like Canton demonstrate a capacity for defusing the revolution, by absorbing potentially revolutionary elements.

A Revolutionary Chia Pao-yu

The hero Ou-yang Shan chooses to epitomize a generation of noble spirits is Chou Ping, brother of Yung, who was too young to take part in the oath-taking ceremony described earlier. Ping's birthright as a blacksmith's son makes him a proletarian only in an ideological sense; in reality he is a contemporary Chia Pao-yu. The scenario of *Three Family Lane* runs parallel, in a much simplified form, to the intricate development of *Dream of the Red Chamber*. As a boy, like Pao-yu, he reveals his unfitness in the eyes of his neighbors. He has tried being an apprentice in a blacksmith's shop and his uncle's shoemaking store, cowherd at the landlord Ho's farm, and later a trainee in another uncle's drugstore — all without success. In all these failures he is the victim either of his honesty or of other people's vicious schemes. These incidents are apparently designed to show that Chou Ping is a rebel against traditional society, where hypocrisy is regarded as a virtue and honesty as stupidity.

The author portrays Ping as irresistibly good-looking, with 'a broad forehead, large eyes and high straight nose'. Like Chia Pao-yu, he simultaneously captures the tender hearts of two female cousins — Ou Tao, the second daughter of his mother's younger sister, and Chen Wen-t'ing, the fourth daughter of his mother's elder sister. Although Ou Tao's father is a shoemaker, this proletarian family background does not prevent her from being slender and beautiful like Black Jade. She is described at various times as 'the dark goddess of mercy', 'the weaving fairy', and 'the queen of *jen-jih*'. Wen-t'ing, the comprador's daughter, is also as good-looking and calculating as Precious Clasp. In the later book, however, the delicate feelings of feminine jealousy, enmity, sympathy and rivalry between the two girls are largely left unexplored.

The tragic ending of the love affair is not unlike that in *Dream of the Red Chamber*. Black Jade, the frail beauty, pines away when she realizes that her love for Pao-yu is merely a dream. She dies a victim of the feudal marriage system, based on an arbitrary and compulsory arrangement by the older generation. The death of Ou Tao is also caused by another evil the Communist revolution attempts to eliminate along with feudalism, namely, imperialism. One June day in 1925, a marching crowd, 100,000 strong, is domonstrating against imperialism in support of the workers' strike in Hongkong. Chou Ping, Ou Tao and the two Chen sisters are among the demonstrators. As they are approaching the Shakee area, which is garrisoned by a platoon of foreign soldiers of unidentified nationality, a low ranking officer gives the order to fire. A massacre is sparked off by accident. Ou Tao, carried forwards by the human wave, finds herself shouting anti-imperialist slogans, and is soon brought down by a bullet.

This is the death of the heroine. Since she is a telephone operator who truly belongs to the ranks of the proletarians, she can be called a martyr. Yet her death is so abrupt, so accidental and so impersonal that it creates no lasting impression on the reader. Ou Tao is cut down in the prime of youth, but it is not clear by whom or for what purpose. The answer 'by imperialism' is only an expression of a concept. It is an ideological explanation that does not satisfy the emotions. Her presence among the protesting workers can be ideologically explained as support for the rights of workmen against imperialist exploitation or even for national independence. But nothing in the narrative explicitly describes the exploitation of workers by imperialists or the humiliation of Chinese by foreigners. In fact, this is the first time Ou Tao and Chou Ping encounter anonymous foreign soldiers.

The death of Ou Tao is presented not only as the climax of the first half of *Three Family Lane* but as the turning-point in Ping's life. He is now determined to dedicate himself to revolution. Revolution, as he understands it, is his personal vengeance for the loss of his girl. When he is asked by a fellow member of a Red Guard platoon (*ch'ih wei tui*) why he has joined the revolution, he answers without hesitation, 'Me? For revenge!'[7] After several years of bitter struggle his understanding of the revolution remains on this level.[8] This view is clearly a heresy, for in Communist theory there is nothing personal in the revolutionary struggle. Even more unforgivable in the view of party theoreticians is the fact that as the hero of a generation of noble spirits, Chou Ping should find courage and conviction from the tender heart of a young woman.[9]

The immediate effect of Ou Tao's death on Chou Ping is similar to that of Black Jade's on Chia Pao-yu. Ping is so completely overwhelmed by grief that he lies broken-hearted in bed for several days. The noisy activities of the strike fail to rouse his attention or interest. As soon as he is able to get up, he wanders outside aimlessly and finally finds himself standing in front of a newly-raised tomb. Inside the small, earthen mound is buried his beloved Ou Tao. He sighs, cries and pours out his sorrows to the silent grave. His behavior is so typical of Pao-yu that there is no question of plagiarism. In his deep anguish, he hears a voice behind him. It is Chen Wen-t'ing, softly persuading him to go home with her. 'Come, let's go home,' she says. 'Cousin Tao has become a spirit, and you're a man of earth. You can't match her. Let's go.'[10] Almost identical words are uttered by Precious Clasp in her attempt to console Pao-yu for the loss of Black Jade.[11]

Chou Ping's love for Ou Tao does not diminish with the passing of time. At the wedding ceremony of his sister and Wen-hsiung, Ping is reminded of his own unhappy love affair. Walking away from the wedding party, he meets a few worker friends and seeks consolation in

[7] *Three Family Lane*, p. 298.
[8] *Bitter Struggle*, pp. 654—5.
[9] Ts'ai K'uei, 'Chou Ping hsing-hsiang chi ch'i-t'a — Kuang-yü *San chia hsiang* ho *k'u tou* ti p'ing-chia wen-t'i' (The image of Chou Ping and Other Problems — Concerning the Evaluation of *Three Family Lane* and *Bitter Struggle*), *Wen-hsüeh p'ing-lun*, No. 2, April 4, 1964, p. 62.
[10] *Three Family Lane*, p. 150.
[11] *Dream of the Red Chamber*, Chapter 109.

drinking at a small restaurant. Drunk and depressed, he recites the first few lines of Pao-yu's poem 'Weeping Over Black Jade's Spirit Tablet'. This is not the only place where there is a direct reference to *Dream of the Red Chamber*. The episode of planting a magnolia tree in memory of Ou Tao on the first anniversary of her death is also just the kind of thing Pao-yu would do. As Ping finishes the planting, with the help of a twelve-year old maid of the Ho family, he says to the tree, 'May you ever be green!' When the girl jokingly asks him why he talks to the tree as though it were a person, Ping suddenly becomes serious. 'Who says it isn't?' he says in earnest. 'She's a person. She left this world a year ago, but she must still be alive. Look at the magnolia, then you'll know. As long as the tree lives she is alive. Can't be wrong.'[12] This sort of talk is typical of the sentimental Pao-yu. When his favorite maid, Bright Cloud, dies, Pao-yu believes that she has become a hibiscus fairy, and recites a poem of lamentation in front of the flower.[13]

This scene is unintentionally witnessed by Chen Wen-t'ing from the second floor porch. She thinks to herself that Chou Ping's emotionalism, so like Pao-yu's, must be the reason why girls fall in love with him.

When she overheard Chou Ping say that there was not a second person like Ou Tao in the whole world, she became unhappy and murmured:

'At best Ou Tao can be a Bright Cloud. What's so marvellous about that? Even if she's not Bright Cloud but Black Jade, so what? In any case, she can't be Precious Clasp. The role of Precious Clasp must be played by me.'[14]

In the end, Ou-yang Shan manages to depart from the dénouement of *Dream of the Red Chamber*. When Chou Ping goes underground as a wanted revolutionary, Wen-t'ing begins to forget about him. Although Ping writes several emotion-charged love letters to entreat her for a rendezvous, she is frightened as well as bored and simply ignores his pleading. As a practical-minded girl, she consents to marry a Kuomintang bureaucrat, at his father and brother's urging. But the love letters expose Ping's whereabouts and lead to the arrest and execution of his eldest brother Chin.

The involvement of Chou Ping in the revolutionary struggle remains peripheral. During the three-day Canton uprising, he serves briefly as a communications orderly for Chang T'ai-lei, takes part in the fight against the intervention of Japanese marines, and later joins in the defense of Kuanyin Shan. When the uprising is suppressed, Chou Ping

[12] *Three Family Lane*, p. 203.
[13] *Dream of the Red Chamber*, Chapter 78.
[14] *Three Family Lane*, p. 204.

escapes arrest through the protection of his influential relatives. He is given a travel allowance to seek refuge at the mansion of the Kuomintang magistrate Chang Tzu-hao, husband of his cousin. When he is tired of life in Shanghai, his cousin recommends him as a teacher in a missionary primary school in Chennan village, not far from Canton.

It is in Chennan village that he resumes his revolutionary activities. When his second cousin and her husband form a land reclamation firm and establish an experimental farm, some of his former worker friends, now out of work, are hired. This gives Ping an opportunity to organize them into a Red Guard unit. This group seems to be a spontaneous organization with no definite political goals, because it has no contact with the party underground. They usually gather at a peasant's house to listen to Ping's talk about current affairs. The description of their activities is as arid as it is meaningless. The author arbitrarily inserts random incidents, in which the Red Guard unit beats up local bullies who try to abuse innocent girls, and steals a shipment of grain to help starving peasants when the village is flooded. These exploits earn them the reputation of 'ten bandits', much to their pride and delight. As a whole, *Bitter Struggle* seems to have no central plot and the random events are strung together without any plan.

Unlike *Three Family Lane*, which exhibits a realistic touch, the story of *Bitter Struggle* is permeated with a quality of unreality. The picture of a teacher of a missionary school, joined by former factory workers in a village, engaging in aimless disruption is utterly absurd. But this very absurdity suggests that a Communist writer, no matter how willing a propagandist, cannot fabricate a convincing story of revolutionary struggle, when the reality clearly rules out such a possibility.[15] At the same time, even in this arbitrary arrangement of events to suit the formula of revolution, the author still has to move the locale of the story to a village. This suggests how totally ineffectual the organizational endeavors of the Communist Party were in urban areas around 1930.

The Mysterious Communist

The author's revisionist approach is reflected in the character not only of the hero but also of the party cadre. The description of a cadre poses a number of problems for a novelist. First, the emphasis on the notion that the people liberate themselves, under the guidance of the Party, often reduces the role of cadres, in many novels, to a supporting

---

[15] The impossibility of Chou Ping's organizing the Red Guard unit in Chennan village, so close to Kuomintang-controlled Canton, is also pointed out by a Communist commentator. See Ts'ai K'uei, *op. cit.*, p. 68.

position. Secondly, since the cadre represents the Party, he must be carefully handled so as not to tarnish the Party's name. Very few human errors are allowed him, because he is supposed to have been 'steeled' in past struggles and to have been reborn as a pure-blooded child of the Party. Finally, unless the part a cadre plays in the story can be logically explained, he will remain a lifeless puppet. It is extremely difficult for a novelist to portray such a character, with such severe restrictions.

In *Three Family Lane* and *Bitter Struggle* Ou-yang Shan treats the cadre character as a mysterious being. Although there are a number of Communists in the novel, who take part in the Canton Uprising, run errands, or are otherwise involved in a variety of organizational activities, most of them have regular jobs as sailors, bus drivers and factory workers. These people are Communists but not professional cadres. The author also briefly describes well-known party leaders such as Chang T'ai-lei, the real leader who died of an assassin's bullet, Tao Chu, later governor of Kwangtung and one of those purged in the Cultural Revolution, and Yeh Chien-ying, who is still prominent in Peking, and a host of others. But these leaders have no bearing on the development of the story and so do not concern us.

The only professional cadre is a man named Chin Tuan, who turns up on four separate occasions. He is a mysterious figure who suddenly shows up without warning and equally suddenly disappears without a trace. The author gives us this profile of him:

> He was a tall man in his thirties from Kiangsu, sallow and skinny, with a square face and high cheekbones. The man had a warm personality and also something mysterious about him.[16]

The author takes only two pages to describe the first appearance of Chin Tuan in a secret meeting with the second of the Chou brothers. Obviously a low-level cadre, he gives Chou Yung a quick assessment of the political situation, instructs him to join a current affairs discussion club, and leaves immediately.

We encounter Chin Tuan for a second time when Canton is briefly taken over by the Communist insurgents. He is among a group of political prisoners released by Chou Ping. Talking casually with other people, he tries to break the fetters with a hammer. When Ping inquires about his health he says, 'My health is always good. The Kuomintang tried to ruin it, but to no avail!' This time he occupies less than a page.

We find him next in Shanghai, arrested by a plainclothes man in a solitary side street. Again the brave, strong Chou Ping overpowers the secret service man and rescues him. After congratulating the hero, Chin

[16] *Three Family Lane*, p. 279.

Tuan attempts to get away in a great hurry. When Ping suggests that they maintain contact, Chin Tuan 'smiled mysteriously and said: "It's hard to say. If you don't see me for a month, I shall probably be in Canton or Peking again. But it doesn't matter. If I don't come to see you, I'll send over somebody else." ' He never does.

Only Chapter 74 is devoted to the activities of the Party. A liaison station is established under cover of a cotton and silk fabrics store; Chin Tuan, now somewhat thinner, his cheekbones more marked, is apparently the man in charge of the operation. The store, however, never functions according to the original plan, and a later reference reveals its closure, due to a swift change of political circumstances.

Altogether the author spends less than ten pages in an 828-page novel on this party functionary, and his treatment of the cadre is almost contemptuous. The man is not only physically unimpressive but also seems ill. He behaves pretentiously, as though he were a cadre of great importance. But twice in his four appearances he is a captive. There is a certain sarcasm in Ou-yang Shan's description of this cadre, which reflects the author's opinion of party functionaries.

It is difficult to see why Ou-yang Shan makes this man mysterious but not omnipotent. One possible explanation is that the author wants to adhere as much as he can to historical accuracy. After the Shanghai massacre of Communists and the failure of the Canton uprising, the Communist revolutionary movement went underground and reached a low ebb in urban areas. But fiction is not history. Since Ou-yang Shan writes about the revolutionary struggle, he should have no difficulty in introducing somebody more capable and less amorphous than Chin Tuan. The author probably has his reasons.

It seems clear that Ou-yang Shan does not want to build up the image of a cadre. Had the author gone to certain lengths in the characterization of Chin Tuan, then this cadre would necessarily have to direct the struggle unfolded in the novel. In that case, the hero Chou Ping would have had less opportunity to make mistakes, not to mention his aimless wandering in Shanghai and Canton and involvement with his rich relatives. The author's main purpose is to describe the three classes — the landlord-bureaucrat, the comprador-capitalist, and the proletarian — and relations between them in the '20s and '30s. In those days, a revolutionary-minded petty bourgeois intellectual could not neatly sever the ties of kingship and friendship. The hero Chou Ping, after the disaster of the Canton uprising, has been trying to make contact with the party underground through most of the story and has still not become a party member by the end of the second volume. The lack of connection with the Party gives the author more freedom in describing the behavior of Chou Ping.

Bitter Struggle ends with Chou Ping waiting in a park for a secret meeting with the mysterious Chin Tuan. He has waited from early morning until dusk, but the man fails to show up. Since Ou-yang Shan has been denounced and will probably never resume his unfinished work, we will never know what might have happened to the hero in the subsequent volumes. But the ending of the story may serve as an important clue. The hero Chou Ping is to fight for the revolutionary cause in his own way, not as an agent of the highly-disciplined party. He will remain his own master, doing things to his own taste, including mistakes and follies.

The way the author treats the only cadre in the novel and his relations with the hero is highly significant. The cadre never tries to cultivate close ties with the hero, nor does he try to train the hero to become a party member. On the other hand, the hero is always trying to make contact with the underground party and has an unshakeable determination to get into the organization. This arrangement allows several interpretations. First, the author may have attempted to show how ineffectual the party's organization was during that particular period. This is probably a fact and the author wants to reflect the reality. Secondly, the author portrays a hero with many faults, but wants the responsibility to rest with the Party. Chou Ping's errors are due to his youth and immaturity, but his youthful eagerness could have been transformed into positive strength if the party cadre had given him a guiding hand. Finally, the author may consider the cadre incidental to the story, and deliberately spent little space on him. That is to say, for the novel to be published at all, the author must assume an ideological stance. Certainly Chin Tuan has little impact on the development of the story. The cadre exists simply to furnish the novel with the essential ideological trappings — its relationship with the Communist revolution is apparent rather than real.

Inter-Class Relationships and the Villains

There is a natural tendency in any ideology to simplify the complexity of reality. The Chinese Communist view of a class society is one of intense class struggle, but Ou-yang Shan, while recognising the existence of classes, minimizes class antagonism. This disregard for the party view of class relationships is consistent with his portrayal of villains. The orthodox treatment of a villain, as one whose behavior can be explained solely on the basis of material motives, is not followed. Early in the story the author does relate some hearsay about the crooked ways in which the two rich families have made large fortunes. The wealth of the Chen family is attributed to opium-smuggling by some people and to a connection with a European merchant by others. In the case of Ho, it is also rumored that his late father made a large sum out of unethical dealings as a prison warden, yet when Ho himself was still in his twenties, he worked as a tax collector and later, in the years of famine, was in charge of relief. Similar stories hinting at immoral practices proliferate in the non-Communist fiction of the May 4th Movement vintage. Ou-yang Shan makes no attempt to describe concrete instances of the methods of exploitation used by the comprador Chen or the landlord Ho, apart from Ho's taking in his wife's niece as human mortgage in lieu of overdue rent. Since the two families are not presented as enemies and exploiters of the people, they never become targets of strikes, demonstrations and armed uprisings in Canton. They are bystanders, watching the revolutionary movement with a certain sympathy and even making small contributions to its cause.

There is no fundamental conflict between the money-making and status-seeking members of the two rich families and the revolutionary-minded Chou brothers. The villains are not ruthless oppressors, nor is the hero Chou Ping an uncompromising revolutionary. In the tangled family relationships, the hero, when still a schoolboy, was cared for and supported by the comprador and the landlord. Later, the Chou brothers are betrayed and their involvement in the revolutionary struggle is made known, but the motive for the betrayal is entirely private and personal. Chen reports the whereabouts of the Chou brothers to the authorities because he wants to prevent Chou Ping from becoming his youngest daughter's lover. Similarly, Ho Hsiu-jen, the landlord's son, informs on them in order to settle a personal account with the second Chou brother, who had earlier eloped with the girl who is now his wife. Feelings of fatherly concern and lover's jealousy are thus presented as stronger than class antagonism.

On the other hand, the hero Chou Ping is not fighting any individuals. Although apparently disgusted with the decadent life of the other families in Three Family Lane, he does not want to destroy them. Determined to eliminate evil social forces, he finds them, in his young mind, elusive and indefinable — his political enemy is the Kuomintang in the abstract. When faced with a real Kuomintang official Chang Tzu-hao, the husband of his cousin, Chou Ping not only fails to fight him but stays for more than a year at his official residence in Shanghai, and tutors his two children. For his part, though well aware of Chou Ping's involvement in the Canton uprising and his persistent aspiration to become a Communist, Chang never seeks to take any action against him, though it is clearly his duty as the Kuomintang magistrate of Chapei district to do so. Family ties are strong enough to allow two men of opposite political beliefs to live under the same roof.

Although Ou-yang Shan may not have been aware of it, the negative characters in *Three Family Lane* and *Bitter Struggle* are villains not according to any ideological yardstick, but simply by conventional social norms. In the traditional social structure, consanguinity serves as the solid, unbreakable foundation upon which other personal relationships are built. In such a schema, a man becomes a villain if he betrays his kinsman, no matter what his justification. He will incur public disgrace if he mistreats his poor relatives, as Ho does when he abuses his teenage niece. Unethical methods of money-making, such as opium-smuggling, swindling and embezzlement are also condemned. In the development of the story, viewed from the ideological perspective, the existence of the villains has no bearing on the revolutionary typhoon then sweeping over south China.

In the absence of a normative theory of villainy, the sociological interpretation of the behavior of negative characters has never been disputed. Many other novelists have done exactly the same. It is Ou-yang Shan's shift from the social to the political aspect of the villains' lives which creates ideological problems. In an attempt to explain the changing attidues of the younger generation in the Ho and Chen families, he attributes them to the influence of the landlord and the comprador. These respectable gentlemen have repeatedly urged their sons and daughters to stay away from the Communist-led workers' strike. Their only hope for deliverance from the Communist riots is the leadership of Chiang Kai-shek. The conversations between the two gentlemen themselves and between them and their youngsters, though realistically constructed, could be disturbing to Communist theoreticians.

At one point, the landlord Ho gives this piece of advice to the comprador Chen: '... There're men of all types among them. Chiang Kai-shek, for instance, is a complicated character. Today he still looks like a leftist. The trouble is, he and Chan-tang[17] are a bit like two tigers on the same mountain; he's too ambitious. If Chan-tang can keep tabs on him, he'll be a useful man.'[18] Elsewhere, Ho admonishes his son Hsiu-jen, then a university student of law and politics, by saying, 'Recently, I observed, Mr. Chiang Kai-shek's ability and leadership yield nothing to Chan-tang and his insight and willpower perhaps surpass the latter's. Even among Peiyang lords you can find few to match him. For the time being, he still has some wild talk, but once he matures, he will no doubt become the pillar in the swift middle stream.'[19] A few minutes later, Ho continues, 'The riots stirred up by the Communists can last for only a few days ... Chiang Kai-shek is a man of shrewd strategy, far-sighted plans, unusual wisdom and great courage ...'[20]

---

[17] Another name for Hu Han-min, then acting marshal in the revolutionary government at Canton.
[18] *Three Family Lane*, p. 134.
[19] *Ibid.*, p. 172.
[20] *Ibid.*, p. 173.

After the Chungshan Warship Incident, Chen again discusses politics with Ho in his living room. When Chen concedes that Chiang Kai-shek has some qualities, Ho says, 'You're wrong. That fellow Chiang just has some qualities? To tell the truth, he's simply outstanding, a man of boundless courage and penetrating insight.'[21]

The landlord Ho's words leave Chen no peace of mind, and he is particularly worried about his children's involvement in the strike. He is not concerned about his son, the smart, elegant Wen-hsiung, in whom he has complete confidence. As a matter of fact, Wen-hsiung has already resigned as a delegate of the striking workers and has been rewarded with the position of assistant manager in a foreign trade firm. It is his second daughter, Wen-t'i, and fourth daughter, Wen-t'ing, whom Chen is deeply concerned for. Some time ago, Wen-t'i, a liberated girl of the May 4th Movement, has defied his authority and eloped with her cousin Chou Yung. Although she has returned after a brief sojourn in Shanghai, she has not completely severed her relationship with the young man.

Then there is Wen-t'ing who is deeply in love with Chou Ping and spends much of her time at the headquarters of the workers on strike. If the comprador does not stop her in time, she may very well follow in her sister's footsteps. That day Chen sternly warns his two rebellious daughters, 'It's not that I want to hurt you. What else can I do? Just think, they call me comprador and want to overthrow me. If it were not for the foresight, guts, and iron grip of Generalissimo Chiang, I might have been struck down myself, who knows? . . .'[22]

Their father's strong language causes the sisters many tears. Actually, the young ladies have already seen the light. Only a few days before, Chou Yung had brought Wen-t'i an issue of the journal *Chung-kuo ch'ing-nien* (*Chinese Youth*) and enthusiastically recommended an article with the title, 'Analysis of the Classes in Chinese Society'. Both sisters have studied the article and are deeply troubled by it. Hiding in a second-floor room, they begin to talk about its contents.

Chen Wen-t'i sighed deeply and cried out: 'Ah, liberty, liberty, how many people have died for you, yet how many more have been fooled!'
Puzzled, Wen-t'ing asked: 'Why? What's wrong with liberty? Isn't it beautiful and noble?'
The elder sister said: 'Yes, who says it isn't? But, it's only a beautiful, noble shadow, an illusion. Anyone who chases this shadow will suffer the ordeal of sorrow. I'm a liberated woman, like a piece of cloth dyed black with no hope of being bleached white. How I envy our sisters, married by an arbitrary arrangement. They live peaceful and happy lives!'

[21] *Ibid.*, p. 189.
[22] *Ibid.*, p. 225.

The younger sister protested: 'How can you say that! You've a job, a lover, and have earned independence and freedom! How many sisters who're still jailed in the prison of the feudal system are looking at you with amazement and admiration and would love to change places with you even for one brief day! Why have you become so vulgar?'

Unperturbed, the elder sister said calmly: 'Vulgar? Yes. I've nothing against this sort of criticism. In the past, if someone had encroached on my sacred freedom and prevented me from associating with men, wouldn't it have been much better? But no one did! Everyone respected my liberty, and now I must suffer!'

Wen-t'ing felt warm, suffocated and frightened, and jumped up from her chair. Fanning herself vigorously, she felt as if the dusk outside the window was pressing in on her, leaving her breathless. Wen-t'i sat there, quiet and motionless, as if all was lost and nothing mattered any more. Suddenly, the younger sister shouted out: 'What is it you're afraid of? Poverty? Gossip? Afraid that you two will become political enemies? Why have you become such a coward?'

The elder sister admitted: 'It's true, quite true. With you, why should I pretend? You know yourself, we've been married for more than six months now, but we haven't even built a home. The financial situation can't be improved overnight. The unusual treatment we've had from society won't suddenly change. But I'm more frightened by the political development. You must realize how cruel and ruthless politics are!'

The younger sister said, full of sympathy: 'Yes! It's the heresy of class struggle which has possessed him. He thinks he has seen the light and goes wild. Who can say, I bet he'll declare *us* his class enemy one day. He'd dare! I bet he will!'

The elder sister wiped away the sweat from her face, and said: 'Yes, of course! That will be the climax of the tragedy. If that Mr. Mao had told us the truth six months earlier, everything would have been entirely different. But now it's too late, too late, too late!'[23]

From the literary point of view, this is a masterly scene, the most exciting in the entire novel. The portrayal of the psychological state of the sisters shows Ou-yang Shan's descriptive power at its best. It is a penetrating analysis of the inner feelings of a woman who has won her freedom by a revolt against family, society and tradition, only to find the taste of freedom full of bitterness. The strugle of Chen Wen-t'i is a struggle of an individual against the values surrounding her. Not only are her family, society and tradition solidly against her, but political struggle now joins in to tear her apart. The strength of the narrative does not lie only in the realistic depiction of Chen Wen-t'i as the victim of the stormy era. Wen-t'i is typical of many Chinese women, who have

[23] *Ibid.*, pp. 212–13.

successfully freed themselves from the oppressive system, only to find themselves naked and helpless. It is the individual's fight against forces larger than life that gives Chen Wen-t'i's story its power.

We can perhaps visualize Ou-yang Shan's own state of mind during this particular stage of the creative process. He could not be so eloquent and persuasive if he were not totally involved in the agony of his heroine. If so, the ideological implication is that at certain moments Ou-yang Shan himself felt some uncertainty about the results of the Communist revolution. Why, he might have asked in spite of himself, is it necessary that so many people should be victims of the revolution? Are they not innocent, helpless people? How much better if things could be changed without bloodshed and suffering! An ambivalent feeling, maybe, but nevertheless genuine and honest.

A party theoretician, however, would react to the story with horror. The author implies that the love-affair between Chen Wen-t'i and Chou Yung ends tragically because of the political struggle between classes led by the Communists, rather than the oppressive system. After all, Chou and Chen have successfully challenged the old system and become husband and wife without waiting for anyone's blessing. It is class antagonism which now forms an insurmountable barrier between them. It is a frightening thought that their incompatibility is created by a political treatise. And its author is Mao Tse-tung!

All that followed was the logical consequence of this. Ou-yang Shan's *Three Family Lane* is a revolutionary novel only in appearance; in substance it is anti-revolutionary. In talking about the class struggle he 'reviles one thing while pointing to another'. It is a favorite trick of intellectuals, who sugar the pill to camouflage their attacks.

The question remains: Is the repudiation of Ou-yang Shan's work justified? The answer must be yes. It is not that Chairman Mao's name has been profaned. There can be no doubt that the name of Mao Tse-tung is mentioned with good intentions. There seems to be no doubt that Ou-yang Shan was and remains a dedicated Communist author. A fundamental problem — a purely impersonal and detached one — is the effect of the novel on its readers. How would the readers react to the constant mention of Chiang Kai-shek and the praises piled on him? Whether the words are said by reactionaries like the landlord Ho and the comprador Chen may make little difference to the average reader, basically lazy and indiscriminate. Might the story evoke nostalgic feelings among the readers? Or worse still, would some of them actually feel after reading the novel that it might be no bad thing if Chiang Kai-shek were to remain in power? Would they sympathize with Chen Wen-t'i or even the comprador Chen, when reminded by them of the fate of some people who have become victims of the revolution? Above all, would the novel ferment doubts in the readers about the cause of the revolution? The answers to these questions are sufficient to place Ou-yang Shan under suspicion of hidden anti-revolutionary motives.

The Ou-yang Shan Affair

Before we discuss the Ou-yang Shan affair, we must first explore his real motives in writing the novel. When *Three Family Lane* was first published it was advertised as the story of the struggle between the revolutionary and counter-revolutionary forces as seen through the lives of a worker's family, a comprador family and a landlord family. They represent the three major classes in Chinese society, and *Three Family Lane* is supposed to be a microcosmic study of the class struggle in the turbulent 1920s.[24] That this is a false claim is clear. What Ou-yang Shan tried to portray is something far more complicated. In order to reflect the people and social environment of that period truthfully, the author chose as the hero of the story a young man whose personality defies categorization. In his own words, Chou Ping

> on the one hand, has the thoughts and feelings of a craftsman, so that in everyday life he is close to workers of all trades and crafts. But he also has the traits of an intellectual, such as his drive for personality liberation and his desire to improve his position through study. Chou Ping is such a man, with these two contradictory forces struggling inside him.[25]

Ou-yang Shan asks the readers to judge for themselves from his behavior which class Chou Ping belongs to, or which is the dominant influence on his personality.

This is an extraordinarily bold proposition, for the author must have known that Communist theory forbids vagueness. The twilight zone is always dangerous ground. Ideology demands black and white dichotomy; a man is either a revolutionary or a counter-revolutionary. As a Yenanite who personally heard Mao deliver 'Talks at the Yenan Forum on Art and Literature,'[26] he should have been aware of this,

[24] See the cover blurb of *Three Family Lane*; also Chao-yen, 'Prelude to a Revolutionary Epic – After Happily Reading *Three Family Lane*', *op. cit.*, p. 5.
[25] Ou-yang Shan, 'Talks About *Three Family Lane*', *op. cit.*
[26] Ou-yang Shan, according to my friend Edward Chan who knows him personally, sat in the front row when Mao delivered his 'Forum Talks'. This is supported by an article which claims that Ou-yang Shan, who had the privilege of taking part in the Yenan rectification campaign personally led by Chairman Mao, was unable to resist the temptations of city life. See Yü Tzu, 'Ou-yang Shan teng jen ti li-tzu cheng-ming liao shih-mo?' (What Have the Examples of Ou-yang Shan *et al.* Shown), *Wen-i pao*, No. 4, February 25, 1952, pp. 10–11.

and probably was. But he was determined to break through ideological restrictions by making a petty bourgeois intellectual the hero of his story. He tried to cover himself by turning *Three Family Lane* into an imitation of *Dream of the Red Chamber*.

The repudiation of Yü P'ing-po, the scholar who worked on *Dream of the Red Chamber*, in 1954, was not a rejection of the classical novel but an attack on Yü's 'bourgeois' method of textual research. The value of the novel was reaffirmed, on the basis of a new, materialistic interpretation. *Dream of the Red Chamber* is said to reflect the unavoidable demise of the feudalistic, beureaucratic landlord class. Both the hero Chia Pao-yu and the heroine Black Jade are viewed as rebels against the feudal family, and their love-affair symbolizes the first protest againt the arbitrary marriage system.[27] This new interpretation has become established since, and has led Ou-yang Shan to assert that *Dream of the Red Chamber* also portrays class struggle.[28]

Ou-yang Shan seems to have reasoned that if *Dream of the Red Chamber* is considered a work of class struggle, *Three Family Lane*, a direct imitation of the same story, cannot possibly be attacked on ideological grounds. But *Dream of the Red Chamber*, a monumental achievement in Chinese literature, has acquired an aura of immortality, which puts it beyond the reach of ideological attack; it does not follow that inferior work by a contemporary novelist will enjoy the same immunity. Ou-yang Shan's ingenious device fails to protect him from the criticism of theoreticians, who are sensitive to any ideological deviance. Thus we find verdicts such as this:

> *Dream of the Red Chamber* takes the side of a rebel against the feudal landlord class in the middle of the eighteenth century. *Three Family Lane* and *Bitter Struggle* take the side of a capitulator to the landlord and comprador capitalist classes in the era of proletarian revolution in the twentieth century.[29]

The interesting aspect of the Ou-yang Shan affair is not his denunciation but the way he was denounced. There have been no comments on the literary quality of *Three Family Lane* and no charges of plagiarism. There has been no mention of the characterization of villains, which, from the ideological viewpoint, warrants a volley of invective. The denunciation focuses almost exclusively on the character-

---

[27] Li Hsi-fan and Lan Ling, 'Kuan-yü *Hung lou meng chien lun* chi ch'i-t'a' (Commentaries on *A Brief Study of Dream of the Red Chamber* and Other Problems), *Wen shih che* (*Literature, History, Philosophy*), No. 9, 1954.

[28] Ou-yang Shan, 'Talks About *Three Family Lane*', *op. cit.*

[29] Shanghai Revolutionary Mass Criticism Group, 'A Reactionary Novel Which Commemorated an Erroneous Line — Comments on Ou-yang Shan's "A Generation of Noble Spirits" ', *Chinese Literature*, No. 3, 1970, p. 102.

ization of Chou Ping as a petty bourgeois intellectual.[30] In a mass
campaign launched in Canton to condemn Ou-yang Shan,[31] the hero's
bourgeois traits also become the target of attack. Workers at Canton
Tractor Factory and Canton Paper Mill refuse to accept Chou Ping as
one of their rank; students at Chungshan University and Canton
Municipal 28th High School express disgust at his love affairs. In
summing up the discussions, the staff reporter Tso P'ing of *Wen-i pao*
concludes that the hero of *Three Family Lane* is a completely
unreformed petty bourgeois, and that Ou-yang Shan has attempted
through this character to spread all kinds of poisonous petty bourgeois
thoughts and feelings.[32]

A synopsis of the discussion of Ou-yang Shan's novel is also
published in *Wen-hsüeh p'ing-lun*.[33] An editorial lists the author's
major errors. First, Chou Ping's attitude toward the revolution
combines the fantasy of a petty bourgeois intellectual and the frantic
pursuit of an ideal. Secondly, the author clearly approves of Chou Ping
and sympathizes with him, instead of reproving him. Thirdly, the novel
distorts the history of the revolution and class struggle during this
particular period. Finally, by emphasizing the physical attraction of the
hero and heroines, the author is subscribing to the aesthetic theory of
the bourgeoisie. According to the aesthetic theory of the proletariat,
the editorial explains, beauty rests not in the outward appearance but
in the spirit — and beauty of the spirit depends on whether a person
possesses the revolutionary ideal and moral character of a proletarian.[34]

---

[30] Ts'ai K'uei, *op. cit.*, p. 64, and Lu I-fan, 'San chia hsiang ho *k'u tou* ti ts'o-wu
ssu-hsiang ch'ing-hsiang — Chien yü Miu Chün-chieh, Lu Tsu-p'in, Chou Hsiu-
ch'iang san t'ung-chih shang-chioh' (The Erroneous Thought Tendency of *Three
Family Lane and Bitter Struggle* — To Consult with Comrades Miu Chün-chieh, Lu
Tsu-p'in and Chou Hsiu-ch'iang), *Wen-hsüeh p'ing-lun*, No. 5, October 14, 1964.
[31] At the time he was under attack, Ou-yang Shan held five different titles and
was virtually the symbol of authority in Canton literary circles. He was
concurrently the deputy director of the Bureau of Culture and Education of
Kwangtung Provincial Government, deputy director of the Department of
Propaganda of Kwangtung Provincial Party Committee, head of the general staff
of Kwangtung Provincial Party Committee, chairman of Kwangtung Provincial
Association of Writers and Artists, and chairman of the Kwangtung chapter of
All-China Writers Association.
[32] Tso P'ing, 'Hsiao-tzu-ch'an-chieh-chi ti tzu-wo piao-hsien — Kuan-yü *San chia
hsiang, K'u tou* ti t'ao-lun tsung-shu' (Self Expression of the Petty Bourgeois — A
Summary Report of Discussions concerning *Three Family Lane* and *Bitter
Struggle*), *Wen-i pao*, No. 10, 1964.
[33] Editorial, 'Kuan-yü *San chia hsiang, k'u tou* ti p'ing-chia Wen-t'i' (On the
Question of Evaluating *Three Family Lane* and *Bitter Struggle*), *Wen-hsüeh
p'ing-lun*, No. 6, December 14, 1964.
[34] *Ibid.*, p. 110, and Lu I-fan, *op. cit.*, p. 16.

All the polemics, along with the accusations by the masses, waged against Ou-yang Shan offer us an opportunity to probe into the motives of the massive attacks on a single author. The dispute seems to have illustrated the function of novel in a revolutionary order. One basic point raised in Mao Tse-tung's 'Yenan Forum Talks' is that the literature and art of any society reflect and in turn perpetuate the value system of that society. No doubt, literature and artistic works perform a social function, but Mao's view is essentially different from that held in the West. Works of literature and art articulate issues, styles and trends to attract public attention in the West; they reflect problems and promote changes in China.

The function of creative writers and artists, as Mao points out in his 'Yenan Forum Talks,' is to serve the cause of the revolution. According to this criterion, *Three Family Lane* and *Bitter Struggle* inevitably come under suspicion. Consequently, the author's motives are questioned. Although little is known about the early life of Ou-yang Shan, it is certain that he was a *bona fide* member of the League of Left-Wing Writers in the 1930s. He took part in the Yenan rectification campaign, and one of his early novels, *Kao Kan-ta,*[35] received a general accolade. There is no question about Ou-yang Shan's credentials as a dedicated Communist novelist.

Ou-yang Shan's involvement in the League of Left-Wing Writers, however, may be a liability rather than an asset. In the early '30s the League played an important role in creating widespread anti-Japanese sentiment and discrediting the Kuomintang government for its failure to resist Japan. With the effect of the persuasive power of literature and art on the Kuomintang regime still fresh in the memory, the Communist leadership has always been extremely sensitive to any hint of dissidence in creative works. From the campaign against the motion picture 'The Life of Wu Hsün' to the Cultural Revolution, the leadership has always taken swift action to denounce ideas discordant with the goals of the Party.

Ou-yang Shan tried to portray urban life in the late '20s and early '30s, honestly, according to his own observation. He describes the values, norms and aspirations of young intellectuals realistically, without considering their effect on contemporary life. The critics who judge his work use the criteria of the '60s. There is a world of difference between traditional society and socialist society three decades later. Individualistic aspirations and pursuits have given way to collective goals and efforts. A new system of values, norms and beliefs has been built, based on an entirely different material

---

[35] Ou-yang Shan, *Kao Kan-ta* (Peking: New China Book Store, May 1949).

foundation. Thus, the issue is whether to ignore the impact of Ou-yang Shan's novel on Chinese youth for the sake of historical accuracy or to denounce it in the interest of party goals. For the Communist leadership, with the enduring memory of the turbulent, divided China of the last hundred years, the choice is never in doubt.

2

THE FORMATIVE YEARS –
THE VILLAGE

The village is always important in Chinese Communist fiction. It was in the countryside – in the great expanse of north China with its mountains and rivers, loess fields and dilapidated hamlets – that the Chinese Communist Party struck root, developed and spread all over China. The Communist victory was born of a marriage between the Party and the peasantry. Thus a majority of Communist novels portray village life, the sufferings of the peasants, and guerrilla warfare, in the familiar setting of rugged terrain, *kaoliang*[1] fields, and earthen caves.

While the party leadership has always encouraged the selection of themes of peasant life, rural struggle and land reform, novelists themselves have also delighted in writing about the countryside. During the Yenan years most Communist novelists lived in villages, came to know peasants, and developed a sense of belonging. With the illiterate and honest country folk, they resisted the bone-piercing cold of north China's severe winter and sweated on the open fields under the scorching summer sun. These experiences must have made an indelible impression. Many are of peasant stock themselves and truly sons of mother earth. Consequently, the best novels are those of peasant life and struggle, from Ting Ling's *Sun over the Sangkan River* and Chou Li-po's *Hurricane* to Liu Ching's *Builders* and Hao Jan's *Bright Sunny Days.*[2]

The peasants in most novels, however, play a more or less passive role, and their class-consciousness has to be awakened by cadres. It is the Party which generally points out to them the direction of the political struggle and leads them to victory. The backwardness of the peasants, as described in the works of Ting Ling and Chou Li-po, fails to answer a historical question: why for many centuries before the birth of the Communist Party China had witnessed numerous peasant risings. Something beyond organizational skill, propaganda techniques and

---

[1] A kind of tall-growing sorghum, like corn in appearance.
[2] All these novels will be discussed in subsequent chapters.

political ideology is needed to explain them. Otherwise, how can we account for the Ch'en Sheng and Wu Kuang revolts at the end of the Ch'in dynasty, of the Yellow Turbans and Red Eyebrows of the Han dynasty, of Chang Hsien-chung and Li Tzu-ch'eng of the Ming dynasty, and more recently the Taip'ing and Boxer rebellions?

But the initiative of peasants is not to be overstressed, for the Party is of an unusually jealous nature. To overplay the role of the peasantry in the revolutionary struggle might easily lead to the charge of opportunism. On the other hand, to present peasants as if they were chessmen to be deployed by Party cadres would sterilize the novel. It would become like a puppet show, which may arouse the interest of the gathering at a village temple fair but would not satisfy the taste of a more sophisticated audience. In order to solve this obvious contradiction — to avoid ideological heresy and at the same time to maintain artistic authenticity — Liang Pin creates conditions for the rebellious peasants and the revolutionary party to find each other in his excellent work *Keep the Red Flag Flying* and its sequel *Sowing the Flames.*[3] This timely link makes it natural that the peasants in their fight against the ruthless oppression of the landlord should gain the backing of the Party, which is glad to recruit mass support in its political struggle. This combination helps to make the story not only a first-class political novel but also a brilliant artistic achievement.

[3] Liang Lin planned to write a six-volume saga. *Hung-ch'i p'u* (Peking: Chinese Youth Publishing House, January 1958), revised edition (Peking: People's Literature Publishing House, September 1959) is translated by Gladys Yang under the title *Keep the Red Flag Flying* (Peking: Foreign Languages Press, December 1963).

Po huo chi (*Sowing the Flames*) (Peking: Writers' Publishing House, December 1963) is the second volume. No English translation is available, but an excerpt, covering chapters 14—18 (pp. 150—215), titled 'A Tale of the Green Woods', can be found in *Chinese Literature*, No. 3, 1961.

Chan k'ou t'u (*Fighting the Invaders*), the third volume, is reported to have been serialized in *Hopei Literature*, starting in 1962, but I have not been able to trace a copy of this journal.

According to the author's grand plan, Volume IV will be centered on the establishment and consolidation of the anti-Japanese guerrilla bases in Hopei, Volume V on the two-front war policy and tunnel warfare, and the final volume on the Civil War and the Communist victory.

In the two years since its publication, *Keep the Red Flag Flying* has sold over 878,000 copies. See Fang Ming, 'How Liang Pin Came to Write *Keep the Red Flag Flying*', *Chinese Literature*, No. 7, 1960, p. 124.

Historical Realism

Keep the Red Flag Flying and *Sowing the Flames* depict the life of two peasant families in central Hopei, against the background of the stormy events of the late 1920s and early 30s. Hopei has produced countless legendary heroes since the warring states of ancient times. Liang Pin's admiration for the gallantry and heroism of the ancients, developed during his boyhood, is reflected in his dauntless characters.[4] They are tough and generous, always ready, as an old saying goes, 'to help friends even if it means a knife between the ribs'. The friendship between the Chu and Yen families goes back a generation, like the rancor between them and the landlord Feng family.

The feud between Chu Lao-chung and Feng Lan-chih is traced back to the days of imperial rule, when the hero's father, a forthright peasant and expert boxer, raised havoc in the willow grove to stop the landlord from seizing twenty-four *mou*[5] of public land. This face-to-face confrontation cost him his life and forced his son to flee from the village. The failure of personal prowess as a weapon against the landlord and his henchmen led the peasants to try another means of righting injustice. When Feng Lan-chih attempted to raise 5,000 silver dollars demanded by a bandit chief by a tax on the peasants, twenty-nine poor men joined together to take the case to court.[6] They lost their case, first in the county court, then in the provincial court, and finally in the higher court at Peking. This lawsuit, which dragged on for three years, eventually forced many of them to sell their houses, land and oxen. A few were completely broken by the weight of the blow.

In these two episodes the seeds for revenge are sown and the logic for revolt established. A familiar scene in the old traditional romances shows peasants setting off with spears, knives and swords to build a stronghold in the mountains. An old saying has it that when people are pressed too hard by local bullies and corrupt magistrates they have no choice but to resort to arms. But *Keep the Red Flag Flying* is not a story of heroic bandits in the vein of *Water Margin*.

The story opens with the return of Chu Lao-chung, now over forty, with a wife and two sons, and the avowed goal of settling his blood

---

[4] Liang Pin, 'Wo Tsen-yang ch'uang-tso liao *Hung-ch'i p'u* (How I Wrote *Keep the Red Flag Flying*), *Wen-i yüeh-pao*, No. 5, 1958, p. 53.

[5] A *mou* is about 0.16 acre.

[6] A similar incident actually happened in Wangkangchen, a village like the one described in the novel. See Fang Ming, 'How Liang Pin Came to Write *Keep the Red Flag Flying*', *op. cit.*, p. 126.

score with the Feng family. At the railway station he unexpectedly comes across his childhood friend Yen Chih-ho. Yen who has just sold his only ox to pay for the lost lawsuit is unable to face his wife, mother and children. He has decided, like Chu twenty-five years earlier, to seek his fortune in Manchuria.[7] The reunion of the old friends gives Yen strength: he returns with Chu to fight the landlord.

In the first thirteen chapters, covering roughly one-fifth of the novel, the author gradually builds up the tension between the landlord Feng and the peasant families of Chu and Yen. In incident after incident, the peasants suffer further humiliations and blows at the hands of Feng. The old feud is rekindled by new hostilities, but the angry peasants are reduced to a state of helplessness and despair. Then almost by accident Yun-tao, the elder son of the Yen family, encounters the party organizer Chia Hsiang-nung one spring evening when he goes out to look for odd jobs.

The contact between the Party and the infuriated and vengeful peasants sets the stage for collective political action. Family feud or personal revenge, however, is not the theme of the novel, for the Party is not an avenging god to right private wrongs. The private blood debt has to be transformed into class antagonism, so that the novel will not depict quarrels between families but the struggle between classes. The landlord Feng personifies the evil forces of feudalism; Chu Lao-chung symbolizes the revolutionary masses. The problem faced by novelists in cases like this is the inevitable pull towards making the characters stereotypes. Obsessed with the concern for ideological purity, novelists may easily deprive their characters of life and reduce them to abstract notions.

Liang Pin is able to skirt the ideological problem which other authors who deal with later periods of the revolution must face squarely in order to stress the correctness of Party policy. In the late 1920s and early 30s the Communist Party was burdened with internal divisions over the problem of revolutionary strategy. In 1925–6 the Party began its organizational work in Kaoyang and Lihsien, where the story takes place. The more militant activities were directed by Li Li-san and Wang Ming, from 1929–32. The failure of their radical policy eventually resulted in their demotion. Thus Liang Pin is able to

---

[7] It was common in those days for peasants, hard pressed by local landlord bullies, to flee from their villages and go to Manchuria. At a discussion meeting held in the same normal school that Liang Pin describes in the novel, one student tells the story of his uncle, who went to Manchuria and returned to become a cadre after the liberation. See 'Huo-chung tsai ch'ing-nien ti hsin-chung jan-shao – Hopei Pao-ting shih-fan hsüeh-hsiao hsüeh-sheng tso-t'an *Hung-ch'i p'u* (Flames Kindle in the Minds of the Young – Students at Paoting Normal School in Hopei Discuss *Keep the Red Flag Flying*), *Wen-i pao*, No. 9, May 1958, p. 15.

turn the story into a tragedy, which is not only historically accurate but also in accordance with the verdict of the Party.

As a Party man, Liang Pin is very conscious of ideological correctness, and twice in the postscript to *Sowing the Flames* says how much a writer can benefit from reading policy documents.[8] Since he writes about north China around 1930, he can concentrate on the activities of the peasants rather than the Party. Historically, the struggle was led by the special committee in Paoting; in the story the Party work is directed by a cadre who works as a school teacher. Although the Party enforces strict discipline and absolute obedience to its orders, no concrete examples are given. The Party is thus not the embodiment of abstract notions, policies and ideology, but is shown in everyday operation, through its representative, Chia Hsiang-nung.

Two events, the pig-tax resistance campaign and the student movement at Paoting No. 2 Normal School, occupy the major part of *Keep the Red Flag Flying*. The incidents take place within a year and a half of each other, about a hundred *li*[9] apart. They are linked through Chiang-tao, the younger son of the Yen family, who takes part in the pig-tax resistance campaign and later as a student leader organizes the protest against the Kuomintang policy of non-resistance. By the end of the first volume, there is a hint that the Party-directed student action, which results in several deaths and many arrests, is probably a policy mistake. The logical next step is to take the struggle to the countryside, in the form of a peasant rising. The story of *Sowing the Flames* focuses on the Kaoyang-Lihsien rising in which the peasant guerrilla force suffers a crushing defeat.

Liang Pin is a very serious author: the novel is the fruit of his life's work. Born in Hopei in 1914, he became a member of the Communist Youth League at the age of thirteen. As a student at the No. 2 Normal School in Paoting, he took part in the demonstration and witnessed the suppression of the student movement by the Kuomintang authorities. During the years of the War against Japan, he did cultural work in the Hopei-Chahar-Shansi Border Region. There he once met an old man of about sixty, of medium height, with a broad forehead and sharp nose. After losing three sons in the revolutionary struggle, the old peasant remained an energetic and optimistic man. He made a powerful impression on Liang Pin, who portrayed him in a short story, *The Father of Three Bolsheviks*, in 1942. The story was later converted into a five-act play *The Thousand-Li Dyke*. He also wrote a short story *Folk Who Resist Japan*, another five-act play *Rich Harvest*, and a novelette

---

[8] Liang Pin, 'Hou-chi' (Postscript), *Sowing the Flames*, p. 659 and p. 667.
[9] A *li* is about ⅓ mile.

The Father. From all these works the characters and structure of *Keep the Red Flag Flying* and its sequels gradually took shape.

A graphic report in a review article gives us a glimpse of Liang Pin in the war years:

> At that time, Liang Pin and I were both working in Lihsien, but I lived several miles away from him and to reach him had to cross five enemy lines and three observation posts. The village where he was staying was less than a mile from a Japanese post. In those days every household kept its gate closed, the streets were virtually deserted and the whole village was silent. If someone ran a short distance down the street, people would cock their heads to listen, wondering whether the enemy had come. I remember slipping quietly into his courtyard once. As soon as he saw me he laughed and ran out of his room. His face was tanned and he had grown a moustache; stripped to the waist, with a coarse towel thrown over one shoulder, he looked just like a peasant.[10]

In addition to his personal experiences as a participant in the protest in his student days, and as a party cadre in the guerrilla base areas, he spent many hours in 1953–4 interviewing those who joined in the Kaoyang-Lihsien uprising and several times visited the villages he describes in his novel. Following the publication of *Keep the Red Flag Flying*, the editorial board of *Wen-i pao* called a special discussion meeting in February 1958. It was attended by the author, Liang Pin, Hou Chin-ching, an editor on the journal, Ts'ao Ch'eng-tsung,[11] Chang Chin-hsi,[12] Ch'ang Ming,[13] and Tsang Po-p'ing.[14] The following excerpts from their discussion[15] show that Liang Pin has been meticulous about the accuracy of historical facts.

> *Ts'ao Ch'eng-tsung:* In those days China was a semi-feudal and semi-colonial country. People like Yun-tao and Chiang-tao (whose

[10] Fang Ming, 'How Liang Pin Came to Write *Keep the Red Flag Flying*', *op cit.*, p. 125.
[11] Ts'ao Ch'eng-tsung, then the treasurer of the Lihsien county government, appears in *Sowing the Flames* as the treasurer Ts'ao. He is now deputy director of the Bureau of Supervision in the Ministry of Transport.
[12] Chang Chin-hsi, then the head of the Communist Youth League in Poshieh and Lihsien, is the model for Chiang-tao. He is now a division head in the Materials Procurement Department, Bureau of Construction Works, Peking Municipal Government.
[13] Ch'ang Ming, then the secretary of Poshieh-Lihsien County Party Committee, is now the secretary of the Party Committee in the State Economic Commission.
[14] Tsang Po-p'ing, one of the leaders of the student movement at Paoting No. 2 Normal School, is now a deputy director of the Seventh Bureau, Ministry of Machine Building.
[15] 'Lao chan-shih hua tang-nien – Pen-k'an chü-hsing *Hung-ch'i p'u* tso-t'an-hui chi-lu che-yao' (Recollections of the Old Warriors – Summary Report of Talks at the Discussion Meeting on *Keep the Red Flag Flying* Called by this Journal), *Wen-i pao*, No. 5, March 1958.

families saved all their earnings as hired hands and gradually became middle peasants, so their children could afford to attend school and sometimes even college) actually joined the revolution. Many of our leading comrades came from a family background of this kind.

Chang Chin-hsi: The Pig-Tax Resistance Campaign is led by Chiang-tao in the novel. There is a vivid description of Chiang-tao speaking to the crowd from a cart and Yen Ping's response from below. Actually, this campaign was launched by the students in the village normal school, under the leadership of the Party. Of a total of 52 students, 48 were members of the Communist Youth League. Whenever there were any Communist activities going on, we skipped our classes. During my three years in the normal school, I attended classes for a little more than forty days. (*Laughter*) Were the Party not so deeply rooted in our part of the country, the normal school would have been closed down long ago. In those days in our school, as we were having our meal, we would start singing the *Internationale*. The county Public Security Bureau (police headquarters) was located next to our school, but all the same we played the role of hero and stood on the wall, facing them and singing the *Internationale*. There were some of our men in the Public Security Bureau. Even the headquarters of the Kuomintang in those days worked for the Communist Party, under the KMT banner.

Ch'ang Ming: . . . On the twelfth day of the eighth moon in 1930 we organized an uprising in the Poshieh-Lihsien area, following the Li Li-san line . . .

Chang Chin-hsi: That evening I went to your home to get the big flag, remember?

Ch'ang Ming (*nods, laughs*): . . . and planned a military coup to take over political power, to organize the Red Army, and establish the Soviet system of government. We prepared leaflets, proclamations of the People's Government, and appointed a Red Army commander, a commissar, and so on. (Ho Ch'ing-yü was the chairman of the Soviet type government, Chang Chao-feng the Red Army commander, and I political commissar.) Because of the mistaken policy, this uprising was unsuccessful. But there were some results: we killed a landlord's son, distributed the landlord's grain among poor peasants, declared the goals of the Party publicly, and broadened our political influence.

Tsang Po-p'ing: The student protest at Paoting No. 2 Normal School was led by the Paoting Special Committee of the Party. When the struggle was well under way, the school was surrounded by enemy troops. (We were only 59 students; the enemy mobilized more than 1,000 soldiers.) We were completely isolated from the outside world and fought the soldiers all by ourselves. (At 3.30 on the morning of July 6, 1932, according to Tsang Po-p'ing, the Kuomintang soldiers broke in, hand-to-hand combat ensued, eight students were killed, the others arrested. After a trial by the military tribunal, four were executed and the rest given sentences of eight or ten years.

A comparison of the narrative in the novel with the recollections of the participants shows that Liang Pin scrupulously follows every detail of the event. Accuracy is of primary importance whenever the activities of the Party are presented. Nevertheless, had the author concentrated on the operations of the Party, the novel would have become a tedious work of propaganda. Liang Pin is an artist first and propagandist second. His subject is the peasants, their deep attachment to the land, their anger towards the predatory landlord, and their generous friendship to each other.

Keep the Red Flag Flying is a historical novel. Unlike a history, a historical novel does not have to be factual on every count. What matters is the author's ability to reconstruct the spirit and mood of the era. A basic criterion in measuring the success of a historical novel is the creation of typical characters who play key roles in an important historical period. Any exaggeration of the role of principal characters would not only impair historical truth but also debase the artistic quality of the novel. Liang Pin's brilliant achievement depends on his perfect honesty in characterization. All the many characters in the novel, the apathetic scholar, the gallant bandit, the idealistic girl student, truly belong to the turbulent 20s and 30s. *Keep the Red Flag Flying* makes one feel as though one is reliving those years of imminent Japanese invasion, student protests, peasant unrest, and general social disorder and chaos. For an impartial reader it is almost irrelevant that the novel is written by a Communist author, about Communist activities. The author has successfully revived the general mood of the era and turned a page of history into a drama full of life.

The Traditional Hero in a Revolutionary Age

To describe a peasant hero in a transitional period in a manner that will satisfy ideological demands and at the same time will not distort reality is indeed a great challenge. Ideology instructs that peasants rise spontaneously to join the Communist revolution in an effort to overthrow the oppressive system. But Chinese peasants have been crushed under the weight of authoritarian rule, prohibitive social conventions, and Confucian moralistic principles. To rebel against authority is something totally against their habitual mode of thinking. The author must elucidate the motivating forces of the peasant rebels. This is made more difficult by the fact that there are no ready models for reference. Before Sino-Soviet relations deteriorated to breaking-point, Chinese novelists could read not only Soviet authors of the revolutionary and post-revolutionary periods but also such classical masters as Tolstoy and Dostoyevsky.[16] Even so, the heroes in Russian novels cannot be adapted to the Chinese setting. The hero must be Chinese, think Chinese and act Chinese. There can be no substitute. The only comparisons are to be found in a few classical Chinese novels which have been positively reevaluated by the leadership.

They are indeed a logical source, for there must be some connection between the heroes of classical novels and the heroes of the new era. The traditional type of hero rebel, as exemplified in *Water Margin*, is usually a persecuted man who wants not only to avenge himself but to right social injustice. Most of the 108 bandits occupying the marshes were forced to revolt, either by the oppressive, wicked landlords or by greedy, corrupt officials. Chu Lao-chung, the hero of *Keep the Red Flag Flying*, comes to fight the landlord-bully Feng Lan-chih in almost exactly the same way.

Chu Lao-chung is no ordinary peasant. He has inherited his unyielding character from his father, who had the courage to fight the landlord Feng personally. The death of his father not only sowed the seeds of a family feud but forced young Tiger Chu to run away from his native village. He wandered to Peking and then worked for a while as a carpet-weaver in Tientsin. When it struck him that weaving weft after weft would lead him nowhere, he shouldered his bedding-roll and sought his fortune in Manchuria of legendary wealth. For twenty-five years he has done all sorts of odd jobs: digging *ginseng* (a herb) in the Long White Mountains, fishing in the Black River, and washing gold dust at Hailanpao. Without this education, he would never have become an undaunted revolutionary.

At the opening of the story, he is already in his early forties, heading home with the stubborn thought, 'I've a debt of blood I must go back to settle!' So nothing is more natural than his hatred for Feng Lan-chih, the symbol of the landlord class in the small village of Soching. The family feud is further intensified by the incident of the redbreast, a rare bird, which the landlord wants to grab from the boys of the Chu and Yen families as his pet, without success. This leads to a second incident when Ta-kuei, Chu's elder son, is forcibly conscripted for the warlord army, by order of Feng, as village chief. Chu chokes with anger and the desire for revenge. At one point he grasps a chopper, but manages to swallow his fury and nurses his wounds to buy time. It is the personal blood debt, mixed with a sense of injustice to be righted, that finally leads Chu to join the Communist revolution. Although the author is very much aware of the limitations imposed by ideology, he does not ignore artistic criteria. It is clear to him that he has to give ideological

---

[16] D. W. Fokkema, 'Chinese Criticism of Humanism: Campaign Against the Intellectuals 1964–5', *The China Quarterly*, April/June 1966, pp. 68–70.

explanations for the hero's joining the revolution. This is supplied by the background of Chu's past life. As Liang Pin puts it, 'a person's character is inseparable from his past experience, that is materialism.'[17]

The resemblance between Chu Lao-chung and the legendary heroes of *Water Margin* is indeed remarkable. When the news of Yun-tao's imprisonment makes Yen Chih-ho ill, Chu decides to see the young man on Yen's behalf. He thinks of what he could do to help Yun-tao. One idea that flashes into his mind is the example of the outlaws of Liangshan, who raided the execution ground. He abandons the idea only because he realizes that it will not work.

The influence of traditional heroes of *Water Margin* on the characterization of Chu is sometimes very obvious. He is reminiscent of Wu Sung, one of the outstanding characters portrayed by Shih Nan-an. For instance, the scene of Chu's leaving Yen Chih-ho to see Yun-tao in a Tsinan prison is unmistakably adapted from *Water Margin*:

> Chu called Mrs. Yen and told her husband in her presence: 'Tomorrow I'm going to Tsinan to save Yun-tao. You must be very careful here at home. Don't go down to the fields till it's light, and close the gate early at night. Look after your pigs, dog, chickens and ducks, and don't let them do any mischief that might start a quarrel. Now those devils know that we're in trouble, they're sure to do all they can to ruin us. Mind you do nothing to anger them while I'm away. Even if they stand at the gate and swear, or call Yen Chih-ho names, don't say a word. When I come back, we'll settle scores with them. Just do as I say, Chih-ho. You're my good brother. If you don't listen to me, I'll have something to say to you when I come back.'[18]

Liang Pin writes in a mandarin with a Hopei accent which is very close to the Shantung vernacular in *Water Margin*. But even with much of the flavor lost in translation, the similarity is clear when the above narrative is compared to Wu Sung's farewell to his elder brother:

> After they had drunk about five cups of wine Wu Sung ordered the soldier to fill the cups again, and then taking his own cup in his hand, he addressed Wu Ta-lang: 'Elder brother, today I have been ordered to go to the Eastern Capital, and I have to start on my journey tomorrow. I expect to be gone not less than forty days, or two months at most. Now you have always been rather weak, and when I am abroad I am afraid that you may be insulted. If you have been selling, say, ten lots of cakes each day, then beginning from tomorrow I want you to sell only five lots. Every day go out late and

---

[17] Liang Pin, 'Man-t'an *Hung-ch'i p'u* ti ch'uang-tso' (Some General Observations on the Creation of *Keep the Red Flag Flying*), *Jen-min wen-hsüeh*, No. 6, 1959, p. 18.
[18] *Keep the Red Flag Flying*, p. 181, Yang, pp. 199–200.

come back early. Do not drink wine with men. When you return home lower the screen, and lock the door. Avoid all scandal. If anybody insults you, do not have a row with him, but wait until I return, when I will discuss the matter with him. If you will take my advice, then drink this wine.'[19]

As a matter of fact, the author himself implicitly admits the influence of classical models on his characterization:

> In portraying the characters, my experience has been that it is easier to draw traditional characters than new characters. Traditional characters are easy to draw, for they have lived through a considerable period in the old society and have relatively fixed behavior patterns. The new characters are still developing, waiting for you to define and create them, and therefore more difficult to sketch.[20]

This reliance on traditional models for his peasant hero helps the author produce a solid, substantial image. Chu Lao-chung turns into a man of flesh and blood. His personal qualities, such as honesty, straightforwardness, and a capacity for enduring hardship, can be found in average peasants. But he also has qualities rare among ordinary peasants: unusual generosity, nerves of steel and dauntless courage. His towering figure stands out among his friends and neighbors. That Chu is not a typical peasant has never been questioned or criticized. On the contrary, many Communist commentators hailed the treatment of this character as a successful example of the theory of combining revolutionary realism with revolutionary romanticism.[21]

A few episodes described in the novel may serve to illustrate Chu's extraordinary qualities. The first link between the Communist Party and the peasants is established through Yun-tao. When Yun-tao asks his father's permission for regular meetings with an unusual man named Chia Hsiang-nung, the prudent peasant refuses. Then the young man goes to seek advice from Chu Lao-chung. Chu listens attentively and hears him say that Chia could very well be a Communist. This is Chu's reaction:

[19] Shih Han-an, *Shui Huh* (*Water Margin*), trans. by J. H. Jackson (Shanghai: Commercial Press Ltd., 1937), Vol. I, pp. 325–6.
[20] Liang Pin, 'Some General Observations on the Creation of *Keep the Red Flag Flying,' op. cit.*, p. 23.
[21] For instance, Feng Chien-nan, 'T'an *Hung-ch'i p'u'* (Comment on *Keep the Red Flag Flying*), in the Chinese edition of the novel, pp. 485–6. The theory of combining revolutionary realism with revolutionary romanticism is the guiding principle in the portrayal of heroes. Although the theory is attributed to Mao Tse-tung, it was never disclosed when and in what circumstances he spelled it out.

'A Communist?' Chu laughed exultantly. 'I heard about them in the northeast. It seems that in the Soviet Union the workers have come to power and downed the capitalists and landlords. The poor resisted . . . If you've found backing like that, you can go a long way!'[22]

Such talk comes naturally to Chu, for he is a man of rich experience and has no fear of political involvement. Ordinary peasants whose experience is limited to a small village would not be capable of such a straight-forward reaction and unequivocal attitude.

The generosity and open-mindedness of Chu are reflected in seemingly trivial details which are nevertheless important in the characterization of the hero. The author accomplishes this by contrasting Chu with the self-absorbed and narrow-minded Yen Chih-ho. Yen, for instance, is unhappy at being treated as if he were a stranger in his own house by his son and the party organizer Chia. When he complains to Chu, the latter simply laughs it off:

'Chia Hsiang-nung is here again.'
'What does he say?' asked Chu.
'How do I know?' Yen answered coldly. 'They're a cosy little family. When you're out of the room, they chat and laugh and discuss things together. The moment you go in, they pull long faces and stop talking.'
Chu chuckled. 'Chih-ho, you should know better than that. They have their own business to discuss. Cough before you go in. And when they want to talk, just leave them alone.'
Yen tossed his head. 'After all this, they still treat me as an outsider!'
'We're not in their confidence yet, that's why! Later, when we are, we can sit talking and laughing with them too.'[23]

One thing which distinguishes *Keep the Red Flag Flying* and its sequel *Sowing the Flames* from other novels of the genre is that the hero Chu Lao-chung is never over-shadowed by the cadre Chia Hsiang-nung. Even in the presence of Chia, people rush over to meet Chu. In the eyes of the peasants, Chu is a hero while Chia is just a party leader. They consider it a great honor to make the acquaintance of Chu, whose name is known among young and old in all forty-eight villages.

The author understands the distinction between a hero and a party man very well. Throughout the story of nearly one million words Chu remains a peasant hero, though he becomes a party member after the pig-tax resistance campaign. Even the description of the ceremony of initiation is different in the case of Chu. When Yen's younger son,

[22] *Keep the Red Flag Flying*, p. 114, Yang, p. 123.
[23] *Keep the Red Flag Flying*, p. 304, Yang, p. 338.

Chiang-tao, is initiated into the Communist Youth League, the author describes how Chia prepares a flag with the hammer and sickle on it and puts it up on the wall. Then he explains to the young man the meaning of the party flag and the discipline a League member must observe. After that, he tells Chiang-tao to raise his clenched fist; together they sing the *Internationale*. But the ritual for Chu's initiation is cut to a minimum. And it is conveniently conducted by Chiang-tao. After having explained to Chu and other peasants the discipline, rights and duties of a Communist, the young Youth Leaguer admits them to the Party under a red flag cut out of the paper used for writing New Year couplets. It is quite natural to have the student Chiang-tao go through all the details of the ritual, but it would seem pretentious and comic for Chu, a middle-aged, illiterate peasant, to have to sing the *Internationale*.

The individuality of the hero is not compromised after he becomes a Party member. He remains an upright, courageous peasant. When the news of the students besieged in Paoting Normal School reaches him, he goes with Yen Chih-ho to see if anything can be done to help Yen's younger son Chiang-tao, not because he is a Party member, but as the friend of a man whose son is in trouble. After arriving in Paoting, he helps send supplies — flour, oil and salt — to the beleaguered students, entirely on his own initiative. Although he fails to save Chiang-tao, he manages to rescue a wounded student by disguising himself as a rickshaw puller.

The author is consistent in his portrayal of a peasant hero. In the second volume, *Sowing the Flames*, Chu is appointed the commander of the Soching brigade during the Kaoyang-Lihsien uprising. Thus, he is no ordinary Party member but elevated to a status higher than the rest of the peasants. But the author clearly feels that Party membership and his position as commander still do not give the hero sufficient distinction. Something more dramatic must be added to give Chu Lao-chung the necessary stature.

When the peasants of the forty-eight villages gather on the bank of Thousand Li Dyke, ready for military action, a yellow steed with a long mane suddenly appears in the field and dashes around on the bank of the river. It is the landlord's horse, which has been turned loose after its master was taken captive by the rioting peasants. Chu Lao-chung orders Ta-kuei, his elder son, a young man, to ride the horse. Ta-kuei jubilantly jumps onto the horse, but is thrown to the ground by the furious beast. Enraged, Chu starts to tame the unbridled horse himself. There follows an exciting description of the struggle between man and horse. In the end Chu conquers the unruly horse completely, amid thunderous shouts and prolonged applause from the soldiers of the peasant Red Army and the people of the forty-eight villages, lining the river bank.

In this episode tradition again reasserts itself. Horse-taming has always been a favorite device of story-tellers, for showing the unusual strength and valor of a hero. Hsieh P'ing-kuei's superhuman qualities are recognized the moment he tames a high-spirited horse in _Hung-tsung lieh-ma (The Red-Maned Steed)_. Kuan Yü's crimson horse, Liu Pei's white horse, and Ts'ao Ts'ao's yellow horse faithfully serve their masters in many a conquest in _Romance of the Three Kingdoms_. The incident is inserted here to reinforce the fearless character of Chu as well as to symbolize the change in the position of landlord and peasant. Such daring, bravery and skill would be totally out of place in any ordinary peasant. It is, however, only natural for Chu, who used to break in wild horses in the days when he roamed the vast grasslands of Manchuria.

Historically, the Kaoyang-Lihsien uprising was a disaster, and the author has to adhere to the facts. _Sowing the Flames_ has a tragic plot, and the calamitous ending gives the tale a pathos a success story could not match. Many familiar figures fall; Chu's best friend, Yen Chih-ho, is seriously wounded. A non-Communist writer would probably let Chu be killed in a dramatic hand-to-hand battle, and thus intensify the tragic impact of the story. Liang Pin, a first-rate artist, must have thought of this, but he has other things to consider. Defeat in the Communist vocabulary means a temporary setback which only serves to invite a redoubled attack. As a hero who epitomizes the invincible forces of the peasant revolution, Chu must live to lead the unfinished fight. The story ends with his organizing underground resistance in the villages struck with the 'white terror', while his son leads the remnants of the peasant force to build the guerrilla bases in the Taihang Mountains. Such an ending may be necessary when we recall that _Sowing the Flames_ is only the second of a six-volume epic story. The main characters must survive to serve as a link to the succeeding stories.

The characterization of Chu Lao-chung as a peasant hero seems impeccable. He is indeed an ideal hero, who embodies all the good qualities of a peasant revolutionary. Chu has no rich relatives to tarnish his class status. He never seeks help from the landlord or begs favors from the authorities. When Feng Lan-chih seizes Ta-kuei for the warlord army Chu does not crawl to he landlord's door to plead for his son's release. In Communist parlance, he is a poor man with backbone, who knows the class enemy, and never compromises on a revolutionary's principles.

Chu's heroism, however, is disturbing to some Party theoreticians, who feel he is not quite appropriate as the model of a flawless hero. There is unanimous agreement on the outstanding characterization of Chu as a peasant hero in the first half of _Keep the Red Flag Flying_. But some critics have misgivings about Chu remaining the peasant hero after he has become a Party member. They complain that nothing in the portrayal of Chu as a Party man indicates his involvement in organizational activities.[24] This touches on a fundamental contradiction in the portrayal of Communist heroes. A hero must have something unique about him, something which distinguishes him from the rank and file. On the other hand, the Communist Party is an organization which operates on the basis of order, discipline, and collective action. Once a man joins the Party, he has to accept orders, observe the discipline, and act in co-ordination with other members. Yet no one can be a hero if he cannot act on his own free will. The author is well aware that if the character of Chu is to be consistent throughout the story, his Party role must be reduced to bare essentials. Faithful to his artistic sensitivity, Liang Pin maintains Chu's hero image by making his Party role inconspicuous.

In portraying a hero, the author must make his positive traits reflect the value system of the society of which he is a part. As a product of the old society, Chu Lao-chung, a peasant revolutionary, resembles in many ways the righteous rebels or fearless warriors in classical novels and popular tales. Chu's qualities are exceptional valor, nerveless composure, and a noble spirit, qualities shared by Wu Sung of *Water Margin*, Hsieh P'ing-kuei of *The Red-Maned Steed*, and Kuan Yü of *Romance of the Three Kingdoms*. These legendary heroes have been revered by Chinese people for centuries because their outstanding traits epitomize the norms and values of Chinese society. Chu Lao-chung is only a contemporary version in this durable hero tradition.

Heroes of personal distinction served a great function in a society plagued by famine, drought, banditry, pillage, burning, assault, killing, and war. When helpless people were at the mercy of foraging bandits, predatory landlords, plundering soldiers, or greedy magistrates, they longed for a Wu Sung or a Kuan Yü to deliver them. The role of traditional heroes was to buttress justice and order in a ruleless society. Chu Lao-chung is a hero of this type, who opposes the landlord on personal terms, and even when he is commander of the peasant insurgents, fights against the forces of the warlords and the Kuomintang army with raw courage. The Party leadership in the Kaoyang-Lihsien uprising is more symbolic than real, and the peasants, without training or discipline, use home-made weapons. At times like this, heroes of legendary stature appear. Thus, the author's occasional imitation of classical novels is never damaging. On the other hand, by using Chia

---

[24] Feng Chien-nan, *op. cit.*, p. 493; also Hu So, 'Ke-ming ying-hsiung ti p'u-hsi – *Hung-ch'i p'u* tu-hou chi' (The Lineage of Revolutionary Heroes – Reflections After Reading *Keep the Red Flag Flying*), *Wen-i pao*, No. 9, 1958, p. 19.

Pao-yu as his model for Chou Ping in *Three Family Lane*, Ou-yang Shan has created a pseudo-revolutionary. This shows that in spite of all the arguments about *Dream of the Red Chamber* as a story of revolt against the feudal system and Chia Pao-yu and Black Jade as rebels against traditional marriage system, it remains simply a love story. Chou Ping, a modern Chia Pao-yu, cannot be other than a sentimental young man. It is a sound policy to treat classical works as a rich heritage for creative inspiration, but sheer plagiarism will inevitably result in a character full of contradictions.

The Other Peasant

A story is not an epic if the events described are not led by an extraordinary man, a hero. The extraordinary qualities of the hero, however, cannot be made conspicuous except by contrast with ordinary men. The supporting characters do not exist for their own sakes, but rather as a foil for the hero. In *Keep the Red Flag Flying* Liang Pin professes to focus on 'the fearless heroes of three generations of the Chu and Yen families in order to reflect the historical truth that Chinese peasants down the centuries have had a revolutionary, fighting tradition.'[25] Nevertheless, he stresses a difference between the two characters. Chu Lao-chung is unmistakably presented as a valiant hero; Yen Chih-ho, though a mason in his spare-time, is described as a typical peasant.[26] There is no doubt that Chu is an unusual man; he has seen Peking and Tientsin, and has been 'steeled' for twenty-five years in the harsh wilderness of Manchuria before throwing himself into the fierce struggle. By contrast, Yen Chih-ho is an ordinary peasant. Like the overwhelming majority of Chinese peasants, Yen has never set foot in the broad outside world except perhaps for an occasional trip to the provincial capital, Paoting.

Yen Chih-ho is portrayed as 'a man with both backward elements and a potential for progress,' in other words he is a typical man in the middle, according to Shao Ch'üan-lin's definition.[27] Yen can be quite definite. When he hears that Chu Ming and twenty-eight other men are carrying on a lawsuit against the landlord Feng Lan-chih, he feels for them and says, 'Count me in!' That single sentence costs him an ox. But the heavy price he pays for taking on overwhelming odds tames his

---

[25] Liang Pin, 'Foreword' to the English translation, p. v.

[26] Liang Pin, 'Some General Observations on the Creation of *Keep the Red Flag Flying*,' *op. cit.*, p. 20. His word for 'typical' is *tao-ti ti*.

[27] Shao Ch'üan-lin has singled out Yen Chih-ho and others as typical of the middle character. For a discussion of men in the middle, see Chapter 9.

temper and teaches him to be prudent. Without encouragement, he would quickly surrender himself to an invisible force called fate. When his older son Yun-tao tells him about his encounter with the Party organizer, Chia Hsiang-nung, and the latter's suggestion that they hold regular meetings, Yen lowers his head in silence. After considerable thought, he says, with a sigh, 'Those three lawsuits I fought with Feng Lan-chih taught me a lesson I won't forget in a hurry. Let's not meddle in anything, but go about our business with bent heads.'[28] This reaction is typical of an ordinary peasant who has come to understand the futility of fighting against fate. Life is a combination of hardship and endurance; defiance will only end in catastrophe. But the incident also serves to strengthen the fearless character of the hero Chu Lao-chung. When Yun-tao goes to consult Chu, he is given unqualified support.

There are many examples of this contrast. Yen's meekness, submission, and lack of willpower help bring out, by comparison, the bravery, broadmindedness, and determination of Chu. When Yen's younger son Chiang-tao asks for his permission to continue study in the normal school, this is how Yen reacts:

> Yen lowered his head to consider this for some time. He puffed out a mouthful of smoke, cleared his throat and said slowly: 'In times like these, I can't see my way to it. A full day's work on the scaffolding only brings in fifty cents. No one builds in a bad year like this. I'm busy at this windlass day and night, but at the market a load of vegetables fetches less than half a dollar. A sack of millet sells for four or five dollars. Nothing we can grow is worth anything. What's to be done? . . .' The burden of living lay heavy on Yen Chih-ho. His mother was old, Yun-tao was away, there was only his wife to help keep the family going. To provide for Chiang-tao's schooling as well was beyond him. He turned to look at the boy from under his long, dark lashes. 'Take some of the load off my shoulders, lad!' he said. After this appeal he was silent. He frowned and lowered his long lashes again.[29]

Chiang-tao knows his father and sees the futility of arguing with him. He goes to seek the advice of Chu Lao-chung, whose response is totally different. 'You'll study if I have to sell my trousers and pawn my jacket!' Chu's intervention settles the matter, and he keeps his word. When Chiang-tao is about to go to school, Chu sells his calf for ten dollars and brings the money to Yen's place. Yen is deeply grateful, and then secretly withdraws five dollars from the fifteen he has meant to give Chiang-tao. Details such as this are not only profoundly

---

[28] *Keep the Red Flag Flying,* p. 113, Yang, p. 122.
[29] *Ibid.,* p. 152, Yang, p. 167.

touching but also reflect the striking difference between the personalities of the two men.

Though the author describes the prudent, submissive side of Yen's
personality as a foil to Chu's unyielding perseverance and optimism, he
does not ignore Yen's positive side. For instance, Chiang-tao's talk
about resisting taxes and levies brings this reaction from Yen:

> 'Resist taxes and levies, eh? H'm, we should have done that long ago.
> How is a man to live in times like these? Fighting every other day,
> taxes on everything. Since we lost our Treasure Trove, the few *mou*
> of sandy soil we have left don't produce enough to pay the grain tax.
> But for my trowel, we'd have been eaten by dogs. How is a man to
> live?'[30]

Such talk from Yen is somewhat unexpected. In order to smooth
over this sudden change in Yen's attitude, the author skilfully brings
the talk of tax resistance and revolution to a level which Yen can grasp.
When Chiang-tao mentions that the pig-tax resistance campaign is to be
led by the Communist Party, Yen asks if they would get their Treasure
Trove back after a revolution. It is important for him to associate the
great task of revolution with the trivial matter of the two *mou* of fertile
land that have been lost to the landlord. The word 'revolution' can
only be understood by Yen in relation to the recovery of the lost land.
By linking the two, the author maintains the unity and consistency of
Yen's characterization.

Yen Chih-ho makes little contribution to the pig-tax resistance
campaign. He is often worried over where this dreadful affair may lead.
But when he sees Chiang-tao standing on a cart addressing the crowd
about the meaning of resisting the pig tax, he is overjoyed and very
proud of his son. Later he also joins the Party, but he still does not play
any significant role. In *Sowing the Flames* Chu Lao-chung is the hero
commanding a brigade of peasant insurrectionists; Yen Chih-ho is
reduced almost to a shadow. He participates in the Kaoyang-Lihsien
uprising, but only because he is carried forwards by the irresistible tide
of revolution.

He remains weak and emotional when he can actually be tough and
avenging. This again is done to contrast with the heroism of Chu. When
Feng Lan-chih's mansion is broken into by the insurgent peasants and
the landlord himself taken captive, this is how Yen behaves in front of
his enemy:

> Yen Chih-ho was so angry that he went over and dealt the landlord
> a sound kick. He wept at the memory of the misfortunes the bully

---

[30] *Ibid.*, p. 234, Yang, p. 258.

Feng Lan-chih had caused his family, forcing husband to separate
from wife, father from son.

'Feng Lan-chih!' he cried, 'you've treated us peasants worse than
dung, you've bullied my family for three generations!'

Years of suffering and injustice welled up in him, he breathed
noisily, held up his trembling hands, and burst out wailing.

Chu Lao-chung was furious to see Yen Chih-ho in such a state.
'Chih-ho! What the hell are you doing! You're supposed to put the
enemy on trial, why cry? Weeping like this in front of him! Now, I'll
show you!'[31]

During the Kaoyang-Lihsien battle, Yen Chih-ho proves his bravery
and is wounded twice. When the peasant Red Army is totally crushed,
Yen, his leg wounded, virtually crawls back home. This unfortunate
man has had more suffering than anybody else. His older son has been
sentenced to life imprisonment in Tsinan because of his Communist
affiliation, his younger son has received twelve years in Paoting for his
role in the student protest, and now he suffers severe leg wounds. But
the moment he sees Chu Lao-chung, he asks a series of questions
instead of the emotional outburst one might expect.

Yen Chih-ho again asked where Chia Hsiang-nung was, and learned
that he was still alive. The flame inside him was suddenly rekindled,
and he straightened himself up. 'Good! He's still alive!' Then he
asked again: 'Brother! How many men do we have?' As soon as he
learned that they still had more than ten rifles, Yen Chih-ho's mind
quivered a bit. 'Good!' he said, 'In the past we didn't even have a
single gun, now we've more than ten rifles. We can certainly carry
on!'[32]

This description of Yen's state of mind, in spite of all his mental and
physical wounds, is somewhat inconsistent with his usual weak
personality. Given his emotional nature, Yen would not show that kind
of calmness and composure. It seems particularly unlikely that when he
finally sees Chu Lao-chung after the torture of crawling home
wounded, he can not only restrain himself from any emotional gesture
but can actually be so calculating as to inquire about the strength of
their fighting force. The only possible justification for this transformation is that Yen has been steeled by his battle experience. In any event,
it seems obvious that the author has deliberately applied the theory of
combination of revolutionary realism and revolutionary romanticism.

In any case, the author has on occasion deliberately stressed the
positive side of Yen's character. This assumption is substantiated by

[31] *Sowing the Flames*, p. 361.
[32] *Ibid.*, p. 592.

Chang Chin-hsi, who participated in the events described in the novel, and served as the model for Yen's second son, Chiang-tao:

> Comrade Liang Pin's portrayal of characters is fine and truthful, but the transformation of Chiang-tào's parents still seems too sudden and too easy. My parents, old folk, were obstinate in their way of thinking. In particular, the fellow who contracted for the tax was the person nobody in our village dared to ruffle. The news of our leadership in resisting the tax spread quickly. When he got wind of it he made his way to our house. 'Brother Chien,' he said to my father, 'your son wants to raise hell resisting the tax, so you've got to guarantee all the payments!' My father was dumbfounded. As soon as I stepped into our house, my parents knelt down and begged me to stop. My parents-in-law also invited me to their home and treated me with delicacies for the same purpose. I had to sneak out. The ideological struggle within our family at that time was far more bitter than the book describes. It was never easy for my parents to change. Something must be added to the description.[33]

Despite these shortcomings, there is no question that Yen Chih-ho is one of the most successfully portrayed characters in the novel. Liang Pin promised to make Yen a typical peasant, and he does not fail us. The occasional strengthening of Yen's conviction in the revolutionary cause and his determination in the struggle is not a serious inconsistency in Yen's personality. Until the very end of the second volume, Yen continues to be a weak-willed peasant Communist. As a matter of fact, he is always more peasant than Communist.

Landlords as Villains

The political significance of the behavior of villains depends on whether it becomes a crucial ingredient in the class war. Its function is to foment the revolutionary struggle in the unfolding story. This is how Liang Pin portrays villains in this story of intense class struggle. The target of the peasant uprising is the landlord Feng family, and the villains fit neatly into categories. The two main negative characters, Feng Lan-chih and his son Kuei-t'ang, readily fall into the two types of

[33] 'Recollections of the Old Warriors — Summary Reports of Talks at the Discussion Meeting on *Keep the Red Flag Flying* Called by this Journal', *op cit.*, p. 32.

landlords, as ideologically defined.[34] Feng Lan-chih is a man of strictly
conventional ideas. He believes in the orthodox means of making a
fortune — through rent and interest. His philosophy is 'however much
you get by other means, it's like a half-dried turnip — goes mouldy once
it rains!'

Feng Kuei-t'ang belongs to a different generation. He has studied law
in the university and served for a while as an army officer. He feels that
the poor must be allowed food and clothes. 'When their stomachs are
full, you are more secure.' His methods of money-making are also
different; he wants to develop commercial crops like cotton, peanuts
and beans, to set up an oil press and a few cotton presses, and to open
general stores with goods from abroad. For him this is a quicker way of
making a larger fortune, without antagonizing the peasants. This
difference in outlook between the generations leads to many arguments
between father and son.

In *Keep the Red Flag Flying*, the struggle between the peasants and
the landlord takes the form of resisting pig tax. The Feng family has
purchased the pig-tax rights for 4,000 silver dollars, in anticipation of a
huge profit. Old Feng has allowed his son to enter this apparently
routine business transaction with the local magistrate, for in his
memory no peasants in this area ever revolted against government tax.
The pig-tax resistance campaign would indeed have been impossible,
had there not been a member of the Communist Party to organize it,
but even this shrewd Communist organizer would not have been able to
stir the village people to open rebellion, but for the feud between the
landlord Feng family and the peasant Chu family. That first violent
confrontation eventually leads to the ransacking of the landlord's
mansion in *Sowing the Flames*. The logical sequence of events
inevitably culminate in a large-scale peasant uprising.

As a partisan writer, Liang Pin has scored an outstanding success in
translating the concept of class antagonism and class struggle into a
powerful, moving human drama. He accomplishes this difficult task by
bringing the historic revolutionary struggle to a personal level. It is not
abstract ideas of justice and equality which make a revolution relevant

---

[34] Exploitation by the landlords is defined as 'renting land, plus money-lending,
hiring of labor, or simultaneously carrying on industrial commercial enterprises'.
See 'How to Analyze Class Status in the Countryside', in Albert P. Blaustein (ed.).
Fundamental Legal Documents of Communist China (New Jersey: Fred B.
Rothman and Co., 1962), p. 292: also in Theodore H. E. Chen (ed.), *The Chinese
Communist Regime: Documents and Commentary* (New York: Praeger, 1967),
p. 204. This document was first promulgated by the Democratic Central
Government in Juichin, Kiangsi, in 1933 and reaffirmed by the Government
Administrative Council of the Central People's Government on August 4, 1950.

to the villagers, but personal grievances, individual sufferings, and the small tragedies they share.

The feud between the Feng and Chu families, which forms an introduction to the book, is intensified by two direct confrontations. Significantly, both have nothing to do with rent or interest. One occurs when Feng Lan-chih, who has an obsessive interest in pet birds, first tries to buy and then to snatch a rare specimen from the boys of the Chu and Yen families. The conflict is a private one, yet at the same time suggests the essential quality of an oppressive socio-economic system. Feng's behavior reveals his unhesitating use of his own power and status, in defiance of public feeling.

When the boys refuse to sell him the bird, Feng Lan-chih whines to his son Kuei-t'ang that his only pleasures in life are tobacco and birds, but he cannot have that redbreast. Kuei-t'ang laughs, 'That's easy,' and sends their steward Li Te-tsai for the bird. Although there is no direct description of the Feng family's habitual treatment of the poor, it is implicit in the following dialogue:

> 'Mr. Feng wants that bird. Hand it over.'
> 'Uncle, don't the classics say: "A superior man does not take something others love"? My brothers are fond of that bird and don't mean to part with it.' He nodded and winked.
> 'Pah! What do you kids know of the classics? Hand it over! Then I'll tell the master: "Yen Yun-tao sends this as a gift to you, sir." And you never know what that may lead to.'
> 'Can't be done, uncle! Don't you know the saying: "Do unto others as you would be done by"? We don't want to part with it, and that's that.'
> 'That isn't the point. The ancients said: "If you help others, others will help you." Suppose he's angry and won't rent land to you? Suppose you want to borrow money, and he won't lend it, at no matter what interest?'
> He started into the house, but Yun-tao blocked the door, holding out his arms to stop him. 'It's the truth I'm telling you. The bird isn't here. Ta-kuei has it.'
> Li Te-tsai glared at him in angry silence, then made off in search of Ta-kuei...[35]

Despite all his efforts, Feng Lan-chih is still unable to obtain the bird and this wounds his pride. The author makes the best of the tension he has skilfully built up and moves swiftly to another incident. An opera is performed at the market-place as part of the New Year celebrations, and Chu Ta-kuei goes with Yen Yun-tao to see it. Old Feng, as the village head, is leading soldiers to conscript young peasants for the

[35] *Keep the Red Flag Flying*, p. 92, Yang, p. 98.

warlord army and Ta-kuei is immediately seized. This, of course, is a calamity to a poor peasant family, which depends on the young to work the fields.

Feng Lan-chih thus salves his wounded vanity by causing the Chu family great misfortune. With a little patience, he knows, he can sooner or later get even with the Yen family. He does not have to wait very long, for only two or three years later Yen Yun-tao is arrested and imprisoned at Tsinan for his participation as a Communist in the Northern Expeditionary Army. Li Te-tsai's earlier warning 'suppose you want to borrow money from him' is now borne out. When Yun-tao's father turns to Feng Lan-chih for a loan he is flatly refused. But the money is urgently needed in order to get Yun-tao out of prison, so poor Yen Chih-ho has to sell his two *mou* of Treasure Trove to Feng for eighty dollars. Feng Lan-chih feels satisfied both because tragedy has befallen the Yen family and because he has obtained one of the few good plots he has been eyeing.

It is relatively easy to draw landlords as villains in the old society, where they truly wielded social and economic power. When landlords are described as ruthless and heartless, peasants, by contrast, are seen as innocent and persecuted victims. This effect can be produced whether they are villains by ideological standards, or only according to conventional criteria. Either way, the reader sees the sufferings they cause, and readily sides with the victims. The reaction is personal and psychological, and therefore intense.

In spite of this, a novelist must still be wary of turning villains into anti-heroes, as Ou-yang Shan does in *Three Family Lane*. If villains are too powerful or too cunning in their confrontation with heroes, they may appear to overpower or outwit the heroes. Serious complications may result: the author may be suspected of belittling the heroes or deliberately magnifying the villains. This is what Liang Pin experienced in his description of the negative characters in *Keep the Red Flag Flying*.

> When I was finishing the third volume Comrade Fang Ming said to me: 'You should pay close attention to the negative characters, for if they overpower the positive characters from the beginning to the end, there will be a problem.' Yes, it can become serious and turn into an ideological problem.[36]

Liang Pin solved this problem by reducing the space devoted to negative characters, while at the same time emphasizing their characterization so that they remained conspicuous.

[36] Liang Pin, 'Some General Observations on the Creation of *Keep the Red Flag Flying*', *op. cit.*, p. 23.

The Party Organizer and the Problem of Wrong Leadership

Ou-yang Shan's approach of avoiding describing the cadre as far as possible is also adopted by Liang Pin in his treatment of Chia Hsiang-nung. In *Keep the Red Flag Flying* Liang Pin keeps Chia behind the scenes as long as possible. But there is an important difference. Ou-yang Shan describes Chin Tuan as a mysterious figure; Liang Pin portrays Chia as a man with human feelings and weaknesses. Before coming to the Kaoyang-Lihsien area, Chia has worked in a Tientsin factory, after two years of high school education. As a Communist in the factory, he organized the opposition to the civil war against warlords and their corrupt rule and was subsequently arrested. His torture in prison has left him permanently scarred; his lips still quiver and his hands shake. So Chia is not portrayed as a tough man, whose health is immune to ruin; on the other hand, his physical handicaps have little effect on his organizational work.

As the first secretary of the county Party committee, he performs Party functions while teaching in a primary school. Chia is not a grim, austere Party worker, but a modest and affable man. When he first sees Yen Chih-ho he calls him uncle, takes a puff at the pipe offered him, and talks about vegetables and farm work. He even takes off his gown, turns the windlass, and waters the vegetable patch. When he is invited to have a meal with the family he makes the customary refusal, but is not adamant. He is quite different from, and much more natural than cadres in some other novels, who would stiffly observe the Party discipline that a cadre should not freely accept anything offered by the people.

The author evidently feels that a cadre need not be irreproachable in attitude, style and emotion. Chia's friendly and casual style in dealing with peasants is not unique. As a matter of fact, the Party leadership always encourages field workers to befriend the masses in order to win their confidence and support. But Liang Pin has gone a step further in the characterization of Chia Hsiang-nung. Chia is not just amiable and helpful but also capable of showing his impatience and temper. A very busy man, he has to do organization work among the peasants, to write up reports for the county Party committee, and at the same time cope with his school teacher's routine. The author describes how Chia feels about the pile of student compositions after he has wrenched his brains to finish a report to the Party committee:

When at length he had finished he glanced at the calendar. Tomorrow was Saturday and he had another composition class. He had not yet corrected the last set of compositions. He clenched his teeth and dropped his pen on the table with a sigh. 'How time flies! Another week gone!' Reading through what he had written, he found it unsatisfactory, crumbled up the paper and chewed it. From his bookcase he took a pile of exercise books, forty or fifty altogether, thinking: 'I shall have to stay up again all night.'[37]

This is quite different from the stereotype of the cadre whose happiness increases in direct proportion to the amount of work he has to do. Here is a man who is tired and overworked, who would prefer a good, sound sleep. He is not the type of cadre whose strength is inexhaustible because he is nourished not on a miserable diet of coarse steamed bread and preserved pickles but on the spiritual food of ideology.

His fatigue changes to impatience, when two pupils drop in to ask him to chair an argument over whether the misery of Chinese peasants is due to exploitation by imperialism and feudalism or to a threefold exploitation by imperialism, warlords and politicians, and local landlords. It would appear impossible to deny two lovely, awakened children the satisfaction of an answer. But Chia's reaction is a surprise:

Chia laid his pen on the table. 'No, I can't! Do you mind going? I'm up to my ears in work. I've no time to talk.' With these words, he pushed them out.[38]

As the two pupils leave, still arguing, the orderly and the cook come in one after another. They ask how many guests Chia entertained the day before and complain about the confusion caused by his endless flow of visitors. By this time Chia's patience wears thin, and he flushes with temper. He tells them – two men of the laboring masses – to charge him whatever they like and to advance his salary from the accountant's office if necessary. Then he shows them out and bolts the door. These details seem trivial, but they are important to show Chia a man of flesh and blood, not just a specimen.

In both the pig-tax resistance campaign and the student protest at Paoting Normal School, Chia is in fact the organizer, but remains inconspicuous. This is of course necessitated by the real situation, for the Party was then operating underground, and Chia could not expose his true identity. But there is another reason. By making Chia more or less invisible, the author can then concentrate on the hero. A simple rule of art dictates that the supporting role should not divert the reader's attention from the main character. But this artistic principle contradicts the demands of Party doctrine which require the subordination of individual heroism to collective action. This point has been raised by Chang Ming, who was the secretary of the Kaoyang-Lihsien Central County Party Committee at the time:

[37] *Keep the Red Flag Flying*, p. 228, Yang, p. 251.
[38] *Ibid.*, p. 229, Yang, p. 253.

The principal character[39] in the novel is Chiang-tao, but his relationship with the Party and other comrades is not shown clearly enough. The victory in the pig-tax resistance campaign depended on the leadership of the Party and the collective efforts of the comrades. Then there is Chia Hsiang-nung. A section in the book describes how after correcting students' homework, he thought for a while and started to draft directives and write instructions. This kind of narrative raises a problem, for it fails to show the power of collective leadership in the Party organization . . . It was possible and feasible at that time to gather a few people together, call a meeting, and discuss problems. As a matter of fact, many of our activities, such as drafting instructions and assigning work, were usually decided after discussion at the county committee meetings.[40]

The comments are obviously made from viewpoint of a professional cadre who is more familiar with Party rules than artistic criteria. A ranking cadre himself, Liang Pin is clearly not oblivious of Party rules either. But as an artist, he has to follow the logic of characterization. He takes pains to explain why he has drawn Chia as he is:

The character of Chia Hsiang-nung is something I have never attempted before. When I started this long novel I felt a lack of confidence. I realized the difficulty of depicting a leading cadre, but how could a party leader be spared in a book like this? After careful consideration, I decided to make his appearances as few but as forceful as possible. Now I feel this is exactly the reason why this character is unsuccessful. The less confident I was and the less frequently he appeared, the less successful became his characterization. Had I given him more opportunities to appear, and then polished and condensed these episodes after the first draft, the result might have been a more powerful image. Of course, the main problem is that I did not have much knowledge of this character. In order to make up for this major defect, I shall strengthen the portrayal of Chia Hsiang-nung in the second volume.[41]

In *Sowing the Flames* the author keeps his promise by devoting a sixth of the entire book to Chia Hsiang-nung. On many occasions he shares the limelight with the hero Chu Lao-chung. The author also tries to stress Chia's Party character, without neglecting the human aspect of the cadre. Under the strain of heavy work, Chia is still able to respond to the sight of the setting sun, colorful clouds, and soaring larks. He still shows interest in the healthy stalks of *kaoliang* with their deep green

[39] '*Ku-kan*' or 'backbone' is the word used in the original.
[40] 'Recollections of the Old Warriors – Summary Report of Talks at the Discussion Meeting on *Keep the Red Flag Flying* Called by this Journal', *op. cit.*, p. 31.
[41] Liang Pin, 'Some General Observations on the Creation of *Keep the Red Flag Flying*', *op. cit.*, p. 22.

leaves and the yellow and white flowers of cotton plants. He is not ashamed to admit that he misses his family and longs to visit his parents and the place where he spent his childhood. Above all, he still calls Chu Lao-chung 'Uncle Chung' instead of 'Comrade Lao-chung', though the latter has become a fully-fledged Party member. The change of address would immediately suggest organization and discipline, and at the same time reduce the cordial relationship between the two men to impersonal comradeship. In short, even as the commander of the peasant Red Army personally directing the Kaoyang-Lihsien uprising, Chia Hsiang-nung has not been turned into a concept but has remained a man.

During the fierce battles, Chia, as commander of the peasant insurgents, tries to appear calm. But the author unmistakably conveys the impression that his outward serenity is maintained by a great effort of will, not by pretentious bravery. When peasants fall one after another under heavy enemy fire, Chia feels genuine pain. To him the casualties are not merely a question of numbers.

Finally, as the uprising turns out to be a decisive failure, Chia hands over the responsibility for leadership to Chu Lao-chung and leaves to make a personal report to the provincial Party special committee. No doubt, he will have to shoulder the entire responsibility for the unsuccessful military operation and answer every criticism levelled at him by senior comrades at a closed-door Party meeting. Accompanied by Ta-kuei on his way to board a ship on the river, he stops at a peasant's thatched hut for the night. Smoking the pipe offered him by the host, an old peasant, and listening to his talk about the land distribution and the failure of the Red Army, Chia says:

> 'Kind-hearted man, old daddy! We've failed, we must beg your forgiveness and that of the poor laboring people, for we shouldn't have failed. But this is our first uprising, we haven't organized it carefully enough, we've no military experience, so we've failed! failed! . . .'
>
> As Chia was speaking, he felt a great weight of sorrow and two large tears dropped on the pillow. Then he opened his wet eyes to look around and stretched out his right hand.
>
> 'Failed,' he said. 'We deserve to be held responsible by the people in the Kaoyang-Lihsien areas, but we shan't always fail. We'll carry on and raise our Red Flag again![42]

Sowing the Flames is a historical novel, so the tragic ending of the story is a foregone conclusion. In tracing the historical development of events, the author has recreated a number of brave people, whose strong feeling and unreserved dedication give life to a minor episode in

---

[42] *Sowing the Flames*, pp. 549–50.

the long, bloody revolution. Historically, the Kaoyang-Lihsien uprising of September 1932 is at least comparable in terms of size and strength to the Hunan Autumn Harvest Uprising of 1927, led by Mao Tsetung, but no account of this event could be found. The only reference is a condemnation of the 'Leftist' adventurism of Wang Ming, 1931–2.[43]

Here lies a dilemma which must have haunted the author throughout his work. Both the Paoting Normal School student movement and the Kaoyang-Lihsien uprising were directed by Wang Ming's so-called 'Leftist' adventurist line. Can raw material of this type, connected with a heretical policy, be used in a literary work? Hypothetically, it is possible if the whole operation is described from the viewpoint of repudiation. Had the author done this, the quality of his work would have degenerated to the level of propaganda pure and simple. But more important, from the practical point of view, is the involvement of many real people, who are not only still alive but actually holding high office. An outright denunciation of the mistaken policy would not only antagonize those who participated in the events, but also enrage Li Li-san and Wang Ming, who were still influential when the novel was being written.

The author solves this problem with great caution and skill in the first volume. He avoids describing the role of Party professionals played in the Paoting Normal School student protest, and thus makes the movement seem a spontaneous outburst of students' patriotism. In the conversation of the participating students some doubts and reservations about the direction of the movement are voiced, but the author stops short of a direct attack on the mistaken policy. By this means the role of the cadre is reduced, and the author is able to concentrate on the principal character.

This treatment of the Paoting Normal School incident, however, makes the actual participants unhappy. They make the political point that the heroes are too individualistic and the Party's organizational nature and collective function are not properly reflected. It is by no means unlikely that they feel that their role in a major political movement has been belittled. Obviously in response to criticism from the Party functionaries, the author devotes more space to the description of cadres in his subsequent work. Thus in *Sowing the Flames* not only does Chia Hsiang-nung occupy the center of the stage for a large part of the novel, but additional cadres are also briefly

[43] For instance, 'Appendix: Resolutions on Certain Questions in the History of Our Party', *op. cit.*, pp. 177–87; also Hu Ch'iao-mu, *Chung-kuo kung-ch'an-tang ti san-shih-nien* (The *Last Thirty Years of the Chinese Communist Party*) (Peking: People's Publishing House, 1951).
Wang Ming was one of the so-called twenty-eight Bolsheviks, and served as General Secretary of the CCP from 1931–2.

introduced. The whole uprising is directed from the top, the participants, peasants and cadres alike, show great courage in the fight, and the failure, as Chia explains to the old peasant, is due to the lack of organizational and military experience. The author deliberately omits any reference to the problem of the wrong line. Indeed, if the question of the correctness of the policy were to be raised, then the author would either have to abandon the entire plan of using the uprising as the major event of the story or produce a strictly propaganda work based on the official verdict of Party history.

The question of wrong leadership is so serious that the author could hardly overlook it. In fact, even the name of the leading cadre, Chia Hsiang-nung, seems to have been carefully chosen to contain hidden meanings. 'Hsiang' is the abbreviated name for Hunan province, 'nung' means 'peasant', and the two words together mean 'Hunanese peasant'. The surname 'Chia' sounds the same as 'chia' meaning 'false' or 'fake'. Thus the name Chia Hsiang-nung can mean 'fake Hunanese peasant', as a reference to the wrong leadership (the true leader being a Hunanese peasant named Mao Tse-tung).[44]

Despite all the precautions taken by the author, the description of the heroic struggle of the peasants and selfless dedication of the cadres gives the impression that the uprising is not a total failure in the political sense. It suffers a disastrous defeat from the military viewpoint, but again the reader may accept the explanation that this is really because the time was not ripe or the Communist Party had not yet gained sufficient experience in military operations. This may very well be the case, but this interpretation has not been sanctioned by the leadership. As a result, the novel gives the impression of being an apologia for Wang Ming's 'Left' adventurist line which was officially censured in the resolution passed at the Seventh National Congress of the Chinese Communist Party in April 1945. This is precisely the reason offered for repudiating the novel during the Cultural Revolution.[45]

---

[44] I have not invented this far-fetched interpretation. There has been one school of research on *Dream of the Red Chamber* which interprets the name Chia Pao-yu as 'fake precious stone' or 'fake Great Seal of the Empire'. These scholars argue that *Dream of the Red Chamber* is actually a nationalistic novel with a hidden message calling the Han people to overthrow the Manchus, who were then occupying the Chinese throne. To support their thesis they point out the many political crime cases, in which scholars concealed their anti-Manchu feelings in overtly harmless poems and were later arrested, prosecuted, and convicted. Liang Pin may have had this interpretation in mind when he chose the name Chia Hsiang-nung.

[45] The Revolutionary Rebel Corps of the People's Publishing House, 'Shih-san-pu ta tu-ts'ao tsai na-li?' (Where Are the Thirteen Great Poisonous Weeds?), *Feng lei pao* (*Wind and Thunder Journal*), May 23, 1967; also 'Ch'üan-min wen-i heh-ch'i hsia ti ch'an-p'in – Hai-jen ti tu-yo, sha-jen ti hsiung-ch'i' (The Product of All-People Literature Black Banner – Harmful Poison, Murderous Weapon), *Wen-hsüeh chan-pao* (*Literary Battle Bulletin*), June 7, 1967.

We should not, however, regard the ideological invective, launched in the heat of the Cultural Revolution, as the authoritative verdict on the leadership problem. Judgment rendered at a calmer time should be a more reliable indication. Yao Wen-yuan, who has achieved great prominence as a result of his role in the Cultural Revolution, never raised any ideological questions in his evaluation of *Keep the Red Flag Flying.*[46] On the contrary, he places Liang Pin's Chu Lao-chung and Liu Ch'ing's Liang Sheng-pao[47] on the same artistic plane with Lu Hsün's Ah Q. According to Yao, while the story of Ah Q reflects the tragic fate of the poor peasant during the old democratic revolution led by the bourgeois class, Chu Lao-chung represents the awakened revolutionary peasant in the period of the new democratic revolution, and Liang Sheng-pao typifies the new revolutionary peasant in the era of socialist revolution. Yao's view perhaps reflects the leadership position more accurately towards the central theme of the novel than that expressed in the short-lived polemical publications of the Cultural Revolution. In his assessment, Yao clearly has not lost his historical perspective. Characters such as Chu Lao-chung and Chia Hsiang-nung must be appraised in the light of the time and circumstances under which they live.

[46] Yao Wen-yuan, 'Ts'ung Ah Q tao Liang Sheng-pao' (From Ah Q to Liang Sheng-pao), *Tsai ch'ien-chin ti tao-lu shang* (*On the Road to Progress*) (Shanghai: People's Publishing House, 1965), pp. 301–16.
[47] See Chapter 8.

3

THE UNDERGROUND STRUGGLE IN "WHITE" AREAS

I INTELLECTUALS AND REVOLUTIONARIES

Underground struggle is a crucial part of the over-all revolutionary movement of the Chinese Communist Party. It was carried out in vast areas not under direct Communist control and extended over a quarter of a century. Since the Communist Party was vying for leadership with rival political authorities, be it the Kuomintang or the Wang Ching-wei puppet regime, it adopted two parallel strategies, legal and illegal. Legal struggle took place within the laws established by the governing authorities. Since in the areas controlled by the Kuomintang or the puppet regime very little political freedom was tolerated, the Communist Party usually operated illegally, i.e., underground. Whenever feasible, both legal and illegal methods were used. The Party's operational tactics also varied significantly, according to the nature of the work, the targets for attack, the strength of the enemy, the situation in the base areas, and finally its own military progress. The goals of the Communist Underground can be generally identified as recruiting support from among students and intellectuals, infiltrating the ranks of the enemy, effecting disintegration and defection among the enemy, building the basis of mass support, and above all broadening the Party organization in 'white' areas.[1]

Novels of underground struggle make a fascinating study, for they offer us an opportunity to understand the clandestine aspect of Party work. No other sources yet uncovered give such vivid accounts of the tactical maneuvers and operational methods of the Party underground. These are intriguing topics and will be explored in the next chapter. The novels also provide clues for understanding why students, writers, teachers, college professors and other intellectuals, mainly products of Western-type education, joined the Communist movement in large numbers. The heroes and villains, when considered in relation to the perspectives of novelists of different backgrounds, provide subtle

---

[1] Some of the tactical as well as strategic principles are outlined in 'Resolution on Certain Questions in the History of Our Party' as an appendix to *Selected Works of Mao Tse-tung*, Vol. III (Peking: Foreign Languages Press, 1965), pp. 198–9, 202–3.

studies of these intellectuals. Their support of the movement was one of the most important reasons for the victory of Communism in China, but they also created unexpected problems for the Party in the post-liberation period.

These novels are written by two types of authors: intellectuals who never became Party men and professionals who spent most of their time in underground work. When these events occurred the intellectuals were either activist students or leftist writers. Obviously interested in the underground struggle, they never took part in the secret organization. They were observers, at best peripheral workers, but not underground cadres. As authors, they are eager to prove their support for the cause by presenting it as a struggle between good and evil. But such efforts are not entirely successful, for their works betray their perspective as non-revolutionaries.

The behavior patterns of principal characters portrayed by the two groups of novelists exhibit a fundamental difference. The heroes in the novels of non-Communist authors love to quote poems by Shelley or to admire Tolstoy's long white beard; their counterparts in the works of professional cadres are the products of Chinese culture. The difference is due as much to attitude as to training. The villains in the romanticized novels of non-Communist authors are much less interesting, perhaps because they have had no personal experience of a Kuomintang official, a general in the puppet army, or a plainclothes man to draw upon. On the other hand, since the cadres used to deal with such characters in their real work, they are able to produce a more accurate picture of their adversaries. Characters based on real people are always more vivid and forceful than fabrications.

Any attempt to probe deeper beneath the superficial resemblance of the stories requires an investigation of the background of the authors. Their education, family origin, and professions will throw light on the bewildering incongruity between the stories they have produced and the underlying messages they actually convey. Even as petty bourgeois intellectuals, their support for the Communist cause and admiration for the courage and dedication of underground workers must be considered sincere, but in a subtle way they reveal their own aspirations and concerns, which are remarkably inconsistent with the cold reality of ruthless underground struggle. Even their descriptions of blood and death, resemble the scenario of a Peking opera, rather than the secret torture room or the execution ground.

We shall start with one of the most controversial novels, *The Song of Youth* by Yang Mo.[2] The story deals with the Communist-led student

---

[2] Yang Mo, *Ch'ing-ch'un chih ko* (*The Song of Youth*) (Peking: People's Literature Publishing House, rev. ed., 1960). Four instalments of the novel in English translation appear in *Chinese Literature*, Nos. 3, 4, 5 and 6, 1960, pp. 3–48, 46–105, 45–92, and 80–137.

movement against the Kuomintang policy of non-resistance, at a time
when China had already lost its northeastern provinces and was under
the immediate threat of further invasion by Japan. It covers a period
from the Mukden Incident on September 18, 1931[3] to the student
protest march of December 9, 1935. It is partly autobiographical: the
heroine is clearly identifiable with the author. Yang Mo admits this
herself:

> My personal experience in life has determined my choice of Lin
> Tao-ching as the heroine of the novel. Lin Tao-ching is not myself,
> but her life contains the elements of my life. My family was similar
> to the family of the great feudal landlord to which Lin Tao-ching
> was born. My father also resembled her father. He raped Hsiu-ni,
> who drowned herself after she became pregnant. The difference is
> that I was not born by Hsiu-ni.[4]

It has never been disclosed whether Yang Mo ever joined the
Communist Party. An introductory note to the English translation of
the novel in *Chinese Literature* briefly states that Yang Mo, born in
Hunan in 1915, is a scenario writer of the Peking Film Studio and has
written a number of essays and short stories.[5] In her own writings and
lectures,[6] she tells about her selfish, ruthless and decadent
landlord family, the break with her father after graduation from high
school, and the search for a teaching job in primary school. She lived
for several years in one of the small apartments near the red-brick
hall of Peking University, came to know some Communists, and was in
the liberated area during the anti-Japanese War. She admits that Lin
Tao-ching's life before she joined the Party is based largely on her own,
but the heroine's Party life is a composite picture of many people she
used to know.[7] In the intense discussion of *The Song of Youth*, which
lasted for four or five months in 1959, Yang Mo was addressed as

---

[3] On this date, the Japanese invaded Mukden and began their fourteen-year
occupation of Manchuria.
[4] Yang Mo, 'Shih-mo li-liang ku-wu wo hsieh *Ch'ing-ch'un chih ko*' (Forces That
Encouraged Me to Write *The Song of Youth*), *Chinese Youth Daily*, May 3, 1958,
cited in T. A. Hsia, 'Heroes and Hero-Worship in Chinese Communist Fiction',
The China Quarterly, No. 13, January/March 1963, p. 122.
[5] *Chinese Literature*, No. 3, 1960, p. 3.
[6] Yang Mo, 'Forces That Encouraged Me to Write *The Song of Youth*', *op. cit.*;
'Pei-ching sha-t'an ti hung-lou – wo tsai *Ch'ing-ch'un chih ko* chung i Pei-ta wei
pei-ching ti yüan-yin' (The Red-brick Hall on Peking University Campus –
Reasons for Choosing Peking University as the Background in *The Song of
Youth*), *Kuang-ming jih-pao*, May 3, 1958; '*Ch'ing-ch'un chih ko* tsai-pan hou-chi'
(Postscript to the Revised Edition of *The Song of Youth*), *Kuang-ming jih-pao*,
January 19, 1960; Chang Pi-ying and Ch'en Ch'in-p'ing, 'Fang *Ch'ing-ch'un chih
ko* tso-che Yang Mo' (An Interview with Yang Mo, Author of *The Song of Youth*),
Chinese Youth Daily, August 9, 1959.
[7] Chang Pi-ying and Ch'en Ch'in-p'ing, 'An Interview with Yang Mo, Author of
The Song of Youth', *op. cit.*

58   *Heroes and Villains in Communist China*

'comrade'. The term, however, can be used in a general sense and does not necessarily suggest her party membership.

The author of the second novel *Annals of a Provincial Town*[8] has an even more unusual life story. Born in 1910 in Amoy to a merchant father who did business with overseas Chinese in Southeast Asia, Kao Yun-lan met a Communist teacher at the age of sixteen and joined the Youth League the following year as a high school student. Later in Shanghai he became a member of the League of Left Wing Writers. When the Kuomintang authorities started rounding up leftist writers, Kao fled to Amoy and discontinued his association with the Communist Party.

During the war years, Kao was first a high school teacher in Malaya and then drifted across the strait to Sumatra when the Japanese occupied the peninsula. There he made a living by selling soap and wine, but by the time the Japanese surrendered he had become the manager of a prosperous trading company. He apparently led a kind of double life, living the life of a rich merchant in public, and writing stories and novels at night. Arrested as a 'Red capitalist' by the British authorities, he was deported in 1949. Upon his return to Tientsin in 1950, he took part in the activities of the Chinese Democratic League, which he joined in Malaya in 1946.[9]

Annals of a Provincial Town is based on a Party-organized prison raid in 1930. As it occurs in the novel, however, the time is 1937. The change of time is apparently made to suit the over-all political situation in China more closely. In 1937 the Communist Party had established its headquarters in Yenan and the war with Japan was under way. The author spent three years and three months on the novel, and revised it six times. Some chapters he even revised a dozen times.[10] The last manuscript was sent to a man in charge of propaganda and publication on May 19; on June 13, 1956, he died. The novel was published posthumously.

Adventure, Love and the Conflict of Values

There are remarkable similarities in the perspectives of the two non-Communist authors. Underground struggle is viewed as a task full

[8] Kao Yun-lan, *Hsiao-ch'eng ch'un-ch'iu* (Peking: Writers' Publishing House, 1956). It is translated into English by Sydney Shapiro under the title *Annals of a Provincial Town* (Peking: Foreign Languages Press, 1959).
[9] This biographical information is based on Chang Ch'u-k'un, 'Wang-yu Kao Yun-lan ho t'a-ti i-chu *Hsiao-ch'eng ch'un-ch'iu*' (My Friend Kao Yun-lan and His Posthumous Work *Annals of a Provincial Town*) which appears as an appendix to the novel. Chang is the Vice-Mayor of Amoy.
[10] Kao Yun-lan, '*Hsiao-ch'eng ch'un-ch'iu* ti hsieh-tso ching-ko' (The Process of Writing *Annals of a Provincial Town*), *Annals of a Provincial Town*, p. 316.

of adventure and mystery. Perhaps in their youth the secrecy of the work had appealed to them. They may also exaggerate the distant memory of an encounter with real Communist underground workers. Both *The Song of Youth* and *Annals of a Provincial Town* are stories of colorful, romantic adventure, rather than the tough, dangerous missions they really were.

As in romance of any language, love inevitably occupies a prominent place. Communist writers do not neglect the theme of love, but treat it seriously, on principle. Once a man falls in love with a woman or vice versa, he means it and sticks to it. The attitude towards love is symptomatic of political belief. Once a man becomes a Communist, he sticks to this belief, body and soul. When described by non-Communist writers, love becomes complicated. It is always triangular. Two comrades love the same woman and each tries to give up his claim so that his comrade will enjoy the happiness he so richly deserves. Such treatment of course complicates the story and makes it more interesting. But it also bespeaks an attitude toward the Communist Party's strict demand for political chastity. It reflects a profound and deep sealed sense of conflict, a conflict which can take a variety of forms. On a higher level, it can involve a conflict of values in the author. Is it Communism or simply nationalism, or some unspecified goal, that he is seeking to promote? In such a fundamental conflict, which involves politics, the victory of Communism is usually more apparent than real. We shall return to this point later.

In *The Song of Youth* the heroine Lin Tao-ching falls in love with three men. She loves at least two men at any given time. While she is cohabiting with Yu Yung-tse, in the fashion of the liberated woman of the May 4th tradition, she is secretly in love with Lu Chia-chuan. Yu is a student of history at Peking University who wants to be a scholar and to have a secure academic position. Lu is also a student, but at the same time a leader in the Communist organization at Peking University. Yu is described as a vulgar man, physically undistinguished; by contrast, Lu has a 'handsome face', 'kindly, brilliant eyes', and 'an ardent, radiant smile'. It is not at all clear whether it is Lu's good looks or his revolutionary zeal which attracts Lin to him. Naturally enough, Yu becomes a jealous 'husband', although they are not legally married. And domestic quarrels ensue.

Seeing Lin Tao-ching intensely absorbed in books such as Marx's *Poverty of Philosophy* and Engels' *Anti-Duhring,* Yu would cynically call her 'the great disciple of Marx'. To this Lin would retort, 'Anyway, far better a disciple of Karl Marx than a disciple of Hu Shih.' The argument then escalates. Yu says:

'Revolution! Struggle! What high-sounding terms! But I've never seen any of these young gentlemen and ladies who profess to be revolutionaries going down into a mine. After all, it's much more comfortable just to shout about the proletariat and the bourgeoisie!"[11]

The argument leads to no conclusion, but the conflict between the two trains of thought is real. It is symbolic of the opposing tendencies then prevailing, the one, urged by Hu Shih, that students should concern themselves with study and leave politics alone, and the other, argued by progressive scholars, radical students and Communist leaders, that they should be involved in political activities to save the country from oppression. The theory of revolutionary involvement wins when Lin Tao-ching deserts Yu Yung-tse, as Nora does in Ibsen's *A Doll's House.*

Lin Tao-ching's love for Lu Chia-chuan remains on the platonic level, for Lu is arrested by the Kuomintang gendarmerie as the Chinese Nora abandons her comfortable petty bourgeois life. She is soon attracted to Chiang Hua, another Communist student leader, while Lu is undergoing torture in prison. For his part, Chiang, knowing Lin loves Lu Chia-chuan, his comrade and best friend, still cannot resist this very attractive girl. He does not reveal his inner feelings until the death of Lu is confirmed. On one occasion Chiang's love for Lin is expressed like this:

Chiang Hua looked at Tao-ching's eyes, clear and transparent as lake water, and her pale, beautiful face, and watched her open manner and ardent talk. Suddenly he could not speak. For a long time he had loved this young and passionate woman comrade. . . Today he realized that she was not only a courageous comrade but also a tender woman longing for emotional consolation. In her eyes he sensed her inner void and loneliness. Then what about himself? Hadn't he already waited in painful expectation for long time?[12]

Lin's feelings are described, as seen by Chiang Hua. The immediate question is whether Lin really has those feelings of emptiness and loneliness. The woman had left Yu Yung-tse's warm apartment and his jealous, therefore passionate, love in search of revolution. Can a girl, by this time already a Party member, intensely involved in underground work, still feel her life is empty and lonely? If so, the work must be meaningless and unexciting. And the Party organization has failed to fulfill her psychological need. Or rather, is her real aim in leaving her first lover, an academic type, to look for a knightly hero who exists only in her youthful imagination?

Even more surprising is the description of Chiang Hua's state of mind. He is supposed to be a Communist of proletarian origin. After

[11] *The Song of Youth*, p. 161, *Chinese Literature*, No. 4, 1960, p. 102.
[12] *Ibid.*, pp. 518–19.

leaving elementary school, he has worked as an apprentice in a Shanghai printing shop. This type of background is often supplied to show the revolutionary's class purity. By working part-time, he has managed to become a student of philosophy at Peking University. His experience as a leader of workers on strike and protesting students apparently has not hardened him. Or has he been converted into a petty bourgeois by the softening effect of university life? To show that Chiang Hua is more a student than a Communist, we need to quote the following narrative:

> Say it? Not say it? Where should I start? . . . His dark face blushed. He rubbed his two large hands restlessly over the fire — as if to cover up his excitement. Twenty-nine years old, except for one transient infatuation, Li Meng-yü (Chiang Hua) had never felt the weight of such passionate love. He had endured in silence, letting slip the opportunity for countless happy moments. But now he would not wait any longer, would not let himself and his beloved suffer. So he raised his head, tenderly took Tao-ching's hand, and did his best to control his trembling. In a low voice, he said frankly:
> 'Tao-ching, today I dropped in to see you, not to discuss our work, I'd like to ask you — tell me if our relationship could become more intimate than comradeship?'[13]

The feelings may be genuine, but are not those of a Communist. At least, the way the feelings are expressed is definitely not Communist. When a man regrets the passing of youth and the lack of a woman's love, these are universal human feelings. To suggest that any relationship could be more intimate than comradeship is not consistent with Communist terminology. A lot of things a man cannot talk about with his sweetheart, his wife or his parents can be openly discussed with his comrades. Here Chiang Hua is of course referring to a sexual relationship that will satisfy his physical desires. As comrades and very close friends, Chiang and Lin have talked about everything, shared their fate as Communists wanted by the Kuomintang gendarmerie, and warmed and encouraged each other in moments of desperation. The idea that the most intimate relationship exists only in the union of man and woman, both body and soul, is most un-Communist.

The triangular love-affairs in *Annals of a Provincial Town* are even more complicated. Two comrades fall in love with the same girl, and at the same time one of them has a wife, also a Communist, who works in a different place. Ho Chien-ping, who has been away on a party assignment for two years, returns to Amoy only to find his girl already in love with another man. The man, Ch'en Szu-min, happens to be a comrade who teaches at an elementary school, and secures a position for Ho in the same place. Watching the kind of concern his girl Ting

[13] *Ibid.*, p. 566.

Hsiu-wei shows to Szu-min, Ho first 'felt something like lead pressing on his heart' and then 'sensed an unexpected feeling of jealousy'. He thus faces a dilemma: he is jealous but also blames himself for the selfish feeling. He thinks that he has no right to demand love from the girl he loves and at the same time he has no right to prevent his comrade from being loved by his girl.

On the other hand, Szu-min is also suffering remorse. He knows that he has no right, as a married man, to love his comrade's girl. After a considerable emotional upheaval, he finally tells both of them that not only is he married, but he also has a two-year old girl. As a result, Chien-ping and Hsiu-wei quickly recover their early intimacy. But the author refuses to abandon this intricate love episode. Szu-min suddenly leaves Amoy for more than a month. When he returns he is almost a different person, thin and ill. Ho quickly learns that Szu-min's Communist wife has been arrested and executed.

Ho Chien-ping is once more ill at ease. He cannot decide whether he should tell his girl about the death of Szu-min's wife. The thought that the news may drive Hsiu-wei away from him makes him tremble. When he realizes that the trembling is the result of his own weakness and selfishness, he begins to hate himself. One day, he sees the silhouette of a couple from a reading room — his girl raising her head from Szu-min's shoulder and wiping away her tears and Szu-min's face also drawn with sorrow. Chien-ping immediately flees from the scene. He does not know that the two have just witnessed a tragedy, the death of a boy laborer who fell from the scaffolding.

Chien-ping runs straight to the home of Li Yueh, his best friend and the leader of the Party underground. He pours out his feelings and declares his determination to withdraw. Li Yueh coldly criticizes this attitude as a sign of great male chauvinism. He points out that Hsiu-wei ought to be able to make up her own mind, and Chien-ping must respect her decision. She is not a commodity which can be presented as a gift. The love story ends in a melodramatic fashion. Szu-min is seriously wounded during the jail break and in order not to hinder the escape of Chien-ping, also injured, he jumps into the sea and drowns himself. Thus, Chien-ping and Hsiu-wei become lovers with a clear conscience.

As a love episode, the story is as stale as a glass of overnight wine. It has been told and retold by countless authors, since the literary revolution undermined the system of arranged marriage. What is interesting is the insertion of such a threadbare triangular love-affair in a story of underground struggle. The relationships are no further complicated by the existence of comradeship, which could easily be replaced by some other relationship, such as brotherhood. The criticism by Li Yueh of Chien-ping's great male chauvinism is particularly inappropriate to his own position as the leader of the underground organization. It is strange that Li Yueh has not looked at the conflict over a young woman from the point of view of its effect on the unity of two comrades and above all on Party work. The only explanation seems to be that although the author has tried hard to be ideologically correct by mouthing clichés,[14] he does not think in Communist terms when he is dealing with matters which are ostensibly apolitical.

The thesis that love has political implications and that there is a difference between the petty bourgeois and Communist approach to the theme of love is supported by a comparison between the Chinese texts and their English versions. Since only portions of *The Song of Youth* are translated, the exclusion of the passages quoted above cannot be used as conclusive evidence. But in the English version of *Annals of a Provincial Town* the whole triangular love story is deleted. A possible explanation of its inclusion in the Chinese edition is the difference in time. In 1956, when the novel was first published, the propaganda department may have been less strict, or overlooked the political implications in the love triangle. This ideological loophole, however, was closed when the novel was rendered into English.

The amputation of the story has restored ideological consistency in the novel but has not improved its quality. Whether Kao Yun-lan could produce a better novel if he did not have to worry about ideology is certainly open to question. But in the process of writing it, he has undoubtedly been confronted with this conflict between art and politics. Perhaps the most interesting character in *Annals of a Provincial Town* is Liu Mei, a petty bourgeois artist and self-proclaimed progressive. Once he has a debate with Ho Chien-ping on the subject of art and politics.

'I must explain,' he said solemnly. 'I paint two kinds of pictures — creative works of art and propaganda. None of my art works convey any message. None of my propaganda works can be considered art.'

His tone was soft and modest. To his surprise, Chien-ping promptly contradicted him.

'I don't agree with you. All art is propaganda. The two are inseparable!'

The smile left Liu Mei's face. 'According to that view, art is a dead thing, a mere instrument of politics. . .'

'Right. Art is a political weapon.' .

'A political slave, you mean.'

'No, not a slave, but it should serve politics.'

---

[14] For instance, as Ho Chien-ping was being taken to the execution ground, he thought to himself, 'Dear Chairman Mao, at the moment I fall, my heart is with you . . .' p. 164. Significantly, this passage is omitted in the English version.

'That's vulgar utilitarianism, an insult to art!'
'What insults art is bourgeois culture! The dissolute culture of the capitalist class!'
'Art knows no class. It is above class. Twentieth century art is not restricted by the bounds of reason. It is the product of emotion, nothing else. That is why we advocate giving full play to the ego, going back to nature, to the primitive. We worship abandon. We believe that only wild abandon can produce great works! . . .'[15]

The debate reaches no conclusion, perhaps because the author is himself uncertain. We do not know whether the author's six revisions were made to improve the novel technically or for ideological reasons. He acknowledged the enthusiastic assistance of some comrades and friends, and admitted that the novel had given him hard time. He said further:

> In the process of contemplating and writing, I continually pruned the formulistic, conceptual rubbish and naturalistic siftings. It can be said that in pursuing the path of socialist realism, from theoretical research to actual application, I had to feel my way at every step.[16]

We do not know what Kao Yun-lan's real feelings were. He probably believed that literature should reflect politics, as so many leftist and progressive writers did, but it is certainly possible that he also thought that all artistic work should maintain its autonomy. Once art is used as a pure political weapon, it becomes, as Liu Mei eagerly points out, the slave of politics. It involves a conflict of values in the conscience of a non-Communist writer. For dedicated Communist writers, no such conflict exists in their work. They always pursue artistic excellence within the bounds of ideological conformity.

The Metamorphosis of a Petty Bourgeois Intellectual?

A secondary theme in *The Song of Youth*, no less important than the description of the role of the Communist Party in the patriotic student movement, is the transformation of a petty bourgeois intellectual. Lin Tao-ching once tells Chiang Hua that her father is a landlord but her mother a farm-laborer. There are thus both white bones and black bones in her. Only after she meets a very good man who teaches her to look at things and people from the class viewpoint do her white bones begin to wither away. The process of transformation of Lin Tao-ching from a petty bourgeois student to a revolutionary is the author's

[15] *Annals of a Provincial Town*, pp. 84–5, Shapiro, pp. 94–5.
[16] Kao Yun-lan, 'The Process of Writing *Annals of a Provincial Town*', *op. cit.*, p. 316.

theme.[17] At first, Lin is only angered by the sufferings of herself and poor people, then she posts revolutionary slogans all on her own under the cover of darkness, and finally after a year of imprisonment she becomes 'steeled' and is accepted into the Party. The metamorphosis of Lin from a girl who cannot accept the cruel reality to a lone heroine, and eventually to a revolutionary fighter, seems clear. But after all that physical and psychological struggle, does Lin Tao-ching really become a proletarian revolutionary? The question has become the subject of a prolonged debate.

It all started with an article by a critic named Kuo K'ai, who argued that Lin remains a petty bourgeois student throughout, and that the novel has had a harmful effect on young readers.[18] His contention is more systematically developed in a later article which urges:

> We are all materialist. A person's way of thinking is formed in the environment where he lives, not brought with him from his mother's womb. Although Lin Tao-ching's mother was a farm-laborer, she left the child when she was very young. Therefore, she has no influence on the formation of Lin Tao-ching's class-consciousness, thoughts and feelings.[19]

Kuo K'ai elaborates on his theme by arguing that blood relationship should not be confused with class character. Class character is determined by a person's economic status and social environment; blood relationship, a genetic phenomenon, cannot influence a person's class character. The author Yang Mo thinks that Lin has black bones and can easily be transformed. Therefore, with a few light touches a 'proletarian fighter' is created. The criticism is a fundamental contention which questions the ideological soundness of the novel's thesis. The novel, however, has been positively evaluated by party leaders of literature and art. As a result, widespread discussions are encouraged, and a meeting of real proletarian workers is even called to review the novel.[20] The conclusions of the group discussion are in favor of the

[17] Yang Mo, 'T'an-t'an Lin Tao-ching ti hsing-hsiang' (Talks on the Image of Lin Tao-ching), *Jen-min wen-hsüeh*, No. 7, 1959, p. 103.
[18] Kuo K'ai, 'Lioh t'an tui Lin Tao-ching ti miao-hsieh chung ti ch'üeh-tien – P'ing Yang Mo ti hsiao-shuo *Ch'ing-ch'un chih ko'* (Brief Commentaries on the Shortcomings in the Characterization of Lin Tao-ching – A Review of Yang Mo's Novel *The Song of Youth*), *Chung-kuo ch'ing-nien*, No. 2, 1959, pp. 37–40.
[19] Kuo K'ai, 'Chiu *Ch'ing-ch'un chih ko* t'an wen-i ch'uang-tso ho p'i-p'ing chung ti chi-ko yüan-tse wen-t'i – Tsai p'ing Yang Mo t'ung-chih ti hsiao-shuo *Ch'ing-ch'un chih ko'* (Commentaries on Matters of Principle in Literary Creation and Criticism in the Discussion of *The Song of Youth* – A Second Review of Comrade Yang Mo's *The Song of Youth*), *Wen-i pao*, No. 4, 1959, p. 34.
[20] 'Kung-jen t'an *Ch'ing-ch'un chih ko'* (Workers Discuss *The Song of Youth*), *Wen-i pao*, No. 6, 1959.

author, and most other commentators agree that Yang Mo has successfully created a genuine proletarian heroine. The various views are best summarized in an article by Ma T'ieh-ting:

> Man is a class animal but also lives in a complex society full of class contradictions. Therefore, the proletarians may be influenced by the thoughts of the bourgeois; those who came from the bourgeois or feudal families may also reject their own class and join the proletariat. After they have joined the proletariat, they may still retain a large or small tail which belongs to their original class. Thus, it is rather common that there is blackness in whiteness or whiteness in blackness.[21]

This is a crucial argument in defending the political reliability of bourgeois. or petty bourgeois turned Communist revolutionaries. It is a refutation of Kuo K'ai's theory of mechanical materialism. Nevertheless, it is a political or theoretical argument, not a literary criticism. From the literary point of view, Kuo K'ai is in effect correct in saying that Lin Tao-ching is never really transformed, although his analysis failed to establish this point.

One effective way of characterizing a person is to show their inner feelings in reaction to the environment. At the opening of the novel, Lin Tao-ching runs away from her step-mother and landlord family to seek temporary shelter with her cousin, who is a school teacher in Peitaiho, the Chinese riviera. When she first sees the sea she cannot conceal her schoolgirl's delight.

> 'Look at the sea. How beautiful!' The girl turned her head. 'How lucky you are, living in this beautiful place!'
> 'What's so good about it? You can't fish, you get nothing to eat. We don't care in the least whether it's beautiful or not...'[22]

The sea in the resort area is a schoolgirl's dream; to the porter, a true proletarian, it is nothing but a large body of water where you cannot fish. The author cleverly contrasts the imaginative cast of mind of Lin Tao-ching, then a teenage girl, with the feelings of the porter. But when Yang Mo claims that Lin has undergone the first revolutionary test through her participation in the class struggle in the countryside,[23] she

[21] Ma T'ieh-ting, 'Lun *Ch'ing-ch'un chih ko* chih ch'i lun-cheng' (On *The Song of Youth* and Its Commentaries), *Wen-i pao*, No. 9, 1959, p. 43.
[22] *The Song of Youth*, p. 5.
[23] Yang Mo, 'Tsai-pan hou-chi' (Postscript to the Revised Edition), *The Song of Youth*, p. 627. According to the author, seven chapters were added to the first edition to give Lin Tao-ching the opportunity to undergo revolutionary test in the countryside, the lack of which had been pointed out in Kuo K'ai's article in *Chung-kuo ch'ing-nien*.

either merely assumes an ideological stance or is unable to portray character transformation. Lin's involvement in a village riot places her in danger of arrest. As she is being escorted to safety by a hired hand of the landlord, the flight is turned into a scene of dreamy beauty:

> The two were running through the sleeping fields without saying a word. The cool night breeze stirred the dewy leaves of *kaoliang*, the rustling branches of poplars, the phosphorescent water of the stream, and also the pretty excited face of Lin Tao-ching . . . How beautiful was the summer night! Stars shone crystal clear in the boundless dark sky; grasshoppers, crickets and sleepless frogs, and cicadas, hidden in the grass, by the ponds and in the foliages, were singing their gentle love-songs. Then the vast, still fields sound asleep, the emerald-green crops, the bubbling flowing stream, the curved path extending far into darkness, the wild flowers and leaves spreading aroma, the dense yet refreshingly intoxicating air, and above all the life of revolutionary struggle, so like a legend, were all so enchanting that they gave a special kind of aesthetic joy.[24]

This purple passage does not accurately reflect the mental state of a girl running for her life. Lin Tao-ching cannot be so oblivious of her danger as to be lost in girlish elation. Yang Mo seems to have been carried away when she uses 'emerald-green' to describe crops (*pi-lu ti chuang-chia*) at night. It is clear that Yang Mo is more interested in conveying the imaginative power of an adolescent mind than the hardened attitude of a girl revolutionary.

Lin Tao-ching has never grown beyond the state of a motherless child longing for maternal care and affection. There is no lack of orphans in Communist literature. In most cases they are boys, little dare-devils, running errands for older Red soldiers or cadres. When little girls occasionally appear they serve as nurses in field hospitals. Such youngsters also miss parental love, but their psychological void is always filled by the Party, the army, or the organization. The process of transformation is accomplished only when the Party has truly replaced the parents in a young mind. But for Lin Tao-ching, the Party never takes the place of a mother. Even after she has become a Communist underground worker, her longing for motherly love has not diminished. She even likes to imagine the older woman, a senior cadre under whom she works, her mother. This state of her mind is best revealed in an extract from the diary she keeps.

> Ostensibly we are mother and daughter earning a living as washer-women, but in reality she's a member of the District Party Committee and I'm a liaison worker. When she hands me an important and urgent document, she fixes her kind, steady eyes on

---

[24] *The Song of Youth*, pp. 347–8.

me and gives me quiet, motherly instructions: 'Hsiu-lan, take this shirt to Mr. Wang. Be careful with it!' Whenever she gives me an assignment like this, I feel a surge of indescribable energy, and her kind steady gaze seems to set my heart on fire. She watches me as I walk out of our old ramshackle gate, while I inwardly assure her: 'Dear mother, I promise to carry out this task!'[25]

Instead of turning Lin into a hardened revolutionary whose loneliness disappears as a result of intense involvement in undercover activities, Lin still feels a psychological emptiness. The heroine remains an orphan girl, and in her imagination she turns a senior woman cadre into a mother image. This is of course totally possible. It may even be argued that many Chinese intellectuals have never become true believers even long after they have become cadres. But this is exactly the point urged by Kuo K'ai, who tried to show that Lin never really changed. Ironically, if we accept her own explanation of her motives at face value, Yang Mo's attempt to portray the process of metamorphosis of a petty bourgeois intellectual, merely shows that such a transformation is impossible.

Romanticization of Communist Heroes

If Lin Tao-ching was not transformed into a Communist revolutionary, many other Communists in *The Song of Youth* also remain petty bourgeois intellectuals. The romanticization of underground struggle is reflected in many ways. As a result, the Communist heroes become fleeting and amorphous dream-like figures. As if nothing shows the nature of underground work better than the pseudonyms acquired by a Communist, the novelist gives everyone at least two names. As soon as Lin is initiated into the Party, she gets the false name of Hsiu-lan. Later, when she is assigned the task of organizing student activities in Peking University, she changes her name to Lu-fang. It is never made clear why it is necessary to abandon her first pseudonym Hsiu-lan. In the same manner, we are informed that Chiang Hua's real name is Li meng-yu, Lu Chia-chuan's pseudonym is Feng Shen, and Cheng Chin's real name is Lin Hung. There are occasionally people without names, such as the grandma Lin encounters when she is fleeing from the police after organizing a student protest. The author perhaps does this to create an aura of mystery and secrecy, but she also makes the heroes less real and substantial.

Another way of making the Communist heroes more intellectual than Communist is to describe their admiration for Western culture.

---

[25] *Ibid.*, p. 450, *Chinese Literature*, No. 6, 1960, pp. 117–18.

This again shows the difference in perspective between non-Communist and Communist authors. Yang Mo tries to depict Lin Tao-ching as a revolutionary, yet on the wall of her room hangs a portrait of Tolstoy. Hsu Hui is another Communist leader in Peking University, but her room in the dormitory is decorated with a picture of Montesquieu. When Lu Chia-chuan feels restless he asks Lo Ta-fang, another comrade, to sing the *Marseillaise*. Once, addressing a student rally on the campus of Peking University, Lu talks like this:

> 'Fellow students! Comrades! The rule of reaction must soon come to an end. The people are rising!' Lu Chia-chuan, still erect on the platform, dignified and unruffled, seemed oblivious of the shooting as he calmly concluded his speech. 'As the poet Shelley says: "If Winter comes, can Spring be far behind?" '[26]

If the use of pictures of Tolstoy and Montesquieu is a deliberate ploy to conceal their identity as revolutionaries, it is certainly a clever measure. But that is not their purpose. The girls have a genuine admiration for these great Western thinkers. As for Lu Chia-chuan, he apparently has no interest in hiding his Communist identity. He appeals to the revolutionary zeal of the audience, calling them comrades and urging them to overthrow the reactionary rule. Interestingly, he has obtained his inspiration not from any Communist treatises but from a famous verse of the romantic poet Shelley.

There is a good deal of admiration for Western culture in the literary works of the May 4th vintage. Unless an intellectual can quote Western poets, novelists and philosophers freely, he has not proved his rich reservoir of knowledge. This propensity clearly still exists in non-Communist novelists. We find the same exhibitionist tendency in Kao Yun-lan's *Annals of a Provincial Town*. Ho Chien-ping's fierce attack on Liu Mei's view that art should be separated from politics apparently meets ·the approval of Szu-ming, another Communist in the company. When they walk out of Liu's house, Szu-min makes a most unlikely observation. He calls the art teacher 'a character from a Moliére comedy'. On another occasion, Kao Yun-lan describes a Communist named Pei-hsün like this:

> When Pei-hsün had been working in Shanghai he was known as the 'Long-legged Deer' because he was so tall and thin. In the Soviet Union he went up from 120 to 230 pounds. Big and fat, he looked something like that famous picture of Balzac.[27]

If the novel were intended for Western readers, the comparisons with a comic character in Molière or Balzac at least convey a visual image. To

---

[26] *Ibid.*, p. 134, *Chinese Literature*, No. 4, 1960, p. 81.
[27] *Annals of a Provincial Town*, p. 200, Shapiro, p. 191.

Chinese readers they would probably make sense only among students of Western literature in the pre-Communist period. But in a novel written for the masses, such comparisons are quite out of place. Nevertheless, these two authors could not resist showing off their knowledge of Western culture.

Whether a character rings true as a Communist or is merely an intellectual in disguise is not a question of merely calling him a Communist. It is his feelings, his perceptions and his behavior which reveal him as one type or another. One of the most successful women Communists in this novel is generally considered to be Cheng Chin (or Lin Hung).[28] But on close examination, Cheng Chin remains a romanticized figure. In reality there were many female Communists as fearless and dedicated as male revolutionaries, but Yang Mo has not given us an example of one. We have to wait for the appearance of Sister Chiang of *Red Crag* and Ho Wei of *The Thundering Yangtse* for a convincing figure. Cheng Chin fits the novelist's romanticization of the Communist revolution perfectly.

After being tortured, Lin Tao-ching is jailed in a small cell with a schoolgirl who still cries 'mamma' in her sleep and Cheng Chin, a hardened woman cadre. The moment she regains consciousness,

> Tao-ching's eyes were riveted upon that pallid face, so warm and expressive. She now saw that her companion was a beautiful woman in her late twenties. Her face was pale yet lustrous as marble, and her large black eyes sparkled like jewels in that murky cell.
> 'She's like a Greek goddess!' This incongruous notion flashed across Tao-ching's mind.[29]

If the notion of a goddess were related to a desperate longing for superhuman power to rescue her from danger, as Lin is semi-conscious after her faint, it might make more sense. But Lin is in full control of her faculties, and is able to scrutinize the fine features of the woman and to compare them to marble and jewels. Thus the comparison to a Greek goddess reveals only the novelist's deliberate romanticization of Cheng Chin, the legendary figure of whom she has probably heard so much. The fact that the goddess is Greek instead of Chinese has the same significance. This is further evidence of the admiration for Western art, or perhaps even for the physical beauty of Western woman, as popularized by the plaster figure of Aphrodite.

Later, when Lin feels better she confides to Cheng Chin that she is not a Communist but wants to devote her life to the Communist Party. This is Cheng Chin's reaction:

[28] See, for instance, Ma T'ieh-ting, *op. cit.*, p. 38; and Huang Chao-yen, 'On *The Song of Youth*', *Chinese Literature*, No. 6, 1960, p. 140.
[29] *The Song of Youth*, p. 386, *Chinese Literature*, No. 6, pp. 86–7.

Cheng Chin listened attentively, and her face grew grave. Some time passed before she raised her head to look Tao-ching in the eyes.

'You mustn't think that being arrested is the end of everything, or that death is sure to follow. Wherever a Communist finds himself, even in prison, he can go on working for the revolution. We must work to the last moment, to our last breath. We want to see with our own eyes a Communist China, to welcome the coming of that day . . . ' She glanced from Tao-ching to Shu-hsiu and her black eyes flashed with joy as she went on to describe *the brilliant prospects of Communism; China's future when she had become a country of independence, freedom, equality and prosperity.*[30]

In the Chinese original the two clauses 'the brilliant prospects of Communism' and 'China's bright future when she had become a country of independence, freedom, equality and prosperity' are separated by a semicolon, as here, while in the official English translation the two are linked by an 'and.' According to the Chinese text, the brilliant prospects of Communism are equated with China's bright future as a country of independence, freedom, equality and prosperity. There is a fundamental difference between the two versions. The vision of Communism in Cheng Chin's mind is a China of independence, freedom, equality and prosperity. This is clearly the vision of Chinese intellectuals, but different from that of the Communist. The Communist vision is above all of a classless society.

This interpretation is consistent with Cheng Chin's understanding of struggle and revolution as revealed in another conversation. She tells her cellmates about studying at a Marxist-Leninist university, that is, the three years she has spent in a Soochow prison:

'Every morning when the steam-whistle of a nearby factory blew, about two thousand political prisoners — women as well as men, not to mention some serving other sentences — used to get up. After exercising by marking time on the spot, we would sit on our beds to study. Some of us were sentenced to death, others to life imprisonment, others to fifteen, ten or eight years in prison. But no one was willing to waste time, we all flung ourselves conscientiously into our work. Some learned English, others Russian, Japanese or German. Naturally, political theory was a course everyone took. I learned German and later even taught it.'[31]

---

[30] *Ibid.*, p. 389, *Chinese Literature*, No. 6, 1960, p. 89, my italics. I have made minor alterations to the English translations, where it seemed necessary to clarify the sense. In this case, the last sentence, *Chung-kuo chiang-yao ch'eng-wei i-ko tu-li, tzu-yu, p'ing-teng erh fan-yung ti kuo-chia*, is translated 'when she had become a free, independent, classless and prosperous country'. It is a distortion to render the author's term *p'ing-teng* as 'classless' instead of 'equal' or 'equality'.
[31] *The Song of Youth*, p. 390, *Chinese Literature*, No. 6, 1960, p. 90.

The description is written by someone who has never been in a political prison. The novelist, carried away by her imagination, seems to have forgotten that she's describing a camp fenced in with barbed wire, not a boarding school. Although political theory is said to be taken by all the political prisoners, no details are given. The enthusiasm for learning foreign languages may be found among university students of foreign literature, but certainly not among those political prisoners marked for death or long imprisonment. It is hard to see the connection between the mastery of several languages and the Chinese Communist revolution.

Cheng Chin then goes on to describe her Communist husband, who has died a martyr's death. He is described as 'tall and handsome, musical, a man of genuine taste and a writer of no mean ability'. He is always overflowing with energy. She and her husband were students together in the Soviet Union, and were very much in love.

'... He was a stickler for personal cleanliness, and whenever he could get a little water he rubbed himself down. He was tall and handsome, with big eyes and jet-black hair. Even some of the jailers came under his spell. He had a persuasive tongue, and wherever he went he did propaganda work. Sometimes he sang, in his fine, clear tenor voice. His splendid character made those jailers who still had some conscience left treat the prisoners less cruelly.'[32]

This elegant Bolshevik, intelligent and cultured, urbane and polished, speaking fluent Russian, is no doubt a perfect match for Cheng Chin, a Greek goddess with marble face and jewel-like sparkling eyes, who speaks both Russian and German. There is a certain logic in this bizarre novel which is supposed to tell a story of bloody struggle in 'white' areas but instead creates a type of Communist fairy-tale. The Chinese Communist revolution has been the dream of girls like Lin Tao-ching (or Yang Mo) who like to think they speak foreign languages fluently and imagine themselves in tête-à-tête with handsome, gallant male comrades who are equally at home in English and Russian. This romanticization of the revolution and of revolutionary heroes apparently still persists, even when the reality has proved different. We are informed that from late 1958 to early 1960, in just over a year, 1,700,000 copies were published,[33] and doubtless a still larger number of people read the novel. The widespread interest in the novel suggests a romantic return to an earlier intellectual fantasy about the revolution. Small wonder that the leadership was alarmed that people pursued the

---

[32] *Ibid.*, p. 394, *Chinese Literature*, No. 6, 1960, p. 94.
[33] Huang Chao-yen, 'On *The Song of Youth*', *op. cit.*, p. 138.

shadow of a hybrid revolution, instead of seeing it as an indigenous revolution led mainly by cadres of peasant origin.[34]

Yet the revolution was won by peasant revolutionaries in dusty cadre uniform and cloth shoes. The real underground workers, as we shall see from the works of actual participants, are earthbound and Chinese. The masses, who have known such people in those tempestuous years, would easily recognize them.

Earthbound Revolutionaries and the Tradition

In contrast to the romanticized heroes in the stories of non-Communist novelists, underground workers portrayed by those who actually took part in the operation are Chinese and traditional. Some of them are also educated, but they appear more at home in the company of Yüeh Fei (*The Life of Yüeh Fei*), Chao Yün (*Romance of the Three Kingdoms*) and Tih Ch'ing (*Five Tigers' Conquest of the Western Frontier*), the heroes of vernacular tales. In this section we shall discuss Li Ying-ju's *In an Old City*,[35] with occasional references to Szu-ma Wen-sheng's *Storm over the T'ung River*.[36]

During the War of Resistance against Japan and the Civil War, Li Ying-ju spent several years as an underground worker in the areas occupied by the Japanese and the Kuomintang.[37] *In an Old City*, a story of the underground struggle against the Japanese and their puppet security troops in Paoting around 1943, is based on the author's

[34] *The Song of Youth* was once more denounced during the Cultural Revolution as a work praising the leadership of Liu Shao-ch'i and P'eng Chen in the North China Bureau.

[35] Li Ying-ju, *Yeh-huo ch'un-feng tou ku-ch'eng* (Peking: Writers' Publishing House, 2nd ed., 1961). Two instalments translated by Gladys Yang appear in *Chinese Literature*, Nos. 11 and 12, 1965, pp. 3–68 and 36–96. *In an Old City* is its English title. A literal translation would be *The Battle Between the Brushfire and the Spring Wind in an Old City*, derived from a verse by the Tang poet Pai Chu-i. The lines read: 'Even brushfire will not burn it up,/For the spring breeze will blow it to life again.' From its publication in December 1958 to June 1959, the novel was reprinted thirteen times and sold over 724,000 copies. See Mao Hsing, 'Tui shih-nien lai hsin Chung-kuo wen-hsüeh fa-ch'an ti i-hsieh li-chieh' (Some Insight into the Development of Literature in New China in the Last Ten Years), *Wen-hsüeh p'ing-lun*, No. 5, October 25, 1959, p. 5.

[36] Szu-ma Wen-sheng, *Feng-yü T'ung-chiang* (*Storm over the T'ung River*) (Peking: Writers' Publishing House, 1964).

[37] Li Ying-ju, 'Preface', *In an Old City*, pp. 1–2; also 'Kuan-yü Yeh-huo ch'un-feng tou ku-ch'eng' (On *In an Old City*), *Jen-min wen-hsüeh*, No. 7, 1960, p. 113.

personal experience in those years. His role in the underground operation is vividly reported by a reviewer of the novel:

> In the autumn of 1943, I was sent by the leadership to Paoting, then the capital of the puppet Hopei provincial government, to consult with Comrade Li Ying-ju about a temporary job. We agreed to meet in a municipal park. I went there early that day and waited in a pavilion. No sooner had I sat down and got a chance to enjoy the surrounding views than someone yelled from a distance the real name I used in the liberated areas. I was startled. Following the direction of the voice, I saw a man in an ankle-length gown walking towards me. It was Comrade Li Ying-ju.[38]

The second novel describes Communist underground operations in Tz'uchow, a town near Ho City (another name for Amoy). From the viewpoint of both time and place, this novel should be considered with *Annals of a Provincial Town*. I have not done so, for two reasons. First, although the author spends considerable space on the underground struggle against the Kuomintang authorities in Tz'uchow, his main theme, like that of *In an Old City*, deals with the co-ordination between urban underground work and rural armed struggle. This is a principle formulated by Mao Tse-tung. Secondly, though there is no biographical information about the author, it is clear from his style that Szu-ma Wen-sheng must have been an underground cadre. The college students and high school teachers in this book never show a trace of Western influence. In both novels, the impact of the New Literary Movement is more subtle, discernible only in writing techniques.

The opening paragraphs of *In an Old City* describe two men walking under cover of darkness. Unlike Yang Mo's self-indulgent description of Lin Tao-ching's escape, Li Ying-ju does not merely describe the landscape, but reflects the nature of the task and the circumstances under which it is carried out.

> It was late at night as Old Liang, setting a brisk pace, led Political Commissar Yang Hsiao-tung along a winding path. Old Liang had a Mauser pistol stuck into the red ox-hide belt round his black padded jacket, which was tight at the wrists, and fitted him like a sheath. With his quick springy stride and agile alert appearance he looked like a man you could count on in a fight.
>
> He was keeping some distance ahead, to reconnoitre and ensure Yang's safety.
>
> To start with they strode along the frozen path, then switched to its withered grass verge and, nearing a village, took cover in a wood

---

[38] Fang Ming, 'Yeh-huo shao pu chin, ch'un-feng ts'ui yu sheng — Tu *Yeh-huo ch'un-feng tou ku-ch'eng*' (Even Brushfire Will Not Burn It Up, For the Spring Breeze Will Blow It to Life Again — After Reading *In an Old City*), *Wen-i pao*, No. 1, 1959, p. 15.

where elms, willows, mulberries and sophoras thrust a tangle of bare gaunt branches towards the sky. Old Liang crouched down to listen. All was quiet. He straightened up and, still keeping well ahead, made for the village.[39]

From the first few lines, the reader's attention is caught by the danger and suspense of underground work. He holds his breath as the two approach the village and prepare to face the enemy lurking in the darkness. *In an Old City*, however, is not a story of adventure but of fine characterization of men and women involved in a dangerous task. The scene of the reunion between Yang Hsiao-tung and his old mother is as touching as it is artistically subtle. Before Yang leaves for the provincial capital, under Japanese occupation, he goes home to see his mother. It is seven or eight years since he last saw her. The author, through the minute details of the old woman's every move, portrays a mother's heart:

His mother climbed on to the *kang*[40] and draped her quilt over the window, then reached for the matches. She struck the first so hard that it snapped into two. And instead of using the second to light the lamp she held it up to look at her son's face before groping unsuccessfully for the wick. When with the third match the lamp was finally lit she turned round and gripped her boy's hands, peering into his face.[41]

This is the beginning of the author's endeavor to build up a profound mutual attachment between mother and son, in order to strengthen the later twist of the plot. At this moment, the mother is only deeply disappointed that her son has to leave after only a brief stay. Before his departure, Yang without much difficulty succeeds in persuading his mother to serve as a liaison worker. She agrees, on three conditions: that he must keep well under cover, that he must get married within a year, and that he must come home for the approaching New Year.

The story of ruthless, bloody struggle is considerably softened by the theme of love and the presence of fine female characters. Apart from the revolutionary's mother, there are two sisters with distinct personalities. The elder sister, Chin-yuan, is a young widow, the mother of a little girl; the younger sister, Yin-huan, has had a high school education and works as a hospital nurse. Chin-huan is bold, outspoken and quite capable of being firm. There is 'a hint of temper and arrogance in her intelligent eyes'. She apparently loves Old Liang,

---

[39] *In an Old City*, p. 1, *Chinese Literature*, No. 11, 1965, pp. 3–4.
[40] A brick bed which is kept warm in winter by burning charcoal or other fuel underneath it.
[41] *Ibid.*, p. 16, *Chinese Literature*, No. 11, 1965, pp. 11–12.

captain of the armed work team, but treats him with a certain amount of sternness. On the other hand, Liang, fearless and defiant in facing the puppet soldiers and enemy agents, becomes gentle and tender in dealing with this young woman. Chin-huan is broad-minded enough to tell Yang Hsiao-tung to share the only *kang* with her and her daughter. After assuring him he need not worry about the enemy, she says with a twinkle that if by any chance the enemy comes, she will say that Yang is her husband just back from a trip. Though a seasoned cadre, who usually feels at home under any circumstances, Yang feels ill at ease to hear such talk.

Only with a stainless character like this can a woman face danger without hesitation. She often smuggles messages for the Party underground, carrying the little girl on her back. On one occasion, when she is escorting Yang back to the city, she is arrested, through the betrayal of a turncoat. The chief Japanese adviser, Tada, tries to use persuasion to get information from her, when torture has failed. Then he takes a liking to Chin-huan, and develops other designs on her. Chin-huan suggests a private meeting, then rams a strong hairpin of bone straight through Tada's gullet, but the wound is not fatal, and the Japanese manages to put five bullets through her.

No doubt, Chin-huan makes an outstanding revolutionary and a valuable comrade, but it is Yin-huan, her gentle, emotional sister, who captures Yang's heart. At their first meeting Chin-huan suggested that they all slept in the same *kang*. One would have enormous respect for such a woman, but would be unable to fall in love with her. On the other hand, Yin-huan's feminine shyness and reserve radiate great attraction. When Yang first arrives in the city Yin-huan as an underground worker has to brief him about conditions under enemy occupation. The conversation takes place over a bowl of rice and cabbage and beancurd soup in a small restaurant.

> . . . But although she was obviously pleased by his arrival her smile was constrained and she bent her head most of the time, as if afraid to meet his eyes, holding her chopsticks awkwardly in her right hand and nervously crumpling the table-cloth with her left.[42]

The subject of love is treated with great caution. It is not that the author avoids describing Yang's sensual urge for the pretty young nurse. Chinese novelists rarely look at love as the manifestation of carnal desire. It is Yang's hesitation in dealing with the problem of marriage which shows the author's prudence in treating the subject. Even with the blessing of Hsiao, Yang's immediate superior, he still seems unable to let himself fall in love with the girl. His indecision results from a

[42] *Ibid.*, p. 25, *Chinese Literature*, No. 11, 1965, pp. 16–17.

conflict between Yang's feeling for Yin-huan and his sense of responsibility to the Party. This is clearly described:

> Watching her beautiful, slim figure from behind, Yang Hsiao-tung murmured: 'Truly a good girl! . . .' After an inner struggle, he sighed, calling his own name, 'Hsiao-tung, Oh, Hsiao-tung! Did the Party send you over here to push ahead the work in the city, or for you to pursue your own personal happiness? Don't you realize that even if those who work under you look at your leadership in terms of principle, many more are watching your life style? You're only twenty-eight, still young. Why not let this problem wait till you have been working for another five or ten years? I know, some people might object to this attitude including your own mother. But this is nevertheless the correct attitude, which a Communist should gladly adopt.'[43]

The leadership's encouragement to Yang not to neglect his personal problems, especially his marriage, is a sign of care and concern on the part of the organization. But a Communist should not lightly accept the generosity of the leadership. The more considerate the leadership, the more dedicated a Party man should be. So the advice from Hsiao, the department head, that Yang should seriously consider marrying Yin-huan, a reliable but inexperienced comrade, is not enough to convince him. There must be pressure from another direction. It would be most appropriate if such a marriage were the wish of an aging mother. In *Storm over the T'ung River* the marriages between Lin T'ien-ch'eng and Ts'ai Yü-hua, two college-educated intellectuals, and San-to and K'u-ch'a, two village cadres, take place only at the insistence of their respective parents, as well as with the blessings of the leadership. But the author of *In an Old City* goes a step further, by making the proposed marriage the last wish of a mother who has died for the revolution.

From the technical point of view, the meeting between Yin-huan and Yang's mother, who has been arrested and jailed in a secret place, is awkwardly managed. Such a meeting, under the watchful eyes of puppet secret police, is simply impossible. But viewed from the angle of love and marriage, it is necessary and logical. The occasion gives the mother an opportunity to exercise her maternal authority over her son's marriage. Yang's mother pulls off a ring with a red stone from her finger and gives it to the girl.

> 'Hsiao-tung's dad gave me this when we married,' she said. 'For years I've been hoping to pass it on to my son. It's been the dearest wish of my heart to slip this ring on to the finger of the girl he loves. Dear Yin-huan, please take it, won't you?'

'Me, aunty? Oh, no. Hsiao-tung wouldn't dream . . .' Confusion was making Yin-yuan incoherent. She took a grip on herself. 'I'll give him this myself. As for me, aunty, I hardly know what to say. You've no daughter, and I've no mother. Let me look on you as my own mother.'[44]

The narrative is typical and traditional. Although Yin-huan has been deeply in love with Hsiao-tung for some time, she has to say 'no'. It is a 'no' said in spite of herself, a 'no' which the old lady knows means 'yes'. The ring is certainly the most precious thing in the world to Yin-huan, yet she has to say that she will return it to Hsiao-tung. Offering herself as a daughter is another way of expressing agreement and gratitude. Only the most devoted daughter-in-law behaves like a daughter.

As an underground worker, Yin-huan makes few contributions but creates many problems. She would quickly lose her head in a difficult situation. After the meeting with the old lady, she cannot even wait until her appointment with Hsiao-tung that afternoon. She must act immediately to rescue Yang's mother. She thinks of Councillor Kao who has some influence with the puppet regime, although he actually works for the Party Underground. On her way to the Kao mansion, she comes across the councillor's nephew, another non-Communist working for the underground. Not knowing that the young man has just become a turncoat, she tells him of the imprisonment of Yang's mother and of her appointment with Yang at a certain hour and place, and begs for his help. The information of Yang's whereabouts is quickly related to the puppet secret service and Yang is arrested.

When the puppet officers fail to buy Yang with money and women they take him to an upstairs window and let him see his mother in a room on the opposite side. The threat to his mother's life leaves Yang speechless, but he finally answers gruffly that they can kill him and his mother as well. Seeing that Yang is quite determined, the secret police drag him to a balcony on the third floor of the other house, barely three paces away from his mother. The scene which follows highlights the drama of conflict between loyalty to country and the Party on the one hand and love between mother and son on the other.

'. . . What can I say? You mustn't think, Hsiao-tung, that I hold this against you. No. I'm proud to have a son like you. Proud and glad. I'm not going to make it harder for you. Oh, there's something I forgot to tell you.' Her thin, ravaged face lit up, but she kept her voice down so that no one else could hear. 'I've chosen you a girl who'll make you happy. I gave her my red ring, and she didn't refuse it . . .'

[44] *Ibid.*, p. 366, *Chinese Literature*, No. 12, 1965, p. 65.

The door to the balcony opened and Lan Mao came out to part them, claiming that what they were discussing had nothing to do with signing a confession. The other secret-service men crowded onto the balcony too. Lan Mao raised his voice to ask Kao Ta-cheng:
'Shall we take the son first? Or first beat the mother up?'
'Have them both strung up,' ordered Kao.
'One minute!' begged Mrs. Yang. 'Let me say one last word to him.' She took her son's head between her hands and stroked his hair, bathing his cheeks with her hot tears. But when she saw the pity and grief on his face, she pushed him abruptly away.
'I'm not going to make things harder for you, Hsiao-tung, my son. For the victory of the War of Resistance, for the happiness of future generations, mind you hold out to the last!'
In two swift strides she reached the balustrade and slipped over. She flung herself down, head first, from the third floor.[45]

This is the most touching and poignant scene in the novel, and provides a striking contrast between the villains and the heroes. The ruthless and beastly nature of the puppet officers is brought out in their vicious scheme to torture mother and son in each other's presence. No matter how tough a man is, he may not be able to bear the sight of the suffering of those he loves, especially his own mother. Yet for Yang Hsiao-tung there is no choice. This has nothing to do with Communism. In traditional popular tales, when a hero has to choose between love for his country and love for his parents, he always chooses the former. This scale of values is deeply rooted in Chinese culture.

The dilemma is also faced by the mother. To the Chinese way of thinking, a mother is responsible for whatever her son becomes. If behind every great Chinese man is a great woman, this woman is not his wife but his mother. The image of great mother has been a favorite theme of Chinese novelists for centuries.[46] Like Hsiao-tung, Mrs. Yang also has no choice. As she has made Hsiao-tung what he is, she must make a further sacrifice, even if it costs her her life. Suicide is the only possible outcome.

In an Old City is a story of underground struggle – a phase in the Communist revolution to overthrow the old system – but paradoxically it is as traditional as any classical novel. Perhaps the paradox is more apparent than real. At this phase of the revolution the fight is against the corrupt rule, foreign domination, and above all, the destruction of values and norms held sacred by the Chinese. Only those who have a deep faith in Chinese culture can fight effectively against forces alien to the Chinese. Those who have been influenced by foreign cultures

---

[45] *Ibid.*, pp. 389–90, *Chinese Literature*, No. 12, 1965, p. 76.
[46] For instance, Yüeh Fei's mother in *The Life of Yüeh Fei* and Hsu Shu's mother in *Romance of the Three Kingdoms*.

would find it difficult to defend values and beliefs about which they have doubts.

The ending of the story is also traditional. The engagement between Yang Hsiao-tung and Yin-huan is not the climax of a love story but the fulfilment of a mother's last wish. Yang has escaped from prison and is joined by Yin-huan. Then something happens:

As he turned to take the cup, the light made the ring on Yin-huan's finger sparkle. Forgetting his thirst, Yang stared at it in amazement.

Yin-huan looked down to see if something was wrong. When she realized that he was staring at his mother's ring, her hand trembled so much that the water spilled and she had to put the cup down.

'Where did you get that ring?' he asked.

'It's . . .' She hung her head in confusion and was silent for several minutes. But what need was there for concealment after all that had taken place? She took a deep breath and told him the whole story.

'. . . How could I refuse your mother anything at a time when her life was in danger? Could I add to her distress? But now I'll return it to its rightful owner.' She pulled off the ring and handed it to him.

Yang took it, immeasurably touched by his mother's love and the goodness of this staunch, warm-hearted comrade-in-arms. He stared at Yin-huan in silence as if seeing her for the first time, until the girl began to blush and lowered her eyes. At that he made a decision and, stepping forward, repeated what she had said:

'Now I'll return it to its rightful owner. Please give me your hand.'

. . .

He slipped the ring on her finger. 'You have some feeling for me, haven't you? The fact is, I fell in love with you long ago. The first evening I came to the city and you lent me your cardigan, I was drawn to you by your sweetness and kindness.' He took her in his arms and stroked her hair . . . [47]

The description of Yang's psychology subtly makes clear the Chinese scale of values. Yang's first reaction is to realize his mother's profound love. Then he recognizes the generosity and consideration of Yin-huan as a good comrade. His love for the girl has to take third place. Only after showing concern for one's mother and considering the significance of the matter in his working relationship can a man think of his own happiness. Yang's way of expressing his love by merely taking the girl in his arms and stroking her hair is also typical. As the author himself explains, the way the Chinese display affection is not necessarily by warm caresses and embraces; merely looking in each other's eyes can be an emphatic way of expressing love. [48]

[47] *Ibid.*, pp. 411–13, *Chinese Literature*, No. 12, 1965, pp. 85–6.
[48] Li Ying-ju, 'Preface', *In an Old City*, p. 2.

The Dark Side and Villains

Although in *The Song of Youth* and *Annals of a Provincial Town* the authors have tried to expose the dark side of the old society and describe villains, their attempts are largely unsuccessful. Both Hu Meng-an, department head at the Kuomintang Peking municipal headquarters, and Chao Hsiung, head of the Political Security Bureau in Amoy, are stereotypes without individuality. It is Szu-ma Wen-sheng who boldly describes whores, pimps, opium-smokers and gamblers, in *Storm over the T'ung River*. Unfortunately, the author paints these characters with sweeping strokes as background figures, without going deeper into their characterization. Only in *In an Old City* do the villains take definite shape and bustle with life.

One such powerfully-drawn character is Kao Ta-cheng, commander of the puppet security forces. A tall, brawny man with a pair of sunglasses perched permanently on his hawk-shaped nose, Kao always takes with him a whole squad of bodyguards, each armed with at least two weapons. Once he gives a banquet in celebration of the 'success' of a military operation, and tries to read a speech written by his staff. It is a formal speech in the classical style. 'In co-ordination with the Great Imperial Army of Japan, our troops penetrated deep into the mountains to exterminate bandits. After bloody battles under the leadership of my colleagues, the brilliant success of the operation was made possible . . .' Apparently the literary style of the speech is not to his taste, so he abandons the prepared text and gives an impromptu rendering of his favorite personal story:

'I was born in Pachow, Hopei, found my way into the underworld society at 13, and started my own business at 15. I slept on tree trunks in the dark pine wood, and went for a shit in the great hall of a county yamen. At 18 I became a hooligan in the streets of Tientsin, cutting local rowdies down to size. I first earned my name by challenging Two-head Tigress. That woman with a wen on her head was a terror — you didn't dare to rub her up the wrong way, a look alone would scare the hell out of you. It was winter when I first went on a visit to her. I went in and without a word lay down flat in her bed. Then I called out: "Bring a light! Heard a Two-head Tigress round here? right? Today Dad Kao's going to ride her!" A cigarette was handed to me, but Two-head Tigress made a signal not to light it. I said: "Bring a light!" Two-head Tigress picked up a piece of red hot charcoal with her bare fingers from the stove. I thought to myself, "Here we go!" Rolling up my trouser and slapping at a fat, meaty spot, I said "Put it here first, darling, I'm going to rest a bit, then I'll have a drag!" She gave me a stare and did as I told her. You could hear a pin drop. The charcoal burned my flesh, making a long sizzling noise. It was like being slowly cut into by a knife. After a minute, the charcoal turned from red to white. "Come on, let's have another," I shouted. Her gang couldn't take it any more. That was how I drove away Two-head Tigress.'

To show he was not lying, he rolled up one trouser-leg to show off his scar.

'Two-head Tigress didn't give up that easily. She had a crowd of toughies backing her up. The third day she brought over her master and a dozen thugs. Without a word, they beat me up, leaving nowhere untouched. It was then my eyeball was gouged out. People tried to persuade me to leave the place. Others wanted to take me to hospital. But I wouldn't go. Instead, I told my men to carry me to the door. Let Tigress come to pick up the pieces. I had two choppers placed by the door. Tigress came again with her men. I lay under the blade of one chopper and had the other ready too. "Come on!" I shouted, "Anyone who objects to me, Kao, holding this territory, come and lie down here, and both our heads will be cut in half." This scared the hell out of them, and that was how One-Eyed Dragon Kao Ta-cheng became boss...'[49]

Kao Ta-cheng belongs to a type which defies any neat definition but comes close to what Mao Tse-tung calls 'lumpen-proletarian' in his analysis of Chinese society.[50] This type can be further divided into two sub-types. One type, to which Kao belongs, bullies people, lives on the fear of the innocent, and controls all kinds of illegal business such as brothels, gambling houses and opium dens. These people have no concern for the suffering of those who fall into their clutches. The other sub-type is represented by Wu the Seventh, in *Annals of a Provincial Town*. He is a boxer, and an expert in treating broken bones. He has a natural sympathy for the poor and weak, and unyielding hate for the rich and powerful. He regards friendship as the best guarantee of loyalty and betrayal of trust the worst form of vice. The former type is completely rejected by the Communist and regarded as an enemy of the people. The latter, however, is viewed as having good qualities and a capacity for reform. Once their individualistic traits are removed, men of this type can become brave and dependable revolutionaries. Wu the Seventh belongs to this *hao han* (manly fellow) type, and is later recruited into the Party.

The story told by Kao Ta-cheng shows a man who prevails by a complete disregard for life and limb, to the point of mutilation. That a fearless man can totally overpower another by cutting off not his opponent's limb but his own is a legend almost ritualistically revered in the Chinese underworld. As the undisputed boss of a bunch of

[49] *In an Old City*, pp. 316–17.
[50] 'Analysis of the Classes in Chinese Society', *Selected Works of Mao Tse-tung*, Vol. I (Peking: Foreign Languages Press, 1965), p. 19.

desperadoes, Kao demands from his men total subjection to his personal authority. He tells them the story of his past not just for egoistic satisfaction but to show them the kind of man he is. Other wrongs he can forgive, but any defiance of his power will be strictly punished. He observes no norms, conventional or otherwise.

Another vividly-portrayed villain is Kao's regimental commander Chao. This man used to own a grocer's shop, but found an official position in the puppet troops more lucrative. By sending many gifts to top Japanese officers, he bought himself a Commission and soon became commander of a regiment. When he learns that Commander-in-Chief Kao is going to call the roll, in order to receive more supplies and salaries than the actual number in his regiment calls for, he fills the ranks with non-soldiers. Even coal-miners and street hawkers are brought in to fill the vacancies temporarily, for the benefit of Commander Kao's inspection. But Kao proves equal to Chao's crooked ways. Wearing civilian clothes, and without the usual escort of bodyguards, Kao pays an unexpected visit to Chao's camp and learns all about his tricks. Finally, the two come face to face and start bargaining like pedlars. The regimental commander demands that 900 men should be on the payroll, but Kao agrees to accept only half that figure. Like a good merchant, Chao comes down to 600. Kao retorts by telling his regimental commander that he would do very well, with no pay at all. He says Chao's pocket should be bulging at the seams from the profit earned from the smuggling of salt and grain the month before. He calls the regimental commander a sly old fox, in a voice which reveals a hint of appreciation for such talent.

Once when the entire puppet army is out looking for the Reds, the regimental commander still does not forget his habit of bargaining. He does not want his men placed in the front line and comes up with the excuse that his troops are not really at full strength. Kao is truly angry with him this time. 'Damn it,' he shouts, 'you're supposed to be regimental commander! Even a whore can't raise her price once her panties are down. Shut up with your nonsense! At the front I enjoy letting my pistol do the talking.'[51]

It is indeed remarkable that the author does not hesitate to use dirty language when they suit the personalities of the characters. Such delightfully wicked characters totally disappear in novels portraying the new society. As a result, many stories of the Communist society are like hospital food, sterile but tasteless. No doubt, men like Kao Ta-cheng and the regimental commander, a plague on society, cannot exist in a healthy environment. As materialists, the Communists believe that a

[51] *In an Old City*, p. 338.

person's vocabulary is a reflection of his social origins and personal experience. A good nice man talks with propriety. Stories describing the post-revolutionary period seem to suggest a deliberate effort to sterilize the language for the health of the society.

Comparison of the Authors' Perspectives

There are conspicuous dissimilarities between *The Song of Youth* and *Annals of a Provincial Town* on the one hand and *In an Old City* and *Storm over the T'ung River* on the other. If we use the method of quantitative content analysis,[52] the computer would probably say that the novels describe two different countries. There are indeed two Chinas. One China is the product of universities, missionary works, treaty ports, and Western cultural influence. The other China exists in the vast interior and the old cities and is the result of millennia of an ancient civilization, with its values and norms remaining intact. Both Chinas are there, one no less real than the other.

The problem with *The Song of Youth* and *Annals of a Provincial Town* is that the authors attempted to incorporate two different value systems, without much success. Had they tried only to portray lives of university students and school teachers within the limits of the college campus and modern and semi-modern cities, the characterization of heroes would have been more consistent and plot development more logical. While this is impossible under the demand for ideological adherence, there is an obvious incongruity between the life styles of the characters and their political behavior. Consequently, a pseudo-reality is imposed on the reality. An admirer of Montesquieu thus becomes a dedicated Communist. And a 'Greek goddess' who speaks Russian and German shouts slogans such as 'Long Live the Chinese Communist Party!' and 'Communism is invincible!' when she is taken to the execution ground. Or a person who quotes Molière believes that art should indeed serve politics.

No such conflict of values exists in *In an Old City* and *Storm over the T'ung River*. The heroes are of the traditional type, fighting against the occupation of foreign troops or against the corrupt rule of the reactionary. Alien domination and corrupt government are the two major evils against which traditional heroes fight to the death in popular tales, from *Sui T'ang yen-yi (Heroes of the Sui and T'ang*

---

[52] I have toyed with and subsequently abandoned the idea of using quantitative content analysis, because it is unfeasible and time-consuming. A simple fact is that the machine is used for the sake of economy. Even if the resources were available, it would be silly to invest tens of thousands of dollars and two years of a research team's time to improve accuracy by, say, 5 per cent.

Dynasties) to *The Life of Yüeh Fei*. Their most powerful weapon in fighting against overwhelming odds is an unshakeable belief in traditional norms: loyalty to their country and fellow countrymen, filial piety to their parents, and trust among friends. Chin-huan is a contemporary counterpart of Hua Mu-lan and Yang Hsiao-tung, a twentieth century Yüeh Fei.

If we move away from these obvious contradictions and consider the basic themes of the novels, we find the problem does not exist only on the technical level. A skilled novelist could easily overcome these shortcomings by making the heroes' personal behavior more consistent with their political activities. Let us suppose that Lin Tao-ching does not compare Cheng Chin to Greek goddess, and Lu Chia-chuan does not quote Shelley's poem. Would they then become real Communists? The answer is still 'no'. Their perception of the revolution is different. Their vision of China after the success of the revolution, that is, after the victory over foreign control and corrupt rule, is of 'a country of independence, freedom, equality and prosperity', modelled on France or perhaps the United States. This vision of China has been shared by many intellectuals, Yang Mo and Kao Yun-lan included. It persisted for a long time until it was finally translated into action during the Hundred Flowers period in 1957, when intellectuals demanded the end of Communist monolithic rule and the establishment of a multi-party system. This vision is developed from reading college textbooks, journals and newspapers, and books in foreign languages, intended for entirely different audiences. It has no roots in Chinese soil, since it does not take into account the inherent problems of China. It is certainly true, as *The Song of Youth* shows, that Lin Tao-ching (or Yang Mo) has seen the sufferings of displaced peasants and unemployed workers, but she is not one of them (despite her partial black bones) and has not lived their lives. She would feel that these poor people could be saved, but never thought that they would make better and more determined revolutionaries. For Lin Tao-ching and Cheng Chin, the revolutionaries should be those who are well versed in political theory (assuming Marxist-Leninist theories are included), fluent in foreign languages, and competent in arguing the revolutionary case. They are as masculine and handsome in appearance as they are suave and elegant in manner. This is a romantic fantasy of revolutionary heroes. Yet such an image is remarkably consistent with the vision of a 'Westernized' China.

I am not suggesting that independence, equality, prosperity and even freedom are not the goals of the Communist revolution. Nevertheless, these goals are understood and defined in a peculiarly Chinese way. The strength of *In an Old City* is its earthbound quality. Yang Hsiao-tung never talks in such sweeping terms. The only promise he makes his mother is that once the war is over and the revolution successful, he would accompany her on a visit to Peking and Tientsin. Other characters, such as Old Liang and Han Yen-lai, are even less articulate. But from their personal experience and simple-minded dedication, they perhaps have a better understanding of the revolutionary cause. They have no doubt that they share the fate of other hungry Chinese, and that something is fundamentally wrong. While they certainly have never entertained a vision of land reform or communization, they feel that the poor should fight together for their common cause.

The difference between the two types of characters is a difference in approach, in understanding the nature of the revolution, and in visualizing the future of China. It is a difference between two forces: dedicated revolutionaries and petty bourgeois sympathizers. They were united in fighting the common enemies in the course of the revolution but parted company when the task was mapping out the future of China.

4

THE UNDERGROUND STRUGGLE IN "WHITE" AREAS

II. THE PRISON STRUGGLE

Fiction of the Communist underground operation in 'white' areas reaches its apogee in *Red Crag*,[1] one of the few intrinsically outstanding novels under consideration. The difference between *Red Crag* and its predecessors, such as *The Song of Youth* and *Annals of a Provincial Town*, is that between a genuine gem-stone and a glass imitation. It is also far better than *In an Old City*, both in technical skill and in its insight into the psychology of underground workers. Here, a number of Communist underground workers are shown as participants in a highly-disciplined collective struggle without losing their individuality. From the political viewpoint, the revolutionaries, now steeled by experience, have also become more sophisticated. *Red Crag* reflects the extraordinary degree of dedication some Communists have achieved: their devotion to the revolutionary cause is total, grown into the bones and marrow, intact even in death.

The story takes place in the mountain city of Chungking, one year before the Communist takeover. After several military setbacks, the Kuomintang authorities plan a last-ditch rearguard fight. Their best hope is to repeat the scenario of the war against Japan, when Chungking was used as a temporary bastion for the defense of China's northwest in the hope that some drastic changes in the international situation may divert attention elsewhere. At worst, the Kuomintang can lay the foundations for anti-Communist guerrilla and underground operations after the fall of Chungking. On the Communist side, the task of the Party underground is to build up a broad base of mass support, to organize workers to prevent the destruction of factories and communication systems, and to form rescue teams to save political

---

[1] Lo Kuang-pin and Yang Yi-yen, *Hung yen* (*Red Crag*) (Peking: Chinese Youth Publishing House, 1962). Three instalments in English translation can be found in *Chinese Literature*, Nos. 5, 6, and 7, pp. 3–32, 3–57, and 64–95.

prisoners. The last goal has been given priority, for the imprisoned Communists are mostly natives of Szechwan, who could make an invaluable contribution to the government of a newly liberated area. Under the circumstances the struggle becomes extremely intense and unusually cruel.

The book opens with the establishment of an alternative liaison post, under the cover of a bookstore. The man in charge of this operation is Fu Chih-kao, who usually works as a bank accountant. Overjoyed with this new opportunity, he tries to use the bookstore as a basis for mass work, such as publishing a progressive magazine and developing contacts with college students. His goal is to broaden his personal influence, so that when Chungking is liberated, he will have accumulated a certain amount of political capital.

This, however, is in direct conflict with the instructions he has received that the liaison office should be completely separated from mass work. Far more serious, of course, is Fu's consideration of his personal interests. The Communist Party functions like a machine, with all parts in their proper places. When a party member fails to perform the work assigned to him and begins to think in terms of personal gain, the machine immediately malfunctions. It is only one step from considering personal advantage to betraying the Party to save one's skin. The Fu's arrest leads to the collapse of the liaison post and the capture of other cadres.

The liaison office is only a small link in the larger network of the Party underground. Fu has contact only with his immediate superior and a few others with whom he worked in the past. No horizontal connection exists between members. Thus his betrayal leads merely to five or six more arrests. For the major part of the novel, the authors focus on the struggle in prison, the war of nerves between the Kuomintang secret service and political prisoners, and finally a well-organized jail break.

From Memoir to Novel

While most Communist novels are based either on research or on personal experience, *Red Crag* is the artistic version of an earlier memoir.[2] The authors themselves were political prisoners in Pai House and the Coal Pit, two of the best-known concentration camps under the

[2] The memoir by Lo Kuang-pin, Lin Teh-pin and Yang Yi-yen first appeared under the title 'Tsai lieh-huo chung teh-tao yung-sheng' (Immortality in Blazing Fire) in *Hung-ch'i p'iao-p'iao* (*The Red Flag Fluttering*), No. 6, 1968, pp. 183–204. An expanded version (74 pages) was published by the Chinese Youth Publishing House in 1959. Lin Teh-pin took no part in writing the novel.

control of the Sino-American Co-operative Organization (SACO).[3] Pai House was converted from the former mansion of the Szechwan warlord, Pai Chu. Ironically, it is called 'Fragrant Mountain Retreat', after the pen-name of the Tang poet, Pai Chu-i. This camp can hold some hundred prisoners. The Coal Pit, reconstructed from a deserted coal mine, can hold five or six hundred inmates at most. The period of imprisonment for Communists averages only a few months, for many were secretly disposed of to make room for new arrivals. In Pai House alone, more than two thousand political prisoners were executed within ten years between 1939 and 1949.[4]

Among the high-ranking political prisoners was General Yeh T'ing, captured during the Southern Anhwei Incident of January 1941.[5] First jailed in a concentration camp in Shangjao, he was later moved to Cell 2 of the Coal Pit. There he kept up his spirits by composing poems, from one of which was derived the title of the memoir by Lo Kuang-pin and his associates:

In blazing fire and boiling blood
I must seek to attain immortality!

The non-Communist general, Yang Hu-ch'eng, was also held there. Yang had been forced into exile after the famous Sian Incident.[6] When the Japanese attacked at Lukouch'iao on July 7, 1937, Yang sent a cable from San Francisco saying that he wanted to return and join in the war against Japan. He did so, despite the warnings of friends. As soon as he arrived in Shanghai, he was put under house arrest. Before long he and eight others, including his wife, children and secretary, were arrested and jailed in a Hsifeng camp. Later he was transferred to

---

[3] It is certainly open to question whether the memoir should be treated as an objective source of information, since it is written by three Communist authors. *Hung-ch'i p'iao-p'iao*, a Communist publication of revolutionary memoirs, anecdotes, and biographies, is used as an important source by such a reputable research center as the Union Research Institute in Hongkong. The archives of the Nationalist Government and the Kuomintang Party must have documents of the Communist underground activities in Chungking and political prisoners in the camps, but they will remain classified for the foreseeable future.

[4] *Hung-ch'i p'iao-p'iao*, No. 6, p. 185.

[5] In January 1941 Chiang Kai-shek's troops ambushed the New Fourth Route Army and wounded and captured its commander Yeh T'ing, in violation of an agreement on a united front with the Communists against the Japanese invaders.

[6] In December 1936 Generalissimo Chiang Kai-shek went to Sian to assume personal command of the north-east army under Chang Hsüeh-liang and the north-west army under Yang Hu-ch'eng in a military campaign against the Communist troops in Shensi. Both General Chang and General Yang wanted to fight the Japanese, and ordered their soldiers to mutiny and arrest Chiang Kai-shek. The Communists succeeded in persuading the two generals to release the Generalissimo when he agreed to halt the civil war and to co-operate with the Communists in a policy of military resistance against further Japanese invasion.

Pai House, and his imprisonment was leaked to the press. On a pitch-dark night in September 1949, Yang and his entire family, including a six-year old girl, were murdered by Kuomintang secret service men.

Of ranking Communists the best known were Lo Shih-wen, secretary of the CCP's Szechwan Provincial Committee, and Ch'e Yao-hsien, political commissar of the CCP's Szechwan Military Affairs Committee. They were captured in the spring of 1940 and secretly executed on September 17, 1946. They do not appear as characters in *Red Crag*, but their names are frequently mentioned by the political prisoners. Their presence is also felt in the wide-spread stories which have acquired the force of legend through continual retelling. The authors describe a piece of pencil left behind by Lo and Ch'e now used by Ch'eng Kang for writing the prison version of the Party underground paper *Forward*, and their handwriting on the pages of books in the prison library to suggest the link between the two martyred leaders and the struggle in progress. The prison songs written by Yeh T'ing and Ch'e Yao-hsien, powerful expressions of their unwavering conviction and lasting optimism, are quoted as an inspiration for sustaining the morale of political prisoners in their darkest moments.

Incorporated into the novel are the true stories of a few Communists of lower rank. Chiang Chu-yün, who appears in the novel as Chiang Hsueh-chin, better known as Sister Chiang, was arrested and jailed in the Coal Pit. The incident in which she witnessed the head of her husband, P'eng Yung-wu, (P'eng Sung-t'ao in the novel), smeared with blood and gore in a wooden cage hanging on the city wall of Fengchieh is one of the most moving scenes in *Red Crag*. The actual happening was itself so appallingly memorable that the authors had no need to dramatize it.[7]

Two other Communists associated with the publication of *Forward* were Ch'en Jan and Ch'eng Shan-mou, who are the main characters in the novel. Ch'en Jan, acting manager of a certain factory, was entrusted with the responsibility of cutting and running the stencil. The job of Ch'eng Shan-mou, an electrical engineer, was to receive the broadcasts of the New China News Agency on short-wave radio. Both were betrayed by a turncoat and held separately, in Pai House and the Coal Pit. In the novel Ch'en Jan appears as Ch'eng Kang, who mimeographs *Forward* in a repair shop of the Yangtse arsenal, of which he is manager. Ch'eng Shan-mou acquires the fictional identity of Liu Ssu-yang, a student at Chungking University with a bourgeois family background.

Some minor characters in *Red Crag* are also modelled on real persons. General Huang I-sheng, a political prisoner in Pai House, is described as

[7] *Cf. Hung-ch'i p'iao-p'iao*, No. 6, pp. 189–91 and *Red Crag*, pp. 69–79.

an associate of Dr. Sun Yat-sen. He opposes the policies of Chiang Kai-shek and sympathizes with the Communist cause. His real name was Huang Hsien-sheng, who served as deputy commander under Chang Hsüeh-liang. Hu Huo is a bespectacled non-Communist, imprisoned years earlier with three other high school students for unknowingly walking into the prohibited area where the concentration camp is located. His real name was Hsüan Hao. What happens to the character in the novel is remarkably true to what happened to him in real life. The last man mentioned in the memoir is Hsu Hsiao-hsien, leader of the prison Party organization in Pai House. With a few strokes Chi Hsiao-hsien (Hsu's fictional name) is vividly painted as a senior cadre, physically weakening yet mentally sharp and alert. He calmly accepted the responsibility of writing the *Forward* by hand, when the jail warder tortured the innocent Hsüan Hao to find out the source of the secret paper. The narration of this incident in the memoir is almost identical with the description in the novel.

One interesting thing about the memoir is that the authors never report what happened to them. It therefore seems misleading to call this non-fiction work a memoir. A logical explanation, however, can be given. As a general practice, Communists never advertise themselves. No doubt they were themselves imprisoned in Pai House and the Coal Pit from 1948 to 1949.[8] They must have had their share of physical torture and the terrible experiences of prison life.

While the earlier version of *Immortality in Blazing Fire* is expanded from an article to a monograph of some length, the novel is by no means a further inflation of the original material. It is an artistic work in its own right. According to a close acquaintance of theirs, in the process of writing the novel the authors had access to secret documents in the Communist Party archives, interviewed former Kuomintang agents, and discussed their material with the then leaders of the Chungking Communist Party underground. They spent nearly ten years on it, and re-wrote the book completely three times, with six major revisions. The length of the novel was finally trimmed from three million Chinese characters to some 400,000.[9] The authors have nevertheless described the characters with great psychological insight unlike other Communist novelists hitherto. Their powerful portrayal of the psychology of both political prisoners and jail warders gives life to the fictional characters. Through their narrative power the historical figures of the memoir come to life again. The reader becomes deeply involved. The unusual popularity of this novel bears witness to the

[8] *Hung-ch'i p'iao-p'iao*, No. 6, p. 183; also Fang Ching-ching, 'Red Crag Hits a Million Sales', *Peking Review*, No. 35, Aug. 31, 1962, p. 19.
[9] Ma Shih-t'u, 'Ch'ieh shuo *Hung yen*' (Speaking of *Red Crag*), *Chung-kuo ch'ing-nien*, No. 11, 1962, pp. 20−1.

success of the authors. With:n a year of its publication, the novel won the widest public attention, and excerpts from it were recited at literary gatherings and on radio programs. It was also converted into a modern stage play and a Peking opera,[10] and its film version was released by the Peking Film Studio in the summer of 1965.[11] In the meantime over five million copies have been sold and it is still a best-seller.[12] Its Japanese translation by Miyoshi Hajime sold over 200,000 copies in less than a year.[13]

The Communist Underground versus *the Kuomintang Secret Service*

Red Crag describes the last battle between the Communist Party underground and the Kuomintang secret service before the end of the Civil War. In January 1948, when the story unfolds, the Communist forces have already gained control of the vast territory north of the Yangtse River. Within less than a year, towards the end of the story, the People's Liberation Army is bombarding the outskirts of Chungking. During this brief period the Communist underground struggle and the Kuomintang counter-intelligence reach white heat. The Communist Party underground is preparing for the take-over by collecting all kinds of data concerning social conditions, class relationships, the economic and financial situation, production figures, and the activities, movements, plans and locations of the Nationalist armed forces. At the same time, they organize workers, students and people of progressive ideas to prevent the Kuomintang secret service from demolishing factories and disrupting water and electricity supplies at the last minute. Finally, they try to absorb scattered armed groups and to persuade the Kuomintang troops to defect. Their work can be summarized as publicizing the policies of the Communist Party, uniting with the masses, and accelerating the dissolution and collapse of Kuomintang control.

On the other side, the Kuomintang attempts to break up the Communist underground organization. As the undercover struggle intensifies, the Kuomintang secret service plants two men in Chungking University. Li Chi-kang pretends to be a leftist student and editor of a radical student sheet in the university and Ch'eng K'o-ch'ang pretends to be Li's cousin who is out-of-work and shares Li's bed. Li's radical

---

[10] Fang Ching-ching, *op. cit.*, p. 19.
[11] 'Red Crag on the Screen', *Peking Review*, No. 34, Aug. 20, 1965, p. 25.
[12] Chao Yang, '*Red Crag*, a Modern Epic', *Chinese Literature*, No. 5, 1965, p. 90.
[13] Wen Chieh-jo, '*Hung yen* tsai jih-pen' (*Red Crag* in Japan), *Wen-i pao*, No. 3, 1964, pp. 29–31.

attitude and his open attack on Kuomintang policies quickly attract the attention of the Communist Party underground. As a man out of a job, Ch'eng K'o-ch'ang spends most of the day in the bookstore which serves as an alternative liaison post for possible emergency use. Ch'eng's habit of reading leftist journals and Soviet novels has not escaped the watchful eyes of the salesman in the bookstore. Ch'eng would never have been able to infiltrate the Communist underground organization, if Fu Chih-kao, the man in charge of the liaison post, had not been interested in personal gain. Fu regards Ch'eng as a young man with progressive ideas, who can help him in his ambitions to expand the bookstore and publish a journal; as a result, Ch'eng is invited to help with store management work.

Through the infiltration of this undercover agent, the Kuomintang secret service arrests Fu Chih-kao. The authors spare no efforts in elucidating the capitulation of this soft-centred Communist. For several years Fu has been chief accountant of Tachung Bank. This is the first time the Party underground entrusts him with an important task. Fu has misgivings about his immediate leaders who have often criticized his working style and never really trusted him. Working in the bank seems to have weakened his dedication to the Party. He has become so accustomed to a comfortable life that he cannot endure the imagined hardships of prison. Therefore, even before any physical torture is applied to him, he defects to the Kuomintang side. Accepting the offer of the post of special commissioner with the rank of colonel, he willingly co-operates with the Kuomintang authorities.

The betrayal of Fu Chih-kao leads to the arrest of Hsu Yun-feng, Fu's present superior, Sister Chiang, Fu's past superior, Ch'eng Kang and Liu Ssu-yang, the two men connected with the publication of *Forward*, Yü Hsin-chiang, Hsu's liaison worker, and Shen Ming-hsia, Liu's sweetheart and assistant. The Party underground immediately severs its relationship with them, so the machine remains basically undamaged. Here the party discipline demonstrates its effectiveness, for as a rule an underground worker is strictly forbidden to maintain contact with other members.

After rounding up these Communists, Hsu P'eng-fei, head of the Second Department of the Kuomintang Northwest High Command, is thrilled by this important breakthrough. The Second Department had recently been formed as an agency in charge of the entire secret service network of the army, gendarmerie, police, and plainclothes men, and Hsu had been under enormous pressure to destroy the Communist underground organization. Now he is confident that these men will offer sufficient clues for him to strike at Communist undercover operations. Mao Jen-feng, director of the Intelligence Bureau of the Ministry of Defense and Hsu's immediate boss, personally takes part in the investigation.

The methods of dealing with arrested Communists used by the Kuomintang secret service, as described in the novel, are varied and sometimes considerably sophisticated. According to the file in the Second Department, Hsu Yun-feng is a high-ranking cadre, though his exact responsibility remains unclear. When a series of threats and offers fails to get anything out of him, a different approach is decided upon. A banquet is prepared, reporters and cameramen alerted, and ranking Kuomintang officials invited to participate in a staged show. If Hsu Yun-feng would only so much as raise a glass, the cameramen would catch the act and a prepared story reporting the co-operation between the Communist underground leader and government authorities would reach the headlines. They calculate that this would dissolve the morale of the Communist Party underground. As an experienced cadre, Hsu Yun-feng proves equal to the trickery. He foils the ruse by saying candidly that they want his co-operation because he has certain amount of influence among the workers. If he clinks glasses with them, he would be despised by the masses and would be of no use to them at all.

When this strategy fails Mao Jen-feng, boss of the secret service, invites Hsu for a private talk. Unlike Hu Meng-an in *The Song of Youth*, whose only strong point is chasing women, Mao is a shrewd and competent master agent. He has a profound knowledge of the Communist organization and knows how to strike at his opponent's weakest point. He says casually that he has met many Communists of greater importance. He points out that men as high-ranking as Chang Kuo-tao[14] and as well-versed in Marxism as Yeh Ch'ing[15] have deserted the Communist Party. According to the Communist Party rule, the moment Hsu is arrested he is no longer a party member. The new relationship between Hsu and the Kuomintang is not that between two rival parties but that between an individual and the government. A man must support his government. After this eloquent argument, Mao Jen-feng suggests three options. First, Hsu can demand conditions for his co-operation. Secondly, Hsu hands over information of the Communist underground organization and a list of important leaders, he promises that this would remain absolutely confidential and the source of information would never be revealed. If Hsu no longer wanted to be involved in politics, the government would be perfectly willing to send him to Macao or Hongkong. Mao Jen-feng does not mention the third possibility, which both of them know to be physical torture and bleak prison life.

---

[14] Chang Kuo-tao was at one time a commander of the Red Army, who split with Mao Tse-tung during the Long March.
[15] Yeh Ch'ing was a Communist theoretician who later defected to the Kuomintang side after his capture.

Mao Jen-feng's soft talk, combined with threats, generally works, but he fails to understand the essence of a Communist's organization life or realize that Hsu Yun-feng is steeled by party discipline. He knows the weakness of human nature and does not expect Hsu to decline an attractive offer. But Hsu chooses prison life, a seemingly hard decision, but on close examination the only logical choice. The logic of such a choice will become clear when we discuss the psychology of collective struggle.

Liu Ssu-yang, the other main character in the book, receives entirely different treatment. He is neither tortured nor threatened on arrest. Instead, Hsu P'eng-fei appears to have a genuine interest in his case and a willingness to help. In their private conversation, Hsu points out Liu's bourgeois background and then presses him further:

'Belief? Isms? All this is nonsense! The Communist Party stresses class origins. What class do you belong to? Your elder brother entered business after serving the government. He's established branches of the Szechwan Pharmaceutical Company both in Chungking and Shanghai. Can't he be counted a member of the bourgeoisie with that huge estate? Then, your origin, thought and style! Aren't you a target for "threefold investigations and threefold rectifications?" I've studied Communist documents carefully. Once the Communist Party gains power, do you think the Liu family's millions can be saved? Wouldn't you, a Communist of an impure family background, be kicked out by the Communist Party? . . .'[16]

After this analysis, Hsu P'eng-fei presents a simple demand. If only Liu Ssu-yang will publish a statement in the newspaper to the effect that he repents his past Communist affiliation and wants to be a new man, he can be immediately released. The argument falls on deaf ears, so Liu is taken to the Coal Pit. After a short period of imprisonment, Liu is again brought to the Second Department. He is released when his second brother personally guarantees his future conduct. As soon as he reaches home, he realizes that he is under house arrest. The next day he reads a newspaper story about his release as a sign of the government's sincerity in peace talks with the Communists.

Outraged by this fraudulent method, Liu is also deeply worried in case the Party underground takes the story of his repentance at face value. He must get away immediately and contact the Party to clarify his case. In the early hours, just before he tries to escape, a stranger knocks at his door. The man declares that he has evaded the vigilance of the plainclothes men to enter the house and tears apart the hem of his shirt-sleeve to produce a slip of paper. When soaked in water, the slip reveals that he is Comrade Chu, sent to investigate Liu by Li

[16] *Red Crag*, p. 196.

Ching-yuan, deputy secretary of the Chungking Party underground. Now Chu tells Liu that Li was highly displeased with his newspaper statement. Liu's party membership has been suspended until his case is cleared. While Chu is looking into his case, Liu must guarantee Chu's safety in his house. This will be a test of Liu's loyalty to the Party.

After protesting his innocence without success, Liu agrees to write a personal statement to set his own position straight as well as to expose the trickery of the Kuomintang. Then Chu conveys Secretary Li's instructions that Liu should also write a report of the party organization in prison, so that the Party underground can work out a plan to rescue the imprisoned comrades. This places Liu in a dilemma. According to the party rule, the secret information Chu demands must be disclosed to an immediately senior cadre and then only orally. Liu realizes that Chu too is surrounded by the enemy. On the other hand, Liu is deeply disturbed that his loyalty to the Party is being questioned. Refusal to write the report will no doubt increase the suspicions of the leadership. After a considerable inner struggle, Liu decides not to write the report. Hearing this, Chu seems surprised and slightly displeased. He tosses the statement Liu has written on the desk and leaves the room.

Liu Ssu-yang is already on his guard. A Communist observes and thinks in a systematic way uniquely Communist. Even with his bourgeois, intellectual background, Liu has learned, thanks to the months of imprisonment in the Coal Pit, to think and observe in the Communist way. His brief imprisonment is perhaps the only period in his life when he has had a chance to live with other Communists. It has been his political schooling; he has come to know how a genuine Communist talks and behaves.

The authors are very skilful in describing Chu's conduct, and subtly reveal the difference between an authentic Communist and a sham. Although Chu has familiarized himself with lines of conversation between Communists, he shows his true color from time to time. A cigarette dangling from his lips shows his frivolity. When he presses Liu to write the report he lacks the consideration with which a comrade usually treats another in trouble. Liu's suspicion is further reinforced when Chu begins to use the loss of his membership as a threat for obtaining the secret information about the party prison organization. A true Communist would hardly be so rash as to intimidate a comrade in order to get top secret information when it can be legitimately obtained through the establishment of mutual trust.

Walking slowly in the garden in the cool air of early morning, Liu comes to realize the dangerous situation he is in. Just at that moment, the milkman appears as usual to make his early morning rounds. As Liu walks over to take a bottle, the man picks up a bottle and hands it to him. Casting a significant glance at Liu, the milkman says, 'This one is yours.' Catching the cue, Liu promptly withdraws with the bottle to his room. There he discovers a note sealed in the top layer of the bottle cover. It is written in Secretary Li's own handwriting, warning him to make no attempt to contact the Party underground and urging him to escape at the earliest opportunity. Liu of course never gets that opportunity.

Ch'eng Kang is the third Communist to become the target of the Second Department for information about the Communist activities in Chungking. He is immediately put to torture without going through the stage of persuasion. Hsu P'eng-fei remembers that the mere sight of sundry torture tools and a threatening gesture made Fu Chih-kao an informer. He hopes that tough measures will produce the same effect on Ch'eng Kang. Hsu seems also to have calculated that Ch'eng Kang may not talk. In that case he can still use Ch'eng Kang's suffering to shock Hsu Yun-feng. But he is unsuccessful in both cases.

Ch'eng Kang's youthful body refuses to die from the serious wounds inflicted on him. He is then carried to Pai House, chained in heavy shackles, and put in solitary confinement. When he gets better he is taken out for medical treatment to a special clinic operated by SACO. An American doctor tells him through an interpreter that he will be injected with some penicillin before surgery. As soon as the liquid flows in his blood vessels, Ch'eng Kang feels a strange sensation and sees hallucinations. The injected liquid is a kind of 'truth serum' usually applied to mental patients for obtaining information about their early lives.

In a semi-conscious state, Ch'eng Kang sees Hsu Yun-feng standing in front of him. Comrade Hsu wants him to make a report of the prison party organization and to reveal the address of the Party underground. The address had been given to him the day before his arrest. At that time Secretary Li Ching-yuan had told him to hand over the work of *Forward*, for the Party underground had decided to change the mimeographed sheets into a printed paper. Ch'eng Kang's next assignment had not yet been determined, but Li gave him the address for contact. Now his superior Hsu Yun-feng needs that information, and Ch'eng Kang must tell him.

The address is top secret; its disclosure may endanger the security of the entire Party underground in Chungking. Even in delirium, his professional alertness tells him that it should not lightly be revealed, even to Hsu Yun-feng. He tries to see Hsu's face more clearly and to remember where he is. Then slowly it comes back to him that he is under medical treatment in a special clinic. The vague figure of Comrade Hsu gradually turns into the tall shape of a foreign physician in white uniform. The questions seem to come from another shadowy figure also in white. Then Ch'eng Kang says that he knows no address.

When the plainclothes man disguised in physician's uniform persists in asking questions he is stopped. The doctor says that the effect of the truth serum lasts only briefly, so the second figure quickly fades away.

Later in a conversation with Liu Ssu-yang, Ch'eng Kang describes the experience he has gone through. Then he adds that that sort of drug has no effect on revolutionaries like them. Its effect does not last long; besides, those who are armed with the willpower of true revolutionaries will never lose control. Liu agrees that they can resist the enemy's frontal attack. With a sense of unease at the memory of his own experience, he points out a revolutionary's individualistic thinking as his weak spot. The enemy nearly succeeded by taking advantage of his fear of being misunderstood and his eagerness to prove his loyalty to the Party.

Failure to obtain information directly from the political prisoners forces the Kuomintang secret service to take other measures. One day four more political prisoners are thrown into the Coal Pit. Three of them are high school students, actually teenagers, who have been arrested for participating in a demonstration against Kuomintang policies. The fourth, a reporter, has been severely tortured and his leg is still in a plaster cast. He appears to be quite willing to tell the story of his past connection with the Communist Party and is eager to join in the prison struggle.

Almost by intuition Yü Hsin-chiang senses something strange about this leftist reporter. In Sister Chiang's experienced eyes, the reporter's ultra-leftist behavior suggests an act. Shen Ming-hsia reaches the same conclusion from another angle. The reporter has declared that he underwent *p'i-ma tai-hsiao*,[17] one of the cruellest forms of torture. As prisoners are well aware, in this method of torture the prisoner is repeatedly beaten with a club with thousands of nails and then wrapped up in a bandage. When the bandage gets stuck to the skin, the jailer pulls it off, along with the skin, gore and all. As a medical student at Chungking University, Shen Ming-hsia knows that *p'i-ma tai-hsiao* cannot be treated with a plaster cast on one leg.

They put their hypotheses to test. During a break time, Yü Hsin-chiang stays in the cell, scrubbing the floor. He has a message in his pocket. As if scrubbing makes him warm, he carelessly takes off his jacket and tosses it on the floor. Then he goes out with the basin to fetch clean water. As soon as Yü leaves the room, the reporter who has been keeping an eye on him sneaks in and fumbles for a quick glance at the slip of paper. Half an hour later, the howling voice of the Owl, one of the worst jailers, is heard in the cells. Under merciless beating, The

[17] Literally, 'wearing white mourning garments and hemp jacket'.

Owl pleads his innocence, when charged with carrying messages for the political prisoners for a bribe of one hundred silver dollars.

Yü is secretly jubilant for getting even with that blood thirsty brute once, at least. At the same time he is delighted that the true identity of the 'reporter' has been verified. The man is a 'Red Flag agent'.[18] With careful planning, the prisoners give the 'reporter' a sound beating. He is rescued by the jailers and carried away half dead. Yü Hsin-chiang never finds out that the 'reporter' is the very Ch'eng K'o-ch'ang on whose information he and others were arrested.

The methods of Communist underground work and Kuomintang counter-intelligence are as ruthless as they are ingenious. The artistic skill of the authors is demonstrated in the best tradition of Chinese classical novels, with their complicated plots and dramatic suspense. Although the suspense frequently makes the reader hold his breath, *Red Crag* is by no means an adventure story in the vein of spy tales. It is the characterization of political prisoners that makes the novel a masterpiece of its kind.

Images of Hardened Communists

The authors of *Red Crag* give equal attention to a number of characters rather than focusing on a single hero. For some time Communist theoreticians have stressed the need for creating several equally heroic characters in collective action. The danger, from an artistic point of view, is that the individuality of the heroes is likely to become blurred. In *Red Crag*, the authors have managed to avoid this. This may explain why the novel was never attacked, even during the Cultural Revolution, although the story dealing with the struggle in a 'white' area clearly falls into the scope of work under Liu Shao-ch'i's leadership.

Few Chinese novels can match its brilliant characterization. Even the author of the celebrated *Water Margin* concentrates on only half a dozen characters. Lo Kuang-pin and Yang Yi-yen are two new authors whose creative talent has not been tested elsewhere. Their unusual achievement perhaps owes a good deal to the real men and women, real events in the concentration camps, and above all the authors' own experience.

Among the political prisoners, Hsu Yun-feng is portrayed as a senior cadre, whose main experience is in underground work. The moment he steps into the bookstore, he knows something is wrong. There are piles of white paper around, new empty bookshelves, and radical and

[18] So named because the agent disguised himself as a Communist.

progressive journals on display. From questioning the salesman Ch'en, a comrade, he learns that Fu Chih-kao has decided to enlarge the bookstore in violation of his instructions. Then he discovers that a non-Communist has been hired. Fortunately, the man is away, so Hsu examines his belongings. He finds some poems written by this man, but immediately identifies them as plagiarisms from Ma Fan-t'o, a well known Communist poet. He suspects that he is trying to win the trust of the Party underground. Informed that the man has told Comrade Ch'en not to leave the store that evening, Hsu promptly concludes that the man must be a plainclothes agent, Ch'en is in danger, and the bookstore must be immediately abandoned. A series of other decisions are made. He phones Fu Chih-kao who comes to see him a few minutes later. Hsu tells Fu of the dangerous situation and stiffly warns him not to go home again but to meet him at a certain market-place for instructions about his transfer next morning. Hsu also makes another phone call to Li Ching-yuan, deputy secretary of the Chungking Party underground, and arranges for a conference in a tea house.

But Fu Chih-kao ignores his warning and takes chances to bid farewell to his wife. He is met at his house by plainclothes men. The next day as Hsu and Li are discussing alternative plans over a cup of tea among noisy haggling merchants, Fu leads Kuomintang agents to arrest Hsu. Knowing that he has no chance of slipping away and that Fu does not know Li, Hsu instantly covers the escape of Li by diverting their attention to himself.

When Hsu rejects Mao Jen-feng's propositions, his fate is sealed. His torture is not directly described in the novel. One day the prisoners in the Coal Pit see a motionless body carried in on a stretcher by plainclothes men. Only a pair of bleeding feet locked in iron shackles can be seen motionless outside the blanket. The wounded man is thrown into unoccupied Cell 7 on the second floor, totally isolated from other prisoners. For several days a jailer is seen taking half a bowl of rice gruel into the cell and then taking it out untouched. The prisoners all share an uneasy sense of ill omen. Several days later, an extraordinary thing happens.

At dawn one morning the political prisoners are startled by the heavy clanking of shackles knocking on the coarse floor. Over the sound of the chains a voice is heard singing:

Arise, you cold and hungry slaves!
Arise, you prisoners of the world!

The song strikes home; from all directions powerful voices join in the song, and not even the threats of the jailers can stop them.

The scene has the force of a resurrection. Hsu Yun-feng's stubborn will has won a battle against his badly injured body. His song poses a fresh challenge to the enemy, and at the same time is a message of reassurance to his fighting comrades; a veteran is rejoining the ranks.

The Second Department has kept a wary eye on Hsu and is uneasy that he may become a leader of the prisoners at the Coal Pit. Before long he is transferred to Pai House and confined in a dungeon, where he is not only separated from other prisoners by two iron trap-doors, but even his identity is kept secret. Sealed alive in a coffin-like stone crypt, Hsu refuses to give up hope. When his eyes get used to the darkness he studies every piece of mortar. He slowly works out that the dungeon is dug into a cliff, with only one side built of huge blocks of stone. He begins to plan how a passage could be made, for escape at the critical moment.

Working day and night with rusty pieces of iron from the fetters left behind by previous occupants, Hsu manages to dig loose a large piece of mortar. A tunnel is finally opened, but it never occurs to him that he himself should escape. He knows that the nearer the Red Army gets to Chungking the greater the danger for the political prisoners. The opportune moment for an escape is on the eve of the liberation of Chungking; and then the action must be co-ordinated with the Coal Pit.

Hsu Yun-feng never gets a chance to use the tunnel himself. As the Communist big guns are heard in Chungking, Hsu P'eng-fei decides to execute the political prisoners secretly. He has an extreme hatred for Hsu Yun-feng whose refusal to co-operate has rendered him helpless in destroying the Chungking Communist underground. All his plans for demolishing important factories, establishing guerrilla bases, and planting undercover agents have met with failure. Before he orders the execution of Hsu Yun-feng, Hsu P'eng-fei decides to visit this stubborn Communist and to have the satisfaction of seeing the expression of a man who knows he is about to die. Even at this last encounter Hsu P'eng-fei has to suffer another setback.

'There's a little news I don't wish to conceal.' Hsu P'eng-fei smiled viciously as he studied Hsu Yun-feng's confident face. 'The Communist victory is already in sight, yet what a pity you can't witness it! What does Mr. Hsu feel, here and now, facing his own death?'

Hsu Yun-feng was unperturbed, smiling. 'This I can tell you without reservation. As an ordinary worker, mistreated and oppressed in the old society, I finally chose the revolutionary road and became a man feared by the reactionaries. Looking back at the road I've traveled, I've only a sense of pride. I'm happy to witness the victory of the proletarians in China. The surge of the revolutionary tide, like the wind blowing away scattered clouds, proves that my ideal coincides with the wish of all the Chinese people. That gives me infinite strength. Since ancient times, who has not died? But there can be no higher glory than to link your own life with the ever

youthful revolutionary cause of the working class. This is what I
feel, here and now.'

Slowly standing up and unhurriedly walking up to look into Hsu
P'eng-fei's face, Hsu Yun-feng smiled again. 'What then is your
feeling at this very moment?'[19]

This dialogue brings home the contrast between a dedicated
Communist and a selfish Kuomintang official. Throughout the novel,
Hsu P'eng-fei is never a caricature of a corrupt, incompetent enemy. He
is a worthy adversary, shrewd, calculating, ruthless. His weakness, as
seen by the authors, dedicated Communists themselves, is his selfish
pursuit of personal gain. He can sacrifice his own men in order to pacify
the anger of factory workers. He fights his colleagues every inch of the
way and even disrupts their plans for the sake of his own success. When
Chungking faces the imminent attack of Communist troops the first
idea that occurs to him is to have an aeroplane waiting to pick him up.
He expects to see Hsu Yun-feng's despair and suffering, for it is simply
inconceivable to him that a man can face death with a smile.

Hsu Yun-feng, whose whole heart is in the accomplishment of the
mission the Party has entrusted to him, is the exact opposite. Indeed,
he wants to do more than the Party asks of him. It is his glory to
surpass the heroic deeds of the martyrs who serve as shining examples.
But Hsu Yun-feng represents more than just a hardened Communist.
His unbending character is typical of Chinese heroes of the best
tradition. The last words Hsu so composedly utters, if the Communist
terminology were omitted, could very well have been spoken by Wen
T'ien-hsiang, author of the immortal *Song of Righteousness*, who
attempted to save Sung China from destruction single-handed.

Hsu Yun-feng's aggressive heroism is matched by the quiet, almost
patient resolve of Sister Chiang. Among dedicated Communists there
are many equally determined women. We already had a glimpse of such
a heroine in Lin Hung of *The Song of Youth*. Lin Hung, however, is too
fleeting and hazy a figure. Only in Sister Chiang do we see a
sharply-focused portrait of a revolutionary woman.

The courage of Sister Chiang is powerfully conveyed in the
description of an incident before her arrest. Assigned to work with her
husband Peng Sung-tao, political commissar of the Mount Huajung
Detachment in northern Szechwan, Sister Chiang sees her husband's
bloody head in a wooden cage hanging high on the city wall. Hot tears
in her eyes and a feeling of suffocation in her chest, she restrains herself
with great effort. She feels she has no right to give way to her personal
grief while she has a job to do.

In the next few pages the authors describe how despite her mental

---

[19] *Red Crag*, p. 560.

tumult she continues her journey. Her bravery is not depicted directly but reflected in the behavior of another woman. She is a sturdy old woman with greying hair, known to friends and foes alike as Two-Gun Grandma. The old lady would never so much as raise an eyebrow at gunning down her enemies. But that day her movements are unusually hasty and awkward. She tells Sister Chiang that Comrade Peng is out on a mission and will not be back for a few days. A meal is quickly prepared without waiting for Sister Chiang to wash. Awkwardly, she knocks over an empty winecup with her sleeve. Finally, Sister Chiang cannot wait any longer and tells the good-hearted old woman that she knows everything.

> Tears trickled down Grandma's wrinkled old face. She flung her arms around Sister Chiang. She did not say a word.[20]

The scene shows Sister Chiang's capacity for taking the greatest personal tragedy. Boundless sorrow and stormy emotion are contained. It would be clumsy from the artistic point of view to attempt the description of her suffering. In an even voice, she says, 'I know everything.' This simple sentence conveys what a whole chapter could not expect to accomplish.

In the concentration camp Sister Chiang is tortured. The jailers use sharp needles to stick into her fingernails, but she refuses to talk. When the plan for escape is completed, the enemy acts ahead of time. She is soon taken away from the Coal Pit.

> When Sister Chiang heard her name called she instantly knew everything. She was unusually calm, without agitation, fear or sorrow. The dawn was arriving, and the first rays of the morning sun could be seen. This was the moment so many people had been longing for! At this moment her whole body was full of hope and happiness, and she smiled. Standing up and walking to the wall, she picked up a comb. In the dim light of early morning, looking into a broken mirror on the wall, as usual she unhurriedly combed her hair.
> Sister Chiang changed into the blue *ch'i-p'ao*[21] and then put on her red knitted sweater. She brushed the dust off her clothes, as usual, and straightened out some creases.
> 'Ming-hsia, give me a hand to straighten my clothes.'
> Sun Ming-hsia knew that Sister Chiang always kept herself neat and tidy. This habit she never changed even in the concentration camp. As a result, calm Sister Chiang always gave others the impression of high spirits and dignity. At early dawn this day Sister Chiang was unusually calm and meticulous. Gradually, Sun Ming-hsia sensed a certain special dignity in Sister Chiang. Could that be the feeling of deliberate martyrdom? She immediately squatted at Sister

---

[20] *Red Crag*, p. 77, *Chinese Literature*, No. 5, 1962, p. 23.
[21] A long gown worn by women.

Chiang's feet, tenderly flattening the creases at the hem of her clothes. Her tears spilled over in spite of herself. As if unaware of all this, Sister Chiang bent down to wipe the dust of her shoes.

Sun Ming-hsia dried her tears and turned around to collect Sister Chiang's belongings. Sister Chiang took another look at the mirror and turned to try a few steps in the room as if she were preparing for a happy dinner party or an important ceremonial occasion. Then she quietly walked to 'The Prison Flower'.[22] The infant was sound asleep. After gazing at the child for some time, she could not help bending down and kissing her on the cheek.

Raising her head, she saw Sun Ming-hsia hand over to her a cloth bundle with her clothes wrapped up.

'Sister Chiang, here are your clothes for changing into.'

Sister Chiang took the bundle, glanced at it, and returned it to Sun Ming-hsia.

'I no longer need them.' Sister Chiang smiled.

The clothes bundle dropped from Ming-hsia's hand. She could no longer restrain her tears and threw herself into Sister Chiang's arms crying out:

'Sister Chiang! Sister Chiang!'[23]

It is a quiet scene without commotion. The narrative has the effect of the stillness before a storm or the suffocating peace before a major battle. The details suggest the uncompromising principle of a dedicated revolutionary; even in the face of death, Sister Chiang does not want to be untidy in front of the firing squad. Her calmness shows the poise of a person who feels the satisfaction of a task accomplished, with nothing left to be done. Her last words as she leaves Sun Ming-hsia are: 'If it should become necessary for us to die for the ideals of Communism, we should be ready to do it – without blanching, heart beating no faster . . . and I know that we can.'

Among the prisoners in Pai House is an old madman with a headful of white hair and a bushy white beard all over his face. At breaks he can be seen mechanically running in circles round the prison walls. He had gone mad three years before, when he was taken to the execution ground with Lo Shih-wen and Ch'e Yao-hsien, two leaders of the Communist Party in Szechwan. Both Lo and Ch'e were shot, but this old man became insane and was spared.

Since then he never spoke to anyone. The leaders of the Communist Prison Special Committee know only his name, Hua Tzu-liang, but have absolutely no information about him. The general assumption is that he was an innocent bystander mistakenly arrested by Kuomintang plain-

[22] An infant girl born in prison to a woman political prisoner who never revealed her identity. After she was shot, the child became the darling of all the women prisoners and was called 'The Prison Flower'.
[23] *Red Crag*, pp. 506–8.

clothes men. The theory appears sound, for there have been many similar cases. The insanity of the old man is so total that when Hu Hao, a non-Communist prisoner, was being ruthlessly tortured and his howls were piercing the nerves of all the prisoners, Hua Tzu-liang seemed perfectly unaware of what was happening. Ch'eng Kang once said with unconcealed disgust, he simply could not understand how the man was still alive when his nerves were dead.

The madman can still do some work, though like an automaton. The jailers let him cook meals for the prisoners and accompany plainclothes men to the market to carry groceries. The prisoners are unhappy with this insane cook, for he often burns the rice. But the jailers are satisfied, because of his reliability.

One day during a break, Ch'eng Kang and the prison party leader Chi Hsiao-hsien are discussing matters in a secret hide-out under the wooden floor of the prison library. The library is the result of a hunger strike led by Lo Shih-wen and Ch'e Yao-hsien years before. The director of the prison had finally consented to clearing out a large room to serve as library. The place is messy and dusty. Kuomintang propaganda pamphlets, texts for training plainclothes men, and cheap American paperbacks are mixed with Communist writings and Russian novels in random heaps. Deep in the piles of yellowing journals and torn books is a spot, where the nails of the wooden planks have been loosened and the earth underneath removed. It is here that Ch'eng Kang and Chi Hsiao-hsien are talking about the problem of making contact with the Party underground outside, while the deputy party secretary Yu, the librarian, is stationed at the library entrance to act as sentry.

Ch'eng Kang tells Chi that he has an address. The problem is to find the right man to send out with the message. Chi mentions the name of Hua Tzu-liang, but Ch'eng Kang strongly objects to the suggestion of trusting a madman. He looks on the old madman as an ordinary person who has been arrested in error by some stupid Kuomintang agents. He uses two convincing arguments. First, the worst thing that can happen to a Communist is the sense of loneliness resulting from the severance of contact with the organization. Since his imprisonment fifteen years ago, Hua has never attempted to get in touch with the prison party. Ch'eng Kang's second point is that a man can withstand his own sufferings but cannot listen to the torment of another without feeling.

At this point they hear Yu's voice loudly reciting a Tang poem, the agreed danger signal. Ch'eng Kang quickly picks up a piece of rock and prepares for an attack on the intruder. Moments later as the floor planks are removed a white head appears.

'Hua Tzu-liang!' Ch'eng Kang shuddered and instantly jumped at this man, who should not have appeared.

'Wait.' Hua Tzu-liang faced Ch'eng Kang and waved his hand. The crazy, neurotic look completely disappeared. He smiled and then turned his shining eyes to Chi Hsiao-hsien: 'I want to see you on business.'

'You want to see Old Chi?' Ch'eng Kang gripped Hua Tzy-liang by the neck.

'Wait a minute.' Chi softly stopped him. Ch'eng Kang turned and his eyes met Chi's. Chi Hsiao-hsien nodded, as a signal that Ch'eng Kang should let go.

'Who are you?'

To answer Chi's question, Hua Tzu-liang moved a step closer and said clearly and sincerely:

'A Communist.'

'Why have you come?'

'The Party needs me to function now.'

'Whom are you looking for?'

'The secretary of the Prison Party Special Comrade Chi Hsiao-hsien.'

'Who told you?'

'Comrade Lo Shih-wen.'

'When?'

'October 18, 1946.[24] The day Lo Shih-wen and Ch'e Yao-hsien were martyred, and I was accompanying them to the execution ground,' Hua Tzu-liang answered calmly. 'Fifteen years ago, I was the Party secretary of the Mount Huajung base area. The secretary of the Party Provincial Committee Comrade Lo Shih-wen was my superior. But in the eyes of the enemy I was only a suspect. On the way to the execution ground, Comrade Lo Shih-wen figured that the enemy brought me to the execution ground only to see if I was really a Communist. So he instructed me to use insanity indefinitely as a cover in order to fool the enemy. At the sound of the first shot, I turned mad.'

Ch'eng Kang's clenched hands relaxed. Chi continued his questioning:

'Why did you wait until this moment to make contact?'

'The provincial party secretary assigned me a special task. I was not allowed to have any association with anybody until the most critical moment.'

'What if I were no longer around?'

'If you were killed, I would look for your successor Comrade Yu.'

'Your assignment?'

'Let the enemy believe that I'm truly insane. Then get in touch with the Party underground. Second, arrange the prisoners' escape.'

Ch'eng Kang looked at Hua Tzu-liang, unable to control his inner

---

[24] The date differs from the one given in the memoir. There can be two explanations: first, the date in the novel is fictional, or, the difference by one month and one day results from the fact that the date in the memoir is based on the lunar calendar.

turmoil. What a veteran comrade was this man in front of him, who
pretended insanity while making long-range plans, enduring unusual
hardships, and engaging in a protracted struggle!

Chi Hsiao-hsien suddenly posed a new question:

'Your code for contact?'

'Let us get ready for this great day!'

Hearing this code, Chi Hsiao-hsien's eyes were suddenly wet. The
code had been given to him and Comrade Yu on the eve of Comrade
Lo Shih-wen's death, when he was appointed secretary of the Party
Prison Special. It had been sent in by the Party underground, and
was a quotation of the last sentence from 'On Coalition Government'. In order to protect the interests of the Party in this
complicated, difficult and dangerous place, Hua Tzu-liang had
executed the instructions of the leadership precisely. His lack of
contact with the organization was completely understandable. How
noble were his perseverance and courage!

'Comrade, how welcome you are! All these years you practiced
running. You've always been preparing for the escape!'

Hua Tzu-liang tightly held the hand Chi Hsiao-hsien gave him and
said:

'I know you and Comrade Yu have kept an eye on me all these
years. Yet not until now have I met the necessary conditions to get
in touch with the Party underground . . . ' Hua took out a piece of
folded paper and handed it over to Chi, saying:

'This is a message to the Party from the comrade in the dungeon.'

'You've already made contact with the comrade in the dungeon!'
There was unusual excitement in Chi Hsiao-hsien's normally steady
voice. 'Who is he?'

'Hsu Yun-feng.'

'Old Hsu!' Suddenly Ch'eng Kang was both surprised and
overjoyed. 'He's been kept in the dungeon?'

Hua Tzu-liang gave a slight nod.

Chi Hsiao-hsien did not immediately open Hsu Yun-feng's note.
Instead, he asked Hua:

'Right now, what do you need?'

'The address.'

Chi Hsiao-hsien turned to Ch'eng Kang. Ch'eng Kang instantly
answered in a low voice:

'318 Linshen Road. Anp'ing Life Insurance Company.'[25]

This lengthy quotation portrays the extent of the dedication sought
by undercover Communists, the role of the leadership at a particular
level, and the functioning of the organization. Hua Tzu-liang's devotion
to the Party and to the mission it has entrusted to him shocks even such
hardened Communists as Ch'eng Kang and Chi Hsiao-hsien. Ch'eng
Kang, especially, finds such protracted, single-handed struggle beyond

[25] *Red Crag*, pp. 477–9.

his comprehension. On an earlier occasion, Ch'eng Kang is described as suffering an acute sense of anxiety when the leadership ceases to contact him for a few months. A Communist working underground and surrounded by the enemy is like a child in need of attention. The Party performs the function of a large family which constantly provides care and comfort to an insecure mind. Liu Ssu-yang also cannot do what Hua Tzu-liang has done, Liu always needs the understanding and trust of the Party to sustain his fighting morale. In comparison with Hua Tzu-liang's solitary execution of a painfully uncertain assignment, even Hsu Yun-feng's undaunted bravery and Sister Chiang's unperturbed courage seem to have paled. In a completely hostile environment, the man has denied himself the consolation of comradely companionship. Pretending insanity which is viewed as the result of cowardice in the scoffing eyes of other Communist prisoners, Hua has to steel himself. What control, to give no sign that things are not what they seem!

The narrative also reveals how the Communist system functions. Even in his isolation Hua Tzu-liang is still a part of the organization. He is carrying out a task assigned to him by the leadership of the Prison Party Special while the leader himself has been dead a long time. In a unique situation such as Pai House the prison Party organization has lost contact with the Party underground. In the absence of instructions from the leadership on a higher level, the senior cadre is automatically in charge. When he knows that he is going to die, he can appoint a successor and give assignments to other members. The Party organization does not die with him. This perhaps makes death easier, for he knows the work left unfinished will be properly completed. The Party will remain alive as long as there is a single Communist left.

The Communist organizational system can be said to be truly airtight. It is a strict rule that secret information must be kept to oneself and related to a second person only when it can produce the expected result. The reason is of course obvious. The more people have the information, the greater the likelihood of a leak. Ch'eng Kang will not share even with Chi Hsiao-hsien, secretary of the Prison Party Special, the address of the Party underground. Chi certainly knows this principle and will not, as the leader and senior cadre, demand Ch'eng Kang to reveal it. Chi Hsiao-hsien is only a man who happens to occupy the position of secretary at a particular time. He does not have the privilege of knowing everything. Ch'eng Kang does not need to worry about what he will do in the case of Chi's death. There will always be someone else to succeed Chi. And Chi has the power to make this appointment, just as Lo Shih-wen appointed him years ago. The address will never be revealed until the moment when this most valuable information has the precise effect required. That will be to achieve co-ordination between the Prison Party Special and the Chungking Party underground when preparations for escape are completed.

There are quite a few other political prisoners who are vividly portrayed and deserve analysis, but space does not allow it. One final example is a nine-year-old boy kept in Pai House. He is not a political prisoner but is kept there with his parents. The little boy's father is Sung Chi-yun, General Yang Hu-ch'eng's secretary and formerly editor of the *Northwest Culture Daily*. When Kuomintang secret agents seized and incarcerated Yang, Sung and his wife were also arrested. The boy was then a nursing infant.

Known to every prisoner as Little Turnip for his unusually large head on an undernourished body, the boy has seen nothing but prison cells, iron bars and barbed wire. Such familiar scenes constantly appear in his dreams. Only once in his nine years of life has he been taken outside the prison walls. On the day of the victory over the Japanese he was taken to a nearby town. Thus, 'town' is not just a word in his reader but a place recurring in his dreams. Nevertheless, even when he is dreaming of the town it turns into a walled place with huge gates of iron bars. Electrified barbed wire grows red above the walls. The people in town wear the same prison clothes as in Pai House. In one nightmare, as he is walking in the streets he sees a commotion.

In an instant, the street was deserted and the house doors locked with big shiny locks. Everyone put his head out through the hole in his door and looked at the sky. Little Turnip looked up too. The sky was blue and cloudless, empty except for a few circling hawks . . . they were Kuomintang agents with wings! They sped like arrows back and forth above the street, casting streaking shadows. One of the keeper-hawks pounced. With iron claws it dragged a man out through the hole in his door. The man's eyes dropped from his head and rolled on the ground, the blacks and whites clearly visible. Suddenly they stopped rolling and stared up at Little Turnip! His heart beating fast, he screamed in terror . . .[26]

This insight into the psychology of the child reveals the powerful impact of prison life. The child's subconscious is always dreaming of the free world outside. Yet the reality of prison life has cast a lasting shadow on his innocent mind that he can never escape. But the young mind constantly struggles to visualize a different world. When Yang Hu-ch'eng and Little Turnip's father are transferred to another camp Little Turnip comes to say goodbye to Ch'eng Kang and gives him as a souvenir a painting he had done himself.

It was a watercolor. Beneath a sky botched with too much blue was a golden mountain with jade green trees. Half an enormous sun peered from behind the mountain and emitted dazzling red rays. In the corner was the title in bold strokes: *Dawn.*[27]

[26] *Red Crag*, p. 389, *Chinese Literature*, No. 6, 1962, p. 46.
[27] *Red Crag*, p. 393, *Chinese Literature*, No. 6, 1962, p. 50.

The boy's clear vision leads him away from cold reality into a colorful, warm world of fantasy. He must have a very powerful imagination, for he complains to Ch'eng Kang: 'I couldn't get it all in. The paper's too small.'

Little Turnip is of course not a Communist, but there is something of the Communist about him. This nine-year-old boy is already hardened by experience. When he first sees Ch'eng Kang he asks him whether he has been tortured. When Ch'eng Kang denies it, the boy does not believe him and checks his twisted fingers. The second question is whether Ch'eng Kang has talked. When Ch'eng Kang says no the boy's comment is, 'You're . . . a good man.' The third question is whether Ch'eng Kang is a Communist. Ch'eng does not answer, because he reasons that he should not discuss such things with a child. But the boy knows more than Ch'eng has realized. He says that he knows, but never tells Ch'eng Kang what he knows. He is much older and more mature than he looks. If he ever survives the dismal life of the concentration camp, he will become a Communist at the first opportunity. He will be a Hsu Yun-feng, a Ch'eng Kang, a Hua Tzu-liang.

The Psychology of the Collective Struggle

A fundamental and legitimate question is this: Is it real, this fierce loyalty of the Communists to their Party? It is true that the authors of *Red Crag* have done a superb job in the characterization of political prisoners, but a fine work of art may not necessarily be a reconstruction of reality. It is true, too, that the story is based on a memoir of real people and events. Again, the authenticity of the memoir itself can be questioned. We cannot and do not wish to verify the details described in the novel, but we can analyze the basic thesis, the unwavering loyalty of underground workers to the Communist Party.

The best place to start the discussion is to look at Fu Chih-kao, the man who has betrayed his party. The authors skilfully reveal the causes for Fu's betrayal. He wants to widen his influence by attempting to publish a magazine and to recruit members from disillusioned students and intellectuals out of work. He returns to his home in spite of the warning of Hsu Yun-feng, for he is afraid that once he is transferred to another post from his present position as chief accountant in a bank, he will have to give up his comfortable life. He is hoping against hope that Hsu may be just over-sensitive as a result of working underground for too long and that he can stay in his present job. These are plausible reasons for Fu's arrest and subsequent defection. But there is a third and actually more compelling reason which Fu Chih-kao uses to defend his case. When Sister Chiang scorns Fu for becoming a turncoat he retorts by saying that since the Party has done nothing for him, why should he die for the Party. He has to bear anguish and distress day and night as an underground worker and then has to accept endless exhortations and criticisms with a smile. What Fu is saying is that the party leadership is partially responsible for his capitulation. An impartial reader gets the impression that Fu is not really trusted. When he is assigned the job of establishing the alternative liaison post he is actually overjoyed at the confidence the Party has shown in him. Up to the time of his arrest and defection, he has tried very hard to do more than his share. In the meantime he has received no new instructions and remains uncertain when and if the liaison post under his charge will be used. He is asked to risk his skin without knowing the true nature of his work. Ch'eng Kang is quite content to sacrifice hours of sleep to publish *Forward*, knowing that the paper will reach all the underground workers in Chungking. Liu Ssu-yang is thrilled to receive news on his short-wave radio, for what he records will be transmitted to his comrades through the party communications network. But Fu Chih-kao is denied the pleasure of knowing the effect of his work.

Underground work is different from other forms of political struggle. An underground worker is surrounded by enemies, both obvious and potential, public and secret. He has no friends; his real job must be concealed from his family and relatives. Working in a completely hostile environment, he longs for the guidance and attention of the Party. Nevertheless, contacts with the organization are few and far-between. Fu Chih-kao lacks the resolution and strength of character essential for this type of work.

An underground worker knows that there is an organization which operates in utter secrecy. It maintains contact with the Central Committee somewhere in the far north, Yenan or Shihchiachuang, as during part of the period under discussion. An underground worker will feel like an orphan when he is given no assignment, no instructions, or is out of touch with the organization. Once he is entrusted with a certain task, he immediately loses that sense of estrangement. He is honored by that trust and eager to prove his worth. The secret party organization suddenly becomes real, yet at the same time remains mysterious, as it is connected with something remote and omnipotent. Ch'eng Kang is ecstatic when after a long worrying period of isolation from the Party Hsu Yun-feng suddenly appears as leader. He can now work under Hsu. And Hsu is sent from Yenan! The same unsettling state of mind must oppress Liu Ssu-yang, when he is told to pack up and leave the Coal Pit. He refuses to go with the plainclothes men. When they take no notice, he insists on having breakfast with his imprisoned comrades. He apparently feels much more secure among his friends in prison. He will be lonely outside the prison walls, even in his own home.

When Liu is re-arrested, he is sent to share the same cell as Ch'eng Kang in Pai House. They have not met before, though Liu is aware that he and Ch'eng Kang have both worked for *Forward*. Seeing the hostility in Ch'eng Kang's eyes, Liu feels a chill running down his spine. He refrains from telling Ch'eng Kang about his role in *Forward*. He knows very well that such an explanation will only increase Ch'eng Kang's suspicion. After briefly exchanging names, each retreats to his own separate world. Liu Ssu-yang feels an acute sense of dejection; he misses the intimate comradeship of the Coal Pit.

By the break, Liu Ssu-yang has almost turned into a pessimist. There is no sign of organized struggle in this camp. He eyes with dismay an old madman running in circles, another skinny old man sitting almost lifeless in the sun, then the intolerably suspicious Ch'eng Kang. When the break is over Liu, thoroughly depressed, reluctantly drags himself into the cell. Then suddenly he is aware of a pair of eyes gazing at him warmly. It is a friendly, engaging gaze. In a short while, Ch'eng Kang has changed into an entirely different person. He produces a note and shows it to Liu. The note comes from downstairs and simply says, 'The man is reliable.' So the organization has welcomed him after all. Only at this point does Liu mention to Ch'eng that they had in fact exchanged messages some time earlier. Before their arrest, Ch'eng Kang had entreated the leadership to send a note to the unknown comrade who records broadcasts from Yenan. He was given a reluctant nod and told that the message must be brief. Finally, Ch'eng Kang managed to put down one line, 'Please accept my revolutionary salute!' Before long he received the reply, also in one line, 'Let's hold hands tightly!' Now at this moment in a tiny cell of Pai House the two comrades meet. Liu Ssu-yang once more feels full of strength and vitality. He has found the organization again. He no longer suffers that keen sense of ultimate loneliness. A lost child has returned to the care and love of his parents.

A Communist alone is harmless and impotent. When he is a part of the organization he can become extremely dangerous. It becomes quite natural for him to make sacrifices for the Party. He has no private life, apart from the life of the organization. The mutual trust between himself and his Party is his spiritual food. It is clearly impossible for Hsu Yun-feng to betray his Party, for once he severs that relationship he is dead, as surely as if he cut his own artery.

When one analyses the way the system functions, one cannot help admiring the chilling efficiency of the system. How desperately dependent a Communist underground worker is on the organization! In *Red Crag* as in other similar novels, the Party underground makes no particular effort to punish a turncoat. It is true that in *Red Crag* Fu Chih-kao is captured by Two-Gun Grandma's men, but their real aim is to rescue Sister Chiang. The immediate steps taken by the Party underground in Chungking are to sever that broken link and to have all cadres transferred to other places or posts. The Party's only concern is that the traitor should cause no further damage. It is not particularly interested in punishing the defector. The reason seems to be that the man will pay for his guilt in breaking off his relationship with the organization and therefore in effect killing his own past life. It is enough to let him be haunted by the agony of living under the shadow of his own past.

Underground struggle is collective struggle. Every underground party man performs the function assigned to him by the Party. In the absence of a personal life, he has to live as a cell in the collective life. He needs work, a new assignment to fulfill his insecure psyche. The tougher the assignment the greater his psychological consolation. No doubt more danger is involved, but the danger is only physical. The psychological satisfaction derived from the Party's reliance on him is an incomparable reward. It is this sense of satisfaction which makes Sister Chiang face death with equanimity and Hsu Yun-feng argue his case with such eloquence before he is taken to the firing squad. If a man lives solely for a cause, knows that he has done his best and that his unfinished work will be carried through to the end by his comrades, he can die in peace and harmony with himself.

The vitality of the collective struggle in an underground operation feeds on the ferocity of the enemy. The tighter the control and the more ruthless the suppression the greater the determination of the underground workers. When a man lives in constant danger, his instincts become much sharper. That explains why Hsu smells something suspicious as soon as he steps into the bookstore. A man also becomes desperately uncompromising and suspicious, ready to see tricks behind the enemy's smiling pose. The trouble with the Kuomintang authorities is their belief that the enemy can either be bought with money and rank or intimidated by torture. Both methods, *Red Crag* shows us, have met with complete fiasco, when dealing with convinced Communists.

5

GUERRILLA WARFARE

The instant picture of guerrilla warfare as popularly conceived in the West is that of a Che Guevara leading a gang of daring, revolutionary soldiers in civilian fatigues, roaming mountainous terrain armed with sub-machine guns. This however, is a highly romanticized vision. Another notion is to compare guerrilla fighters with Robin Hood and his merry men. Such an analogy merely conveys a general moral undertone. A third misconception is that guerrillas thrive on the use of threats and terror against peasants. This is generally incorrect, because a basic principle of guerrilla warfare is reliance on the support of the people. On the other hand, Mao Tse-tung's treatises on this subject provide a theoretical conception, but are of little help in gaining real knowledge of this very complicated military and political operation.

Guerrilla warfare has been the subject of many a lengthy story,[1] usually written by participants whose memories of this prolonged, cruel fight have been haunting them long after the war against Japan and the Civil War were concluded. These stories are popular because they are packed with adventure and action. There must be considerable psychological release in reading horrifying tales of killing, burning, rape and other forms of suffering, that has been so much a part of life during the wars. But most guerrilla war stories are poor in characterization and do not adequately show the implications and the scale of the struggle from the remote north-east to Central China, behind the enemy lines.

The authors of guerrilla war stories share a common background as unskilled but serious writers. They were barely literate, or had only had limited formal schooling, when they first joined the Communist

[1] For instance, Feng Teh-ying, *K'u Ts'ai (Bitter Herb)* (Peking: PLA Literature Press, 1958); Feng Chih, *Ti hou wu-kung-tui (Behind the Enemy Line)* (Peking: PLA Literature Press, 1958); Liu Liu, *Lieh-huo Chin-kang (Heroes in Blazing Fire)* (Peking: Chinese Youth Publishing House, 1959); and Liu Chiang, *T'ai-hang feng-yün (Upheavals in the T'aihang Mountains)* (Peking: Writers' Publishing House, 1962).

114

revolution.[2] In the long years of struggle they were frequently given opportunities to study at training schools in base areas, and gradually acquired some degree of writing ability. Their rich experiences are reflected in the episodes they relate, but they fail to piece them together in a meaningful, coherent way. They lack the artistic skill to tell a good story, and particularly the ability to understand the struggle as an early phase of a far-reaching socio-political-cultural revolution. Their stories can be regarded as crude but truthful records of events in the war years. *The Railway Guerrillas*[3] is a novel of this kind, containing a wealth of information about guerrilla tactics.

Operational Tactics of a Small Mobile Unit

During the Anti-Japanese War a small guerrilla detachment was active along the Lincheng-Tsaochuang section of the Tientsin-Pukow Line, and *The Railway Guerrillas* is a story based on their exploits. The author, then a cadre in the same area, had frequent contacts with this unit. At the end of the war, he visited the railway guerrillas twice and lived with them for a short period in order to gather material for the novel.[4]

The primary task of the railway guerrillas is to disrupt Japanese control in the cities, to intercept enemy ammunition trains, and to provide the base area with intelligence and supplies. In one operation, a counter-move to the Japanese mopping-up campaign, the unit's political commissar outlines a plan which summarizes the basic tactics of small detachments. First, they must outwit the enemy, for the unit has only some twenty men and a dozen pistols. Secondly, they must strike a deadly blow, that is, attack a vital enemy target. Thirdly, the attack must produce wide repercussions, so that the Japanese have to withdraw troops and thus reduce the pressure on the base area. Finally, they must take all precautions to ensure success. The last point is considered crucial for the confidence of a newly organized guerrilla force.

In order to achieve these goals they quickly reach the decision to hold up a passenger train, a job considered within the scope of this

---

[2] For instance, the author of *Tracks in the Snowy Forest* has had only primary school education. See Ma Ching-po, 'Tu *Lin hai hsüeh yüan* hou so hsiang-ch'i-ti' (Thoughts After Reading *Tracks in the Snowy Forest*), *Jen-min wen-hsüeh*, No. 1, 1958, p. 110.
[3] Chih Hsia, *T'ieh-tao yu-chi-tui* (Peking: Writers' Publishing House, rev. ed., 1965), *The Railway Guerrillas* (Peking: Foreign Languages Press, 1966). By the spring of 1965, a total of 905,000 copies had been printed.
[4] Chih Hsia, 'Hou chi' (Postscript), *The Railway Guerrillas*, pp. 568–70.

small unit. The whole operation is meticulously planned. Two guerrillas, who have some experience as engine-driver and fireman, will make their way along the moving train and take over control of the engine. Others, in pairs, will board the train at an earlier stop, disguised as merchants or respectable travellers. Their job is to engage the Japanese guards in conversation and drinking, and disarm them on a given signal. Still others will quickly demolish sections of the track once the train comes to a halt. The most difficult part of the venture is the signal for simultaneous action. The use of a whistle is considered and quickly abandoned, for fear that it may not be heard in the rear coaches with the windows tightly closed. The final decision is that the guerrilla engine operator should press the lever, producing a sharp, squeaking sound which will be the signal for action.

The execution of this elaborate plan proves to be a routine job. The hold-up of the passenger train delays the entire train schedule by hours and produces a shock wave throughout the Tientsin-Pukow Line. Posters plastered on the sides of the cars and handbills distributed among the passengers are effective psychological weapons. The best propagandists turn out to be the passengers, whose exaggerated accounts of the train raid create instant myths about the guerrilla fighters. When the operation is over, the guerrillas get away safely, with loads of military equipment, telephone apparatus, medical supplies, and Japanese-made canned food.

The railway guerrillas seem to have no fixed pattern of operation. Their moves depend on the opportunities available, and little control is exercised by the headquarters in the mountains. Even when they are ordered to go to the base area for a brief period of regrouping and training, the program and schedule are worked out by their own political commissar, and they still wear their civilian clothes and retain their old style and habits. The governing principle appears to be decentralization; every member is encouraged to use his own ideas. Individual ingenuity becomes the rule.

Flexibility is the key to success. When the railway guerrillas are transferred to the Lincheng area, all eighteen men wear the same clothes — dark blue cotton suits with a row of frog-fastenings down the front and rubber-soled black canvas shoes. Everyone carries a pistol, with a piece of red silk fluttering in the breeze. They create a deep impression on the villagers, who are accustomed to seeing guerrillas in threadbare peasant clothes with home-made rifles. But when they return after training in the base area, they find the villages under the tight control of the puppet authorities. Realizing the difficulty of regaining a foothold in the area, they immediately discard their distinct identity, shave off their hair, and put on peasant rags and tatters to mingle unobtrusively with the people. Local conditions determine whether they maintain their identity as an élite unit or abandon it.

The rule of flexibility also applies to the treatment of puppet officials. In one case a landlord who serves as the head of a township is killed, as an example to those who voluntarily collaborate with the Japanese. In another case a puppet head who refuses to co-operate, but is otherwise a 'good fellow', is treated differently. The guerrillas derail trains and fell telephone poles in his area and leave the bodies of Japanese plainclothes men near the town office. The Japanese suspect the township head of collusion with the guerrillas and have him tortured. Consequently, the man is obliged to seek out the guerrilla leader, and promises close co-operation if there are no more incidents in his area. The exploitation of the conflict between the Japanese and the puppet authorities proves more effective in this case.

The guerrillas' life is full of risk; survival often depends on individual ingenuity and occasionally on animal instinct. Hard-pressed by repeated mopping-up campaigns, they have to snatch a few hours' sleep in the open fields. On waking in the early morning, a guerilla will leap to his feet in an instant, so that an enemy would take him for a peasant who had risen early to work the field. Otherwise it would be obvious that he has camped in the field overnight. If hotly pursued, he will jump into a river or a lake. Using a straw to breathe through, he can stay under water for hours. These are only two of the countless tricks used to confuse or trap the enemy.

The activities of the railway guerrillas are only one small aspect of this type of warfare. The over-all task in guerrilla warfare is the establishment, expansion and consolidation of base areas behind the enemy line. It is finally given comprehensive treatment in an excellent novel, *The Thundering Yangtse*.[5] The author started the work in 1954 and did not complete it until eleven years later, in 1965. The novel amply deserves the attention of literary critics and commentators, but because of the disruption of the Cultural Revolution, the only information we have been able to trace is a one-line announcement of its publication.[6] *The Thundering Yangtse* shows us that guerrilla warfare is really a process of realigning social forces, of reshaping the ideas and beliefs of country people, and above all of transforming the pattern of life in China's vast countryside.

The Collapse of Political Control and Revival of the Ancestral Order

The story takes place on the fertile soil of the Lo River basin, situated between the Huai and the Yangtse, from the winter of 1939 to the

[5] Ai Hsüan, *Ta chiang feng lei (The Thundering Yangtse)* (Peking: People's Literature Publishing House, 1965).
[6] *Chinese Literature*, No. 4, 1966, p. 120. The English title of the novel in this announcement is *Storm over the Yangtse*.

spring of 1941. At the beginning of the story this area is virtually a
political vacuum, but towards its end, guerrilla bases are firmly
established in a vast region north of the Yangtse River, under the
command of a reorganized New Fourth Army with Ch'en Yi as acting
commander, Chang Yun-yi as deputy commander, Liu Shao-ch'i as
political commissar, Lai Ch'uan-chu as chief-of-staff, and Teng Tzu-hui
as director of the political department. This extraordinary achievement
is given a graphic, convincing account in this powerful novel.

The strategy and tactics of leadership, the efficacy and discipline of
the organization, the dedication and courage of the fighters are all
important factors in guerrilla warfare, but what matters most is the
people's receptivity towards the idea of revolution. In general, people
loathe changing the *status quo*, of which their familiar way of life is a
part; they support the power structure which maintains stability and
order. Tyrannical and oppressive though the ruling authorities may be,
they are preferable to the destruction and anarchy which are sure to
arise in a revolutionary situation. Only when disorder and chaos are
already widespread is a change, any change, desirable. The chaotic
situation in the Lo valley, as *The Thundering Yangtse* shows, incubates
the growth of the guerrilla operation.

The chaos is caused by the fragmentation of the ruling structure.
The area is plagued with numerous large and small military units —
Japanese infantry, puppet troops, Kuomintang special forces, landlords'
militias, and armed secret societies. The author adroitly reflects the
reign of disorder by describing taxes, excises and fees. The countless
levies include household tax, sandal fees for *pao* and *chia*[7] heads,
entertainment fees, birthday celebration fees, dog tax, ox tax, smoking
tax, smoking prohibition tax, even a grain tax, which has been collected
in advance for the following five years. The widespread confusion is
also shown in the circulation of a variety of currencies. Apart from the
banknotes issued by the Central Bank, the Bank of China, the Bank of
Communications, and the Agricultural Bank, there are reserve notes,
without reserve funds, issued by the puppet government of Wang
Chin-wei, and the military currency of the Japanese army. In addition
to this green, blue and red paper money, promissory notes are
distributed by local trade associations, local landlords, warlords, and
commanders of various armed units. These are crude lithographs, wood
engravings, or simply mimeographs. The areas where these currencies
circulate often correspond to the extent of the military or political
control of the distributors. In localities where no effective control

---

[7] A *pao* was an administrative unit during the Ch'ing and Kuomintang periods,
usually consisting of ten *chias*; a *chia* was the smallest administrative unit at that
time, and consisted of ten households.

exists, peasants resort to a more reliable though primitive means of barter, computed on the basis of catties of grain.

The region is within the jurisdiction of the commanders of the Seventh Special Mobile Column and the 102nd Brigade, under the high command of the Fifth War Zone of the Kuomintang government. The cities are controlled by the Special Mobile Corps of the Kiangsu-Chekiang-Anhwei Pacification Army of the Wang Ching-wei puppet regime. Both sides claim *de jure* government, while neither has *de facto* control. Local landlords keep private armies to protect their mansions and estates, and maintain a semblance of legitimacy by purchasing commissions and titles from the Kuomintang military command. The puppet regime, also interested in the guns and wealth of the landlords, sends its representatives to secure their co-operation. Although the landlords share a common interest in safeguarding their estates, feuds often exist between them. On the other hand, the armies of the Kuomintang and the Wang Ching-wei regime fight each other, but they have friends in each other's camps. Many of them were fellow cadets in the Paoting or Whampao military academies. They not only make secret contacts but actually co-operate on matters of mutual interest. The line dividing friend from foe is thin and ambiguous, but their common goal is to squeeze as much as they can from the helpless masses.

The people on both sides of the Lo River are struggling for survival. The fertile soil of the basin is productive, but they still find it hard to scrape a bare subsistence. Those who want to be good 'old hundred surnames', hand over every penny earned by sweat and toil in taxes, and accept hardship as a way of life. They secretly hope, as did their ancestors, that peace will be restored by a true 'Dragon Son of Heaven'. Their expectation appears not to be vain, for soon news reaches them that a true 'Dragon Son of Heaven' has been enthroned at Kung Bridge Town. Rumor has it that a certain Liu Cheng-en, practitioner of Chinese medicine and geomancy, has returned after a five-year disappearance. Liu has brought with him a twelve-year-old, whom he claims to be a descendant of Emperor Chu Hung-wu of the Ming dynasty. With an impressive beard spreading over his chest, he assumes the role of imperial adviser and claims to have received through divine revelation the Mandate of Heaven for establishing a Society of Heavenly Immortals and forming a Yellow-Robed Savior's Army. The mission of the Yellow-Robed Savior's Army is said to be to capture demons and bogies and to assist the emperor to regain his throne. Messengers are dispatched to villages to recruit followers. Anyone who wishes to join in the Society of Heavenly Immortals must first show his sincerity, secondly must have affinity, and thirdly must pay an initiation fee, determined on the basis of each person's ability to contribute. Since his enthronement, the emperor is in really good business.

While credulous peasants seek salvation in the divine power of the emperor, others revive secret societies for a variety of reasons – personal ambition, self-survival, local defense. The headmen of the Yellow Spear Society, the Small Sword Society and the Flower Basket Society work for Chen Hai-lung, the Sea Dragon King. On the west bank of the Lo a sect of the Red Spear Society under the Skinny Third, headman of the altar of incense, has thirty or forty followers. The Skinny Third strictly maintains a ritualistic service for his esoteric society. The altar of incense is set in an ancestral hall; in front of it a green pennon, lined with a black saw-shaped hem, is hoisted high. At the top left-hand corner of the pennon is printed a *t'ai-chi*[8] and in the center a bizarre animal, part wolf, part hunting dog and part leopard, is embroidered. The animal is known as the Divine Dog kept by the Second Son of God. On the four sides of the society's ensign are embroidered four characters, 'Buddha Protect Bareheaded People'.

The Skinny Third meticulously observes a pre-war sacrificial rite no outsiders, especially women, are allowed to interrupt. In front of the image of the Second Son of God and his Divine Dog, he performs the function of a priest. Murmuring inaudible incantations, he dips a brush into a bowl of cinnabar liquid and then swiftly draws symbols of spells on a piece of yellow paper. When he finishes the drawing, an attendant takes over the yellow sheet, burns it in the candle light, and lets ashes drop into a bowl. This done, the attendant holds a huge earthen jar in both hands, moves it in a circle above the censer, and pulls the cinnabar liquid into the bowl with the ashes.

The Skinny Third will then call a name, and a man immediately comes up to the altar. The man kowtows to the image of the Second Son of God and then to the Skinny Third, he gulps down the whole bowlful of cinnabar and paper ash. The Skinny Third takes out a yellow cloth bag, with a *t'ai-chi* diagram on it, which contains a talisman for resisting knife and bullet and a picture of the Second Son of God and his Divine Dog. With his bony fingers, he hangs this amulet around the neck of the member. This whole ritual service is repeated until everyone has swallowed down a bowl of cinnabar-ash mixture and has an amulet on his chest. Finally, the Skinny Third recites aloud and the members repeat in unison their society vow:

'Let lightning strike and fire burn those who commit sacrilege against god, our father; let lightning strike and fire burn those who

[8] Usually translated 'the Supreme Ultimate'. In this Supreme Ultimate exists the First Cause of the Universe, the co-ordinating point from which the two principles *yin* and *yang*, or the negative and positive elements, proceed. The alternation of *yin* and *yang* produces the Five Agents – Earth, Fire, Wood, Metal and Water. The symbol for the Supreme Ultimate is a circle with light and dark inter-locking segments.

are unfilial to their parents; let lightning strike and fire burn those who are greedy after wealth; let lightning strike and fire burn those who seduce women; let lightning strike and fire burn those who betray the secret of our society.'[9]

The belief of this Red Spear sect is a queer mixture of pantheism, superstition and social norms, not uncommon among secret organizations and societies. It is belief of this kind which turns bare-footed peasants armed with swords and spears into fearless warriors against powerful Japanese and puppet soldiers equipped with rifles and automatic weapons. There are some positive elements in their belief system, such as loyalty, integrity and austerity, which prompt them to join forces with the Communist guerrillas. Nevertheless, their narrow-minded localism, superstitious practices and blind faith in the traditional order are so deeply rooted that they are unable to appreciate the reforms initiated by the Communist revolutionaries. It appears inevitable that eventually they will part company with the guerrillas and rejoin the old forces epitomized in the landlord Li Chin-chai, who has by then become the Kuomintang-appointed magistrate of this county.

The east side of the River Lo is the territory of another sect of the Red Spear Society. Chao Chang-ch'ing, a poor peasant, organized this sect to defend his village when the war broke out. The altar of incense is also in an ancestral hall, but his sect neither worships gods nor practices superstition. The guardian spirit is the Hero Prince, Chen Yü-ch'eng, of the Taip'ing Heavenly kingdom. Outside the hall, more than thirty feet high, is a rectangular yellow banner hemmed all round with red, with two narrow purple streamers on top. The ensign embroidered at the center of the banner is a roaring lion, surrounded by four characters, 'Defend Families Defeat Invaders' in regular writing, every stroke uncompromisingly applied.

Chao is a figure of historical significance, symbolizing the resilient force of revolt in Chinese peasantry. Without going far back into the voluminous chronicles of China, in the last hundred years we find the crucial role men of his type played in the Taip'ing Uprising, the Nieh Insurrection, the Boxer Rebellion, and Sun Yat-sen's revolution. An element of resistance in the blood of peasants like Chao Chang-ch'ing stirred them to take up arms when the country was plagued by flood, drought or war. He and people like him have been fighting guerrilla war for centuries. But until the Communists come to provide them with leadership and ideology, their impact on the mainstream of Chinese history was hardly felt.

Such are the strong undercurrents beneath the tranquillity sustained by apparently well-defined spheres of influence in the Lo River valley.

[9] *The Thundering Yangtse*, p. 49.

Although there are unwritten laws governing the conduct of rival governments, landlords, and secret societies, each schemes to swallow down the other at the first available opportunity. Even the two sects of the Red Spear Society, who join in defending their region against the Japanese and puppet troops, are soon at each other's throats. It is not simply a matter of rivalry but also the result of a tribal feud, compounded by the conflicting personalities of the two leaders.

Into this chaotic yet well-armed region, dominated by complex social and political forces, marches a Communist unit of regimental strength. They are met head on by a file of women, two abreast, with hair tied in high knots, dressed uniformly in black trousers, blue tunics and yellow aprons with purple edging. Each woman carries a bamboo basket on her arm. A few paces behind, two men, both idiots, half-naked despite the freezing weather, wield a broadsword in each hand. Following them is an undisciplined crowd in sundry peasant clothes; everyone wears a broad yellow belt at the waist and holds a yellow-tasseled lance.

Under unexpected attack, the Communist regiment first organizes a propaganda team to try a political dialogue. When this fails, warning shots are fired. Instead of dispersing, the women unfold their white paper fans, vigorously fan the flower baskets, and recite in a sing-song voice, 'The Flower Basket Society, quickly fan away the bogies' bullets!' The soldiers begin to shoot in earnest; the fans and lances are no match. At dawn the next morning, the Yellow Spear Society, the Flower Basket Society and the Small Sword Society are reinforced by some two dozen rifles from the landlord Chen Hai-lung's mansion. Since the attack is anticipated, the secret societies suffer a total defeat. The Red Army is ready to plant a foothold on both banks of the River Lo.

The Growth of a Guerrilla Cell

During its brief stay, the Red Army distributes among poor peasants the grain, clothes and furniture confiscated from the landlord Chen Hai-lung, who has evacuated his mansion to join the puppet regime. But the regiment has to move on. The instructions are that the regiment is to penetrate enemy lines as far as the coast of the Yellow Sea, and that the four cadres left behind to organize a guerilla force must mobilize local people to establish a base; they can expect contact neither with the Party nor the regiment for some time. Thus the theme of *The Thundering Yangtse* is to demonstrate how a guerrilla cell adapts itself in a hostile environment, expands from a single nucleus into a vital organism, and eventually grows into a politico-military leviathan.

The cell is an army of six, including a former company commander, a director of a mass movement unit, one female and one male member of the same unit, and two communications orderlies, Hsia T'ieh-yu, leader of the team, is a veteran soldier. Tough, alert and fearless, he has three years' guerrilla experience. Though a shrewd commander under the most trying circumstances, he is quite capable of giving way to his temper. He is uncompromising in dealing with enemies, but is also a willing organization man who will readily see his own weaknesses and accept others' criticism.

Lin Yeh, former leader of a mass movement unit, now assumes the responsibility of political commissar. He has left Futan University at the end of his third year to take part in the war against Japan. Before he joined the regiment he had been in Yenan. A slender man with anaemia from under-nourishment, he has the thoughtful eyes and pale face of an intellectual. At twenty-three, he has already acquired wide experience of dealing with all kinds of people and has developed a capacity for systematic analysis.

The two most interesting characters, portrayed with force and subtlety, are the girl cadre Ho Wei and the non-Communist Hsing Kuang. Once a textile worker in Shanghai, Ho Wei is straightforward and carefree, with a great ability for making herself at home under any circumstances. She will not hesitate to pull off her sandals, roll up her trousers and step into the paddy fields to help haul the plow or harvest crops. This kind of work Hsing Kuang will not do; Lin Yeh might, but only as a conscious, deliberate act, while to Hsia T'ieh-yu it simply would not occur. In Ho Wei we find a dedicated woman Communist who has absolutely no concern for herself, yet always remains herself, and whose enthusiasm seems part of her natural bent.

Hsing Kuang is an uncommitted intellectual, uncommitted in the sense that he has joined the Communist revolution as an independent individual. Even in the Red Army he has never relinquished his intellectual's eccentricity. For instance, he has made a promise to himself that he will collect a souvenir each time he crosses an enemy blockade. The first time his troops passed a highway closely guarded by enemy pillboxes, he decided to pick up a pebble. As he bent down to do so, he saw a small wild flower and plucked it instead. The flower is still kept in his notebook. During the crossing of the Yangtse he was happy to pocket a glossy beautifully-patterned shell. In his souvenir collection, every item had to be a part of his personal history.

He and Lin Yeh have had many long debates on the question of his party membership. Long ago in Shanghai Hsing Kuang risked his life to work for the Communist Party and later voluntarily joined the Red Army, but he has refused to apply for party membership. He wants to be a writer some day and argues that many great writers are

Communists without formally joining the Party. He insists that everyone must have his own beliefs and convictions and that he has no wish to imitate other people. Lin Yeh agrees that everybody is entitled to his own belief, but a Communist revolutionary cannot fight outside the party organization. In Lin Yeh's view what really worries Hsing Kuang is the rigid organization and strict discipline of the Party which he cannot accept. No revolutionary can depend solely on his own enthusiasm and personal conviction to overthrow reactionary rule. To arguments like this, Hsing Kuang feels like saying that he is not an anarchist, but always refrains. There is something far more complicated, something he is unable to explain clearly. This ambivalent feeling is shared by many Chinese intellectuals when they are confronted with the dilemma of personal freedom *vis-à-vis* organization life.

Later when Hsing Kuang hears the news of Ho Wei's death he instantly files an application for party membership. It is done at a tense moment of emotional upheaval, when all other considerations, rational or sentimental, give way to a passionate urge for revenge. Although Hsing Kuang and Ho Wei are mere friends, they have shared moments of danger and despair. The revenge is for more than the loss of a friend; it is national in scope, totally overwhelming personal considerations and reservations. For years he had been able to hold out even against the more cogent analysis of Lin Yeh, but the news of Ho Wei's death simply devastates all his arguments and instincts against joining the Party. This is the moment of truth for many a Chinese intellectual, who crosses the threshold by signing the application. The commitment is made in full consciousness of its consequences.

These four cadres are entrusted with the task of forming a guerrilla force in a region where outsiders are treated with undisguised suspicion and open hostility. The peasants have been told that the Communists advocate communal sharing of property and, worse still, communal sharing of wives. Even Cheng Wei-fa, a hunter and bachelor of fifty, who should have no worries about all this talk, is concerned lest under Communist control he may have to give up his only pleasure — his two cups of spirits. But he is destined to witness the unbelievable. He has seen soldiers of all brands — Manchu bannermen, landlords' militiamen, infantrymen of northern and southern warlords, Japanese marines, puppet troops, the Kuomintang army, special mobile units — yet none behaves like the Communist soldiers. The peasants turned guerrillas call older men 'uncle' and older women 'aunt' in a tone more deferential than that of their own sons and nephews. A broken bowl will be paid for, with endless apologies, though the cost is negligible. The hunter had always thought that if soldiers burned down a house, there was nothing to fuss about. But these guerrillas are not soldiers in the usual sense.

The organization work begins as soon as the regiment moves out of the area. The cadres adopt different approaches toward secret societies, armed units, merchants and landlords, traitors and enemies. The negotiation with Chao Chang-ch'ing, headman of the Red Spear sect, is carried out by Ho Wei. Aware of what has happened to some other secret societies, Chao at first treats Ho Wei's plea for co-operation with unconcealed distrust and aloof dignity. Even her argument that their policy of 'resisting Japan and establishing a people's democracy' is similar to the Red Spear Society's call for 'defending families against invaders' falls on deaf ears. Chao cynically calls himself 'a muddy leg' who is in no position to unite with the Communist guerrillas in fighting the Japanese. Ho Wei patiently assures him that she was once a textile worker and their regimental commander used to work in a brick kiln, and that the Red Army consists of poor people fighting for the welfare of the poor. Chao has to concede that he admires their exploit of breaking up Chen Hai-lung's mansion and having the landlord's grain distributed among impoverished peasants. What finally moves Chao Chang-ch'ing to join the Communists is Ho Wei herself. The girl soldier, not much older than his own daughter, delights him. She is 'like the silver fish in the Lo River, so transparent that its intestines are there on display for everyone to see'. Her man-like heroic mien is also enormously to his liking. With Chao's conversion, the Red Spear sect and his second in command, Yang Ta-hsing, go over to the Communist side.

Lin Yeh's negotiation with the Skinny Third proves to be much easier. The headman of the superstitious sect wants Commander Hsia to be his sworn brother, and to promise there will be no interference with his society's internal affairs. When these conditions are accepted the Skinny Third joins the guerrillas without actually being converted. The Communist policy of uniting with all forces to fight the Japanese turns out to be costly in this case. The subsequent defection of the Skinny Third almost costs Ho Wei her life.

In order to broaden the basis of support from all strata of society, a meeting of local leaders is called. Invited to attend the meeting are landlords, merchants, chairmen of trade associations, local officials, and professionals. At the meeting the cadres declare the abolition of all taxes, excises and fees and give landlords and merchants assessed figures as contributions to support the guerrillas. The announcement shocks the wealthy who have anticipated a tax allocation, but have hoped to pass the burden on to peasants. The elimination of sundry levies proves to be the most effective measure to win broad support for the guerrillas among the masses.

The policy of abolishing taxes produces repercussions which are not only limited to those who have to pay larger shares. It has also stopped other military units from imposing special taxes, thus depriving them of their main source of revenue. Liu Fu-jen, commander of a few dozen rifles, comes with two bodyguards to negotiate with Hsia T'ieh-yu and Lin Yeh. Using underworld jargon, Liu argues not without eloquence that a good fellow never stands in another's path of fortune. He suggests a familiar method of dividing taxation fairly by separating odd and even number days for each side to collect taxes. The proposition is rejected; instead, Liu is urged to intercept the Japanese supply lines as an alternative. Knowing this to be an impossible task, Liu rises to go, considering the negotiation fruitless. At this point, to Liu's great astonishment, Hsia T'ieh-yu pulls out a thick roll of bills and places it in front of him. Liu picks up the money and departs in a confused state of incredulity and gratitude.

Liu Fu-jen reappears a few days after the Communist guerrillas have killed the puppet chairman of a nearby town. This time he is accompanied by two porters, carrying delicious dishes and matured wine in red-lacquered cases. He announces that he is perfectly aware of the austere life style of the guerrillas and their strict military discipline, but they must accept the small token of goodwill, so that the soldiers can have a celebration party. He insists that he will not have the face to walk out of the door if the dishes are declined.

'I have not come only to present the gift,' Liu Fu-jen confided. 'First, I'm here to congratulate Comrade Ho and Commander Yang (Ta-hsing), and second, I have a few heartfelt words to say. There's an old saying, "If you don't dare enter the tiger's lair, you won't be able to catch cubs." Comrade Ho and Commander Yang have got real guts. They not only entered the lair but caught a fierce tiger.' Liu Fu-jen gave a burst of hearty laughter, which Hsia T'ieh-yu found catching. When the laughter stopped, Liu continued: 'Commander Hsia, I whole-heartedly agree with the anti-Japanese arguments you and Commissar Lin put to me. What Commissar Lin said that day was as precious as gold and jade. I was then so damn stupid that I did not appreciate it. Thinking over what you said to me in the middle of the night, I was totally convinced. I, Liu Fu-jen, chose to fight the Japanese and gathered several dozen rifles. But what battles have I fought? No wonder the people rejected me. Today I come to entreat you, if you think I'm not unworthy, to let me join you; I am sincere, and willing to subject myself to your command. If there are any regrets, I'll be a son of a bitch!'

Hsia T'ieh-yu swiftly stood up and held out his hand, palm up, declaring: 'Good, together we fight the Japanese with one heart and mind.'

Liu also stood up and clapped Hsia's hand with his palm.

In his dealings with friendly troops of all descriptions in the last few years, Old Hsia had come to know the minds of officers like Liu Fu-jen. In the circumstances, to entrust him with a battle assignment would be regarded as a show of confidence, a gesture of friendship. Old Hsia promptly said:

'Willing to fight with us, excellent. Tonight, there's a combat mission.'[10]

Liu Fu-jen voluntarily places himself and his men under the command of Hsia because as a soldier he knows that the guerrilla detachment is a genuine fighting army and has a great future. In this case, Liu's transformation is brought about less by the eloquent persuasion of Lin Yeh and Hsia T'ieh-yu than by the example of a daring move by Ho Wei and Yang Ta-hsing in which the puppet chairman of a nearby town was kidnapped, despite tight security measures, and shot at the outskirts of the town.

Different people join the guerrillas for different reasons; in order to expand their fighting strength, the cadres adopt an open-arm policy. Be it a secret society, a Kuomintang unit, or a landlord's militia, all are welcome as long as their primary goal is to fight the arch-enemy, the Japanese, and their puppet troops. Li Fei-hsieh, son of a landlord, with high school education, brings over his small family army in order to exact a blood debt from Chen Hai-lung. Fei-hsieh's father and Chen had fought a court case over a supposedly auspicious grave site. Chen had never forgotten this old score, since he lost the case and had vowed to get his own back. During a Japanese mopping-up campaign, Chen, commander of the puppet troops, gives orders to burn down the landlord Li's mansion as well as several villages.

Li Fei-hsieh's twenty-odd men are immediately organized into the Second Guerrilla Company and he himself is appointed the company's commander. Self-satisfied and accustomed to the life of a young country squire, Li has little respect for the guerrilla leaders. He is very proud that his men are well clad and equipped with good weapons, while the soldiers of the First Company wear threadbare peasant clothes and do not have a single decent rifle. Only when he learns that Lin Yeh has completed a three-year course in college does he feel any respect for the political commissar.

One day after watching the soldiers of the First Company practise hand to hand combat with broadswords, Li decides to show the company's commander Yang Ta-hsing his feat of pistol shooting. Holding a Mauser pistol in each hand, Li exhibits his skill in shooting two guns simultaneously. He empties two magazines of bullets direct into a distant old willow tree and then challenges Yang for a similar demonstration. Knowing Yang lacks Li's shooting expertise, Ho Wei suggests that Yang should display his swordsmanship.

[10] *The Thundering Yangtse*, pp. 246–7.

Aiming at a dozen coins stacked on a stone, Yang wields his broadsword and with a swift movement splits the pile of coins into two. While one half of the coins stands intact, the other drops with a trailing metallic sound to the ground. The only comment this unusual feat, which demands precision of aim, balance in handling the sword and proper application of strength, evokes from Li is that it is indeed a good trick. Enraged, Yang orders his men to plant wooden poles. Fifteen poles of various lengths are planted at random a few paces apart. On top of each pole is attached the painted face of a Japanese soldier complete with helmet. They look like real enemies.

Standing with one leg firmly on the ground like a golden rooster, Yang Ta-hsing begins to wield his broadsword, first slowly and gradually with increasing speed. Very soon it becomes difficult for the spectators to distinguish man from sword. Suddenly, like a fast-whirling wheel, Yang rings circles around the poles. Seconds later, equally suddenly, he is standing still as a rock. Fourteen of the poles are neatly shortened, exactly one inch below each painted enemy face. The last one is split at the center all the way down to the bottom. Though watching attentively without a blink, Li Fei-hsieh cannot tell how this is done. Only at this moment is he completely humbled.

In the battles that follow, Li proves a good fighter. His heroism, however, is the demonstration of personal valor; he has little concern for disciplined and co-ordinated group action. The Communist Party appears to have a genuine interest in this young man when it offers him an opportunity to study at an Anti-Japanese University. But Li Fei-hsieh views guerrilla war as an adventure in the tradition of gallant rebels and chivalrous heroes rather than a protracted struggle with all its hardships. Instead of accepting the opportunity to undergo training as a revolutionary, he wants to get out of a continual fight under strained conditions. So he proposes to run away with a landlord's daughter who has also joined the guerrillas. When the proposal is rejected by the girl he wounds her and turns into a deserter. For people like Li Fei-hsieh, revolution proves to be too much of an ordeal; they will drop out by a process of natural selection.

The policy adopted by the cadres for the expansion of the guerrilla force and the consolidation of the base area is simple yet extraordinarily effective. The main line drawn is between traitors who help the Japanese, and all other elements who fight the invaders. In order to whip an assorted army into a fighting force, they teach the guerrillas about the meaning of the war against the Japanese, the disciplines of a people's army, and the goals of the Communist revolution. But more important than such political instructions is the style of the Communist cadres. They mingle with the masses, do everything possible to help them, and show no interest in personal gain. Their spirit of self-denial,

above all else, earns the respect and wins the support of all the people
of the Lo River basin.

Guerrilla Strategies

The guerrillas operate in a region where there exist both tangible and
intangible enemies. Their policy of abolishing taxes, reducing rents, and
shifting the financial burden antagonizes the rich and influential. For
the peasants, the new life-style the cadres bring with them poses a
threat to their traditional way of life. The following small incident is
perhaps the most revealing. After Yang Ta-hsing has become a guerrilla
company commander, Ho Wei urges Yang's wife, Ah-yüan, to go out
and talk with other women about equality between the sexes. Ah-yüan
tries to excuse herself by saying that she does not look like a comrade.
The mischievous Ho Wei plays a girlish trick by cutting off Ah-yüan's
hair knot with a pair of scissors. The incident creates a minor crisis.
Women keep a wary eye on Ho Wei in case she is holding a pair of
scissors. Even Chao Chang-ch'ing's seventeen-year-old daughter always
guards her long, large plait when she is taking lessons from Ho Wei.

The greatest challenge to the cadres is the broad influence of the
emperor at Kung Bridge Town. They have underestimated the emperor
and his imperial adviser by treating them as a phenomenon of
superstition in a chaotic period. The problem gets much more serious
when leaflets are discovered everywhere, urging people to join the
Yellow-Robed Savior's Army. The printed handbills are skilfully
designed in the forms most likely to appeal to gullible peasants, such as
'Liu Po-wen Tablet Inscription' and 'Admonitions of the Priest of
Mercy'. Posters written in the style of divine revelation appear on the
walls of nearby towns, inciting people to reject the Communist
guerrillas as a bogey force which does not worship Heaven and Earth,
has no respect for parents, and is sacrilegious to gods and spirits. In
some villages members of the Red Spear Society no longer obey the call
of the guerrillas, and are secretly making banners and armbands for the
Yellow-Robed Savior's Army.

The emperor phenomenon, with its slogan of 'eliminating foreigners
to save China', had been a revival of considerable social force. After
some clandestine contacts were made by the Japanese secret service,
this superstitious clique had changed its color and assumed an open
anti-Communist posture. Araki Kazukuma, head of the Japanese secret
service in the region and author of *The Secret Societies and
Organizations in the Lower Yangtse*, had successfully turned this
superstitious body into a powerful instrument in support of the
Japanese pacification policy.

After careful analysis of intelligence data, the cadres work out a plan to trap the emperor and his imperial adviser. They seize the opportunity of a large temple fair at Kung Bridge Town and without any difficulty capture the entire imperial coterie. The emperor turns out to be a little boy of thirteen and the imperial adviser is clearly the man in charge. Using both as hostages, the guerrillas are able to have the Yellow-Robed Savior's Army dissolved. They take no punitive action against the little emperor, who willingly joins the cultural work team in the guerrilla detachment. The fact that the emperor doffs his dragon robe and wears guerrilla uniform will have an ineradicable effect on the minds of the peasants.

Just as difficult as transmuting traditional social forces into a belief in the revolution is the task of dealing with the Kuomintang troops. Under the policy of a united front, the Communists and the Kuomintang are supposed to have joined forces in fighting the Japanese. The Communist guerrillas entertain no illusion about a lasting coalition but are unwilling and unprepared to antagonize this more powerful political rival. On the other side, the Kuomintang commanders ostensibly maintain an alliance with the Communists while secretly keeping contact with their former colleagues in the Wang Ching-wei puppet troops. From time to time they are ordered by the Kuomintang high command to attack the Communist guerrillas in the flank when the Japanese launch a large-scale offensive against the Communist base area. This delicate relationship is best described by the term *mo*, which suggests deliberateness, circling and evasion of direct friction.

The guerrillas, however, will retaliate with force if attacked by the Kuomintang troops. During one such battle, the guerrillas rout a whole Kuomintang company, take more than sixty prisoners, and capture four automatic rifles. The Kuomintang brigade commander is convinced that it must be the job of Communist regulars, so he sends a staff officer to see Commander Kao for a truce. Under these circumstances, Hsia T'ieh-yu has to pose as the deputy commander. Among the conditions for a truce laid down by the Kuomintang side is the return of captured men and weapons. Hsia agrees to send a representative to negotiate a settlement. Before the Kuomintang officer departs, Hsia gives him a sword as a souvenir for the brigade commander. The Kuomintang aide, shocked to see 'Lieutenant Haramo Muichi' inscribed on the blade, realizes that the sword is one of those called 'the Soldier's Soul', used by Japanese commanders for committing suicide before capture. Seeing that the Kuomintang officer is extremely delighted with the gift, Hsia gives him, in addition, a cloth flag printed with a red sun and a line 'May Our Military Spirit Prevail'.

Ho Wei is sent to the Kuomintang brigade headquarters to discuss truce terms. She is cordially treated, but the negotiation makes no progress. The Communist side agrees to return men and weapons in exchange for guarantee that they will make no future attack; the Kuomintang side refuses to issue such a written promise. At first Ho Wei is bored by the ceremonious treatment, lavish meals, and polite yet fruitless discussions, but soon she finds a way of spending the otherwise tedious days, in conversation with Kuomintang soldiers, aides and officers. Her carefree style and candid talk have a contagious effect which alarms the Kuomintang commanders. They hastily conclude the negotiation and send Ho Wei back, for fear that her words may poison their soldiers. As for the negotiation itself, they do not want to issue a formal statement, and simply forget about the captured men and weapons.

The episode is concluded with the adroit touch of the Japanese sword incident, which shows the difference between the Communist and the Kuomintang cadres and implicitly suggests the success of the one side and the defeat of the other. The Communist guerrillas considered the sword an impractical weapon and the flag useful only for cleaning rifles. The Kuomintang political department director has a different use for the sword and the flag; they are to be presented to the generalissimo. The battle report says that in a fierce combat the commander of the first battalion of the 304th Regiment has demonstrated his unusual courage by killing the Japanese lieutenant Haramo Muichi and capturing his sword and a military flag, and is recommended for promotion. This battalion commander happens to be the son of the brigade commander.

The real enemy of the Communist guerrillas is the Japanese and their puppet troops. Against them regular guerrilla tactics are employed. Their units never stay long on one spot and constantly shift position, sometimes disperse and sometimes concentrate in one place, as the situation demands. When confronted with large-scale offensives, they will evacuate their positions and take the peasants with them. Nothing of any use will be left behind for the enemy. When the enemy is exhausted or in retreat they will intercept or attack from the rear. Tactics such as making a diversion in the east, while attacking in the west, hit-and-run, and night action are frequently used.

As a rule, attack on the Japanese main force is left to Communist regulars. The guerrillas' primary function is to extend their influence and control to peripheral areas where puppet regimes have been established. They do not want to destroy the puppet governmental machinery to form their own political structure; they would have neither resources nor man-power for this. Furthermore, it would be difficult to ward off a Japanese offensive if the base area were over-stretched. So they warn puppet officials to assist the anti-Japanese movement, under cover of nominal co-operation with the enemy. This is enforced by threats, disruption, and actual execution of the worst traitors. Through this policy, the guerrillas gain control of all peripheral towns without actually occupying them. They force the puppet regimes to reduce or abolish excessive and unreasonable taxes, to the great relief of the inhabitants.

The story reaches a climax in the destruction of the building which houses the puppet county government as well as serving as Chen Hai-lung's mansion. The Sea Dragon King, who has earlier defected to the Japanese side, is well aware of the guerrilla strength and has the building heavily fortified. A wide moat is dug around the walls; under the water are planted long sharp bamboo spikes with a coating of poison. Inside the walls are some two dozen pillboxes of various sizes and shapes. Right in the middle are four large round concrete forts with shooting slits overlooking every direction. Chen's spacious, luxurious mansion is situated in the very center of these layers upon layers of fortifications. The place is known as 'the Sea Dragon King's Forbidden City'.

The guerrillas have been wanting to remove this nerve center of the Japanese outer defense in order to open a passage between the base area and the party regional headquarters. Every possible tactic has been considered and subsequently abandoned as impracticable. Then an opportunity suddenly presents itself. The Sea Dragon King is nearly forty-nine, but he is contemplating an advance fiftieth birthday celebration as an auspicious move. His only worry is the possible disruption of this propitious occasion by the guerrillas. The matter somehow reaches the ears of Araki Kazukuma, a captain in the Japanese secret service. Araki, an old China hand, never lets slip an occasion to show his respect for Chinese customs and habits. He views such a birthday party as a great opportunity for promoting his pacification program. Therefore he encourages Chen not only to hold a birthday celebration but to make it lavish and expensive. He will send a platoon of Japanese soldiers to reinforce the garrison troops and promises to grace the birthday banquet with his presence. The matter is settled; large, gold-engraved invitation cards are sent to social luminaries all over the county.

The day finally arrives. Chen Hai-lung's hall is decorated with a huge character of longevity in red and gold, and the sound of firecrackers has not ceased since daybreak. Chen's executive secretary assumes the temporary assignment of toastmaster general, ushering in a galaxy of prominent guests with Araki Kazukuma as the star attraction. Costly gifts are conspicuously displayed, to the admiration of the guests and the satisfaction of the host. The party unmistakably demonstrates the power and influence of Chen Hai-lung.

Hardly are the guests seated when the executive secretary approaches the county magistrate and whispers in his ear. Word quickly spreads that the joint chairman of five townships has brought an unusual guest, a representative of Wang Chin-yung, the grand boss of the Shanghai underworld. This gentleman, a Mr. Lu, happened to be in the area and had heard about the celebration. A charming person who never misses the opportunity of befriending a powerful man, Mr. Lu has selected a few gifts and requests the honor of attending the birthday party. The name of Wang Chin-yung produces a shock wave across the spacious hall. Chen Hai-lung and Captain Araki exchange a puzzled smile and walk shoulder to shoulder toward the door to extend their personal welcome.

The moment he steps outside the hall, Chen Hai-lung's eyes are riveted to the two black-lacquered trays full of dazzling gifts — a golden bracelet, a silver necklace, an emerald ring, a huge silver wine pot — carried by two attendants, dressed in long gowns and black jackets and wearing small round skull-caps. Behind the attendants is a long procession of coolies, carrying cases of fruit, fresh chickens, preserved hams, red eggs, bottles of matured wine, a birthday cake, and longevity noodles. Then a whole pig and a whole sheep, scrubbed white and decorated around the necks with red and green silk ribbons, are each borne on a pole by two coolies. Following the gift bearers is a band which has just finished playing the tune of 'Celebration of Universal Peace'. This Shanghainese is certainly the most extravagant guest. Chen Hai-lung apologises for not coming out sooner to welcome the honorable guest. To this, Mr. Lu simply nods and extends ceremonious greetings for the occasion with a polite smile. Chen immediately recognizes his manner as that of a man who knows his importance, but does not wish to be insulting. Araki Kazukuma also welcomes the guest in fluent Chinese, with an authentic Tientsin accent.

As the host leads the honored guest into the hall, those already seated begin to stand up. The guest turns to the attendants and gift bearers and utters something like 'What a stylish party!' Before Chen has time to wonder about this strange line, his eyes are dazed by a silvery flash. Next moment he finds himself facing the dark muzzle of a Mauser pistol held by one of the attendants. Shots follow the explosion of hand-grenades. Yang Ta-hsing has played the role of Mr. Lu superbly, and the guerrillas quickly kill Araki Kazukuma and capture Chen Hai-lung.

The guerrillas' ploy is a favorite ruse, described in many classical novels and popular tales. In *Water Margin* the third attack of the Chu Village depends for its success on a group of would-be rebels who, posing as officers to infiltrate the Chu mansion, act in concert with the

assault by the heroes of Liangshan. In *Romance of the Three Kingdoms*
Huang Kai's trick of pretended desertion wins Ts'ao Ts'ao's trust and
sends his entire fleet to the river bottom at the naval battle of the
Yangtse. It seems plausible that Chen, with enormous confidence in his
garrison troops and heavy fortifications, as well as in the wisdom of
Captain Araki and the fighting capacity of the Japanese soldiers, is
totally unprepared for this daring stratagem of the guerrillas. Of course,
he has no way of knowing that the joint chairman of five townships
whom he had himself appointed, has been forced into co-operation
with the guerrillas. It is always easy to defend oneself against an attack
from without but impossible to ward off an outbreak of fighting from
within.

Counter-Guerrilla Warfare

Incredible as it may seem, there is a fine anti-guerrilla warfare novel,
that is, anti-Kuomintang guerrilla warfare. It is, of course, seen from the
Communist point of view. In the winter of 1946, with the People's
Liberation Army gaining control of northern Manchuria, Communist
work teams started the early phase of land reform. Under the pressure
of the class struggle, landlords, former officials of the puppet
Manchukuo, and professional brigands joined hands with the battered
Kuomintang forces and employed guerrilla tactics to make hit-and-run
raids on villages. Against the disruptive attacks of such mobile units,
Communist regulars found themselves helpless. Consequently, a small
detachment of thirty-six men was dispatched to search for and destroy
the scattered armed gangs loosely known as the Kuomintang Central
Vanguard Assault Army. *Tracks in the Snowy Forest*[11] is an
autobiographical novel written by the commander of that detachment
about their dramatic and colorful adventure, which lasted for several
months through the winter.

The novel is unconventional in still another sense. The author
himself figures conspicuously in the story, in violation of a well-
accepted rule that a Communist should not proclaim his personal
heroism. He makes no effort to conceal that the story of Shao Chien-po
is based on his personal experience. He stresses, however, that he is not
Shao Chien-po, for such a hero character ought to be portrayed as the

[11] Ch'ü Po, *Lin hai hsüeh yüan* (Peking: People's Literature Publishing House, 2nd
ed., 1959); English translation by Sidney Shapiro (Peking: Foreign Languages
Press, 1962). The novel is very popular and sold over 1,465,000 copies in less than
two years. See Mao Hsing, 'Some Insight into the Development of Literature in
New China in the Last Ten Years', *Wen-hsüeh p'ing-lun*, No. 5, October 25, 1959,
p. 5.

perfect example of a PLA commander.[12] But the self-esteem is too obvious to escape the reader's notice. 'Shao Chien-po,' the author writes, 'his uniform neat and spruce, a smart little automatic in the holster hanging from the brown belt around his waist, was the regimental chief-of-staff, a brilliant handsome young officer of twenty-two.'[13] There is also an unreserved admiration for the girl medical orderly whom he falls in love with and eventually marries:

> Only eighteen, White Dove was very pretty, with cheeks as pink as roses. Deep dimples flickered in the corners of her constantly smiling mouth. Her large beautiful eyes flashed so gaily it seemed they could almost speak. White Dove wore braids which hung beside her ears, and feathery tendrils of hair played about her forehead and temples.
> She was slim and graceful, but very strong. Blessed with a clear, well-modulated voice, she loved to sing and dance. She danced as lightly as a bird; even her walk was nimble and airy. Wherever she went, there was song and laughter. Everyone was enormously fond of her.[14]

The author's narcissism and adoration for his girl, which have been criticized by Chinese commentators,[15] become not entirely distasteful when one thinks of Communist novelists' total self-denial.

As an adventure story, *Tracks in the Snowy Forest* is full of scout tricks, sensational episodes and breathtaking suspense, interwoven with colorful legends and romantic myths. The detachment has to destroy three strongholds far apart and deep in the snow-covered mountains; each attack demands an imaginative stratagem and daring surprise action. The first target is a rugged mountain peak called Breast Mountain, amazingly like its name, where the enemy has built a fortress. The only access is a narrow path in a series of natural stages, each with dozens of rocky steps, flanked on both sides by precipitous cliffs. The Kuomintang guerrillas live in a spacious cave beneath the mountain top with the fairy-tale name of Cave of the Nymph.

The description suggests an unconquerable natural defensive barrier. Even the legends and fairy tales associated with water, stone and cave are not superfluous extravagance. They reinforce the idea of primitive taboo with a sense of mystery. An attack on such a desolate mountain crest is like an attempt to conquer Mother Nature itself. The challenge provokes a bold plan. It is logically assumed that the enemy will rely so

---

[12] Ch'ü Po, 'Kuan-yü *lin hai hsüeh yüan*' (Concerning *Tracks in the Snowy Forest*), *Tracks in the Snowy Forest*, p. 559.
[13] *Ibid.*, p. 1.
[14] *Ibid.*, p. 49–50, Shapiro, p. 53.
[15] Ssu Niao, 'Lun *Lin hai hsüeh|yüan* ti ch'uang-tso fang-fa' (On the Writing Skills of *Tracks in the Snowy Forest*), *Ch'ang-chiang wen-i*, April, 1959, pp. 68–9.

completely on the natural barrier that they do not guard against a surprise attack.

Instead of a frontal attack, the Communists decide to reach the mountain peak and then fight their way down into the Cave of the Nymph through the tunnel to the sky. The detachment climbs up a neighbouring crest called Hawk's Beak, some twenty paces away from the Nipple and overlooking it. Luan Chao-chia, an expert mountain climber and squad leader, slides down a rope to the edge of the cliff and swings over to land on the Nipple. A hemp bridge is built, and the other members hook their arms and legs over the rope and slide over to the other side. When this obstacle is overcome the rest of the operation is easy. The mountain stronghold is taken and the leader, Horse Cudgel Hsu, and his followers are captured in a matter of hours.

The second stronghold is Tiger Mountain, where the terrain is less precipitous, but the fortifications more formidable. The detachment seizes a suspect who turns out to be an adjutant to the Eagle, leader of the brigands at Tiger Mountain. From this man they learn that Tiger Mountain is surrounded by twenty-seven forts connected by several dozen *li* of underground tunnels. The headquarters of the Eagle is at the center of Five Happiness Peaks. Protected by gun batteries with a capacity for cross-fire on the outer ridges, the stronghold of the Fifth Peace Preservation Brigade of the Kuomintang Assault Army appears to be impenetrable.

It is also learned that the man has been sent to collect chickens from peasants for the Hundred Chickens Feast, an annual event held on New Year's Eve, which happens to be the Eagle's birthday. They decide to attack at the middle of the Hundred Chickens Feast. Yang Tzu-yung, a squad leader, disguises himself as Hu Piao, Horse Cudgel Hsu's cavalry adjutant, who is supposed to have escaped from the fall of Breast Mountain. His job is to infiltrate Tiger Mountain and to co-ordinate with the detachment's assault. He is armed with a 'Contacts Map' seized from Horse Cudgel Hsu. The map shows all the cities and hamlets on both sides of the Aristocratic Range with nearly four hundred names, the underground contacts of the Kuomintang Assault Army. The Eagle has been anxious to get hold of the names and locations in order to realize his ambition of controlling the entire Peony River region.

On his way to the bandit den, Yang Tzu-yung kills a tiger, and his shots draw a small gang of armed men. His mastery of bandit jargon enables him to pass the first test when questioned by the men. Led blindfold into Tiger Hall, Yang comes face to face with the Eagle. Presenting the 'Contacts Map' and the dead tiger as gifts, Yang quickly wins the confidence of the chieftain and is appointed deputy regimental commander. On the day of the Hundred Chickens Feast, as master of ceremonies, he manages to help everyone get drunk. When the

Communist detachment finally arrives Tiger Hall is a scene of tumultuous orgy. Victory is achieved without a shot being fired.

The stratagem used for taking the last camp is called 'luring the tiger out of the mountain'. The total strength of the enemy amounts to some three hundred men, ten times that of the Communist detachment. Moreover, they live in a well-entrenched cave built by the Japanese, surrounded on three sides by huge mountains linked in a triangle with summits shaped like steel helmets. Since the Kuomintang commanders have learned the operational methods of the detachment, the old tricks cannot be repeated. The ruse the detachment finally adopts is to invite an attack by the enemy. When the Kuomintang assault force launches a raid on the villages occupied by the detachment the Communist soldiers evacuate the area and then turn back to burn down the enemy camps.

Once the Kuomintang assault force loses its mountain stronghold, it is forced to fight the detachment on the snow-covered grassland. After a number of maneuvers and hit-and-run actions by the Communist soldiers, the Kuomintang force is greatly weakened. Their commanders lead the heavily-battered remnants across the Harbin-Suifenho Railway in an attempt to regroup and lie low in the snow-locked Long White Mountains while waiting for a Kuomintang spring offensive. But they are intercepted and completely destroyed in a final clash at Leelee Temple.

One may conceivably argue that the Communists are masters of guerrilla warfare, and the use of such tactics against them is doomed from the start. Such an argument is certainly correct but can be misleading if one is led to believe that tactical perfection is the primary determinant for success in guerrilla warfare. A fundamental reason for the failure of the Kuomintang policy is that they recruit support from landlords, Manchukuo officials and professional brigands. In another age, against another enemy, this would have been successful. These types, after all, have ruled China for thousands of years. They were appeased, cajoled, bought and absorbed by ambitious dynasty-founders; for over two decades the Kuomintang followed this time-honored policy with apparent success. But by the winter of 1946 they had become social outcasts, and were obliged to seek refuge in the mountains. Unlike the Communist guerrillas, who looked upon the people as their best protection, the Kuomintang assault forces found inaccessible terrain remote from population centers their safe haven. They could no longer treat villagers as kings and princes of feudal times did their serfs. A new age was dawning in the winter of 1946; from then on, the Kuomintang policy clearly became anachronistic.

New Myths and Old Legends

One characteristic common to all guerrilla war stories is that their operations are frequently wrapped in myth. The actual strength of any guerrilla unit is usually far short of the powerful image attributed to it. Stripped of its mythical elements, a naked guerrilla force of a few dozen men armed with light weapons cannot perform miracles. Their unusual intrepidity and remarkable success are greatly assisted by the imagination of the enemy as well as of the people. If peasants do not entertain an exaggerated, often mysterious, image of guerrillas, they will be less willing to give their support at the risk of enemy retaliation. The psychology of the enemy also helps facilitate guerrilla plans and tactics. They look upon guerrillas as ubiquitous and inscrutable and thus inflate the potential damage they can inflict.

Unless a guerrilla force acquires some supernatural traits, its efficacy will be greatly reduced. Superstition is incompatible with Communist theory and practice, but Communists are quite capable of exploiting human psychology to yield the desired effect. At the same time, they will not do anything to dispel certain superstitions if they help spread the image of their invincibility.

The adventures of the railway guerrillas, such as the raid on the Japanese trading company and the hold-up of the passenger train, are promptly converted into short dramatic pieces.[16] Guerrilla actions rendered in the form of a ballad or one-act play are not only entertaining but also perform a political function. Such propaganda will greatly enhance the confidence of the villagers in the ultimate victory of the Communist revolution. The conversion of guerrilla exploits into instant stage shows must be a popular practice, as it is found in other novels.[17]

The most effective way of myth-building, however, is the spontaneous creation and circulation of stories by the peasants themselves. In *The Thundering Yangtse* many rumors about Ho Wei are widely circulated. She is said to be an invisible person, whose comings and goings cannot be traced.[18] After she and Yang Ta-hsing have killed the puppet head of Black Tiger Town and released a number of peasants, a story is disseminated that a girl in a red blouse and skirt was seen unlocking padlocks weighing several catties by a mere flip of the fingers.[19]

The railway guerrillas are surrounded by similar myths. Liu Hung, commander of the unit, is reported to have eyes brighter than electric bulbs; whoever looks into these eyes will involuntary shudder. No

[16] *The Railway Guerrillas*, pp. 231, 236–8, English version, pp. 243, 248–50.
[17] For instance, *Bitter Herb*, pp. 344–8.
[18] *The Thundering Yangtse*, p. 145.
[19] *Ibid.*, p. 268.

matter how fast a train runs, he gives a cough and instantly flies onto it like a swallow. He never misses his target; if he wants to hit a man's left eye, the bullet never strikes the right eye. Li Cheng, the political commissar, is said to be a pale-faced scholar who can solve practically any problems by calling a meeting. He can become invisible and can cast a spell on the Japanese who will then be incapable of discovering the whereabouts of the guerrillas.[20]

Once the railway guerrillas are given the task of supplying the base area with cloth, for the regulars need winter uniforms. They intercept a Japanese cargo train and unlink two freight cars. As villagers, organized into transportation teams, are carrying away bundles of cloth, Japanese and puppet troops arrive at the scene and open fire. Fortunately, the night is dark, with a heavy fog; they suffer no casualties. Not long after the train raid, many stories have spread through the region. Some say that the guerrillas are an auspicious army, blessed with the protection of a heavy fog. Otherwise, hundreds of villagers would have been killed by Japanese machine-guns. Others insist that among the guerrillas is a superman, who forecast the fog several days ahead, like Chu-ko Liang of *Romance of the Three Kingdoms*. Still others claim the knowledge of something more miraculous. Kuan Yü, the renowned general of the Three Kingdoms and now a local guardian god, has lent the guerrillas a hand by fighting the Japanese, for the clay horse in his temple was perspiring after galloping.[21]

There is no doubt that these were widespread myths about guerrillas during the war years. There used to be a tendency among peasants to attribute mythical or supernatural power to heroes they admired. After mouth to mouth transmission, tales tend to acquire a certain aura of miracle. Such deliberate efforts to exaggerate the fighting capacity of guerrillas fit neatly into the Communist scheme of propaganda. Stage plays may be a faithful reproduction of actual events and may produce a powerful impact upon the audience for the purpose of political education, but the effect and durability of such propaganda messages are no match for the myths created by the peasants' own imagination.

Guerrilla warfare is perhaps the most indigenous form of struggle in the Communist revolution; it is peasant life intensified and dramatized. Chinese peasants have for millennia learned to cope with all types of enemies, and Communist guerrillas in a sense are not an innovation but a renovation of rebel forces throughout history. During the numerous, prolonged periods of chaos, peasants and rebels could hardly be distinguished. A peasant driven to despair would turn into a rebel; many Communist guerrillas joined the revolution primarily for survival.

[20] *The Railway Guerrillas*, p. 419.
[21] *Ibid.*, p. 432.

From the political as well as the artistic point of view, a historical link ought to be provided to give the guerrilla war a proper perspective. Such an effort is made by the authors of both *The Thundering Yangtse* and *The Railway Guerrillas*.

The climax of *The Thundering Yangtse*, as noted earlier, is the ransacking of Chen Hai-lung's mansion on the occasion of his fiftieth birthday. After the Japanese captain is killed and the puppet county magistrate taken captive, there remains a platoon of Japanese soldiers, who occupy a large concrete pillbox and refuse to surrender. All schemes and attempts to drive the Japanese soldiers out into the open are fruitless. Finally, the old hunter Chen Wei-fa brings in two cannons which he has unearthed from the backyards of landlords' mansions. On one cannon is engraved a line of characters in regular style, 'The Holy Cannon of the Taip'ing Heavenly Kingdom', and on the other a line of characters in free style, 'Great General's Majesty Radiating in Eight Directions'. These are the big guns which the Taip'ing insurgents used to attack Tseng Kuo-fan's pro-Manchu army. Now, some eighty years later, a new generation of revolutionaries once again use them to destroy the Japanese invaders. Charged with bits of metal and plenty of gunpowder, the cannons are fired. Moments later, the Japanese soldiers hold out the white flag of surrender.

The author of *The Railway Guerrillas* also connects the present struggle with old legends. After their transfer to the Lincheng area, the guerrillas gain a foothold on Weishan Island in the middle of Weishan Lake. The island is small, only ten *li* round, with six or seven tiny villages. The legend that Chang Liang of the Han period lived there as a hermit gives the island significance. Though a founder of the Han dynasty, Chang Liang was first associated with the rebel force led by Liu Pang. There is a clear hint that the guerrillas are engaged on an enterprise comparable to the founding of the glorious Han dynasty.

As though concerned that the parable may be misunderstood, the author gives an additional description of the lake. Lake Weishan is linked with Lake Tushan and Lake Tungp'ing to form an immense expanse of water. Near Lake Tungp'ing is the old site of Liangshan, where the legendary heroes gathered an invincible force to fight the corrupt rule of the Sung emperor, as immortalized in *Water Margin*. It seems as though the railway guerrillas are not fighting alone, for a thousand years ago the heroes of Liangshan had already set a shining example. And their brilliant deeds have been told and retold by countless people down the centuries to this very day.

The juxtaposition of dynasty founders and legendary heroes with contemporary warriors gives the guerrilla war a historical dimension. The guerrillas no longer seem a group of peasants or working men who fight with inferior weapons against powerful enemies. It is not just a war against tangible enemies, be they the Japanese or the Kuomintang troops. The guerrillas, as it were, are writing with their blood the first pages of a new history.

The link between China's past and the Communist revolution is also stressed in *Tracks in the Snowy Forest*, where Chinese cultural tradition is implicitly reflected in the contemporary theme of political struggle. The moral undertone, the triumph of Good over Evil, is adroitly provided in the narration of fairy tales connected with the military operations of the small detachment. As told by Old Mushroom Picker, Breast Mountain is associated with a mythological love story. In time immemorial, a couple at the age of fifty was suddenly granted a daughter by the grace of Heaven. Divine Iris, so named because of her flowery face, grew up to be a girl of unmatched beauty. Riding a small spotted deer with eight-pronged antlers and nimble feet running like the wind, she was the very embodiment of the goddess of hunting. She fell in love with a young man named Hero, who was both a powerful hunter and a gentle flute-player.

As is always the case with fairy tales, the intrusion of a villain disrupted the idyllic life and pure love between the innocent girl and the virtuous hero. When Fat Pig, chieftain of a savage neighboring tribe, carried away Divine Iris, Hero took up his three-hundred-catty bow and mounted his white horse in pursuit. In a fierce battle against Fat Pig and his men, Hero was defeated, after having loosed seven quiverfuls of arrows to no avail. That night, on a mountain peak covered with iris plants, Divine Iris's bitter weeping aroused some immortal power to her rescue. When she awoke from her faint she found herself at the side of Hero and then saw four fairies, dressed in blue, red, apricot yellow, and emerald green, walking towards her. They were 'the Clear Spring Maiden', 'the Spirit of Grain', 'the Nymph of Flowers', and 'the Spirit of Birds'. With a wave of their hands, the fairies turned Breast Mountain into an earthly paradise, with fountains gushing water, grain sprouting from the ground, grass growing on slopes, and birds of all feathers singing everywhere.

The long history of China has bequeathed its mountains and waters with rich fables and legends which have remained unexplored. By connecting the fairy tale with the taking of Breast Mountain, the author seems to suggest a parallel between the legend and the immediate struggle. The Communist revolution is implicitly treated as a struggle between Good and Evil in which the virtuous always prevails over the vile. This recurrent theme in popular literature now finds a place in mass literature. Unlike other authors who simply imitate the form and style of popular tales, Ch'ü Po has suggested an alternative by developing the tradition of popular literature into a new type of mass literature.

A second fairy tale is associated with Leelee Temple where the

Communist detachment finally rounds up the remnants of the Kuomintang assault force. The temple has been built in memory of a victory won by fishermen of the Sungari River over a local bully, a story which unmistakably carries the message of class struggle. It is said that many years ago in a place called Boat Market a couple begot a daughter in their old age. The girl was named Li Lee because she was born on the day her father netted a shipful of *lee* (carp). When Li Lee was sixteen she loved to go out hunting alone. On one of her hunting expeditions, she rescued a small snow-white bird called Leelee from a hawk. She did not return from another hunting trip, but was finally found by a rescue team following the Leelee birds. The girl was sleeping peacefully in the hollow of a tree, without knowing that a fortnight had elapsed. She was thus regarded as the reincarnation of one of the fairy birds. When the rich and powerful supervisor of Boat Market heard the story he wanted to possess her. But he was opposed by all the fishermen in the area.

In the subsequent battles the fishermen armed with spears and arrows were no match for government soldiers whom the supervisor had called to suppress the revolt. Then some divine power appeared to have lent a hand when a violent storm arose from the Sungari River and overturned the soldiers' boats. Riding on the strong wind, the fishermen attempted to sail over the Long White Mountains and to build new homes at Lake Mirror. The towering Four-Square Ledge, however, formed an insurmountable barrier to the despair of the fishermen. Then Li Lee stepped forward and shot at the ledge with her bow and arrows. Her first arrow split the rock, her second arrow shook the mountain, and her third arrow pierced Four-Square Ledge into a tunnel seven *li* long. In an instant the wind dropped and the waves became calm, and the fishermen sailed safely through to the rippleless Mirror Lake. The tunnel known since as 'Carp Gate' is the only route people can take to cross the Long White Mountain in winter.

This lovely myth fits the whole story remarkably well. The fairy tale is an old version of the class struggle in the form of a fable. The battle between Good and Evil, between the weak and the strong, and between the tyrannical overlord and the desperate people is a theme found in most Chinese folk tales. But there is a dilemma to which novelists of mass literature appear to have no solution. In traditional popular literature, the maiden is often the focal point of struggles waged. Her fate at the hands of a scoundrel or under the threat of a tyrant never fails to arouse the reader. This intense personal involvement forces the reader to take sides and to identify himself with the morally superior and physically weak. The theme of mass literature, on the other hand, is not personal but social, in the sense that the class struggle is not waged for personal revenge but for social justice. There are in

Communist novels only conditions to be corrected, inequalities to be leveled, and sufferings to be relieved. When conditions take over from human victims, the reader changes from being an active participant in the unfolding story to a passive observer of developing events.

From Hero Images to Ideological Models

While the disappearance of human victims weakens the sense of identification, the recasting of hero images into ideological models sterilizes mass literature. In *Tracks in the Snowy Forest* the author Ch'ü Po, as commander of the detachment, has drawn the heroes on the basis of his personal observation. The characters remain authentic and real until they are changed to meet ideological criteria.

One charming character is Luan Chao-chia, an experienced mountain climber and a carefree, fun-loving man. As a typical veteran soldier, he never misses an opportunity to crack jokes, often at himself and occasionally to the embarrassment of others. Once he describes how he has tailed a woman suspect for several days. At a railway station people smiled at him, even the women and girls. He thought to himself, 'Why do they all have an interest in me? I'm not that good looking!'[22] Walking into the stationmaster's room, he came face to face with a wierd-looking fellow. The man's face was black with dust, only his eyeballs and teeth showing white; his padded army coat was inside out. Chao-chia could not help laughing at the sloppy-looking soldier, then realized it was his own reflection in a mirror.

He curses freely and never censors his vocabulary. When the detachment commander jokingly criticizes him for taking chances in barging into Tiger Mountain, he says that his sixth sense told him that the detachment had already taken the mountain and a merry party was going on. Then somebody asks him if his sixth sense can tell the fate of the Eagle. Chao-chia's answer is that the Eagle cannot be dead but will not live. He even uses coarse language such as 'capturing the Eagle at the Hundred Chickens Feast is just like . . . ing in one's underwear.' His face reddens when he sees White Dove in the Crowd. When pressed by the others to be explicit, he gives White Dove a glance and says: 'Let's use a civilized expression: catching that thing . . .'[23]

Liu Hsun-tsang is another character portrayed with vigor and force. A strong, husky fellow, Liu moves around like a tank and is actually called Tank. He is brave in fighting, but reckless and quick-tempered in

[22] *Tracks in the Snowy Forest*, p. 331. In the English version it is translated into 'What's so funny about me? I wondered.' p. 318.
[23] *Ibid.*, p. 328. More than a page of the narrative is deleted in the English translation.

dealing with other people. When Tiger Mountain is taken in a surprise attack, the soldiers suffer frostbite after covering three hundred *li* on skis day and night. As White Dove is instructing everyone to massage his legs with snow, Tank Liu grumbles: 'What kind of charlatan are you? What sort of treatment is this! Apply snow to frozen feet? Never heard of this sort of cure! It's like eating salt when you're thirsty or wrapping up with cotton padding when you're warm. You're not making a sacrifice in the temple but abusing the monk!'[24]

Liu also loves fun. As the detachment is recuperating on Tiger Mountain, a sentry patrol spots two suspects and reports to the commander. Tank Liu is ordered to take five men to get the suspects alive. Moments later, a small, thin man is taken in blindfold in the bandit fashion, along with another untied man. Leading his captive to the center of the hall, Tank Liu, imitating a Tientsin magician, prattles: 'Cover up, quick, with the sound of brass gong, change into a monkey king!' He whips off the blindfold; it is Luan Chao-chia.[25]

It is natural for soldiers to get angry when they risk their lives only to be given the cold shoulder. At Suifen Plain the Communist soldiers find the local people simply refuse to talk to them. Only a few elderly women venture out of their courtyards with basins to fetch snow. They melt snow for drinking and will not go farther to the well for water. The soldiers are irritated and blame the villagers for their stupidity and backwardness. Tank Liu calls the village China's number one backward area. 'It must be a bandit lair. Damn it! They should all be shot once we get the evidence.'[26]

The deletion of these vivid and forceful words in the English version deprives the characters much of their personality. Translation of literary work from one language to another is in itself difficult enough. When slang and vigorous and colorful idioms in one language are converted into mechanical expression in another, the effect is like talking to friends in computer fortran. The meaning of the original is either subtly modified or brutally altered, after undergoing a dehumanization process. But the problem in the present case goes beyond the limitations inherent in translation. The fault obviously rests not with the translator but with the person who decides on the deletions. It is the result of a policy which demands changes in characterization in order to meet ideological criteria. The deliberate change from hero image to ideological model is exaggerated in the case of Yang Tzu-yung.

The episode of taking Tiger Mountain by stratagem has been

[24] *Ibid.*, p. 305. An entire page including this paragraph is deleted in the English translation.
[25] *Ibid.*, p. 326. This paragraph is deleted.
[26] *Ibid.*, p. 394. Tank Liu's curses are deleted in the English version.

converted into a Peking opera. The opera has undergone several revisions, and after each revision, some aspect of the rich characterization of Yang Tzu-yung is lost until finally he becomes completely colorless. In order to depict his bravery, the author inserts the incident of killing a tiger, as does Wu Sung or Li Kuei in *Water Margin*, before he enters the bandit lair. The hero thus proves his valor, but finds himself exhausted after the desperate struggle. It takes the author more than two pages to describe the encounter in which Yang empties his automatic's whole magazine of bullets and fires his rifle five times before he kills the tiger. The 1970 printed version of the Peking opera *Taking Tiger Mountain by Strategy* gives this simple parenthetical description, 'Re-enters, throws off his overcoat, pulls out pistol at tiger. The tiger screams and falls dead.'[27] Such a change is not necessitated by the inherent limitation of a different artistic medium, for Peking opera allows endless mime to suggest a character's inner struggle in overcoming fear and horror. It is a deliberate endeavor to recast the character into a nerveless hero.

In the novel Yang Tzu-yung's familiarity with bandit jargon is the means by which he gains entrance to Tiger Hall. In order to convince the Eagle and the other bandit leaders that he is indeed an adjutant to Horse Cudgel Hsu, Yang amuses the bandits by inventing ugly stories between Butterfly Enticer and her open and secret lovers. The opera versions retain some bandit jargon spoken by Yang, but the amorous stories about Butterfly Enticer are conveniently omitted. The way the 'Contacts Map' is presented differs significantly in the two opera versions. In the earlier version the description runs as follows:

Yang (laughs lightly): Please, oh, Brigadier,
  (Holds up the map.)
The map I present to you here.
(Eagle takes the map and examines it avidly while the Invincibles crowd around.)[28]

In the 1970 version not only the Eagle, the original translation of the bandit's nickname Tso-shan Tiao, and his lieutenants the Invincibles are respectively rendered into Vulture and Terribles, but the parenthetical description is also changed:

Yang (laughs lightly. Changing to *hsi pi kuai pan*[29] sings):

[27] 'Taking Tiger Mountain by Strategy', *China Reconstructs*, special issue, February 1970, p. 10. I have seen the movie version of the Peking opera in which the actor's performance is rich and powerful, much better than the script description but still a revision of the original characterization.
[28] *Taking the Bandit's Stronghold* (Colombo: Afro-Asian Writers' Bureau, 1967), p. 34. This is apparently a reprint of an earlier Chinese version of which I have been unable to trace a copy.
[29] *Hsi pi* is the name of a tune and *kuai pan* means 'quick tempo'.

Look, Brigadier Tsui,
This map here I present to you. (Holds up the map.)
(Standing high and looking down at the bandits, Yang holds out
the map as Vulture respectfully flips the dust from his sleeves and
takes it. He examines it avidly while the Terribles crowd
around.)[30]

This description is obviously incredible and absurd. The explanation
given is: 'If negative characters are given the same weight as positive
characters, or if they are shown to be arrogant and in domineering
positions, the result will be a reversal of history, with exploiters and
oppressors ruling the stage.'[31] Thus the earlier stage villains who are
'ferocious and cunning'[32] are turned into shadowy, ghostly figures. At
the same time, the following reasons are given for turning Yang
Tzu-yung into an ideological model:

> The road taken in the portrayal of the hero in the new presentation
> is completely different from that in the original script (issued prior
> to 1963). In the old script, a handful of representatives of the bour-
> geoisie, pursuing their reactionary political aims, did everything they
> could to smear Yang Tzu-jung (yung). Under the pretext of 'truthful
> writing', they actually insisted on stressing Yang Tzu-jung's 'dare-
> devilry and dashing roughness', that is, 'bandit-like airs'. They made
> Yang Tzu-jung hum obscene ditties on his way up the mountain,
> and, in the bandits' lair, flirt with Vulture's foster-daughter, Rose,
> and tell dirty stories.[33]

The striking contrast between the hero images created by the private
observation of a writer and the ideological models built by anonymous
technicians[34] demands an explanation. Ch'ü Po the author was trying not
only to make his heroes lively and forceful but also to reconstruct
an operation by a small detachment in an artistic form. There are many
reasons for the success of the operation, but one of the most important
is the type of men involved. These men put daring plans into action;
only men with imagination, personality and ingenuity can accomplish
the seemingly impossible task. The credibility of a fictitious work

[30] *China Reconstructs*, special issue, February 1970, p. 12.
[31] *Ibid.*, p. 42.
[32] Hsia Shun, 'Kuan-yü *Lin hai hsüeh yüan* ti kai-pien' (Conversion of *Tracks in the Snowy Forest* into Peking Opera), *Chü-pen (Drama)*, No. 7, 1958, pp. 86–7.
[33] *China Reconstructs*, special issue, February 1970, p. 40.
[34] Although the special issue claims that the modern Peking opera on this revolutionary theme has been 'carefully revised, perfected and polished to the last detail with our great leader Chairman Mao's loving care', it is simply impossible to believe that Mao who has a poet's imagination should have had anything to do with it. During the Cultural Revolution it was not unusual that official statements were attributed to Mao in order to give them the appearance of authoritative utterance.

depends on how truthfully the novelist creates the characters, and Ch'ü Po should be given credit for the artistic truth in his characterization. The ideological model, on the other hand, displays a brave posture but demonstrates little heroism.

The reason for this attempt to change hero images into ideological models must be further pursued. It seems to involve more than just an idealization of the hero model. The tendency suggests a process of ossification as a dynamic military operation is converted into an ideological model for exhibition. The problem of how a man should talk never existed in a guerrilla war situation. But once the hero is to be presented as an image for mass emulation, the way he talks, acts and even moves his eyebrows suddenly acquires enormous importance. In an endeavor to make perfect everything associated with the hero, ideology-oriented technicians treat dirty language as something which will tarnish the image of the hero. By eliminating the hero's personal style of expression and behavior, they deprive him of life. It is a great irony indeed that the people who invented and perfected guerrilla warfare should have forgotten how it was fought and won.

6

THE CIVIL WAR

At the outbreak of the Civil War in July 1946, the Red Army was facing overwhelming odds. In terms of numerical strength, the ratio of Kuomintang and Communist troops has been estimated variously from five-to-one to three-to-one, and the Kuomintang enjoyed 'a virtual monopoly of heavy equipment and transport, and air power'.[1] Yet, over a period of three years, the Communist forces took over the entire mainland and drove the Kuomintang regime to the islands off the China coast. It seems incredible that the Kuomintang soldiers seemed like men of straw and their tanks and airplanes like paper toys, wiped out by an army made up almost exclusively of peasants. The Communist victory was won by magnificent military strategy, superior operational tactics, and swift battle maneuvers as well as efficient organization, successful mobilization, and high morale. The formidable fighting capacity of the Red Army is only vaguely understood; the significance of individual campaigns has yet to be analysed by military scientists.

The military victory constitutes the most important, though by no means the only, aspect of the Communist revolution. Many Chinese novelists have attempted to describe the epoch-making military campaigns, but most seem unable to handle a subject which involves tens of thousands of men, highly intricate organization of man-power and material resources, and covers theatres of a thousand square *li*. In the end, they avoid describing the larger campaigns, dwelling on small units, or on some particular phase of a battle; major battles are only indirectly reflected through mass mobilization.[2]

The depiction of large scale military operations demands a cinema-scopic vision, in order to reflect the vast deployment of troops and the pace of battle. At the same time, it requires an artist's brush, rather than a movie-maker's camera, to portray the spirit of war rather than its

[1] John Gittings, *The Role of the Chinese Army* (Oxford University Press, 1967), p. 1 and notes.
[2] There are several well-advertised war stories: the crossing of the Yangtse from western Hopei into Hunan is dealt with in Liu Pai-yu, *Ho-kuang tsai chien (Flames Ahead)* (Peking: People's Literature Publishing House, 1952); campaigns in the central theatre are described in K'o Kang, *Chu-lu chung-yüan (Fight for the Palm in Central China)* (Peking: Writers' Publishing House, 1962); battles in Manchuria between the North-east People's Liberation Army under Lin Piao and Lo Jung-huan and the Kuomintang troops commanded by Tu Yü-ming are told in

outward appearance. This artistic criterion is well expressed by Wu Chiang when he speaks of his writing experience:

> War stories cannot consist only of rifle shooting, bombardment, close combat, bayonet charges, and battle cries. In reality each soldier has thoughts, feelings, and spiritual activity, while he is shooting his rifle, or firing his gun, or charging with a bayonet. His spiritual life is more intense than at normal times. If we only describe actions and neglect mental activity, then we treat man in combat as a moving machine, in clear violation of reality.[3]

The challenge of this difficult task is met with noticeable success only in two novels, Tu Peng-cheng's *Defense of Yenan*[4] and Wu Chiang's *Red Sun*.[5] Although Tu Peng-cheng had little formal education beyond the primary school level, he acquired literary skill by writing short stories and reading classical novels such as Tolstoy's *War and Peace*.[6] As a journalist attached to the Northwest Field Army during the Yenan campaign,[7] he had ample opportunity to observe the conduct of rank and file soldiers and the talent of the commanders. He demonstrates considerable insight in reconstructing the campaign, although his artistic limitations are obvious. The operation of a company level unit, the work of a political commissar, and the execution of the Communist strategy are described in sufficient depth, but the over-all structure of the story is rather loose and diffuse.

Red Sun, describing battles in Kiangsu and Shantung, is better both in characterization and plot structure. Since his participation in the League of Left-Wing Writers as a high school student, Wu Chiang has been engaged in cultural and propaganda work in the Red Army. Although he was the director of the department of propaganda during the campaigns described in the novel,[8] he seems to have given a fairly

---

Hsiao Yü, *Chan ku ts'ui ch'un (War Drum Awakens the Spring)* (Canton: People Publishing House, 1963); and the mobilization of peasants and the role of the militia in the defense of Yenan are portrayed in Liu Ch'ing, *T'ung-ch'iang t'ieh-pi (Wall of Bronze)* (Peking: People's Literature Publishing House, 1952).
[3] Wu Chiang, 'Hsieh-tso *Hung jih* ti i-tien kan-shou' (Thoughts After Writing *Red Sun*), *Wen-i pao*, No. 19, October 1958, p. 42.
[4] Tu Peng-cheng, *Pao-wei Yen-an (Defense of Yenan)* (Peking: People's Literature Publishing House, 1954). Chapter Five 'At the Great Wall', translated by Sidney Shapiro, appears in *Chinese Literature*, No. 1, 1956, pp. 3–63.
[5] Wu Chiang, *Hung jih* (Peking: Chinese Youth Publishing House, rev. ed., 1964); *Red Sun*, trans. by A. C. Barnes (Peking: Foreign Languages Press, 1961). Between its first publication in 1957 and its revised edition in 1964, the novel was reprinted sixteen times and sold over 970,000 copies.
[6] Wei Kang-yen, '*Pao-wei Yen-an* shih tsen-yang hsieh-ch'eng-ti' (How *Defense of Yenan* Was Written), *Chieh-fang-chün wen-i*, December 1954, p. 106.
[7] '*Defense of Yenan*', *Chinese Literature*, No. 2. 1955, p. 160.
[8] 'Chiang-chia wang-p'ai-chün ti chüeh-mu-jen tso-t'an *Hung jih*' (Grave Diggers of Chiang's Crack Army Discuss *Red Sun*), *Wen-i pao*, No. 19, November 1958, p. 13.

accurate account of the battles and a relatively fair appraisal of the
performance of Kuomintang generals.

The Nature and Scope of Conventional Warfare

Defense of Yenan covers the first large-scale war between Communist
and Kuomintang regulars in the Shensi-Kansu-Ninghsia border region
from March to September 1947. During those six months the
Communist Northwest Field Army, some 25,000 men, fought the
Kuomintang forces, ten times their number. The novel treats with
clarity and proportion the Communist retreat from Yenan, the battle of
Chinghuapien, the battle of P'anglungchen, the battle of Lungtung
Plateau, the crossing of the Kansu desert, the march along the Great
Wall, the battle of Shachiat'ien, and the battle of Chiulishan. The entire
theatre of campaign stretches over seven to eight hundred *li* from east
to west and eight to nine hundred *li* from north to south. The battles
are fought on rugged, treacherous terrain under torrents of seasonal rain.
    The strategy for the defence of Yenan is outlined by P'eng Teh-huai:
'If we try to hold Yenan, the burden is on our back. If we retreat from
Yenan, the burden will be shifted on to the back of our enemy.'[9] After
the tactical retreat, the Red Army adopts mobile warfare by massing
overwhelming forces against separate units of Hu Tsung-nan's well-
equipped troops in attempts to demolish them one by one. The first
engagement at Chinghuapien, some twenty miles northeast of Yenan,
results in the annihilation of the Kuomintang 31st Brigade. When the
Kuomintang First Army and 29th Army, a total of sixty thousand
strong, march northward to Suiteh in pursuit of a company which they
have mistaken for the main force, the Communist troops encircle
P'anglungchen and destroy the Kuomintang 167th Brigade. In retaliation, Hu Tsung-nan adopts pincer tactics. He orders his troops in central
Shensi to move northward and the 100th Brigade of Ma Pu-fang and
the 81st Division of Ma Hung-k'uei to press eastward. Avoiding a direct
confrontation, the Communist Northwest Field Army marches day and
night through forests and across the desert toward the east Kansu
plateau. The poorly organized and ill-equipped troops of the two
warlords prove to be no match for the Communist army, and are
completely routed. Then at the major battle of Shachiat'ien, Hu
Tsung-nan's crack 36th Division is put out of action. This battle marks
the turning point for the Northwest Field Army which now launches a
counter-offensive in good earnest. Hu Tsung-nan has to order his First

[9] *Defense of Yenan*, pp. 26–7.

Army and 29th Army to move southward for the reinforcement of his garrison troops in Yenan.

The concluding paragraphs describe the preparations of the Communist troops for an imminent attack on Laoshan, the mountain gateway overlooking Yenan. As the soldiers prepare for action, they are told that the Army Group of Liu Po-ch'eng and Teng Hsiao-p'ing has crossed the Yellow River and penetrated the Tapieh Mountains and the Army Group of Ch'en Keng and Hsieh Fu-chih has liberated a dozen counties and controls over five hundred *li* of railroad between T'ungkuan and Loyang. The news is welcomed with prolonged, tumultuous applause and shouts which shake the whole valley. The last scene suggests a conquering force ready to sweep across the land mass of China:

> A great storm gathered in the north over the Great Wall. Lightning flashes and roaring thunder accompanied this storm that swept irresistibly over the forests and mountains near Yenan, across the Yellow River which has seen battles for several thousands of years, and on into the far distance . . .[10]

Red Sun focuses on critical battles in the east China theatre. The time-span extends from the late autumn of 1946 to May 1947, overlapping that of *Defense of Yenan*. The novel starts with the setback of the Communist army commanded by Shen Chen-hsin and the political commissar Ting Yuan-shan[11] at the battle of Lienshui. The withdrawal from Lienshui is a humiliation that everyone finds hard to swallow, from the army commander to soldiers of the lowest rank. They keep remembering Chang Ling-fu and his 74th Division and nurse their resentment.

After a brief period of recuperation and training, the Shen-Ting Army fights at the battle of Tuszukou in coordination with other troops of the East China Field Army against the Kuomintang main force in Laiwu. In this campaign Li Hsien-chou, the deputy commander of the Hsuchow Pacified Region, commands the 46th Army and 73rd Army with a total strength of well over 50,000 heavily-armed troops. On the Communist side, the entire Third Field Army appears to be mobilized for the siege of Laiwu. When the. campaign is over Lieutenant-General Li Hsien-chou and eighteen generals are captured and two other generals killed in action.

Li Hsien-chou's debacle and the rout of the Kuomintang reorganized 72nd Division in the Taian campaign shatter the confidence of the Nanking government in defending strategic locations in central China. Consequently, Chiang Kai-shek is forced to redeploy his forces. In a

---

[10] *Ibid.*, p. 608.
[11] Both are fictitious names.

tortoise-shaped formation with the 74th Division as the backbone, supported by the three army corps under T'ang En-po, Ou Chen and Wang Ching-chiu, a new all-out offensive is launched against the strongholds of the Communist Third Field Army in the Yi-Meng mountains. This theatre extends over the entire mountain ranges of Yishan and Mengshan in southern Shantung.

On the other side, the Communist Third Field Army arranges its units in a sack formation to trap the Kuomintang 74th Division. General Chang Ling-fu, who has become arrogant and complacent since his victory at Lienshui, moves his 74th Division deep into the mountains and is promptly cut off from the main Kuomintang supply line. The task of a frontal attack on the 74th Division falls to the Shen-Ting Army. Since the Communist soldiers have been longing for a re-engagement with the 74th Division, they carry out the assignment with a will. The deployment of troops on both sides leads to the battle of Mengliangku.

The 74th Division, unlike other Kuomintang units, proves to be a fighting force. But trapped in the Yi-Meng mountains, without reinforcements from the Kwangsi Army, the 7th Division, and the 48th Division, they are running out of munitions, water and food supplies while all escape routes are sealed off. After fighting for several days and nights, Chang Ling-fu withdraws his main force to the towering summit of Mengliangku. The last-ditch fight turns out to be suicidal. On May 16, 1947 Chang Ling-fu met his death and the entire division was annihilated. This campaign is viewed as the turning point from a defensive to an offensive strategy for the Communists in the east China theatre.[12] The novel ends with a description suggesting the totality and single-mindedness of an army, in its endeavor to defeat the enemy:

> As the army commander and political commissar, many of the unit commanders, and the heroic fighters of the Red Flag Platoons and the Red Flag Sections, stood erect on the highest point of the summit of Mengliangku, towering in magnificent isolation in the Yi-Meng Mountains, and looked down at the hills spread at their feet with wide eyes that flashed like the eyes of a hawk, they made a brave picture of greatness and nobility and unity.[13]

Many factors which account for the two successful campaigns also contribute to the ultimate Communist victory in the Civil War. In our attempt to analyse the two novels, we shall pay attention to the combat performance of ordinary soldiers as well as the talent of commanders in

[12] Wang Yü, 'Tu *Hung jih*' (On *Red Sun*), *Yen-ho*, No. 15, June 1957, p. 69; also Ho Kan-chih, *Chung-kuo hsien-tai ko-ming shih chiang-i* (*A Draft History of the Modern Chinese Revolution*) (Peking: Higher Education Publishing House, 1956), p. 340.
[13] *Red Sun*, p. 557, Barnes, p. 671.

planning strategies and directing operations. We shall discuss the Communist troops' fighting strength from the viewpoint of relationships between veteran soldiers and new recruits, between commanders and political commissars, and between commanders and subordinate officers. In addition, we shall suggest causes for the victory of one army and the defeat of the other.

The Hero Company

Since the Yenan years, the Communist military leadership has always given primary attention to the company as the basic unit in army organization. In both *Defense of Yenan* and *Red Sun,* the authors give extensive coverage of an élite company and its commander. A company with a strength of just below one hundred appears to be an optimum-size unit for intensive political as well as military training. During a battle a company is a cohesive force with great maneuvrability. Since the soldiers of a company live together, receive the same training, and fight alongside each other, there is a natural tendency among them toward brotherhood even without political education. Armed with ideology and bearing the title of Hero Company, such a unit can perform feats greater than its size would suggest.

In *Defense of Yenan* the First Company forms the nucleus throughout the major battles. It fights bravely in the battle of Chinhuapien and in the Lungtung Plateau campaign and later takes part in the battle of Shachiat'ien and the battle of Chiulishan. In all this fighting, however, it is only a unit under the command of the Northwest Field Army. Its real combat strength and the heroism of the company commander Chou Ta-yung and other soldiers has to be tested when the company is entirely on its own. Only in operations totally independent of higher command and without support from other units does a company demonstrate its fighting capacity, *élan,* and resourcefulness. This opportunity comes when the First Company is completely cut off from the main force.

When the Communist troops withdraw from the siege of Yulin the First Company is ordered to cover the retreat. After the completion of the mission, it has to fight its way through. Soaked in heavy rain, the soldiers of the First Company fight one battle after another and are finally disengaged from the pursuing enemy. In the small hours of the morning, a file of wounded men plod on in dead fatigue. Suddenly, the scouting squad reports that some enemy soldiers have been spotted. After ordering the company to halt, Chou Ta-yung takes Ma Chang-sheng and Ma Chuan-yu to investigate. They discover animal manure scattered along the road.

Ta-yung halted at the foot of a bluff near the road. He pondered silently, a blade of grass in his teeth.

Ma Chuan-yu picked up a handful of earth and rubbed it in his hands. He was impatient at the company commander's stolidity. Ma Chang-sheng, on the other hand, did not want to interrupt his commander's thoughts but continued to creep forward, trying to find other signs. In spite of his rough exterior, he had a keen mind. He too analysed every stick and stone in his path.

Ta-yung was deep in thought: 'At this time of the year, draught beasts eat grass and discharge wet faeces. The wet stuff must have been discharged this afternoon. The weather is pretty warm. If the faeces had been left there since noon, they would have been dry by now. Then, why have there been so many mules, oxen, and camels passing through this afternoon? Were these draught animals carrying the peasants' own produce? With fierce battles going on, how could peasants drive so many animals on the road? Could it be the enemy who forced the peasants to move grain for them? Could there be an enemy grain station in the village? If there is, we'll destroy it!'[14]

Chou Ta-yung reaches the conclusion that there must be an enemy grain station in the village. He wants to destroy it, but realises that the soldiers are too exhausted to fight. As usual under circumstances like these, an urgent conference is held. Although the company has only thirty-eight men left, everyone is eager to take the grain station. So a surprise attack is launched. The battle is over in twenty minutes; the company rounds up more than a hundred prisoners of war.

The fighting spirit of Communist soldiers is well known, but little effort has been made to understand the source of their morale. It is a mistake to assume that Communist soldiers are deadly fighters simply because they are indoctrinated to sacrifice their lives in combat. They too are vulnerable to bullets, feel the pain of a bayonet wound, and do not enjoy death. Their fighting capacity is to a large extent the result of using their resourcefulness and imagination. When one man cannot solve a problem a conference is called to put the ideas and thoughts of several men together. In *Red Sun* when the Hero Platoon is unable to destroy a pillbox at the battle of Mengliangku, a Chu-ko Liang conference is held to get everyone's suggestions for coping with the situation.[15]

No doubt, ideology, training and military discipline play an

[14] *Defense of Yenan*, p. 352, 'At the Great Wall', *Chinese Literature*, No. 1, 1956, p. 33. The translation in *CL* is unreasonably condensed. The missing sentences are supplied here, for they show Chou Ta-yung's careful reasoning process.

[15] *Red Sun*, p. 472, Barnes, p. 567. The conference is so named because of a Chinese saying, 'The ideas of three shoemakers amount to the wisdom of Chu-ko Liang.'

important part in the execution of battle orders. But more important
than these organizational factors is a deep sense of mutual concern
between a commander and his men and among the soldiers themselves.
They would rather risk their own lives to rescue a wounded man than
let him die in desolation. They would give what little food or water
there is to a dying man even if it means their own starvation. Such
mutual attachment is best shown in the scene of Chou Ta-yung's
rejoining the main force.

All these days the brigade commander Chen Hsin-yun had remained
quiet and kept painful thoughts to himself. Even if Chou Ta-yung
were finished, he could not root him from his memory. Often he
would repeat the same words to the political commissar: 'Ta-yung is
a sharp fellow, nothing could go wrong.' The political commissar
knew from the way he talked that Commander Chen said it only for
his own consolation. Now Ta-yung's voice outside brought Commander Chen immense joy. In order to show his happy mood, he
was toying with the idea of using some harsh words to tease
Ta-yung.

But the moment Ta-yung stepped into the room, Commander
Chen's heart missed a beat, and all his relaxed mood was wiped
away.

Ta-yung had a bandage around his head; his face was dark and
lean, his cheeks were sunken, his eyes and nostrils full of sand. His
black eyebrows had turned yellowish as a result of burning; his eyes
seemed larger than ever. Clay and blood stains, burned spots, and
bullet holes spread all over his threadbare uniform. The sleeves were
burned off from the elbow down, the trousers torn to pieces below
knee level. His bare feet, smeared with blood and clay, were so
swollen that they appeared thick and large.

He stood stiffly in front of the commanders, his mouth quivering
as if he wanted to say something, but his scorched, swollen lips
disobeyed him.

The brigade commander and the political commissar exchanged a
look in silence.

'Back at last!' Commander Chen said, 'I knew you'd come back.
Your regimental commander sent all his scouts and a dozen
cavalrymen to look for you. Didn't see them? Misfortune never
comes singly. All the soldiers have safely returned? Of course, not all
of them. This is obvious! It's obvious! Com — rade!'

There was a certain childlike shyness in Ta-yung's usually brave
and confident eyes. Not knowing what to do with his two hands, he
aimlessly rubbed the edge of his uniform and said: 'It's nothing. We
completed our task of covering the retreat, and I was able to bring
our soldiers to rejoin the main force. On our way back, the enemy
attacked us several times, and we fought back!'

Commander Chen said: 'How easy you make it sound! Look at
me, don't keep looking at the wall. When you withdrew from the

outskirts of Yulin the enemy must have attacked you in force. Then perhaps you also had a few fierce contacts with the 36th Division moving southward!'

The commander took a bowl from the stove and walked to Ta-yung. Pointing at the potatoes, Commander Chen said: 'Come on! You could finish these potatoes in three bites. But chew it slowly. What a pity to swallow them without tasting their flavor!'

As Commander Chen handed over the potatoes, Ta-yung stood up to take them. His sudden movement made him black out, and he nearly fainted. Hastily supporting himself against the wall, he closed his eyes for a moment. When he opened his eyes again he saw Commander Chen's grave expression, his eyes riveted on him. Looking at the wall, Ta-yung realized that the commanders must have been standing in front of the military maps for the best part of the night and perhaps hadn't had a bite yet. The three potatoes must be the entire meal for Commander Chen, commissar Yang, and the staff officer.

Commander Chen urged: 'Eat it! How nice, three potatoes!'

Ta-yung timidly and unconvincingly said: 'I'm not hungry.'

Commander Chen raised his voice: 'What? I won't permit this!'

Ta-yung took the potatoes without daring to argue again. How sharp were the eyes of Commander Chen, how could anyone fool him!

As soon as he took a bite, the images of his men appeared before him. They had said yesterday: 'Company commander, we're so hungry, we can't move!'

Ta-yung collapsed like a heap of mud. With potatoes in his hand, his head drooping, he fell asleep.[16]

Without reading the chapter on the First Company's fighting at the Great Wall, which covers more than a sixth of the whole book, the reader gets the feel of the brutal battles through the description of Chou Ta-yung. He can also see the severity of the food shortage and other hardships suffered by the Communist troops. But above all, the narrative tells of the profound mutual attachment between the brigade commander and the company leader. Chou Ta-yung was an orphan picked up by Chen Hsin-yun during the Long March some ten years earlier. Since then Commander Chen has reared and trained Ta-yung like his own son. A similar relationship exists between the army commander Shen Chen-hsin and the squad leader Yang Chun in *Red Sun*. There have been numerous Chou Ta-yungs and Chen Hsin-yuns in the Red Army. The former have joined the army as orphans; the latter, with their homes destroyed and families slaughtered, are lonely men in their private lives. The Chou Ta-yungs and the Chen Hsin-yuns have found each other in the big family of the Red Army and have become

---

[16] *Defense of Yenan*, p. 443-7. The narrative has been condensed.

deeply attached to each other. It is not just revolution in the sense of political struggle but also war in terms of broken families and drifting lives that unites the two generations of Chinese in a common destiny. The importance of Communist military training in developing a soldier's fighting capacity certainly should not be underestimated. But equally important is his feeling of gratitude toward the Red Army, which makes him fight like a man defending his family and protecting his parents.

It is, therefore, entirely conceivable that Chen Hsin-yun would give the three potatoes to Ta-yung, while the latter would decline it despite his hunger. Or that after only one bite, Ta-yung would think of his famished men. It is natural too that as he awakes to overhear a talk between the brigade commander and the political commissar about the task of escorting grain transportation, he immediately asks for the job. His behavior suggests neither a sense of responsibility nor a show of bravery; Chou Ta-yung has proved both. He simply has an urge to share the burden with others. Without any rest, the Hero Company is on the march again.

Shih Tung-ken, the company commander in *Red Sun*, is quite different from Chou Ta-yung. Known as 'the Block of Stone' not only because of his surname Shih which means 'stone' but also because of his stubbornness, Shih can be completely carried away. Unlike battle-hardened Chou, who can be so oblivious of fatigue as to ask for the new assignment, and who seems to have no human weaknesses, Shih Tung-ken, with his fallibility, is a more lovable man. When the Tuszukou campaign is victoriously concluded his company captures more than one thousand prisoners of war and receives the title of Hero for two squads. At the celebration party held in the regimental head-quarters, he is swamped with wave after wave of toasts and finishes up thoroughly drunk. But he refuses to admit it and declares: 'You say I'm drunk? You just watch while I have a gallop round and see whether I am!'

He actually runs back to his barracks, dons a Kuomintang officer's uniform complete with a long sword, and mounts a captured foreign horse. As he gallops along the highway against the sunset, he takes no notice of the army commander, Shen Chen-hsin, sitting on the hillside. He speeds back and forth, forcing other riders to retreat to the side of the road or to seek refuge in the fields, but is told to dismount by somebody standing in the middle of the road. With his high-fronted peaked cap perched awry, his sword dangling against the horse's belly, he looks sternly at the man who has interrupted his fun. Finally recognizing the man as Commander Shen's bodyguard, Shih cheerfully calls him little devil and jokes with him. Then the impatient voice of the army commander sobers him up, and he dismounts to give a slovenly salute.

Deeply annoyed, the army commander gives 'the Block of Stone' a good scolding but takes no disciplinary action against the drunken man. Shih merely receives an assignment, to write a summary of the battle experience of his company. At first, Shih takes it as a punishment, for he has mastered less than a thousand characters. But he discovers to his pride as well as dismay that the army commander really wants the summary of battle experience, as a means of learning something from each battle. The battle performance of his company will be the focal point, which makes him proud, but the very idea of writing the report appears to him utterly impossible. When the young cultural instructor suggests that the summary should be done on a Marxist-Leninist level, Shih touches his head and says: 'I've got a head up here. But Marxism and Leninism? I haven't got any of that!'

Shih Tung-ken and Chou Ta-yung are both commanders of Hero Companies, but they have entirely different personalities. The army commander Shen, however, treats Shih with the same solicitude that the brigade commander Chen does Chou Ta-yung. Shih is never dealt with harshly for his mischievous conduct. When his company holds a meeting to exchange battle experiences the army commander personally attends the meeting and pays close attention to their discussions.

The most effective method of transforming a peasant army into a fighting force appears to be not discipline but political persuasion. Discipline may make soldiers obedient but cannot turn them into fighters. Although both authors focus their attention on a Hero Company, neither makes it perfect. In both companies there are deserters[17] who tarnish the Hero title. The way deserters are treated is highly significant. In both cases, the deserters receive no disciplinary punishment, while those who form the backbone of the fighting force take the blame.

In *Red Sun* a soldier's desertion causes the squad leader Chin Shou-pen to complain about the difficulty of handling new recruits. He tells Chang Hua-feng how he stays awake at night in order to watch them. But Chang says that as long as they have a pair of legs Chin will never be able to keep an eye on them all the time. Then he confides to Chin his own experience:

'Now listen, when I first joined up I was torn off a strip by the section-leader — the deputy commander of 3 Platoon as he is now. I was very upset by it at the time: I'd only joined the revolution because I was fed up with being kicked around and sworn at by the

---

[17] Desertion must be a very serious problem in the Communist army, especially with those soldiers who have defected from the Kuomintang side. The first chapter of *War Drum Awakens the Spring* deals exclusively with a deserter and his conversion.

landlord, so when I came here and got sworn at just the same I suddenly felt different about things and thought of deserting. All that kept me from running away was that later on Yang Chun, who was then the deputy section-leader, was good to me and helped me and talked things over with me as man to man. If it hadn't been for Yang Chun I might not be sitting here with you now . . .'[18]

These simple words make Chin realize his neglect of the men in his squad. He has never tried to understand the soldiers; on the contrary, he has often lost his temper with them. This little talk helps change his attitude towards the new recruits. In *Defense of Yenan* the desertion of a new recruit is made an occasion for political education. When Li Ch'eng, the regimental political commissar, asks Chou Ta-yung about a deserter, Chou says that the man has been taken back; his tone suggests nothing had happened. But Li Ch'eng refuses to drop the subject and asks why the man tried to run away. Chou explains that the new recruit is afraid of the heat of the desert. Li insists that there will always be people afraid of something; otherwise, no difference exists between Communists and ordinary soldiers. Chou feels a certain injustice in being held responsible and points out that the company's political instructor is away on a training course. But Li Ch'eng accepts no excuse and asks if the political instructor has packed the party organization in his knapsack and taken it along with him. He suggests a party meeting be held immediately. This is how the discussion goes at the meeting:

> Li Ch'eng weighed his words as he said to them: 'There're ninety-six men in your company, but many of them you don't know very well!' His tone was rather calm, not as severe as they'd expected.
> Without waiting for others to respond, Li Chang-kuo promptly said: 'Ninety-six? Our company has altogether ninety-seven men!'
> Li Ch'eng said: 'Comrade, there must be ninety-six.'
> 'Ninety-seven, can't be wrong.' Ma Chang-sheng stubbornly insisted.
> Li Ch'eng asked: 'Hasn't one deserted?'
> 'Ha, he didn't make it!' Li Chang-kuo smirked. He thought to himself: no wonder the political commissar pulled a long face, for he didn't know that Yin Ken-ti did not get away.
> Li Ch'eng said: 'Then still ninety-six. The reason Yin Ken-ti tried to run away is that he still doesn't know why he is fighting and for whom. This sort of soldier does not count, comrades.'
> 'Then don't count him.' Wang the Tiger unhurriedly said.
> Li Ch'eng said: 'Don't count him? That doesn't solve the problem! I've a few other problems for all of us to study.' He asked: 'Where did Yin Ken-ti come from? How old is he? What's his class status? How long was he in the reactionary army? What's his

---

[18] *Red Sun*, p. 67, Barnes, pp. 73–4.

character? Since he joined the First Company, what have the cadres
and Communists done for him? . . .'

The group managed to make a few points. After that, they looked
uneasily at one another.

Li Ch'eng maintained his silence.

Old Sun repeatedly swallowed saliva.

Wang the Tiger said in a low voice: 'Really too busy, unable to
care . . .'

Li Ch'eng said: 'Tiger, revolution has always been a busy job!'

Ma Chuan-yu complained: 'All the new recruits with a good class
background and correct ideology were assigned to other companies.
Those no one wanted were given to us!'

Li Ch'eng said: 'Great! Ma Chuan-yu has dug an impenetrable
air-raid shelter for himself!' After a pause, he said again: ' "Camp of
iron and soldiers of water" is a description of the reactionary army.
Our warriors fight for their own class interests, but why are there
still people who want to desert? The responsibility rests with me and
you, too. Comrades, the Party's entrusted us with this army, wants
us to give it good leadership. Yet, what have we done to lead it
forward? Yin Ken-ti has belonged to your company for three days
already, but, look, you haven't even started to understand him, not
to mention your failure to take care of him!'

Ma Chuan-yu said: 'He just got here, and without resting his feet
he tried to desert. What a coward, he can't be a good fellow!'

Li Ch'eng said: 'How could you say he's no good? Yin Ken-ti
came to join our big family. In the first place, he's received no
attention from the Communist Party members. Secondly, he's not
understood the difference between a revolutionary army and an
anti-revolutionary army. The devil he didn't desert!' He looked at
the left corner of the wall, while his thoughts moved swiftly. After a
while, his eyes sweeping across everyone's face, he said: 'A company
is a fearsome force. Why? Because there's a Party branch in the
company. But look at the fortress in your company – that Party
branch! Comrades, even the loss of a bullet is inexcusable to us
Communists, much worse is losing a soldier. Try to find time for a
branch Party meeting and start by examining this problem, and then
check all the loopholes in your work. Chou Ta-yung must report the
conclusion of your discussion to me during the march the day after
tomorrow . . .'[19]

Who is responsible for Yin Ken-ti's desertion? The regimental
political commissar puts the responsibility squarely on the Party
members of the company and on himself as well. Instead of taking
disciplinary action against the deserter, he is excused for his ignorance
of the nature of the war of liberation. In the political commissar's
mind, it is totally understandable that a man will refuse to fight if he

[19] *Defense of Yenan*, pp. 200–2.

does not know what he is fighting for. If a new soldier does not enjoy the warmth of a large family which has been denied him in the Kuomintang army, then he has every reason to desert the Red Army too. Once a soldier knows the cause of the revolution, shares brotherly love with the others in the company, and develops a sense of belonging, he will become a fearless fighter. Thus, by the fulfilment of their psychological needs, as well as the cultivation of political awareness, the soldiers of the Red Army, with all the differences in their ages, education, accents, and personal backgrounds, are transformed into a formidable force.

The Commander-Commissar Relationship

What Li Ch'eng has done suggests the nature of political work in the Red Army, but more is to be said about the role of the political commissar and his relationship with the commander. In the Communist army above regiment level, leadership is jointly exercised by a commander and a political commissar. The commander is responsible for matters of a military nature; the political commissar as the party representative leads political work throughout the party hierarchy. In addition, there is a political department headed by a chairman (*chu-jen*) at every level from the regiment up, which deals with all aspects of the army's everyday life, its cultural, educational and political activities. The political commissar is spared day-to-day managerial work and allowed to concentrate on matters of policy. The commander and the political commissar together form the nucleus of leadership and consult each other on military tactics. An army is often called after the surnames of both its commander and political commissar, such as the Shen-Ting Army, named after the commander Shen Chen-hsin and the political commissar Ting Yuan-shan. From the battalion down, the party function is performed by a political instructor, and the soldiers' spare-time activities are handled by a cultural instructor.

Leadership by committee, as a rule, tends to create division, but there seems to be no such problem in the Communist army. Two reasons appear to account for the smooth functioning of joint leadership. First, commander and political commissar have different, well-defined responsibilities and each respects the jurisdiction of the other. A second, perhaps more important, reason is that in most cases both have come from the same peasant background and have shared the same experiences in battles. Very often a commander is transferred to another unit to serve as political commissar or vice versa. Their common training and the interchangeability of the two jobs allows each to appreciate the assignment of the other and creates a sense of mutual respect. This is exemplified by the relations between the regimental commander Chao Ching and the political commissar Li Ch'eng and between the brigade commander Chen Hsin-yun and the political commissar Yang K'e-wen in *Defense of Yenan*. Once the regimental commander Chao Ching tells his political commissar Li Ch'eng that during night engagements he called Li's name several times, and the latter always answered him. It is not that he saw Li, rather that he sensed Li's presence. On one occasion the brigade political commissar Yang K'e-wen saves his commander Chen from airplane machine-gun fire by pulling him to the ground. When Chen thanks Yang for saving his life the political commissar says: 'If you put it that way, then you've also saved my life a dozen times.' There seems to exist perfect harmony and co-operation between the commanders and the political commissars in *Defense of Yenan*.

Strains, however, emerge in this relationship when commander and political commissar have different backgrounds. With the participation of intellectuals in the revolution, the homogeneous quality of army ranks undergoes a drastic change. Intellectuals are often assigned to the army as Party representatives to deal with more delicate tasks such as the recruitment of Party members, political education, cultural activities, morale-building, and the correct handling of war prisoners. Under the theory of Party control of the army, commanders who have received their training and promotions mainly through fighting naturally harbor a certain suspicion towards those who have gained rank by the merits of their formal education and non-military experiences. It is a normal reaction for veteran soldiers, who are unable to accept as their peers those whose valor has yet to be tested under gunfire.

Such is the reaction of the regimental commander Liu Sheng toward the newly-appointed political commissar Chen Chien in *Red Sun*. After the Lienshui campaign, Liu Sheng has been promoted from deputy commander to commander, and during the regrouping a new political commissar is sent to share with him the leadership of the regiment. Hearing that Chen Chien has been to a university, Liu Sheng becomes sceptical about their working relationship. He has a rather strong bias against intellectuals, for in his mind intellectuals are good at talking but will show their true colors under hardship. Since he considers himself a country rustic, uncouth and uncultured, he does not think he can get on with a smart-looking, smooth-talking intellectual.

When Liu Sheng complains to the army commander, Shen Chen-hsin, the latter is deeply disturbed. Instead of responding directly to Liu's complaints, the army commander raises a series of questions. He asks if all intellectuals' words do not match their deeds. What does Liu Sheng mean by country rustic and intellectual? Why must he draw a line between 'we' and 'they?' Why does he think that the two of them cannot get on? Liu Sheng is unable to answer these questions and already senses the army commander's displeasure. When he finds some excuse to leave, he is told to stay. The army commander takes Liu's misgivings about intellectuals seriously; he knows that unless Liu's attitude changes, there can be no unity and co-operation in the leadership of the regiment.

The army commander does not directly overrule Liu's objection, nor does he reprimand him. Shen Chen-hsin simply shows his annoyance by taking off his lined woollen overcoat and hurling it to the ground, chain-smoking, and pulling out from his briefcase and scattering all over the table articles such as documents, maps, scissors, and personal letters. He is waiting for Liu Sheng to admit his mistake. Liu's attitude cannot be changed by anyone but himself. So, Liu Sheng first admits his ideological error, then concedes the limits of his ability, and finally says that he is not up to the responsibility of commanding a regiment. Only then does the army commander give his subordinate solemn advice:

'Your only trouble is your pride! The defect is in yourself. Every battle we fight I think we're sure to win, but it doesn't always turn out that way. The second battle at Lienshui was vital, because if we didn't hold the enemy in check they were going to make a deep breakthrough and put us in a nasty fix. So far as this army of ours is concerned it really was a battle lost, a very poor showing. The reasons for our defeat are many, and one of the most important is pride and self-satisfaction on the part of our cadres, a failing which I share, as you do. I had a talk yesterday with four fighters from your regiment and they told me something about the battle. They're brave men, not afraid to die, but we with our pride, our underestimation of the enemy, and our inability to see our own weaknesses, are throwing their lives away! You say that intellectual cadres have certain shortcomings and aren't easy to get on with, but then you're from the country, the same as me; just think about it for a moment: haven't we got our shortcomings as well? Don't other people perhaps find us difficult to get on with? What was the point of asking the Field Army Command to send down a cadre to be your political commissar? And why have they chosen a cadre who has been to university like Chen Chien to come and be your commissar? Be more humble, comrade! You must look harder for your own shortcomings and for other people's good points; don't think that everything about yourself is all right and that everything about other people is all wrong...'[20]

The army commander has detected in Liu Sheng something more dangerous, something which forms the root of his attitude toward the

[20] *Red Sun*, p. 44, Barnes, p. 45.

regimental commissar. It is Liu Sheng's pride and self-satisfaction. His contempt for Chen Chien as an intellectual weakling is the manifestation of this self-esteem, a most serious weakness for any commander to possess. To be a good commander, Liu Sheng must learn humility and must appreciate merits in other people. In reprimanding Liu, the army commander also criticises himself. It is general practice in the Communist army for a superior officer always to share part of the responsibility when one of his subordinates commits an error. Such a practice has a certain healing effect on the psychological wounds caused by the exhortation. It soothes the pique of the junior cadre, whose improved performance in the future is of primary importance.

The talk produces the anticipated result when Liu Sheng promises to take Shen's words to heart. But the army commander clearly feels that something else has to be done to salve his subordinate's ruffled feelings. Noticing the stiffness of Liu's left arm and a burned copper-size hole on his cadre's jacket, Shen immediately inquires about the regimental commander's injury. When he is assured that the wound is not serious, he gives Liu his overcoat. The regimental commander is also invited to have supper with him. All this is done in a most natural way but with the clear purpose of removing whatever hard feelings may have remained between them.

Meanwhile, Chen Chien is also briefed by his superior, the army political commissar Ting Yuan-shan. As Liu Sheng goes to the office of the army commissar, he overhears Ting talking to Chen: 'Whiskers Liu isn't a case of "all courage and no resourcefulness" but of "more courage than resourcefulness". You must give him every assistance, because he's got plenty of good points . . .' Liu Sheng turns away at once and waits for his political commissar some distance away. The incident is revealing; only with mutual understanding and trust between the two lines of command can unity and co-operation be maintained.

Although their respective responsibilities are clearly defined, a good relationship between commander and political commissar is after all a matter of personalities. Even with military regulations and help from the leadership, Chen Chien still has to earn the trust and respect of his regimental commander through his own efforts. He tries hard to be not only Liu Sheng's partner but also his close friend in their private lives. At the battle of Tuszukuo, Chen proves his courage under heavy fire and his thoughtfulness in objecting to Liu's impetuous move. Liu Sheng once again shows his prejudice against intellectuals, he feels that the new political commissar lacks battle experience and turns out to be weak and irresolute, even timid and lost, in a crisis situation. Chen Chien is not disturbed by Liu's obvious annoyance; instead, he offers an alternative plan. Then he adds that if Liu still thinks the best way is to attack with gasoline fire, then he will accept Liu's decision. But he explains why it is not a good tactic to destroy the enemy by paying a heavy price. His deferent tone and candid reasoning finally change Liu Sheng's mind. Liu not only agrees to Chen's idea but also admits to himself that he has misjudged the political commissar.

Like Chang Fei, the rude and forthright character of *Romance of the Three Kingdoms*, Whiskers Liu has an incessant urge to throw himself into every battle. Whenever he is left out of a combat mission, he complains that his regiment has been slighted because of its defeat in the Lienshui campaign. When his regiment is ordered to separate from the main force and to hold control of the Sha River in southern Shantung, he is absolutely unwilling to go. As he cannot very well disobey the order, he hopes his political commissar will find good reasons to change the army commander's mind. He is very upset to hear Chen Chien say that they are unanimous in the acceptance of any task given to them. Later, when he complains because Chen had raised no objection, the political commissar manages to turn it into a joke by saying that the regimental commander is indeed a nice, honest man, who wants somebody else to disobey an order for him.

Holding a strategic point along the west bank of the River Sha while waiting for battle orders, Liu Sheng again becomes restless. Information obtained from the local people reveals that a Kuomintang force consisting of a battalion headquarters and five companies is stationed at a nearby town. Annihilation of this enemy unit is considered an easy task, so preparations are made and a request for permission to attack is sent to the army headquarters. But the request is turned down without any explanation. Liu Sheng is boiling with rage and again complains of his rotten luck. He complains that his regiment has not been treated like the eldest son. But Chen Chien assures him that parents may like the youngest best, but still depend on the first-born. Liu Sheng insists that they have been treated like a son who is incapable of earning money. Tracing back its history, Chen Chien counts the past glories of the regiment and concludes that the Field Army Command will never slight their fighting capacity.

Liu Sheng has not been totally convinced by Chen Chien's analysis, but he changes the subject. He asks Chen about his personality. It is a touchy topic; Chen does not know where to start. An impatient man, Liu characterizes himself as being clumsy in three respects: clumsy of tongue, for he cannot talk persuasively; clumsy of hand, for he cannot write well; and clumsy of brain, for he cannot make the best use of his mind. But Chen Chien says that Liu is straight in three respects: first, speaking straight; second, straightforward with people; third, thinking straight. This conversation not only puts Liu Sheng's mind at peace but also brings the two men closer.

The next morning Liu Sheng helps his orderlies to sweep the house, takes a bath, and has his hair cut and beard shaven. After unpacking, he chooses a thick volume to read. He declares that he is not going to move and will wait to eat the grapes on the vine. At noon he spreads himself out in the mosquito-net and falls fast asleep like a man without a single worry in the world. Before long he is awakened by the cipher-clerk with an urgent signal. After reading the message, he orders his orderlies to have everything packed immediately. Moments later, he is reading aloud the signal to the cadres gathered round him:

> 'The orders of Field Army Command – Commander-in-Chief Ch'en, Deputy Commander Su and Deputy Political Commissar Tan – are that our army shall fly there! Fly! Got that? They want us to grow wings and fly there! Our regiment's position will be at the extreme front of the army, the closest to Mengliangku, the hawk's head and beak!'[21]

Once again Liu Sheng's suspicion of Field Army Command's low estimate of his regiment's fighting capacity turns out to be unwarranted. Once again Chen Chien's patience and perseverance have contained any reckless move his commander might make. The relationship between commander and political commissar as shown in *Red Sun* is considerably more delicate than the simple principle of the Party controlling the army. As the representative of the Party, a political commissar has the ultimate sanction of calling a meeting of the Party committee to deal with a recalcitrant commander who ignores his orders, mistreats soldiers or war prisoners, or otherwise works to the disadvantage of the revolutionary war. In reality this authority of the political commissar is rarely exercised. The role of the political commissar is to guide the commander in the right direction, especially if he is a man like Liu Sheng, emotional, hot-tempered, valiant but thoughtless. In military matters the political commissar is a co-commander, but the commander is still the one to give the orders. Although a decision is jointly made by commander and political commissar, due respect must be shown to the commander. If the political commissar disagrees, as Chen Chien did at the battle of Tuszukuo, he has to be tactful and to present a convincing argument. His job is to assist, to advise, but never to overrule the commander.

A political commissar has to work with enormous patience; it is the keystone of his profession. Actually, the regimental commander Liu Sheng has shown very serious symptoms of misconduct, detrimental to the execution of battle orders. He has disclosed, openly and repeatedly, his dissatisfaction with the top level leadership. The Field Army headquarters, in his view, has no trust in his regiment's fighting capacity, has not treated them as the eldest son, and has not given them the opportunity 'when there is money to be made'. These thoughts are at

[21] *Red Sun*, p. 404, Barnes, p. 485.

the root of the Kuomintang generals' defeat, a subject to be discussed later. But the political commissar Chen Chien never directly criticizes this dangerous trend of thought, but skillfully persuades Liu to have faith in the decisions of Field Army Command. The order for the regiment to hold a strategic position on the River Sha is a chess move. An old Chinese saying that the soft overcomes the hard perhaps best describes the role of the political commissar in the Communist army.

Liu Sheng is nevertheless portrayed as a hero, a tragic hero in the tradition of Hsiang Yü, whose reckless bravery foiled his ambition of empire building. In the attack of Mengliangku Liu Sheng is fatally wounded; the political commissar Chen Chien is ordered to assume the responsibility of acting commander. Liu Sheng's heroism and his dedication to the revolution are vindicated in this touching death scene:

> Hovering on the brink of death, Liu Sheng suddenly became calm. He slowly bent his arm, felt for his wrist and took out his stainless steel watch; next he felt for his breast pocket and took out his large, thick Gold Star pen; then he slid his hand inside his jacket and after groping for some time produced a small wallet, extracted a small paper package from the wallet and took from the package a bank-note for one dollar on the Soviet Bank from the period of the Second Revolutionary Civil War. He clutched these three things in his trembling hand for a moment, then handed them to Teng Hai and said in a voice that was weak yet clear and resonant:
> 'Give these to the organization department. This note . . . was issued to me . . . by the quartermaster on the day I . . . joined the Red Army . . . That was fifteen years ago . . . a souvenir . . .'[22]

The death of Liu Sheng causes profound sorrow among the soldiers of the regiment, for his forthright character had won the respect and affection of his men. Even in death he can still play a crucial part in the assault on the summit of Mengliangku. The political commissar Chen Chien, now also acting commander, manages to turn the soldiers' grief over Liu's death into a desire for revenge. Moments before the attack at dawn, in the cave closest to the peak of Mengliangku, a memorial ceremony for Liu Sheng is held, as well as the front-line ceremony of initiation of new members to the Communist Party. The description of the scene forcibly drives home Mao Tse-tung's theory of the Party's control over the army.

Communist Field Army Commanders

In the above discussion, the superior-subordinate relationship has been illustrated to some extent. The way the brigade commander Chen Yuan-hsin treats the company commander Chou Ta-yung in *Defense of*

22 *Red Sun*, p. 520, Barnes, p. 626.

Yenan and the army commander Shen Chen-hsin deals with the regimental commander Liu Sheng in *Red Sun* indicates a very personal relationship, rather than a formal superior-subordinate relationship. In this section we shall focus on top level military leadership, battle decision-making and transmission, and the anticipation and implementation of orders.

A guiding principle for Communist novelists, in effect a general rule of fiction-writing as well, holds that top commanders and generals should not be directly portrayed. In Western historical novels, kings, prime ministers, and generals are usually minor characters in the story. The novel is a fictional form; any attempt at portraying historical figures will force the author to stick to historical accuracy and reduce the power of imagination. Communist novelists often avoid the portrayal of top leaders for fear of fostering a personality cult. Even Mao Tse-tung never appears in novels, though there is no lack of praise for his wisdom. But the description of P'eng Teh-huai, in *Defense of Yenan*, proves to be an exception. The author gives us this picture of P'eng:

> The Commander-in-Chief P'eng Teh-huai was of medium height. He had the face of an ordinary worker, with two black, coarse heavy eyebrows under which a pair of not too large eyes radiated authority and wisdom. This military genius had the simplicity and integrity of ordinary working people. He stood there, serene and firm . . .[23]

At the battle of P'anglungchen, P'eng Teh-huai explains to the brigade commander Chen Hsin-yun the overall strategy of this operation. He estimates that it will take seven days for the Kuomintang troops to reach Suiteh. His calculation is based on such data as road conditions in northern Shensi, the weather, the weight of equipment carried by the infantry, and the speed of march. Then he considers the likelihood of this unit returning to reinforce the Kuomintang troops at P'anglungchen once the attack is launched. Before they do this, the unit's commander will have to obtain approval from Hu Tsung-nan in Yenan. Hu will need time to give the request consideration and to decide on a number of options. Once a decision is made and a signal sent to the troops in Suiteh, the Kuomintang reinforcement will have to cover the distance between Suiteh and P'anglungchen. After taking all this into account, he concludes that the Northwest Field Army will need at least four days to take P'anglungchen.

Then he invites Chen Hsin-yun to discuss his brigade's plan of assault on the strategic height. Chen analyses the topography of the battle zone and talks about the positions of their firepower, the organization of assault parties, and likely routes for charges. When he mentions

[23] *Defense of Yenan*, pp. 416–17.

earthworks and the use of explosives P'eng Teh-huai, who has been all attention, wants him to be more explicit. The commander of the Northwest Field Army seems meticulous in his battle preparations and a willing listener to the ideas of his subordinates. He always asks if there are any difficulties. Once Chen Hsin-yun says that the only problem is not enough gun shells, but after saying it, he immediately regrets raising this problem. When the battle begins his unit receives eight gun shells.

For about two weeks, the Northwest Field Army has avoided direct contact with Hu Tsung-nan's main force and has waited to destroy Chung Sung's reorganized 36th Division. In Chen Hsin-yun's brigade all want action, commanders and soldiers alike. Chen himself comes to P'eng Teh-huai's cave to request permission to attack. P'eng listens carefully to Chen's report of the enemy moves, raises a few questions, and then gives his own analysis of the military situation:

'Suppose this is the situation.' Commander-in-Chief P'eng put down the candle, looked at the map, and counted his fingers as if calculating something. After half a minute, he said: 'There're at least a thousand enemy troops moving northward along the river. If we attack, the enemy will concentrate on the bank, and their troops on the south side of the river will rush in reinforcements. As a result, we may be able to destroy them and capture seven or eight hundred prisoners, but we'll have to suffer two or three hundred casualties. Another possibility is that as soon as we attack, the enemy will withdraw. We may not gain anything, but expose our position.' He turned around to look at Chen Hsin-yun. 'Once our position is exposed, the enemy main force, a total of seven brigades, will press northward. With such a large force, we'd be unable to bite. And we're short of food. From this point of view, even if we've an opportunity to attack, it's better not to fight this battle.'

'Oh! Not to fight this battle?' Chen Hsin-yun thought to himself.

Commander P'eng looked attentively at Chen for a while and then asked: 'What do you say? Should we attack?'

Chen Hsin-yun felt embarrassed. He said uneasily: 'We'll do whatever the commander decides! But the soldiers cannot wait to fight, and their eagerness . . .'

P'eng Teh-huai shook his head slightly and said: 'I say, no — battle, no battle.' His first 'no battle' was said in a prolonged, slow, questioning tone. The second time his voice was positive, resolute, and unshakeable, like a huge mountain.[24]

The author Tu Peng-cheng spends a total of thirty-seven pages, or six per cent of the entire book, portraying, directly or indirectly, P'eng Teh-huai's great leadership as a field commander and his modesty and amiability as a man. He appears cool and optimistic under the crushing

[24] *Defense of Yenan*, p. 419.

pressure of the enormous enemy strength and is able to turn the most adverse situation to his own advantage. In dealing with his junior commanders, P'eng is depicted as humble in listening to their opinions, but firm in commanding the over-all operation in the north-west military theatre, an affable man who always attracts peasants and children to his side and never shows impatience.[25]

During the campaign of Shachiat'ien, the most critical battle in the defense of Yenan, P'eng personally directs the operation on a nearby hilltop. He stands unperturbed under continuous machine-gun fire from Kuomintang aeroplanes, but the author does not describe P'eng Teh-huai's courage directly. Instead he describes the brigade commander, Chen Hsin-yun. Watching the progress of the battle through binoculars and giving orders through the field telephone, Chen discovers that one of his regiments fails to take a hill after a dozen charges. The regimental commander Chao Ching's report confirms his suspicion that the headquarters of the Kuomintang 36th Division and 165th Brigade are stationed there. The capture of the hill will mean the conclusion of the battle, so he decides to go over there to take personal command of the assault. At this point, the telephone rings again; Chen picks up the receiver:

> 'Chao Ching? ...' As soon as Chao Ching answered 'Hum ...' another voice was heard in the receiver: 'Chao Ching, why must you report my presence to your brigade commander? What's the need? Why worry! The bullets have no eyes ...'
> 'Oh, Commander-in-Chief P'eng is already at the regimental commanding post?' A feeling of shock and emotion galvanized Chen Hsin-yun and instantly spread through him. He shouted into the receiver: 'Chao Ching, is No. 3 there at your side? You must give him best protection, and I'll come over right away.' Chao Ching must have been holding the telephone, saying something to Commander P'eng. Chen could only hear intermittently the calm and unhurried voice of P'eng Teh-huai, 'Very good ... in one swift strike, completely destroy ... don't worry about me. I'm not a new recruit who needs the squad leader to show me how to fight ...'[26]

[25] This portrait of P'eng Teh-huai is considered accurate. See Feng Hsüeh-feng, 'Lun *Pao-wei Yen-an* ti ch'eng-chiu chi ch'i chung-yao-hsing' (On the Achievement and Importance of *Defense of Yenan*), *Wen-i pao*, No. 14, 1954, p. 13; Ma Han-ping, 'Tu *Pao-wei Yen-an* ti chi chang' (After Reading the Serialized Chapters of *Defense of Yenan*), *Chieh-fang-chün wen-i*, May 1954, p. 115; and Pei-ching ta-hsüeh chung-wen-hsi ssu-nien-chi 'Chung-hua jen-min kung-ho-kuo wen-hsüeh shih' pien-wei-hui hsiao-shuo-tsu (The Fiction Section of the Committee on the Compilation of 'History of Literature of the Chinese People's Republic' of the Senior Class, Department of Chinese, Peking University), '*Pao-wei Yen-an* — Chieh-fang chan-cheng ti shih-shih' (*Defense of Yenan* — Epic of the War of Liberation), *Wen-hsüeh chih-shih*, January 1959, p. 13.
[26] *Defense of Yenan*, p. 496.

The willingness of Communist generals to risk their lives in a crucial battle appears to be real, when we think how many of them were killed and wounded. What is unusual is the author's endeavor to portray it. *Defense of Yenan* was published in June 1954, when P'eng Teh-huai was still the commander of the Chinese People's Volunteers in Korea. In September of the same year, he returned to assume the post of Minister of Defense. That was a time when P'eng's prestige was at its height. The book was edited by the PLA Literature Editorial Board and published by the People's Literature Publishing House. It appears that no one could have prevented its publication.

Direct description of a Field Army commander is avoided in *Red Sun*, published three years after the appearance of *Defense of Yenan*. Here Ch'en Yi, Commander-in-Chief, and Su Yü, second in command, are just code numbers; their orders are given by field telephone. But in the brief dialogues where views of the battle situation are exchanged and orders given, Ch'en Yi is portrayed as a man of warmth and humor. While the author of *Defense of Yenan* forces upon the reader the image of P'eng Teh-huai as a great commander who is nevertheless simple and modest, Wu Chiang succeeds in conveying, in a few words, the impression of Ch'en Yi as a casual and witty man. This portrait of Ch'en Yi is regarded by Communist critics as vivid and accurate.[27]

The battle of Tuszukuo has been going on for two nights and a day and is reaching deadlock. As the army commander Shen Chen-hsin is discussing with his deputy Liang Po and his division commander Tsao Kuo-chu ways to bring the battle to an early conclusion, the telephone rings. It is '501', code number for Ch'en Yi, the Field Army commander and concurrently political commissar.

Shen Chen-hsin snatched up the receiver and the clear, familiar voice with its touch of humor boomed in his ear:
'The 200,000 enemy on the southern front have decided to come and join in the fun. They're now sixty *li* from where I am now. Tomorrow their shells may be falling outside my door. The day after that you may be able to smell the sulphur from their shells. How is it with you? Tough? Bitten off more than you can chew? Want me to send reinforcements?'
Over a long period of time Shen Chen-hsin and many other commanders had trained themselves into the habit of always preserving a fully confident voice and manner before their superior commanders. It could only show them up as weak and add to their

---

[27] Liang Ping, 'T'an *Hung jih* ti chi-ko jen-wu' (Talks on Some Characters in *Red Sun*), *Wen-i yüeh-pao*, February 1958, p. 56; Feng Mu, 'Ke-ming ti chan-ko, ying-hsiung ti sung-ko — Lioh lun *Hung jih* ti ch'eng-chiu chi ch'i jo-tien' (A Revolutionary Battle Song, A Heroes' Panegyric — Brief Commentaries on the Achievement and Weaknesses of *Red Sun*), *Wen-i pao*, November 1958, p. 34.

superiors' burdens for them to complain of hardship or haggle or make qualifications. So when '501' paused for a moment Shen Chen-hsin replied calmly and easily:

'There are certain difficulties, but we can overcome them. There won't be any need for reinforcements.'

'Well, then, when are you going to get this battle finished off? Are you still going to be the old bullock pulling a broken cart, creeping slowly along?'

'Tomorrow.'

'What time tomorrow?'

Shen Chen-hsin's eyes sought the views of Liang Po and Tsao Kuo-chu on this and with one voice they told him:

'Tomorrow evening.'

Shen Chen-hsin took the receiver from his mouth and said, waving it at them:

'Too late!'

Liang Po and Tsao Kuo-chu looked at each other and Tsao Kuo-chu's eyes seemed to be saying: 'It'll be difficult to make it any earlier than that.'

Liang Po felt that one should give the strongest possible support to any decision made by the commander in charge of an operation and it was obvious from Shen Chen-hsin's expression that it was going to be awkward for him to make a decision on the time allowed for this battle, so he raised his head and said to Shen Chen-hsin:

'You decide. We'll have to bring it forward a bit if that's the way it is.'

Shen Chen-hsin turned his face and spoke into the receiver in a firm, clear voice:

'We'll finish off this enemy before twelve noon tomorrow. Will that do?'

'All right, then, I'll be expecting news of your victory tomorrow morning!'[28]

The words of '501' show a man who is capable of cracking jokes over a matter of life and death. Ch'en Yi lets his army commander know the severity of the battle situation, but he makes it sound as if it were a ball game. His mention of reinforcements is less to show his concern for the army's ability to win than to express his dissatisfaction with the slow pace of progress. On the other hand, the army commanders have developed a habit of sharing the burden with their superiors. In the process of giving and receiving orders, both sides have carefully taken into consideration potential difficulties faced by the other. Ch'en Yi would never have made the call, had the main force not been under great pressure. Shen Chen-hsin has to decide on an earlier deadline for himself without being told so. The same attitude is shared

[28] *Red Sun*, pp. 168–9, Barnes, pp. 196–7.

by the deputy army commander Liang Po, who is obliged to give his unqualified support to the army commander. When Shen Chen-hsin, with the support of Liang Po, suggests the conclusion of the battle before noon tomorrow, he must have anticipated the deadline as acceptable to the Field Army Commander. Ch'en Yi's last words are said as an expression of confidence in the army commander and a wish for his success, but also as an order that the deadline must be met.

Ch'en Yi's second telephone call comes when the assault on Mengliangku reaches its most critical stage. It is made only minutes after Su Yü has ordered Shen Chen-hsin's army to annihilate Chang Ling-fu's 74th Division before dark tomorrow under any circumstances. If this is not done, enemy reinforcements will break through their outer defense lines and link up with Chang Ling-fu, and the military situation will turn to the disadvantage of the Communist side. Even at this crucial moment, Ch'en Yi does not forget to ask how Shen feels after swallowing several mouthfuls of water at the crossing of the River Sha. It is a reference to the incident when Shen's raft was overturned and he was nearly drowned. Then '501' goes on in his clear, ringing voice:

'. . . If we win this battle we shall have our feet planted firmly on the rocks of Shantung. We shall have the upper hand, we'll be up on the hilltops with our backs to the Yellow River and our face to the South. Chiang Kai-shek will be at our feet, down in the mire. But if we don't win it will be a different story: we shall have to turn our backs[29] to the South and cross the Yellow River. You haven't fought at all badly these past few days and we're very satisfied with you. The holding units have been having a tough time and fighting even better than the units here. They've withstood attacks by over 200,000 men. If you want to stay here in Shantung eating maize and millet you'll have to destroy this enemy within the next twenty-four hours. Haven't you been sending in signals and letters telling us how determined you are to defend the Central Committee of the Party and Chairman Mao? Then you must relentlessly destroy the 74th Division that you are now up against. You must prove your determination with real action . . . The reason we transferred you back from South Shantung was to use you as a surprise assault force,[30] to give you an opportunity of achieving an outstanding success . . . I've come across one of your unit's songs and I like it: "Destroy the 74th Division and make a name for ourselves, plant the Red Flag on the highest peak!" Let's see you singing it and doing it!'

'Our determination to carry out our task and destroy this enemy is unshakeable,' Shen Chen-hsin replied in a firm resolute voice. 'We

---

[29] The Chinese word is 'buttocks' (*p'i-ku*).
[30] The original translation 'as a military working unit' is changed into 'as a surprise assault force', which is a more accurate rendering of the Chinese expression *i-chih ch'i-ping*.

have every confidence. Judging from the way things are going in our positions the 74th Division won't escape this time!'

'You're sure you can do it?'

'Do you think I'd say it if I didn't mean it at a time like this?'

'Then I won't take up any more of your time. Carry out staunchly the orders 502's just given you.'[31]

Unlike the first telephone call where Ch'en Yi asked their opinion, this time he simply re-emphasizes the order that the enemy must be eliminated within twenty-four hours. The names of the Central Committee and Chairman Mao are invoked not only to remind the army commander of the signals and letters sent to the Field Army Command but also to illustrate the gravity and urgency of the military situation. But even under such circumstances, Ch'en Yi never uses threats as Kuomintang commanders often do to their subordinates. He simply makes Shen Chen-hsin reassure him of their determination and confidence in winning the battle.

The accuracy of the images of the two Communist field commanders as drawn by the two authors is of course open to question. There seems to be a certain amount of exaggeration in Tu Peng-cheng's portrayal of P'eng Teh-huai. On the other hand, Wu Chiang's sketch of Ch'en Yi shows a more realistic touch. At any rate, both novelists cannot have gone to great excess in idolizing the field commanders. Since the two Communist generals are real men known to many people, the authors must give a more or less faithful characterization in order to maintain their credibility. Secondly, as there are men of higher authority and stature than the two field commanders, the authors must avoid exaggeration, which may invite displeasure from the commanders' superiors and peers. They seem to have shown a rustic, down-to-earth quality in both P'eng and Ch'en, which is largely consistent with the impressions formed by other authors such as Edgar Snow.[32] The informality and warmth the field commanders maintain in their relations with subordinates appear to have created a pervasive sense of unity in the Communist army.

Kuomintang Generals

The above discussion of the Field Army commanders serves as a contrast with the style of the Kuomintang generals. Both in the campaigns of Yenan and of south Shantung, Kuomintang commanders make serious strategic errors which talented commanders would do

[31] *Red Sun*, pp. 501–2, Barnes, pp. 603–4.

[32] See, for instance, Snow's accounts of P'eng Teh-huai in his *Red Star Over China*.

their best to avoid. In both cases, the Kuomintang troops penetrate deep into the Communist heartland where they have organized and consolidated peasant support during the years of the anti-Japanese war. Thus the Kuomintang units fight like a blind man, totally denied intelligence, through lack of support from local people. They fight in unfamiliar terrain and on Communist terms. All their modern, mechanized equipment is of no avail. Tanks cannot be used to climb mountains and cross rivers; aeroplanes are useful only for disruption and parachuting supplies. The Kuomintang logistic supply line has been so over-extended that shortage of food and munitions thoroughly destroys the morale of their soldiers. While these factors contribute greatly to their defeat in the major battles, a more fatal weakness is the distrust and rivalry between Kuomintang field commanders and their subordinate generals and among the generals themselves.[33]

In the Yenan campaign, the Kuomintang generals show a pride and complacency that virtually amount to insubordination. At the battle of P'anglungchen, the army commanders Tung Chao and Liu K'an ignore Hu Tsung-nan's signal that their troops turn back to reinforce the beleaguered brigade. They calculate that the attack on P'anglungchen is merely a Communist diversionary tactic. Liu K'an thoroughly despises Sheng Wen, Hu Tsung-nan's chief-of-staff, and considers him a man without talent. He resents the fact that Sheng Wen sits comfortably at headquarters and with his random red and blue pencil marks on the military map makes them climb all over the rugged terrain to no purpose.

The same indomitable conceit is also evident in Chung Sung, commander of the Kuomintang 36th Division. After his troops lifted the siege of Yulin and he received the congratulations of the Generalissimo, Chung Sung no longer bothers to conceal his disdain for his army commander Liu K'an. The satisfaction of a man who is confident of his immediate promotion and bright future is shown in his relaxed mood and carefree appraisal of Yulin products, wine and woollen blankets. After he has demonstrated his knowledge as a connoisseur, he casually mentions that his troops will cross the Wuting River to occupy Chench'uanpao and will then head for Shachiat'ien. When one officer reminds him of the army commander Liu K'an's signal ordering the 36th Division to stay at Chench'uanpao for further instructions, he says that he is responsible only to Hu Tsung-nan. Then he goes on to say that he has rejected Liu K'an's order because he wants to prove to Hu Tsung-nan that his troops will reach that strategic town before Liu K'an's 29th Army does. This shocks another officer who

---

[33] This fatal weakness is also reflected in *Fight for the Palm in Central China*, pp. 429–32, and in *War Drum Awakens the Spring*, pp. 331–2.

points out that such a move was not even mentioned at the divisional meeting held earlier. But Chung Sung says confidently that speed is the key to success and he wants to achieve a miracle.

Through this reckless move Chung Sung's troops are surrounded at Shachiat'ien. Now he desperately waits for reinforcements from Liu K'an. When Liu K'an's army shows no sign of moving to his rescue, he declares that he will take note of this inaction. He says that Hu Tsung-nan has sent Liu K'an a warning that if his troops fail to reach Shachiat'ien the following afternoon, he will be turned over to the military court for trial. By then it is already too late; Chung Sung's pride causes his own destruction at Shachiat'ien.

In *Red Sun* similar mutual rivalry between Kuomintang commanders trained at the Whampao Military Academy and commanders of other backgrounds is described even more explicitly. When Li Hsien-chou, deputy commander of the Second Pacified Area of the Hsuchow Pacified Region, is encircled in Leiwu, no reinforcements are sent by the Hsuchow Front Headquarters. Li's chief-of-staff gives him this advice:

'Sir! The trouble with you all your life has been that you hesitate too much. Effective force! Effective force is everything! For you and me to be taken prisoner or to die here is a small matter compared with fifty or sixty thousand men being wiped out in a day! Yes, fifty or sixty thousand! We musn't be taken in by any more of their mischievous schemes. Come on, let's get out of this area as fast as we can. Don't take any notice of them. We're not their "favorite children". They want the enemy to finish us off!'[34]

The chief-of-staff is pleading with Li Hsien-chou to break through the siege in order to maintain their strength. He knows that Li Hsien-chou has been able to hold the title of deputy regional commander because of the fifty or sixty thousand men under his command. Once his troops are put out of action, he becomes a nobody. In the staff officer's mind, the reinforcements' failure to arrive is not because they are bogged down but because Chiang's 'favorite generals' have a vicious scheme to see their defeat at the hands of the Communists. It is a sound analysis, from the personal point of view of Li Hsien-chou, but a subtle admission that they fight the Communists for no other reason than their personal ambition. It is small wonder that such an army is no match for the Communist troops who have the single goal of winning the revolution, with the resolution to sacrifice themselves if necessary. This explains why Li Hsien-chou with his fifty or sixty thousand well-equipped soldiers fails to stand and fight. He has no reason to risk his skin for the benefit of others.

[34] *Red Sun*, p. 197, Barnes, p. 232.

In contrast to Li Hsien-chou, Chang Ling-fu is Chiang Kai-shek's pride and his 74th Division considered one of China's crack forces. He has fought a brilliant battle in the Lienshui campaign, which further enhances his self-esteem. The author spares no effort in characterizing Chang Ling-fu as a man of mettle and a general of no mean ability. On the eve of the major battle, Chang's tall figure stands on the summit of Mengliangku, looking down the Yi-Meng ranges and surveying the battlefield beneath him. Standing next to Chang, Tung Yao-tsung appears short and insignificant, but the chief-of-staff knows how to please his commander. He declaims 'He reins his horse on Yi-Meng's highest peak', and invites Chang to comment on this as a line. Chang Lin-fu cannot conceal his satisfaction and magnanimously shows his approval by saying that when the war is won it should be engraved on the cliff. He never doubts that victory is in his grasp.

Then the chief-of-staff reports in a timid voice that when Chang was asleep last night the enemy had closed a gap in the encirclement. The news comes as a surprise, but Chang immediately expresses his pleasure at the prospect of engaging the enemy. He even shows his scorn for Hu Tsung-nan's capture of Yenan, which in his view is nothing but a hollow victory over a deserted city. As far as he is concerned, victory over the Communists can only be won by meeting force with force. Since his troops are the No. 1 mainstay unit, they are the only ones fit to set an example for others.

In the initial contact, Chang Lin-fu is totally satisfied with the performance of his three brigades and the 83rd Division which is also put under his command. He is especially pleased that the 83rd Division, by no means a fighting force, has done so well since its incorporation into his column. But before long he receives his brigade commander's telephone report that the 83rd Division's main position has fallen to the Communists.

'No! I don't believe it!' he told his informant.

'It's absolute chaos! They came pouring back over my positions as they withdrew and they and my unit mistook each other for the enemy and began fighting. They killed one of our battalion commanders and my men brought in one of their regimental commanders as a prisoner!'

'And quite right, too!' Chang Ling-fu roared angrily. 'I'll have him shot!' Then lowering his voice, he asked: 'How are things with you? Still no movement from the enemy?'

'We're all right. Minor contacts. This 83rd Division should be cleared out, they're only getting in everybody's way here. My men are clamoring to finish them off.'

'Get hold of their divisional commander and tell him my orders are that they counter-attack at once and recover Wanchuanshan for me. If they don't recover it I'll deal with them as prescribed by

military law and disciplinary regulations! Give that regimental
commander a good dressing-down and send him back. Tell him to
expiate his crime with some outstanding achievement! . . .'[35]

In the deteriorating battle situation, Chang Ling-fu reveals his true
color as a haughty general. He has never trusted the fighting capability
of the 83rd Division; now his distrust seems to be borne out. But it
appears likely that the 83rd Division lacks the determination to fight precisely because it has been treated as a step-child. Chang Ling-fu's disdain
for the 83rd Division is apparently shared by Lu Hsin, the brigade
commander who makes the telephone report. Lu urges that the 83rd
Division be got rid of because they are getting in his way. It is certainly
an interesting attitude to treat a friendly unit as if it is a burden. There
is the same arrogance in the brigade commander's impatient voice.
Furthermore, this virus of conceit seems to have infested the entire
division down to the soldiers of the lowest rank. Lu Hsin's men clamor
for a clean elimination of the 83rd Division.

The threat of using military discipline against the retreating
divisional commander betrays Chang Ling-fu's way of treating his
colleagues. After all they are both divisional commanders of the same
rank. By the same token, his display of rage against the captured
regimental commander shows him to be a man who mistakes authority
for leadership. The use of strict military discipline may force a unit to
fight, but in the long run it will only inject a sense of fear in the minds
of both officers and soldiers and sow the seeds for its defeat.

Chang Ling-fu's aloof contempt for other units and his unshakeable
faith in the fighting capacity of his own soldiers have led him to
penetrate deep in the Yi-Meng mountains. His 74th Division and the
83rd Division under his command are surrounded by the Communist
Third Field Army. Outside the perimeter of the Communist forces are
the Kwangsi Army under Li Tsung-jen and Pai Chung-hsi and the
heterogeneous Szechwan troops and Northeastern troops. The Communist encirclement rapidly closes in on him, while the Kuomintang
troops on the outer perimeter are unable or unwilling to come to his
help. Finally, Chang has his troops concentrated on the top of
Mengliangku for a last-ditch fight.

In a small redoubt near the summit of Mengliangku, as the shadow
of death hovers over them, Tung Yao-tsung for the first and last time
gives Chang an honest appraisal of the reasons for their defeat:

'In the battle of Leiwu Li Hsien-chou was surrounded but we units
in the central system wanted to keep ourselves intact and made no
effort to save them, with the result that they were destroyed. Now
it's our turn to be surrounded but will these units of the Kwangsi

[35] *Ibid.*, p. 457–8, Barnes, p. 550.

Army, the 7th Division and the 48th Division, fight to the death and sell their lives to save us? Our mistake was in not seeing this far ahead!'[36]

Even at this final moment, Chang Ling-fu displays his pique and unwillingness to face the truth. He is furious at his chief-of-staff's disloyalty; with a threatening look, he presses Tung to pour out all his complaints. Since everything is lost by now, Tung no longer has any fear and goes on with rare candor:

'I'm speaking as my conscience guides me at a time when death is staring us in the face. I feel that for me this moment represents the few minutes in my whole life when I have been most wide awake. If our party and our country are to be preserved intact the only way is a complete change of ideas. We must put an end to all this scheming and struggling against each other, all this stabbing each other in the back. The Communist Party is united within itself while we are divided among ourselves, cheating and deceiving each other. Ai!'[37]

Chang Ling-fu meets his death moments later; Tung Yao-tsung's words may be viewed as an unflattering obituary for a once-brilliant Kuomintang general. All this is of course the portrayal of an enemy commander by a Communist novelist. But the appraisal of weaknesses in the personality of Chang by an adversary may not be necessarily inaccurate. Wu Chiang has this to say about Chang Ling-fu:

I did not know Chang Ling-fu, only saw his photographs and his body the day after the victorious conclusion of the Mengliangku campaign. As mentioned earlier, the images of characters like Chang Ling-fu were generally formed in my mind a long time ago. In the old society ruled by warlords and the Kuomintang, I met people as ruthless and crafty as Chang Ling-fu. During the war against Japan, I even had contacts with such people and had opportunities to observe their appearance and inner feelings. In our army I did some work among prisoners of war and heard so much from captured officers and soldiers about the lives of people like Chang Ling-fu. From my direct and indirect contacts, I came to recognize that our enemies are not all simple-minded and ignorant . . . Based on historical facts and personal experiences, we must truthfully portray enemies like Chang Ling-fu . . . I kept reminding myself: never make enemy characters lifeless, artificial.[38]

The defeat of Chang Ling-fu may be viewed as the result of his personality traits, conceit, aloofness, and defiance, which are the

[36] *Ibid.*, p. 542, Barnes, p. 653.
[37] *Ibid.*, p. 543, Barnes, p. 654.
[38] Wu Chiang, 'Hsieh-tso *Hung jih* ti ch'ing-k'uang ho i-hsieh t'i-hui' (The Conditions Under Which I Wrote *Red Sun* and Some of My Comprehensions), *Jen-min wen-hsüeh*, January 1960, p. 124.

qualities of lone heroes like Kuan Yü in old romances. The same shortcomings caused Kuan Yü to lose Chingchou, which in turn made Liu Pei's plan to unify China during the period of the Three Kingdoms impossible. But such an explanation is insufficient. Chang Ling-fu has to be treated as the product of the Kuomintang military tradition. The Kuomintang troops were an assorted force, assembled under the nominal command of Chiang Kai-shek since the days of the Northern Expedition in 1927. The strategy adopted by the Generalissimo to hold heterogeneous units together is 'divide and rule.' They were never whipped into a uniform fighting army with a common goal. Yet the Civil War was not a war between generals. It was a struggle for power between two political parties. It was a contest between strategies, organizations, systems, ideas, and visions. At the battle of Mengliangku, Chang Ling-fu was in effect fighting single-handed against the best military machine built by the Chinese Communist Party.

The images of Kuomintang generals are drawn with remarkable consistency by Tu Peng-cheng and Wu Chiang. Their assessments of the Kuomintang failures in terms of its disunity, its generals' pursuit of selfish interests, and above all its lack of a uniform, larger goal are in general agreement. As individuals, Chang Ling-fu or even Chung Sung resemble the Communist regimental commander Liu Sheng in many respects. While Liu Sheng's personal heroism and reckless bravery are held in check by the effective party organization symbolized in the person of the regimental political commissar, the Kuomintang generals are allowed to act in violation of a fundamental military principle that units must act in co-ordination under the field commander. It seems only logical that a disunited army will suffer defeat at the hands of a military force which boasts of its near-perfect organization and unmatched efficiency.

Factors Contributing to the Communist Victory

It seems possible to draw larger implications from these war stories, that is, to suggest underlying factors for the Communist victory. Inferior in equipment and short in man-power, the peasant army from Yenan seems to have achieved the impossible by defeating one of the world's largest and best-armed armies at the end of the Second World War. The Communist triumph bears out Mao Tse-tung's dictum that it is man not weapon that determines the outcome of war.

Mao's thesis needs elaboration. What he means at first glance is that the will of man is the primary factor in winning a war. But there is more to this. Not only must Communist soldiers be educated to know the purpose of the revolutionary war, but also enemy soldiers must be

made aware of their mistake in fighting on the wrong side. When the
battle of Tuszukuo enters the most critical stage the head of the
political department Hsu Kun makes this suggestion:

'Now what about a political assault to tie up with the military one?
Whiskers Liu here says we should use small groups. Let's combine
mass action politically with the use of small groups as well. I think
we should send a few wounded prisoners back as the spearhead of
our attack. They can take some propaganda leaflets back with them
and carry messages by word of mouth. And give them a good square
meal before we send them back. How does that strike you? I think it's a
good idea. That staff officer who came running over in a daze, do you
know who he is? The enemy divisional commander Ho Mang's
nephew. He says the enemy are burying their wounded alive and that
the enemy troops don't know much about our policy towards
prisoners, so I think it would be useful to send a few of them back.
It'll help the officers and men on the other side realize that we're
lenient and humane. The enemy have been dosing their officers and
men with a lot of propaganda about the Communists ill-treating
their prisoners. So if we let a few of them go back it'll open their
eyes a bit. It'll be a useful weapon for attacking the enemy's minds
and breaking down their obstinacy and resistance . . .'[39]

The suggestion of the political department head reveals only one
aspect, and an obvious one at that, of the psychological warfare. The
Kuomintang army has also learned something about the use of
propaganda. Such a suggestion by itself may have some limited effect.
More fundamental is the over-all Communist strategy in the Civil War.
While the Kuomintang fights for the conquest of territory, the
Communists aim at the conquest of minds. Two of the greatest military
strategists, Sun Tzu in the East and Machiavelli in the West, have both
counselled the winning of people's minds as the ultimate determinant
of war. In a slightly different language, Karl von Clausewitz considers
war as the pursuit of a political goal by might when other means have
failed. In an extension of Von Clausewitz's famous dictum without
distorting his message, we may say that the most effective method of
waging a war is the use of political weapons. Mao is not an innovator in
stressing the importance of man over weapon, but he has most
effectively put this theory into practice.

In order to effect the disintegration of the rank and file of the
Kuomintang army, the Communists have meticulously executed a
policy of leniency toward prisoners of war. They send enemy soldiers
back to their own army or to their native villages with good meals or
with a travel allowance. The purpose is of course that they will be the

---

[39] *Red Sun*, p. 173, Barnes, p. 203.

best spokesmen for the Communists. The Communists also give careful
protection to captured Kuomintang commanders because they are more
useful alive than dead. When Li Hsien-chou, the deputy commander of
the Hsuchow Pacified Region, and Major-General Hai Ching-chang,
commander of the 188th Division, are captured, they are given good
treatment. Later, Li Hsien-chou sends a circular telegram opposing the
Civil War; Hai Ching-chang broadcasts his letter to his family over the
Communist radio. Such measures are most effective in dissolving the
fighting spirit of the Kuomintang troops.

But the conquest of the mind of the enemy remains of only
secondary importance. It is the allegiance of the people, especially that
of the peasants in the vast interior of China, that the Communists seek
to win. The support of the peasants will be the strongest possible
defense against attack. During the war of resistance against Japan, the
Communist organizational work in the base area and guerrilla-control-
led regions was so successful that when the Civil War broke out the
Kuomintang was fighting as if in an alien land.

There is a third aspect in the conquest of the mind. It is the
transformation of individual minds into a unified group. An underlying
thesis throughout our discussion, reflected consciously or unconsciously in both novels, is the channelling of interpersonal relations into
an operational pattern which will perform most effectively the function
expected by the Party to achieve the anticipated goal. This is shown in
the political education of soldiers, in the development of company-level
combat strength, in the treatment of deserters, in the cultivation of
mutual respect and trust between commanders and political commissars, and in the transmission of orders from commanders to their
subordinates. In each case, primary attention is given to human
relations. Each man is treated as a man in order not to frustrate his
feelings or to discourage his resourcefulness. At the same time, he is a
part of an organization and must perform his proper function. As a
result, everyone, from Field Army commanders to soldiers of the
lowest rank, knows precisely where he stands and will make the best
use of his brain to achieve a specific goal. When this is completed the
war over mind is won; the war against the enemy becomes merely a
matter of time.

7
LAND REFORM

During the years of development and consolidation of base areas, the Chinese Communists experimented with piecemeal measures of social, economic, and political reform. They abolished heavy taxes and levies, reduced rents, reclaimed swampy land and barren soil, formed a people's militia, established peasant associations, and instituted village-level local government. These may be called pilot projects in relatively secure villages which were used as social laboratories. Such projects, however, were given only secondary attention, while matters of a military nature received priority. The land reform program launched in the autumn of 1947 presented the Communists with the first opportunity to reorganize the broad basis of Chinese society. The full implementation of this extremely ambitious program took more than four years and was not completed until the winter of 1951. The enormous scope of the program defies human imagination: nothing in the history of man is comparable in scale.

The land reform ultimately affects the lives of a quarter of mankind, reshapes the foundation of a society with thousands of years of history, and covers a land mass spreading over approximately 6.4 per cent of the globe's surface area. It is not just an agricultural program, designed to redistribute cultivable land among the hundreds of millions of Chinese peasants. It is a program of many dimensions: economic, social, political, military, and cultural. The ultimate goal of the Chinese Communist revolution is not limited to the seizure of political power; rather, it aims to remake a civilization and reshape the destiny of the Chinese people. If there is one thing which can spark the imagination of hundreds of millions of people to join in this gigantic undertaking, it is land redistribution.

Ting Ling's *Sun over the Sangkan River*[1] and Chou Li-po's *Hurricane*[2] are stories of the implementation of the land reform

[1] Ting Ling, *T'ai-yang chao tsai sang-kan ho shang* (Peking: New China Book Co., November 1949); '*Sun over the Sangkan River*', *Chinese Literature*, Spring 1953, pp. 26–296.
[2] Chou Li-po, *Pao-feng chou-yü* (Tientsin: New China Book Co., reprint, May 1949); *The Hurricane*, trans. by Hsu Meng-hsiung, (Peking: Foreign Languages Press, 1955).

183

program in small villages. Nuanshui, Hopei, the scene of land reform in *Sun over the Sangkan River*, is a village of some two hundred households or a population of about one thousand. Yuanmao where the story of *The Hurricane* takes place is a village in north Manchuria, twice the size of Nuanshui, with four hundred households. But there are much smaller villages with only fifty households or less. If we take Nuanshui as a village of average size, then we can count more than half a million villages which will eventually go through the same process of land reform. If in each case ten cadres take part in the program, it requires an army of five million cadres. The huge manpower necessary is a further measure of the immensity of the land reform program.

Both Ting Ling and Chou Li-po personally took part, and converted their experiences into stories of outstanding quality,[3] not as artistic works but as remarkable social documents. Most characters in *Sun over the Sangkan River* are superficially observed, and are not drawn in depth.[4] They are introduced by a biographical narrative and thereafter hardly characterized at all.[5] These are the comments of unsympathetic critics after Ting Ling has been officially censured, but her close friend, Feng Hsüeh-feng, had this to say in an earlier review:

> Obviously, the author draws characters to serve the purpose of portraying society or life, that is, primarily to serve the purpose of portraying the rural class struggle (land reform).[6]

[3] *Sun over the Sangkan River* won the Second Stalin Prize for Literature and *The Hurricane* the Third Prize in 1951. It is questionable whether the awards suggest an appraisal of the novels' artistic merits by Soviet literary critics. *Sun over the Sangkan River*, however, has been translated into Russian, Ukrainian, Lithuanian, Latvian, Rumanian, Czechoslovak, Hungarian, Polish, Bulgarian, Japanese, German, and Mongolian and is reported to have received considerable attention in these countries. See 'Su-lien ta-shih-kuan tai-piao ssu-ta-lin chiang-chin wei-yüan-hui shou-yü Ting Ling teng ssu-ta-lin chiang-chin' (The Soviet Embassy Representing the Stalin Award Committee Confers Stalin Literary Prizes on Ting Ling and others), *Wen-i pao*, Nos. 11/12, June 25, 1952, p. 7. The same source reveals that *The Hurricane* has abridged Russian and Japanese translations and complete Hungarian and Czechoslovak translations.
[4] Chu K'o-yü 'Lun *T'ai-yang chao tsai sang-kan ho shang*' (On *Sun over the Sangkan River*), *Jen-min wen-hsüeh*, No. 95, October 1957, p. 116. In a footnote the author says that the article was submitted to *Jen-min wen-hsüeh* in October 1949, but was rejected. Its revised version was accepted only after the exposure of the Ting-Ch'en anti-Party clique.
[5] Wang Liao-ying, '*T'ai-yang chao tsai sang-kan ho shang* chiu-ching shih shih-mo-yang ti tso-p'in' (What Kind of Work Is *Sun over the Sangkan River*?), *Wen-hsüeh p'ing-lun*, No. 1, February 1959, p. 67.
[6] Feng Hsüeh-feng, '*T'ai-yang chao tsai sang-kan ho shang* tsai wo-men wen-hsüeh fa-chan shang ti i-i' (The Significance of *Sun over the Sangkan River* in Our Literary Development), *Wen-i pao*, No. 10, May 1952, p. 27.

Feng Hsüeh-feng argues, in effect, that Ting Ling focuses on land reform rather than character and that the characters do not exist for their own sakes but only to illustrate the impact of land reform. He further holds that the strength of the novel lies in its reflection of the peasants' reservations and scepticism toward the Communist victory, and of their fatalistic attitude, which are an underlying theme throughout the story.[7]

The Hurricane was similarly received. Though he considered the novel's characterization rather over-simplified and its plot structure unsophisticated, one commentator nevertheless gave this general assessment:

> *The Hurricane* comprehensively describes the whole process of rural land reform and faithfully reflects the behavior and inner feelings of people of various classes and the struggle between them.[8]

At any rate, Chinese novels such as *Red Crag* and *The Thundering Yangtse* are superior in characterization and dramatization of events. But the two stories of land reform offer exhaustive documentation. They were recommended reading for cadres who were to initiate land reform in the winter of 1951. It was pointed out that cadres could learn about intellectual cadres' weaknesses, the conflict between landlords and poor and tenant peasants, and the mass line policy.[9]

Though a Communist with a personal history going back to the 30s, Ting Ling is a renowned maverick. Her short story 'In the Hospital' and her essay 'Thoughts on March 8', voicing dissatisfaction with Communist practices in Yenan, got her into serious trouble. After studying for two years in party schools, she went to the villages and subsequently wrote *Sun over the Sangkan River*.[10] Because of her rivalry with Chou Yang as well as her arrogance after winning the Stalin Prize, she was attacked again in 1955–7.[11] Chou Li-po is also an uncompromising writer and his *Hurricane* is considered an honest piece of work.[12] Both authors seem serious enough to warrant our accepting their stories as authentic reports of what actually happened in the

---

[7] *Ibid.*, p. 25.

[8] Ch'en Yung, *'Pao-feng chou-yü'* (On *The Hurricane*), *Wen-i pao*, Nos. 11/12, June 1952, p. 35.

[9] Hsiung Pai-shih, 'Wo-men ts'ung *Sang-kan ho shang* yü *Pao-feng chou-yü* li hsüeh-hsi shih-mo' (What Can We Learn from *The Sangkan River* and *The Hurricane*), *Chung-kuo ch'ing-nien*, No. 80, Dec. 8, 1951, pp. 20–2.

[10] Merle Goldman, *Literary Dissent in Communist China* (Harvard University Press, 1967), pp. 22–4, 42–4, and 93–4.

[11] *Ibid.*, pp. 207–16.

[12] T. A. Hsia, 'Heroes and Hero-Worship in Chinese Communist Fiction', *The China Quarterly*, No. 13, January/March 1963, pp. 116–18.

microcosm of a small village during the process of land reform. Although their observations of the problems in land reform are subtle, discriminating, and penetrating, actual problems encountered must have been manifold. Even so, from their stories one can perceive the complexities of land reform and the intricacies of the interaction between cadres and peasants, as well as between political pressures and social forces.

The Work Team and Local Cadres

When the three-man work team arrives at Nuanshui in the lower reaches of the Sangkan River the village had already gone through the initial stage of land reform. A struggle meeting against the landlord Hsu had been held the year before. It was a relatively easy job; in Hsu's absence, everyone dared stand up and make accusations. In the spring, a second mass meeting was organized, to settle accounts with the landlords. Everyone knew who the landlords were, but refused to challenge them for fear of reprisals. As a result, Hou Tien-k'uei, a man of weaker stuff, was chosen as scapegoat. The villagers were bold enough to point accusing fingers at the old man, for he was already so feeble that he had to spend most of his time in bed. Even so, they kept a wary eye on Ch'ien Wen-kuei, the man who had been the unchallenged authority in the village despite the 'change of dynasties'. The villagers proceeded at a measured pace; after each step, they waited for Ch'ien's reaction. When the struggle was over Hou surrendered some grain and land, which were divided among poor peasants. One Hou Chung-ch'uan even secretly returned one and one half *mou* of land to the landlord, but denied it vigorously when the peasants' association investigated the matter.

Things have returned to normal. The villagers have no understanding of political power. The village chief remains the same landlord who served the Japanese in the war years and was overthrown the year before. But he has been reinstated, on the grounds that someone is needed to do the donkey work, and since he is rich, he can afford to put off his own work. The cadre who proposed the reinstatement of the landlord as village chief had received two bushels of grain from him, through a third party.

Other landlords have made the necessary adjustments to cope with the new political reality. Ch'ien Wen-kuei, the man who used to rule the village without assuming the official title, has made all possible arrangements to protect his property. First, he has divided fifty *mou* of land between his two sons and registered them as separate families, although they still live and eat together. He has sent his second son to join the People's Liberation Army, so he has the status of an army dependent. He has married off his daughter to the village security officer and is trying at present to secure the support of the peasants' association by encouraging his niece to marry the association's chairman. The relations between local cadres and landlords have become so entangled that land reform virtually comes to a complete halt.

There are other forces at work. Rumors of all sorts are widespread. Hsu, the overthrown landlord, is said to be on his way back. The Eighth Route Army is not expected to be around very long; the Kuomintang troops are reportedly closing in with modern weapons and American backing. The people's attitude wavers. They begin to behave in accordance with an old saying that it is always best not to take the lead but to leave room for retreat. The local cadres can do nothing to stop the rumors, to squash the talk of a Kuomintang counter-attack, or to assure the villagers of an ultimate Communist victory. As the local people have known them since they wore diapers, they can claim neither special knowledge of current affairs nor forewarning of future political developments.

Superstition is another element which works to undermine the land reform. A widow who claims to possess a certain supernatural power has spread word that a snake was seen under the eaves of her house and that it was Goddess White reverting to her original form. She says she has received a message from this goddess, that the true dragon emperor is holding court in Peking and all China will soon be united in peace. People must behave themselves in order to be rewarded by Heaven. There is a great revival of belief in *karma*. The landlord Hou Tien-k'uei, who founded I-Kuan Tao (One Unity Taoism), again asks people to join the cult. He is telling people, 'In a time of desolation and confusion all men are bound to suffer. But once you become adepts in this religion, you can ride a swift horse to the Western Paradise.' He urges everyone to be a connecting link with the primal Buddha Maitraya. The problems created by superstition are much more profound and pervasive than local cadres can handle. Besides, some of the cadres are susceptible to the influence of superstition themselves. After all, they have been brought up in the same tradition, exposed to the same system of belief, and have accepted gods and spirits as part of the folk heritage.

Cadres are sent from outside to offset the influence of blood relationship and friendship and to cope with well-entrenched social forces. But there is another reason. The local cadres are usually new party members, recruited since the last struggle meetings; only a few can read and write. Serious conflicts, however, soon arise between the cadres sent from outside the district and the local recruits. The outside cadres suspect that land reform has come to a stop because the local cadres have formed an alliance with the landlords. This suspicion appears to be borne out by the facts, but it is often impossible to identify the people who have betrayed the party. In addition to their ignorance of local affairs, the outside cadres have a certain intellectual arrogance. The leader of the work team, Comrade Wen, looks down on local cadres as illiterate, and considers himself well-read. He seems to have hinted that he is a university student or even a university professor. He offers himself as a specialist on political economy, and a gifted leader of the mass movement.

One of the local leaders is Old Tung, chairman of the district workers' union. After three years in the Party, this ex-laborer has learned to write. Whenever he has any free time he loves to sit down and write letters. He always carries envelopes and stationery with the union's official letterhead; it is handy in case he has to write an urgent message. He loves to deliver speeches and always begins with the cliché: 'Land reform is to do away with the feudalistic landlords who exploit the people . . .' After talking about the elimination of worries and fears, he would drag in strikes of Canadian workers and Italian sailors or similar stories he had heard somewhere. He clearly receives great satisfaction from speeches like this, but does not seem to care whether his listeners can make head or tail of what he is saying.

One such talk is cut short by the intervention of the leader of the work team. But Comrade Wen is a man of the same type, though on a slightly higher level. When he takes over the platform, he spends six long hours explaining point by point the directives for carrying out land reform. The next evening, the number of people attending the meeting has visibly decreased, but Comrade Wen is not discouraged. In order to overcome the peasants' fear of the return of the landlords, he reasons that it is crucial to raise their level of political education. This time he starts with the history of man and explains how history is made. Then, analysing the political situation in China and abroad, he talks about the activities of democratic parties in the Kuomintang-controlled areas, the hatred of Kuomintang soldiers for the war, and the military strength of the Soviet Union. In his broad coverage of current affairs, he mentions American correspondents Agnes Smedley and Edgar Snow, the Marshall Mission, and the assassination of the progressive professors Wen Yi-to and Li Kung-p'o by Kuomintang agents. By the time he reaches the point of the War of Liberation, most of his listeners have fallen fast asleep.

Apart from his weakness for making long speeches, the team leader displays another equally serious failing. He is smug and self-satisfied, and always relies on his own judgment. He does not trust the other two team members and regards them as fit only for doing the donkey work or arranging meetings. To his mind the most urgent task in steering a movement is to guide the thought of the masses. He has a strong bias against the local party secretary, Chang Yu-min, because he has been told that Chang was once a member of the *Ko-lao Hui* (Elder Brother Society). On the strength of this preconception, he manages to see traits of banditry in the local party leader.

Chang Yu-min seems to be portrayed as a dedicated party man who has become uncertain because of his inability to identify the target of the struggle. He knows that the landlord Ch'ien Wen-kuei is the worst of their oppressors. But since Ch'ien's son is now a PLA soldier and his daughter has married a local cadre, Chang is no longer sure that Ch'ien should be their target. Clearly, he does not understand the meaning of the mass line, for he feels that the last two struggle meetings have been easy, because the people listened to him. Now he is no longer sure that he can rally the necessary support.

There are activists like Liu Man, who played an important role in the past struggles, in the village. As a matter of fact, Liu had become a party member, but recently his membership had been suspended, due to a quarrel with the security officer Chang Cheng-tien, son-in-law of the landlord Ch'ien. Liu Man is a forthright and hot-tempered man. When he is frustrated he becomes utterly inarticulate. Thus he leaves a very bad impression on the team leader, who considers him insane. The case of Liu Man has frustrated the enthusiasm of other activists.

These are problems encountered in the process of land reform in Nuanshui. Some have their roots in the cultural tradition of the village. A few are created by landlords who have attempted to assume a revolutionary posture in order to bleach out their past anti-Communist record and to neutralize the hostility of local cadres. Still other problems either emerge as the outcome of the usual conflict between outside and local cadres or are caused by the arrogance of intellectuals who have no idea of life in the countryside.

The Masses and the Mass Line

In order to accelerate the pace of land reform, cadres have been urged by the Party to rely on the masses and to follow the mass line. This principle sounds clear and simple, but proves otherwise when it is applied to local conditions. A villager called Hou Chung-ch'uan epitomizes the backward elements. Hou used to be a different man when he was in his twenties. He had two years of schooling, learned to read vernacular tales and plays about brave heroes, chaste women, loyal ministers, and faithful servants, and loved to tell these stories to the villagers. His family had nineteen and a half *mou* of land and lived in a three-room tiled house. He was the envy of other young peasants because he married a pretty girl who bore him a chubby son. Then one lean year he borrowed three bushels of grain from his great-uncle. When

he was unable to pay back the debt the next year, his great-uncle told
him to send over his young wife to help with the housework. As the
demand was not unreasonable, he could not very well reject it. But his
wife was seduced by his great-uncle's older son. His ideal of chaste
women exacerbated his rage when he learned about it. He called his
wife home, gave her a sound beating, and threatened to get a divorce.
That very night she jumped into a well and was drowned. His
great-uncle's son could not forget the woman and urged her family to
file a lawsuit. Hou lost, was jailed for two months, and had to sell land
to pay his fine. Hou's father died a broken man; his mother had to
borrow money for the funeral. After this series of misfortunes, Hou left
home to seek his fortune outside the Great Wall as a camel driver. After
five years of vagabond life, he returned to settle in his native village. By
this time he was a different man and had totally surrendered himself to
fate. His great-uncle and the uncle who had seduced his wife had both
died, and his second uncle, Hou Tien-k'uei, urged him to be a tenant.
This uncle was a kind-hearted, pious man, who advised Chung-ch'uan to
believe in Heaven and the gods. Chung-ch'uan thus became a willing
believer in One Unity Taoism, *karma*, and fatalism.

When Hou Tien-k'uei became the target of attack the previous
spring, Chung-ch'uan was urged by cadres to settle accounts with the
landlord whose father and brother had been the cause of his ruin. Now
over sixty years old, Chung-ch'uan regarded his tenant position as
analogous to that of a servant, and found the idea of disloyalty to his
benefactor repugnant. Since he could find no way out, he went to Hou,
as he was told.

... Hou was lying in bed, and asked: 'Who's that in the yard?'
'It's me, uncle,' Chung-ch'uan had said.
'Oh, you, what do you want?'
'Nothing,' said Chung-ch'uan. 'I just came to see you, uncle.'
Having said this he found a broom and started sweeping the yard.
'Oh! You really are a good sort after all, I thought you'd come to
settle scores too. If you want to settle them you'll have to go to the
King of Hell, and let him decide whose things these are destined to
be! By the way, Chung, you can forget about those $10,000[13] you
owe me. We're the same family. After all these years we can count
on each other's friendship.'
'Oh, that won't do, that won't do ...'
When Chung-ch'uan went out and people outside asked him if he
had settled accounts, he said, 'Yes, it's all settled. I still owe him
$10,000!' Later the Peasants' Association gave him one and a half
mou of land, and he actually returned it secretly.[14]

[13] Actually a small amount due to the unprecedented run-away inflation in
China at the time.
[14] *Sun over the Sangkan River*, pp. 282–3, *Chinese Literature*, Spring 1953,
pp. 191–2.

Hou Chung-ch'uan became a laughing stock in the village; cadres used his case as an example for educating backward elements. They attempted to convince the villagers that land does not yield grain by itself, but only because tenant peasants cultivate it and spread manure to enrich it. They have to live on husks of beans, wheat, and rice after laboring from dawn to dusk, year in year out; landlords, on the other hand, can eat good rice and flour without stirring a finger. Thus peasants should not give grain to landlords. Such arguments are easily understood, but villagers are still afraid of going to landlords and demanding title deeds.

After Li Tzu-chun, one of the landlords, has disappeared, the cadres urge a number of tenants to go to Li's mansion to demand the title deeds. Their taunts seem to have an effect, and some of them agree to go. One elderly peasant is still reluctant, for he argues that only a woman is left behind in the landlord's house. He is reduced to silence when asked if the woman does not also suck his blood. Even when they finally leave the office of the peasants' association, they remain uncertain and reluctant.

They are actually expected. As the tenants stand in the empty courtyard not knowing where to start, Li's wife comes out from behind the bamboo curtain with a red lacquered box. She kneels down in front of the peasants, tears streaming down her cheeks, and begs them to pity a poor woman and her children. She admits the guilt of being a landlord and curses her husband, but asks them to spare her and her children. As she kowtows to the peasants, her two little children start howling. All the peasants who have spoken boldly of getting even with the Lis now find themselves struck dumb. They do not know what to do with the woman, whom they have always thought of as a noble lady. They begin to remember her little acts of charity; a few are terribly moved by her present plight. Somebody sighs, turns, and retreats to the very back of the courtyard.

One of the tenants slipped out, followed by another. The whole group gradually retreated in disorder till only Po-jen was left standing there dazed, wanting to say something, but not knowing how to say it. The woman stood up and said, crying: 'Uncle, sit down a little before you go. You've known us for a long time. Please forgive us for the wrongs we have done you. Please, uncle, be generous. And we, mother and children, will repay you bit by bit. My husband ought to be blamed. See how he's gone off without caring what happens to us, going off like that! I must be fated to be unfortunate! Please uncle take these title deeds to the Peasants' Association, and do say a few good words for me and the children. Our life is in your hands!'

Po-jen looked distressed too, and said: 'Don't cry, we're all old tenants. We can talk things over. It was the Peasants' Association that told us to come. As for the title deeds, you keep them. You'd better have a rest. I'll be going too.'[15]

Peasants all want land. Most of them have labored all their lives without owning so much as a small tract. Land has been their dream for generations, but it has always been beyond their reach. Now the cadres argue that since they work the land, they should be the lawful owners. Nevertheless, the idea of economic exploitation is new to them, and not understood. They are accustomed to the notion that land must be earned by one's own sweat and toil. They do not see landlords as exploiters but as neighbors, friends, or relatives. They believe in fate. The vicissitudes of life are predetermined; some are born rich, others poor. It is impossible to alter a man's destiny; any such attempt is doomed to fail. There are other considerations and reservations. No one knows how long the Communist rule will last, when the Kuomintang will return, and the overthrown landlords with them, and whether they will eventually be held responsible for revolt against the proper order.

The policy of the Communist Party is not to divide land for peasants but for peasants to demand, distribute, and keep land all by themselves. The Party cannot do it for them. It actually did so in the past, only to find some peasants like Hou Chung-ch'uan secretly returning the land to the landlord. Moreover, it is not just a matter of redistributing land; it is a method of political education. Unless peasants are taught their right to own land, the reform is meaningless. Otherwise they will never be their own masters and learn to protect their own rights, even without landlords. If they do not take the initiative in protecting their interests, they cannot be counted on to defend the land against the Kuomintang and the restoration of the landlord class.

Land reform can be accomplished only by mobilizing the peasants, by changing their fatalistic attitude, and by making them aware that it is labor, not land, which produces grain. Such a task cannot be achieved by mere persuasion. The masses must be aroused to see their own poverty, by contrasting their own misery with the luxury and waste of the wealthy, and by fanning their tacit hatred for landlords who charged them high interest and ruthlessly took away their land for old debts. Once peasants are aroused, they are no less ruthless. They will know how to settle accounts and to demand that their blood debts are paid. This is what is called the mass line. The policy does not mean that the masses spontaneously know what they want, how to get what they want, and how to keep what they get. Given the backward state of Chinese peasants, who are illiterate and demoralized by the control of

---

[15] *Ibid.*, p. 229, *Chinese Literature*, p. 159.

the landlord class, they will never be able to take the initiative of fighting landlords by themselves.

To settle accounts with the landlords, the masses must first of all change their peasant mentality. They must forget their social relationship with landlords as relatives, neighbors, and friends, in order to see the economic relationship of exploiter and tenant. The severance of social relations is a necessary first step. It is called in Communist parlance '*hua-ch'ing chieh-chi chieh-hsien*' (demarcating class line). This too is not an easy task. A momentum must be created to focus on the past exploitations by landlords, especially blood debts resulting from exploitation. Once the peasants' hatred for landlords is aroused, events will take care of themselves. The sweet taste of revenge, together with the prospect of taking land from landlords, is sufficient to turn the most docile peasants into blood-thirsty avenging angels.

When the work team and local cadres are facing the difficulty of speeding up the land reform in Nuanshui, a man crosses the Sangkan River to enter the village. He is Chang Pin, propaganda commissar of the county Party committee. Armed with the simple guideline that landless peasants must have land, Chang Pin acts with resolve and expedition. The first thing he does is to call a Party meeting where everyone, including the local Party secretary, makes a public confession of their faults. The cadres must draw a clear-cut class line themselves, so peasants will have faith in them and do the same. At the meeting, a decision is quickly reached to settle accounts with Ch'ien Wen-kuei, the number one class enemy. That Ch'ien is an army dependent and the father-in-law of a local cadre no longer gives him protection, for a class line is drawn to separate him from the rest of the village.

The Party meeting sets up the momentum. The tempo of settling accounts with the landlord Ch'ien is suddenly accelerated. His son-in-law is deprived of his job as security officer and immediately isolated. Anyone who has connived with the landlord loses his Party affiliation and becomes an enemy of the people himself. Such a decision is drastic enough to rectify the wavering attitude of other cadres. After all the tangled relations with the landlord are neatly cut off, he becomes nothing but a culprit at the mercy of the people. A mass meeting is arranged for the next day to allow peasants to pour out their bitterness against the landlord and settle all old scores with him.

Once preparations are carefully made, the only worry is that the peasants may go too far. Chang Pin, the county cadre, does not stay for the struggle meeting, for he knows that from now on events will take their own course and that nothing else is left for him to do here. The conversations between Chang Pin and the local party secretary Chang Yu-min before the former's departure conveys the essence of the land reform:

Yu-min looked at him and he looked at Yu-min. Both realized what the problem was, and after a long interval Pin had to say: 'Whatever happens don't let him be killed.'

'In that case we'd better hand him over to you.'

Pin started thinking hard again. He could not think of a good solution. He was used to working in villages and understood the psychology of peasants; either don't attack or attack to kill. They did not like going through legal procedures, fearing that if they did so, someone they thought deserved death might only be imprisoned. They often felt the Eighth Route Army was too lenient. They were not yet able to take a longer view, but clamoured for revenge, for a clean sweep. The peasants in some villages just killed their hated oppressors under a rain of fists. The district and village cadres all put the blame on the masses, but there were so many people it was impossible to say who was responsible. Pin knew too that the village cadres, just like the masses, worried in case the tables should be turned in future, and were therefore eager to do the job thoroughly. To persuade so many people at short notice was far from easy.

'No need to hand him over to us. The county government can't settle so many cases all at once. Better settle it in the village.'

'Uh huh'. Yu-min realized the difficulty too. He was rather at a loss and said: 'You understand the whole situation, don't you? Whether the people will be enthusiastic or not depends entirely on this.'

'Is that the way you feel too?' asked Pin.

'Most of the cadres feel that way.'

'That means you fear the reactionaries may come back. We ought to correct that outlook. Killing people at will isn't good. We can collect statements of his crimes to give the law court. Execution ought to be legally carried out. In agitating nowadays we defeat landlords on political grounds, wanting them to bow to the people, not necessarily wanting to destroy them . . .'[16]

The policy of the Communist Party is to destroy a landlord not physically but politically. It is not his life but his socio-economic-political power that must be destroyed. Peasants want to kill the landlord, for they are still worried and scared. So are the cadres, who also feel that unless he is disposed of, there remains the danger of his coming back to power. Only by overcoming this fear will people be psychologically armed in the political struggle against the Kuomintang and its power base, the landlord class. The fear can remain, even if the landlord is physically eliminated. His ghost will still live in the minds of the peasants and haunt the village.

There is an even more compelling reason for keeping the landlord alive. Once the landlord is deprived of all economic, social, and political power, he is not only harmless but actually useful as a living warning. This is what is called 'teaching through negative example'.

Both Ting Ling and Chou Li-po make it crystal clear that struggle meetings are engineered by cadres, to provide an opportunity for political education, not only for the masses but also for their own benefit. Even people like Wen Ts'ai, the team leader, and Chang Yu-min, the local party secretary, can learn lessons from the enthusiasm and excitement of the mass struggle. They have always underestimated the power of the masses. The intellectual Wen Ts'ai will never again forget the potential of collective struggle and the capacity of an aroused peasant population. Chang Yu-min, who used to think that class struggle is possible only when people follow the leader realizes the latent strength of the masses.

Ting Ling is a sharp observer, but her penetrating insight is limited to the initial stages of land reform. She is at her best in depicting the tangled social relations in the village, conflicts between outside and local cadres, and differences between the cadres and the masses. By shrewdly describing the psychology of peasants, their inner ambivalence and contradiction, she accomplishes the difficult task of showing land reform not simply as an economic and political revolution but also as a process of transforming the peasant mentality. Her description of protest meetings, on the other hand, is a hasty job. One gets the impression that she rushes to conclusions without considering the importance of the meeting itself. All work, such as exposing the schemes of landlords, uniting with active elements among the masses, and rectifying the wavering attitudes of some of the cadres, is really preliminary to the climax – the mass meeting. But in *Sun over the Sangkan River* the meeting is quickly over, after a few peasants make the accusations, and Ch'ien Wen-kuei admits to all the charges and signs a letter of repentance. Such summary treatment fails to demonstrate the real transformation of the masses. It is in Chou Li-po's *Hurricane* that we get a clearer picture of how mass meetings are used to destroy not a particular landlord but the whole Chinese feudal system.

Struggle Meetings

Land reform in Yuanmao, as portrayed in *The Hurricane*, faces quite different problems. The village has only recently come under Communist control. The fourteen-member work team finds the village totally unprepared for land reform. The peasants' only experience with the Communists is a brief contact with Communist soldiers when a battalion of the Eighth Route Army drove some bandits from the village earlier in the year. But the good impression left on the villagers by the behavior of the Communist soldiers paves the way for co-operation between the work team and the peasants. There are no local cadres or Communists the team can count on to start the land reform.

The work team consists of Hsiao Hsiang, the team leader, Liu Sheng, an intellectual type, Little Wang, a semi-literate young man, Hsiao's orderly, and a ten-man squad of soldiers. As strangers in the village, they first hold a meeting to decide on strategy. Liu Sheng, an impatient man, is for an immediate mass meeting, while Hsiao stresses the importance of initial contact with the villagers and preliminary study of local conditions. When Liu Sheng's view receives the support of the majority of team members, a mass meeting is scheduled for the next day.

The meeting is not well attended. Liu Sheng tries to explain the goals of land reform and to urge peasants to rise against the landlords. When he asks whether they should tackle the landlords he gains the support of a dozen voices. When he asks them to identify the local landlords he is met with only silence. Somebody says that there are no landlords around, but they can tackle them in other villages. Others say whatever the government says goes. They are pleased that the work team is here to help the poor. After this perfunctory talk, people begin to excuse themselves on the grounds that it is late and that tomorrow morning they have work to attend to. The first meeting proves fruitless as no one is willing to speak out.

After the meeting, the work team decides on a different method. The next day they approach only poor peasants and tenants, knowing that these people have nothing to fear as they have nothing to lose. The cadres exchange personal experiences with poor villagers; on the basis of their common background mutual trust and friendship are gradually built. Once local activists are discovered and their co-operation is assured, the team gathers data about the criminal activities of local landlords. With such information available, they are able to decide on Han Number Six as the target for attack.

The real name of Han Number Six is Han Feng-chi. An opium addict, he is lean and bald and looks well over fifty, though he is actually in his late forties. He has been the village head, under the puppet Manchukuo; with the support of the Japanese he has accumulated a large fortune. His land includes ten thousand *mou* on the north bank of the Sungari, over two thousand *mou* in Pinhsien county, and about one thousand *mou* in Yuanmao. He also holds shares in a Japanese timber company and owns one third of the shares of the distillery in a nearby town. After the defeat of the Japanese, Han's days seemed numbered. But he again became the undisputed local ruler when the Kuomintang Vanguard Assault Army incorporated the armed gangs of his two brothers. Seizing this opportunity, he sent his son to join the Kuomintang army. Through these connections, he was appointed the interim head of Yuanmao village. Once again he is in a position to impose taxes on the villagers.

When the work team inquires about Han Number Six no one is willing to discuss Han's affairs. Even Old Sun the carter, usually a talkative man, is silent and changes the subject. The people in Yuanmao have lived too long under Han's shadow to risk their lives by talking behind his back. Those who actually hate Han nevertheless decide to play safe by adopting a wait-and-see attitude. A few have been bought by Han, who solicited their support in exchange for rent exemption. The great majority of peasants entertain a strong doubt about whether the Communist officials are any different from those they used to know. In their experience, a newly-appointed official always likes to pick quarrels with influential local people, but before long they become bosom friends or even sworn brothers. Han himself also shares this feeling and believes that the work team can be purchased. He actually sends his man to deliver a red invitation card to the team leader, begging his honor to dine with him at his 'humble abode'. If the invitation is accepted and the team leader actually dines with him, then everything else is negotiable. Such a scheme has worked so well with officials of Manchukuo and later with Kuomintang representatives that Han is confident that it cannot fail. But he is wrong this time; the invitation is rejected, with a stiff warning.

The second mass meeting is more lively. After several days of working among poor peasants, the team members have won the confidence and trust of some young men. These young peasants become very aggressive at the meeting and talk about the sufferings caused by Han. It is Han who co-operated with the Japanese by conscripting peasants for forced labor. It is Han who seized their land by illegal means, took away their daughters or women simply because they were not bad-looking, and hired them as farm laborers without pay. These stories are familiar to those attending the meeting: the recollections of their old sufferings begin to foment a sense of hatred and a desire for revenge. At this point, the team leader grasps his opportunity and in an almost inaudible voice urges the activist Chao Yu-lin to throw in an inciting question. There follows a series of questions, designed not to inviting discussion but to appeal to mob psychology. 'Is Han a bad man or good man?' 'Should we settle accounts with him?' 'Have we the courage to settle accounts with him?' When the crowd roar positive answers in unison, the inevitable battle cry is 'Let's go and get that bastard!'

Chao Yu-lin leads the crowd with an automatic in one hand and a rope in the other, handed to him by Little Wang of the work team. But on

the way to the Han mansion, someone disappears into the darkness.
Half way there, another starts to lag behind and slips into a roadside
shed. The rest manage to march on, but soon they are met head on by
two men. It is Han and his bodyguard. This unexpected encounter
startles even the activist Chao, who instinctively hides the rope behind
his back. In his usual high-pitched, authoritative tone, Han says that he
has come to offer himself for arrest. His initiative thoroughly disarms
the group, while older peasants all take to their heels. Han becomes
even more arrogant and wants to find out from the team leader why
Chao should come in the dead of night to arrest him for no reason at
all. Unable to match Han's eloquence, Chao becomes defensive and says
that Han can go ahead and accuse him. The first battle with Han turns
into a fiasco; the rope is not used.

Han proves a hard man to deal with. Once in the schoolhouse where
the work team has set up its headquarters, he conceals his hatred and
extends his hospitality by offering the north wing of his mansion for
the team's official use. When his friendly gesture fails he again demands
an explanation for being taken into custody. He is soon joined by his
wife and concubine, wailing and beating their breasts. Before long the
schoolhouse is crowded with Han's relatives and friends; a petition with
names, fingerprints, or seals of over thirty people is produced. They all
vouch for Han's innocence and request that he should be released on
bail. Seeing all this is to no avail, Han tells them to disperse, and asks
his women to send him cigarettes, dishes, and wine. When the food
arrives he calmly invites the team leader Hsiao to join him.

That night, when Hsiao goes out to make a round in the village, a
bullet is fired at him and only barely misses him. The next day rumors
spread all over the village. Hsiao, the team leader, is said to have drunk
wine with Han Number Six. He is reported to have said that as
strangers, they needed Han's help, whereupon the latter had immediately offered his services. The shooting is attributed to Han Number
Seven who has come back from the mountains to rescue his brother. He
had been stopped by Han Number Six, who said that everything was
settled, and the team leader and he had agreed to co-operate. The team
leader is overheard apologizing for the misunderstanding. As the rumors
spread, they become even more convincing. It is said that the team leader
and Han have kowtowed to each other and have become sworn
brothers. Han had gone home to prepare a reception, more expensive
this time, in honor of the work team.

The mass meeting is held as scheduled. A temporary platform is set
up, made of six tables and twelve planks. On the trunks of two poplars
by the platform the team workers have stuck up posters with slogans
reading: 'Peasants of Yuanmao Meet to Settle Scores!' and 'Down with
the Local Despot Han Feng-chi!' Han is led, unbound, to the platform.

Seeing that his family, relatives, and friends are scattered everywhere among the crowd, Han is relaxed, lights a cigarette, and sits down next to one of the cadres. The rumor that Han and the team have been reconciled seems to have been substantiated.

After the meeting is declared open, only three or four peasants stand up to accuse Han. A certain momentum seems to have gathered force when many shout slogans at the prompting of Little Wang of the work team. Some even attempt to get at Han, but the platform is too high for them to reach him. Then Han's men begin to divert the attention of the crowd to some trifles. Others request Han to offer his land voluntarily. Han quickly agrees to part with five hundred *mou* of land, surrender five horses, and offer some worn-out clothes. Many in the crowd begin to feel that they have gone far enough and besides, they have a lot to do in the fields. It is already noon, so the meeting has to be adjourned.

When the meeting is over Hsiao orders the release of Han. The landlord keeps his word and has the horses and clothes delivered to the schoolhouse. They are distributed to needy peasants, but before long all are returned. Hsiao then orders them to be sent back to Han. It has been a total débâcle. Liu Sheng immediately ties up his bedding roll, and is ready to leave. He cannot take any more frustration, and wants to go to Harbin. Little Wang is so angry that he addresses Hsiao Hsiang as 'team leader' instead of, as usual, 'Old Hsiao' or 'Comrade Hsiao'. He actually accuses Hsiao of capitulating to the landlord. Hsiao manages to keep the team from falling apart by this powerful and convincing argument:

> 'I could easily have kept Han in custody — or even put a bullet through him. But the point is — have the masses risen? They must act of their own accord. If we can't work patiently on the masses so that they take their destiny into their own hands and level the feudalistic strongholds to the ground, we can't overthrow feudalism...'[17]

In other words, this is not a struggle against Han Number Six. It is a rehearsal for the exercise of political power by the peasants. Hsiao has in his possession more than sufficient evidence about Han's past criminal activities under Manchukuo. He can easily produce the evidence, call upon witnesses, and have him sentenced to death. But what is involved, however, is not simply a legal case but a revolution, whose purpose is to change the socio-economic basis of power. The landlord is the symbol of the ruling class in the old society; it is not he but the class which must be destroyed. The landlord class cannot be destroyed even if all landlords are eliminated, for pretty soon new

---

[17] *The Hurricane*, Vol. I, p. 101, Hsu, pp. 68–9.

landlords will emerge. It is the idea of exploitation which must be eliminated from people's minds.

The Communist revolution is an enormous task which involves every villager. It is not enough to cultivate a few activists; the masses must be mobilized. The mass meeting is a session in political education. No one can be there without getting intensely involved. If a majority, many, or even a few are not involved in the political struggle, then the meeting has to be declared a failure and another must be called. The meeting must teach the people who exploits and rules them, must show them the connection between economic and political power, and above all must give them a genuine taste of political power. To stand up and accuse a landlord is the first lesson a peasant learns in exercising his right. This is the quickest way to initiate the masses of China into politics. In the process of the mass struggle, he will gradually shed his fear and ignorance and eventually take his destiny into his own hands. If a political party is based on the willing support of the masses, this party is unconquerable. It is this power base the Communist Party sought to build during the land reform.

Political education for peasants is not limited to mass meetings. After the failure of the first meeting, the team members are busily engaged in identifying activists and in helping to set up a peasants' association. With thirty-odd poor peasants as its nucleus, the association forms a land distribution committee, a people's militia, an anti-traitor committee, and a production committee. Poor peasants begin to feel the strength of organization; more join the association. They no longer feel that they are fighting singly but realize that their fate is closely linked to that of many others. After a secret meeting of the team members and local activists, a further mass meeting is called. This time militiamen guard the schoolhouse with spears to bar Han's relatives and supporters from attending the meeting. No platform is raised; a single large table is placed in the middle of the playground for 'the people's tribunal'. More posters appear, including such provocative slogans as 'Landlords Owe Us Blood Debts!' and 'Share out Land and Houses and Claim Back Rents!' Han, hands tied, is brought out by armed militiamen. Since the meeting has been thoroughly prepared, it proceeds as expected. Just as the emotion of the crowd reaches its peak, somebody steps out and slaps Han across the face. Although a few shout applause, more, particularly women, are scared by the sight of blood. This blow turns out to be staged; the man who strikes Han is a tenant who has been promised rent exemption. The ruse is effective. After a suggestion of fining him $100,000 is accepted, Han is again turned loose.

Again there are disappointments, doubts, and frustrations in the minds of many people. Though dejected himself, Hsiao sticks to his linc. Further progress seems difficult, but Hsiao still urges the peasants to hold small group meetings to keep Han worried. The situation is saved by an incident which is brought about by the hard work of the peasants' association, but also shows Han's true face in dealing with his hired hands. The incident involves Han's swineherd, a thirteen-year-old boy, who works like a slave for his bowl of rice. This little swineherd has been persuaded to join one of the discussion groups and is caught sneaking back late one night. Han is genuinely outraged that even this meanest wretch, this little swineherd, should revolt against him. He orders his henchmen to pull off the boy's clothes, rams a rag into the boy's mouth, and whips him into a bloody heap. But Han's house has been under surveillance; the incident is spotted by two militiamen.

When people break into Han's mansion they find no trace of Han, but the boy lying in a pool of blood. A search party soon finds Han hiding in a small shed near the river bank. This time, needing little encouragement, the villagers cry aloud for revenge:

'Beat him to death!'
From all sides the shouts thundered. The peasants raised the sticks and spears in their hands, and surged forward. The militiamen held their spears horizontally to stop them, but the crowd burst through . . .[18]

But Han is not finished off by mob lynching. His life is temporarily spared to allow peasants to pour out charges against him. When all the evidence is piled up it turns out that Han has killed seventeen persons, without counting many others he has secretly murdered. Only then does the team leader disclose that back in 1935 in collaboration with the Japanese he slaughtered nine anti-Japanese Communist guerrillas and more recently, as the local Kuomintang representative, killed another Communist soldier.

It takes almost forty days, three mass meetings, and many more discussion meetings until the destruction of Han the landlord is finally completed. This whole process is worth scrupulous study. Chou Li-po spends more than two hundred pages to demonstrate the logic of the elaborate procedure of mass trial. There is no mistaking the manipulation of crowd psychology by the cadres. The final scene of Han's beating up his little swineherd seems to invite his own destruction. But it can also be viewed as a trap set up by the work team, though this is not specifically stated. The cadres are well aware of Han's temper and his capacity for murderous action against a hired hand who betrays his trust. Although the accusations at the mass meetings have produced an impact on the masses and many of them share the same experience of

[18] *The Hurricane*, Vol. I, pp. 230–1, Hsu, p. 145.

being mercilessly exploited, peasants are not very vengeful people and are always ready to forgive. Time dilutes the bitter memories of what happened years ago; the opportunity to pour out their bitterness also works as an emotional release. Only a new blood crime committed under their very noses can arouse intense hatred for the landlord. The incident appears to be not entirely accidental.

The Communist method seems ruthless. One may ask why the landlord is not disposed of without all this ceremony. But the mass meeting must be viewed as a mechanism for making the masses politically conscious. In order to transform the illiterate, disorganized, and politically innocent peasants into a revolutionary force, they have to be persuaded, shocked, and aroused. The taste of blood is the first act of revolution, just as Adam's tasting of the forbidden fruit constitutes his first act of rebellion against the authority of God and his pursuit of freedom.[19] Once a man has a share in the death of a landlord, his fate is permanently joined with the Communist revolutionary cause. With village after village of peasants behind them, the Communists cannot possibly fail in their revolution.

The Consolidation of the Rural Power Base

`Land reform, which combines economic, social, and political reform, is the most effective mechanism of the class struggle. Once Han Number Six, the symbol of feudalism in Yuanmao, is disposed of, more and more peasants take an active part in the peasants' association. It offers the peasants their first opportunity to administer affairs of common concern, that had been within the exclusive jurisdiction of the landed gentry for over two thousand years. The first important job is to divide Han's property — land, houses, furniture, grain, livestock, clothes, utensils, and everything else. Since all poor, tenant, lower middle, and even middle peasants can expect a share in the mountains of material piled up in Han's mansion, everyone is eager to join in the classification of villagers and the division of the 'fruits of struggle'. In doing this, they learn the first lesson in public administration. 'They had worked out a scale of three classes and nine grades: for instance, Class 1, Grade 1 comprised the poorest peasants while Class 3, Grade 3 comprised middle peasants.'[20] The core of village leadership consists of those poor peasants who have taken the initiative in the mass struggle and who will form the political structure to govern the village.

---

[19] This psychological interpretation of the biblical story is eloquently presented by Erich Fromm in his *Escape from Freedom.*
[20] *The Hurricane*, Vol. I, p. 242, Hsu, p. 153.

Although Han's property is enormous by village standards, it still cannot satisfy the needs of poor peasants. In the process of distributing the 'fruits of struggle', the villagers learn something which points to the future road of the Communist revolution:

> By evening all the clothes, three vats of soya bean oil, one vat of lard, and over three hundred catties of salt had all been distributed to more than three hundred families. Thirty-six horses and donkeys had been given to one hundred and forty-four families — every four families sharing one animal, each family owning, so to speak, one leg of an animal.[21]

Since four families share one draught animal, they have no choice but to co-operate in feeding, keeping and using the animal. It is the first instance of co-operation among neighbors who used to care only about their own business, worry about their own problems, and suffer their own misfortunes. This first step inevitably leads to mutual-aid teams.

Apart from the common share of property, the peasants also learn to think in the long-term. In the absence of exploitation by landlords, they can now produce for their own consumption and can look forward to better days. The old attitude of surrendering themselves to fate and of consuming whatever is available before it is taken away by landlords gives way to a more optimistic frame of mind.

> The twenty pigs defied any attempt at division. Somebody suggested that they should have a feast to celebrate the triumph of the peasants over the landlord. But Chao objected:
> 'We're the masters now, but we must look ahead. It's not the time for us poor people to be feasting yet. I think the Peasants' Association should keep the pigs. At the end of the year, when the time comes to sell them, we'll buy horses. At present, we poor villagers have only one leg of a horse each, but later we should have two legs and after New Year all four legs. What do you say?'[22]

Such a sensible suggestion is supported by everyone without any objection. Chairman Chao Yu-lin has secured a new job for the peasants' association; after the immediate political struggle is over, it will become a permanent organization, the village power center, with the solution of common problems as its primary task. The responsibility for raising and later selling the pigs to buy horses gives the association, in addition to its political power, a measure of economic power.

But these are only the beginnings. The power base of the peasants as well as of the Communist Party has yet to be consolidated. The second

---

[21] *Ibid.*, Vol. I, p. 249, Hsu, p. 157.
[22] *Ibid.*, Vol. I, p. 250, Hsu, p. 158.

part of the novel, though less dramatic and exciting, is crucial in giving a complete picture of land reform. It starts with the return of Hsiao, now county party secretary, leading a new work team to launch another mass movement for eliminating the residue of feudal forces and influences. The time is October 1947, when the *Outline of Agrarian Law* has just been proclaimed.

The class struggle a year earlier produced a number of experienced local cadres who were politically reliable. In the overall shortage of manpower, especially when new areas were liberated and there were new struggles to be waged, these local cadres were transferred elsewhere to assume leadership. Such a process suggests the efficacy of land reform as a means for training cadres who are direly needed as the Communist revolution gains ground in its military operations.

The transfer of local cadres creates a vacuum which allows some opportunist elements to take over the village leadership. One Chang Fu-ying, known as Bad-Egg Chang, has managed to install himself as the chairman of the peasants' association. In the old days he squandered some two hundred *mou* of inherited land on wine and women and later set up a flapjack shop with money borrowed from his relatives and friends. During the first phase of the land reform, he impressed many people by his aggressive attacks on the landlords. When other cadres were transferred he was first elected group leader, then chief of the local militia, and finally vice-chairman of the peasants' association. A shrewd man who can talk and argue, write and count, Chang has been able to plant his coterie in the association, to depose the chairman, and assume the post himself.

Once he becomes chairman, he hires five militiamen to scout and spy for him. He places his sworn brother, a former commissioned officer in the army of Manchukuo, in the position of village head. He has also made another former Manchukuo officer clerk of the association. With these men in charge, the old order is quickly restored. While some landlords are spared and still able to live on rent, a few middle peasants become the target of attack because of old personal grudges. For most of the time, the trio simply enjoy drinking, singing and playing the gramophone in the office of the association. Their only visible accomplishment is the use of the proceeds from the sale of confiscated property to open a co-operative store where cosmetics and women's stockings are sold.

An underlying thesis of the second part of *The Hurricane* seems to be that since revolution does not necessarily change people's characters, there is a need to develop a class character. In the first stage of the class struggle, the landlord is the focal point and all other forces must be aligned to destroy his despotic rule. In this broad alliance, some undesirable opportunists cannot be kept outside the mass movement. In the process of consolidation, however, it becomes urgent to purify the ranks of the village power structure. Since backward elements do not belong to the landlord class, they cannot be dealt with in the same manner, as this would create uncertainty in the minds of other peasants. Yet they must be reformed and their selfish motives eliminated if socialism is to take root in China's countryside.

Selfish motives prove much harder to fight than landlords. The case of Chang Fu-ying may be extraordinary but is by no means exceptional. A peasant may simply want a tract of more fertile land, a better horse, or a few more bits of old clothes. It is important to create a sense of mutual assistance, a sense of common destiny, and a sense of unity among the poor. This can be achieved by cultivating class character to replace individual character. If every peasant learns to view things from his class standpoint, to understand that what is good for the class without property is good for him, and to work for people as poor as he is, a truly indestructible power base can be built up.

The first order of business in Yuanmao under the new dispensation is to set up a poor peasants' and farm laborers' league, as the peasants' association has not been functioning properly. It is a necessary step towards seizing power from those who have usurped the peasant organization. Then there is the unfinished job of settling accounts with the remaining landlords. By much hard work and indefatigable effort, members of the league unearth weapons as well as gold and silver. The hidden articles are dug out not only from the courtyards of landlords' mansions but also from the houses of their poor relatives. After these tasks are accomplished, the poor peasants' and farm laborers' league is abolished and the peasants' association restored.

Once land and other property has been confiscated, the next job is to make a fair distribution. Unlike the previous mass struggle meetings, charged with intense emotion, the meeting for dividing landlords' land and property this time resembles a crude democratic assembly. A method of 'comparative grading' is adopted to classify all the villagers on the basis of personal background, and economic and social status. Everyone is allowed to present his case and to be challenged by other contenders. A poor peasant, for instance, will stand up to claim the first place as the most needy:

'I'm Chu Fu-lin. In my family, we've been hired hands for three generations. Who can beat that?'[23]

People seem to agree that Chu has made an honest living by farming in spring and fishing in autumn. More important, when Han Number

[23] *Ibid.*, Vol. II, p. 200, Hsu, p. 311.

Six escaped from his mansion, Chu's information led to the landlord's capture. This is a great contribution; Chu seems to be assured of the first place. But somebody points out that when Chu was a swineherd he stole corn-cobs in the fields. Serious discussion ensues, centering on the question of whether a hungry boy picking up a cob or two from the landlord's field can be called a thief. When this is rejected, someone else raises another issue. Once Chu as foreman for Snatcher Tang drove the hired hands to speed up their work at the sight of the landlord. Another discussion follows. Some say that was no fault, since in the old society no one could afford to offend the landlord. Others contend that there was still no need to suck up to the landlord. Since the discussion is inconclusive, Chu maintains his good standing. But when someone mentions that Chao Yu-lin's widow ought to be the first, they all remember that Chao was the one who made the first attempt to arrest Han, and who died fighting bandits. The motion to rank Mrs. Chao first receives unanimous approval.

Then Old Sun the Carter suggests that Kuo Chuan-hai, a poor peasant and chairman of the peasants' association, should be the second. The majority agree, and Chu becomes contender for third place. But the little swineherd who had been brutally beaten by Han snatches that position. Mrs. Pai is placed fourth, for her husband has studied in a party school, works in the city as a security officer, and is interrupting his New Year vacation to arrest Han Number Five. The fifth place goes to Big Li, who forged spears for the militia day and night when the struggle against Han was in progress. The sixth place is won by Old Tien whose daughter died under Han's whip rather than confess the whereabouts of her fiancé, a Communist guerrilla, in the Manchukuo days. Only then is Chu able to hold his number seven position without being further downgraded. This method of grading people according to their economic status, political standing, past contributions, and other merits receives the whole-hearted support of the villagers.

The Outline of Agrarian Law of 1947, like all laws, laid down only general principles; its implementation had to be worked out by cadres in accordance with local conditions. The Chinese Communist Party was then groping and experimenting with tentative political procedure. While there is no doubt that the party was interested in building socialism, the nature of socialism had yet to be defined. What happens at the village meeting in Yuanmao is a genuine form of participatory democracy at the local level. The power to decide on matters of a local nature gives the word 'democratic' some meaning in the seemingly contradictory term 'democratic centralism' used to describe the Chinese political system.

Socialism cannot be achieved by political means only; its realization also depends on the refinement of positive traits and remolding of negative traits in human nature. The distribution of confiscated property offers an opportunity to educate the peasant population by allowing their good qualities to be seen, so encouraging a change in the selfish mentality of backward elements. Mrs. Chao has been ranked number one not only because her husband sacrificed his life for the community but also because she herself has been a shining example of virtue. 'She had made up her mind not to remarry, but to bring up her little boy So-chu.' 'Honest and kind-hearted, she had been a mother to the orphaned little swineherd.' These are examples of unselfishness which, though a Confucian virtue, is still needed for building socialism. Mrs. Chao does not disappoint her neighbors. When the grading is completed and it is her privilege as the number one family to choose articles, she picks up a discolored quilt. Others protest that the quilt is no good, but Mrs. Chao says, 'This is all right. It wouldn't do to scoop out the flesh of a melon and leave the rind to somebody else.' Others will have none of this; finally, Old Chu has to rummage through the pile to select a fur coat, a fox-fur cap and a small pair of blue padded shoes for her boy, and a brand-new quilt with a woollen cover for herself. Chairman Kuo Chuan-hai, who has been ranked second, is also willing to settle for anything. Modesty becomes the dominant virtue of the gathering and sets the tone for dealing with public affairs in the future.

Although the refusal to exercise one's privilege in choosing articles of superior quality speaks for an attitude, it does not amount to a real test of the spirit of self-denial. That comes later. Some time after the distribution of the landlord's property, the county party secretary Hsiao comes back to Yuanmao. He is very happy that Chairman Kuo Chuan-hai has got married and that village affairs are now in good hands. Hsiao considers Kuo a very capable man, secretly congratulates himself on having trained a first-rate cadre, and has a plan to make a district party secretary of Kuo.

Hsiao's return to Yuanmao is precipitated by an urgent task. As the Civil War has escalated to fighting between large army groups, there is a great demand for men. Yuanmao must start a movement to encourage young peasants to enlist in the army. The difficulty of the task is obvious: now the villagers with their houses, draught animals, and, above all, land, want to start farming in earnest. In order to meet the target of volunteers for the army, mass meetings, small meetings of activists, and family meetings are held day and night. But in the end, only a few men have applied for enlistment, far short of the number needed.

It becomes clear to Kuo, chairman of the peasants' association, that unless something drastic is done, the task is destined to fail. He comes to a decision and goes to see Secretary Hsiao. Kuo's decision to join the army surprises Hsiao, who asks who is to do the work in the village. But Kuo walks away, saying that Hsiao can find someone else. Only then does Hsiao realize his own selfish motives:

> 'I'm like one of those backward village women, short-sighted and selfish. This concern only for one's own outfit is actually a form of individualism. I'm no better than a backward woman who sees no farther than the scissors on her *kang*.'[24]

The spirit of selfless dedication is the guarantee of the ultimate victory of the Communist revolution. No village is really a strong rear base unless this spirit exists. Kuo's decision to leave his newly wedded wife and join the army immediately inspires many young men to volunteer for the front. Only at this point do we grasp fully the many dimensions of land reform. It is an economic revolution, through which the means of production are redistributed and exploitation eliminated. It is also a social revolution, which not only removes class distinctions but also reshapes customs, norms, and values. Its political implications lie in the change in the village power structure and in the training of new cadres for administering local affairs. The activists who emerge during the process of land reform in each village, are initiated into the Communist Party once the process is completed, and will form the backbone of the political structure. Finally, it has great military significance. In both *Sun over the Sangkan River* and *The Hurricane*, land reform is being carried out while the fighting goes on within earshot. Land redistribution is the surest means of rallying the support of the poor. Once peasants have received land, they will fight the Kuomintang, not just for the Communists, but for themselves. They are determined to defend the land, now theirs, against any attempt to restore the landlord class.

Some Unanswered Questions

Sun over the Sangkan River was completed in June 1948 and *The Hurricane* in December 1948; both novels were published in 1949. It seems clear that neither Ting Ling nor Chou Li-po was able to foresee the future; both had thought of land reform as the ultimate goal of the Chinese Communist revolution. There is this optimistic note near the end of *Sun*:

> All the cadres crowded onto the stage. Cheng stepped forward and declared the meeting open, saying: 'Elders! Neighbors! Our meeting today is to celebrate the return of the land to its rightful owners! We suffered, generations of our ancestors lived

[24] *Ibid.*, Vol. II, p. 335, Hsu, p. 395.

like beasts, but we had no land, nothing to eat and nothing to wear — where had our land gone?'

'Stolen by the exploiting landlords!' answered several voices from below.

'Now the Communist policy is that every peasant shall have land of his own to till. The land is for those who have suffered. Do you approve or not?'

'Yes!'

'In a moment we're going to distribute tickets, stating where the land is. The old title deeds are no longer valid. We're going to burn them.'[25]

The same belief that from then on peasants would own the land was also shared by Chou Li-po. Thus in *The Hurricane* the party policy is announced by Hsiao Hsiang, county party secretary, in an even more unequivocal tone:

'You've been discussing how to redistribute the land. This is an important job, and I hope you'll do it well. After this there will be no more redivision: the Government will issue land deeds to the owners. What's more important to us peasants than land? In such a matter none should yield to anyone else. Men and women, young and old, all have a right to a piece of land...'[26]

This appears to be a promise the Communist Party made to the peasants during the land reform. The failure to implement the policy of 'Land to the Tillers'[27] outlined by Sun Yat-sen caused the downfall of the Kuomintang. The Communist Party counted on land redistribution for gaining the support of the great majority of peasants. Through land reform the Communist Party was able to build a broad, solid basis of political support in China's vast countryside. From the viewpoint of the peasants, acquisition of land had been their sole ambition for countless generations. One of the most touching scenes in *The Hurricane* is the joy of owning land shown by an old couple:

The next afternoon, Old Tien was going to stake the boundary of the land, and his blind wife insisted upon going with him to see what the farm was like. Old Tien led her by the hand until they had passed the North Gate and reached the place by the river. He stopped and she asked: "Is it here, the land?"

'Yes, here,' he answered. The blind woman squatted down to

[25] *Sun over the Sangkan River*, p. 450, *Chinese Literature*, Spring 1953, p. 292.
[26] *The Hurricane*, Vol. II, p. 296, Hsu, pp. 369–70.
[27] 'Land to the Tillers' and 'Control of Private Capital' are the two programs proposed by Dr. Sun Yat-sen, leader of the Nationalist revolution, to protect the livelihood of the people. They formed the basic economic policy of the Nationalist Government under Chiang Kai-shek, but were never implemented.

pat one of the ridges. She stroked a corn-cob, picked up a clod
of sandy black earth, and crumbled it lovingly in the palm of
her hand, letting the soil run out between her fingers. A smile
appeared on her face. It was their own land now. The like of
this had never happened to any of their ancestors...[28]

Such is the deep attachment of Chinese peasants to land which not
only grows grain but also holds the roots of their very existence.
Without land, they are like rootless plants which will dry up in the sun.

But the land redistribution solves China's agrarian problem only
on a temporary basis. The equalization of land distribution does
not ensure that it will remain equally divided among the peasants.
At the beginning of *Sun over the Sangkan River*, Ting Ling describes how Old Ku has acquired more and more land and has
become a well-to-do peasant.

As year after year passed and land changed hands repeatedly,
their hardships began to tell on them. However, thanks to their
hard work they gradually acquired land and became respectable
farmers. Since their family grew fast they needed more and
more land. Because they had many hands and the whole family
of sixteen, men and women, old and young alike all worked on
the land, they were able to conquer it. Their acreage increased
until they had to hire a number of day laborers. People in need
of money sold their property to Old Ku, and spendthrift sons of
ruined landlords' families after a bout of gambling made over
their title deeds to him too. At first he used paper to wrap up
these title deeds, then a piece of cloth, and finally a small
wooden case...[29]

Land reform does not solve the problem of potential reaccumu-
lation of land in the hands of thrifty and able-bodied peasants.
Greed for more and more land is natural to Chinese peasants.
Given the limited area of cultivable land and the prospect of an
ever-increasing population, it appears inevitable that within a short
span of time there will be the need for another revolution and
further land reform.

Then there is the difference between the perspective of a village
peasant, who thinks only of tilling land to raise crops, and the
Communist Party's goal, which is to establish socialism and eventually communism in China. Peasants are content with small plots
separated from other plots by raised earthen boundary ridges. The
Communist Party, however, has much larger aims in mind, such as

[28] *Ibid.*, Vol. I, pp. 256–7, Hsu, p. 162.
[29] *Sun over the Sangkan River*, p. 7, *Chinese Literature*, p. 30.

preventing floods, building dams and irrigation systems, introducing tractors, and mechanizing agriculture. All this will require a collective effort and a complete change in the mentality of small owner-producers. This fundamental contradiction foreshadows difficulties in the development of mutual-aid teams and co-operatives.

From the viewpoint of socialism, land distribution may well be considered a mistake. If the land confiscated from landlords had immediately been placed under communal ownership, the tensions encountered in the transition from private ownership to the mutual-aid team and the co-operative stages might well have been reduced. Peasants never expected the Communist Party to distribute land among them. The Chinese name Kungch'antang can be literally translated 'The Property-Sharing Party'; sharing property was actually expected in many areas to be the Communist policy. Under such a policy middle peasants could still be persuaded to join with the great majority if the superiority of collective farming were demonstrated. The process would certainly have been simpler and less painful.

All this is of course speculation. This hypothetical question is raised in order to make the point that land reform should be viewed primarily as a political program. If what is suggested above had actually become Communist policy, poor and landless peasants would not have become so intensely involved in the class struggle. The distribution of land created the momentum for rallying support behind the Communist Party, then in the process of fighting against the Kuomintang for political control of China. There was no alternative to stimulating the active participation of peasants in the political struggle, recruiting and training them as new party members to meet the acute problem of shortage of manpower, and above all, converting the millions into a dedicated revolutionary army to fight the Kuomintang troops, with their superior weapons and equipment.

Even if the land reform is viewed as a means to achieve political goals, this does not mean to suggest that the Communist policy was a Machiavellian scheme. By studying the Communist approach to solving the problem of backward elements and especially the problem of selfish motives, one can say with relative certainty that the built-in tensions of the land reform had been anticipated and considered soluble. Communism cannot be achieved without changing people's attitudes. There is an unshakeable belief implicit in available Communist documents that people's attitudes can be changed by raising the level of their ideological consciousness, as well as by demonstrating the superiority of collectivism.

8

THE ROLE OF THE WORKER
IN THE REVOLUTION

The traditional conception of the social order in China was hierarchical in nature, with the scholar gentry at the top, sustained by four other classes: the peasant, the craftsman, the merchant, and the soldier. The new conception of the Chinese social order is of a horizontal relationship with three classes, worker, peasant and soldier, on an equal basis. The disappearance of scholars or intellectuals as a class implies the integration of learning and application, or the combination of mental and physical labor. The function of the merchant has been taken over by the state; consequently, merchants have disappeared. In every document, however, the worker is always mentioned first. In a country highly conscious of ceremonies and formalities, this seems to give the worker a more or less preferential status. Workers, particularly factory workers, do in fact earn more, have a higher standard of living, and have gained prominence in society.

The preferential status given to workers is an indication, not of the importance of the role they played in the revolution, but rather the priority the government gives to industrialization and the natural operation of economic forces. There is, of course, an ideological explanation to the preferential status of the worker. In the Marxist theoretical structure of society, workers are the avant garde, the leaders in a proletarian revolution. But this theoretical model does not apply to the reality of the Chinese Communist revolution, where workers virtually played no part. In Communist novels covering half a century of the revolutionary movement, the Chinese proletarians are totally absent, except in the initial stages of the urban struggle. Occasionally, we come across cadres of worker background, but in most cases they were craftsmen, carpenters, kiln workers, or masons, only rarely former textile workers or printers from the city. Even the participation of these people with *quasi*-worker backgrounds does not change the nature of the peasant revolution. Their role in the revolution is usually that of cadre rather than worker. A genuine proletarian revolution is a struggle waged in an industrial environment. Deprived of that setting and the struggle against capitalist exploitation, the worker is no longer a worker but a cadre.

212

Very few novels about workers and their struggle, seen as organized action in an industrial setting, have been published. Among the precious few, *Seeds of Flame*[1] depicts Shanghai workers and their revolutionary rising in 1927. Since then for twenty long years workers have been completely cut off from the Communist revolutionary movement until the reunion of the Party and the workers in 1948 on the eve of the liberation of Manchuria. During this long period, whether in underground struggle, in class struggle, or in the Civil War, workers took no part. Even in stories of the underground struggle, attempts by Communist cadres to build mass support in urban areas largely center on schools, universities and newspapers. There is no description in novels of any attempt to penetrate factories run by the Japanese or the Kuomintang in the war years. Intensive efforts to organize workers to prevent disruption and sabotage by Kuomintang secret agents were made only on the eve of the Communist take-over.

The second novel to be discussed is *Dawn in Wind and Rain*,[2] a story of Anshan steel workers and their role in the restoration of this huge dismantled steel factory. After decades of operating in the most backward, impoverished villages in northern China, Communist cadres, without the slightest idea of steel-making or of the life-pattern of workers, are entrusted with the responsibility of supervising the reassembly of a thoroughly mutilated steel complex. The portrayal of the capacity of Communist cadres to win the support of workers and get them organized is a masterly job. The problem of adjustment between almost total strangers presents a tremendous challenge to both sides, but is overcome in a remarkably ingenious way.

Manchuria soon developed into the industrial heartland of China, with mushrooming factories, in a matter of half a decade. The third novel centers around a steel plant of the Liaonan Iron and Steel Company and describes all the bustle and commotion of industrial activities at the time of China's industrial take-off or the beginning of the First Five-Year Plan around 1953. *Steeled and Tempered*[3] focuses on problems resulting from the accelerated pace of industrialization. It portrays a Communist worker, the conversion of an old-fashioned worker, and the rectification of the incorrect attitude of a third.

[1] Ai Ming-chih, *Huo chung (Seeds of Flame)* (Peking: Writers' Publishing House, 1963). Two instalments in English translation appear in *Chinese Literature*, Nos. 4 and 5, 1964, pp. 3–55 and 23–84.
[2] Lo Tan, *Feng-yü ti li-ming (Dawn in Wind and Rain)*, Vol. I (Peking: Chinese Youth Publishing House, 1959, rev. ed., 1963); Vol. II (Peking: Chinese Youth Publishing House, 1964).
[3] Ai Wu, *Pai lien ch'eng kang* (Peking: Writers' Publishing House, 1958, 2nd ed., 1962); *Steeled and Tempered* (Peking: Foreign Languages Press, 1961).

Although the author Ai Wu is a veteran novelist, his novel is the least imaginative of the three.

Certainly, revolution and struggle are exciting topics, while steel-making, a routine job, inevitably challenges the craftsmanship of the novelist and tries the patience of the reader. But the novels suggest something else. A comparison of the three novels reveals the changing life-style of workers from insecure yet independent individuals to secure but disciplined organization men. The workers in the novels of the earlier periods may have to suffer hunger or tighten their belts, but they fight like heroes for survival or for the revolution. In the new era of socialist industrial reconstruction, they are well-fed and clothed, efficiently organized to perform the task assigned. The novel thus becomes a description of the process of making workers into an efficient production force.

Shanghai Workers and the Insurrection of 1927

Seeds of Flame is a realistic account of urban life and the plight of workers in Shanghai.[4] For more than two-thirds of the book, the author concentrates on the personal lives of Liu Chin-sung, Fan Tang-lin and other workers in the Greater Shanghai Shipyard and their struggle for survival. They take no part in the strikes in response to the May 4th Movement in 1919 and do not demonstrate against the wanton killing of the textile worker Ku Cheng-hung by Japanese police in 1925. Although strikes have been steadily increasing since the founding of the Chinese Communist Party in 1921 and the subsequent establishment of its trade union secretariat, these shipyard workers have not been involved in political unrest until the autumn of 1926.

Shanghai is powerfully and vividly presented, not as an international colony so much as a paradise for Western adventurers. The overthrow of the Manchu court in 1911 appears to have had little effect on the life of the Chinese in this metropolitan city. There are a few signs of change: bannermen have been replaced by black-uniformed police, the yellow dragon flag has been hauled down from the pole of the Kiangnan Arsenal, and pigtails like dead snakes are scattered here and there in the streets. The hand of international capitalism, however, is visible everywhere. The old city wall has been torn down and turned into a main road plied by trolleys of the French-owned Electric Tramways Company. New office buildings are mushrooming, new automobiles of various foreign makes crowd the Bund, and new

---

[4] The author Ai Ming-chih seems to be a native of Shanghai. His first novelette *Shang-hai nien-ssu hsiao-shih (Twenty-Four Hours in Shanghai)*, describing the city under the Japanese occupation, was published in Chungking in 1946.

fashions modelled in high class clubs and luxurious department stores. At nightfall neon lights advertise the latest imported goods, from colorful Japanese fabrics to Hollywood motion pictures. The famous Shanghai Club, an elegant edifice, specially designed for combining business transactions with fun, features Sikh doormen and white Russian waitresses.

If Shanghai, or China, is the victim of exploitation, the capitalist who emerges in the novel is not a caricature of a Wall Street banker, and his Chinese partner not a landlord turned comprador. Their success story is told as though adapted from the pages of Horatio Alger. The first encounter between James and Liu Wen-sheng does not take place in the elaborately furnished office of a business building but at the small hole-like window of an obscure pawn shop. In his shabby Western suit, James manages to make it clear in his strongly-accented Shanghai dialect that he wants to pawn a ruby ring. Liu Wen-sheng realizes that the ring is worth $150, but, as a good pawn-broker, is willing to offer only ten dollars. The ring is finally accepted for thirty dollars after much pleading from James. It thus becomes the symbol of a financial matrimony.

James, the only American in Chinese Communist novels, is portrayed as a man of ideas. He has only just arrived in Shanghai, without a penny in his pocket. The sum he receives from pawning the ring gives him his initial break. He is able to buy a decent suit and give a respectable dinner party. As a result, he raises three thousand dollars and plans to set up in a kerosene business. During their second meeting at a small office in a three-storey building on the Bund, James urges Liu to leave his pawnshop job and become his street broker. Liu is to distribute lamps filled with kerosene free of charge, from door to door. Once people begin to use kerosene lamps, James explains, they will see its many advantages. When the oil in the lamp is burnt up they will buy a gallon, then a second gallon, and a third. At first Liu Wen-sheng is taken aback by this ridiculous idea of giving away lamps and free oil, but is soon totally enchanted by James's description of his great vision.

The partnership between James and Liu Wen-sheng, a classic example of collaboration between foreign capitalist and Chinese comprador, is presented without malice. The author even describes their initial frustrations. Some people frown at the mere mention of kerosene, while others accept free lamps only to trade them in for sweets at second-hand stores. Since Liu Wen-sheng knows how to use his glib tongue, their business soon picks up. In one year they move into a new tall, modern building exclusively designed for James Enterprises. In less than ten years James Enterprises have a hand in every profitable area, with subsidiaries ranging all the way from egg-processing to ship-building.

Seeds of Flame is a story of the lives of workers rather than of class struggle. As a cameo figure, James never turns into a predatory capitalist. Even his Chinese partner, the comprador Liu Wen-sheng, is a minor character who never assumes the role of villain. When the New American Shipbuilding Corporation, a subsidiary of James Enterprises, attempts to take over the Greater Shanghai Shipyard and creates labor trouble, Liu never adopts oppressive measures. By posting notices to recruit workers at the shipyard, he manages to take the steam out of the labor trouble.

If the plight of workers is caused by exploitation, this is not explicitly stated in the novel. The predicament of the hero, Liu Chin-sung, a shipyard worker, is caused by a debt he has incurred to pay for his marriage expenses. He first went to Liu Wen-sheng, a distant cousin, to borrow money, but was turned down. The incident may show the comprador's lack of concern for a relative, but hardly represents conflict between two classes. In fact, the foreman Foxy Min, who charges Chin-sung 30 per cent monthly interest on a $20 loan, is more of a villain. Mao Tun in his review of *Seeds of Flame* points out that the author portrays personal conflict with force but describes class contradictions only in general terms.[5] When an author tries to portray life according to his own observation he is inevitably governed by the logic of the story.

As a shipyard worker, Liu Chin-sung has many opportunities to play a part in organizing workers, but he shows neither understanding of nor interest in the labor conflict. When the post-war depression hits Shanghai in 1924 and the shipyard lays off men, workers become restive. Chin-sung, however, is confident that as an able-bodied, skilled worker, he will not be fired. When the take-over of the shipyard by New American appears imminent he stills expresses his doubts that anyone would be so unscrupulous as to make thousand of workers jobless. Even when the strike is under way and he takes part in it, he still thinks that all their efforts will be in vain. Finally, the loss of his two sons forces him to view life and this world with a deep sense of hostility and to throw his energy into the Communist-led revolution.

Another worker the author uses considerable space to portray is Fan Tang-lin. Fan shows his clear thinking and resolve when he emerges as the leader of the workers striking to prevent the shipyard from being taken over by New American. The failure of the strike so angers and frustrates him that he leaves his wife and four children to join the revolutionary army in Canton. There in the general confusion he finds

[5] Mao Tun, 'Tu liao *Huo chung* i-hou ti tien-ti kan-hsiang' (Thoughts After Reading *Seeds of Flame*), *Shuo-huo*, No. 2, 1964, p. 66.

himself a member of the Kuomintang,[6] and later is promoted to the rank of platoon leader in the revolutionary army. When his troops enter Shanghai he learns about the plot to slaughter Communists and striking workers. Instead of informing his friend Liu Chin-sung, now a group leader in the picket corps, Fan makes a protest at a Kuomintang army cadres' meeting, is arrested, and commits suicide.

Mao Tun, who has been a friend of the author for some twenty years,[7] apparently senses the revisionist approach in the plot structure and character portrayal. He regards the backward aspect in Liu Chin-sung's personality as over-emphasized, but still stresses the hero's ultimate transformation into a Communist revolutionary. Deeply disturbed by the character of Fan Tang-lin, Mao Tun comments that Fan's behavior suits a petit bourgeois rather than an industrial worker. Somehow, he still tries to rationalize the heroes' deaths with this speculation.

Perhaps the author uses this arrangement to make a point. Liu Chin-sung, who used to be more backward, is able to fight to the finish and to die a glorious death because he is under the Communist leadership. Fan Tang-lin, who was once more progressive, ends in suicide because he is not led by the Communist Party but has unwittingly joined the Kuomintang.[8]

This explanation seems to be intended as a line of retreat for the author to fall back on in case of ideological attack. The author's purpose, however, is clear enough. He meant to tell a story of workers in Shanghai during the tumultuous decade from 1918 to 1927. He focused on their private lives and personal misfortunes, at least in this first volume,[9] and largely left out the theme of class struggle. In doing so, he followed the logical sequence of events; thus, both Liu Chin-sung and Fan Tang-lin turn out to be not heroes of the revolutionary struggle but victims of power politics.

If the workers are less than revolutionary, the revolutionaries themselves are not all dedicated idealists. Ma Chieh-min, a Communist

---

[6] At that time the Kuomintang had formed a coalition government with the Communists in Canton, and joined forces with the revolutionary army to defeat warlords and unify China. Once the revolutionary army had taken Shanghai, in April 1927, Chiang Kai-shek purged Communists from the ranks of the army and massacred many workers of the picket corps, which was organized largely by Communists.

[7] Ai Ming-chih's 1946 novelette *Twenty-Four Hours in Shanghai* was published in a series edited by Mao Tun.

[8] Mao Tun, *op. cit.*, p. 63.

[9] The author planned to write a trilogy, but his project was apparently disrupted by the Cultural Revolution and is unlikely to be resumed.

organizer and intellectual, once complains to his district party secretary Chung Hua about the backward state of the Shanghai workers and attributes their political apathy to the impact of imperialist domination. He says that one day he and his girl, disguised as workers, went to a textile factory. Standing among the workers, they distributed handbills and called for the overthrow of warlords and imperialists. Ma thought it one of the most eloquent speeches he had ever made, and was particularly satisfied with the way he introduced terms such as 'Bolshevism' and 'Soviet'. The workers immediately noticed their fair complexions but mistook them for soap salesmen. Very soon they began to think the couple were plainclothes men sent by warlords, and drove them off with blows and curses. Ma Chieh-min is terribly frustrated, for the workers had failed to appreciate what he was doing for them.

Ma's involvement in the Communist movement is motivated primarily by personal political ambition. He and his girl love to go for a walk in the almost deserted side streets after a hard day's work. One October evening in the dreamy moonlight, Ma unfolds his vision of Shanghai under Communist rule. It will be a great satisfaction to him, he confesses, to see those now living in Western-style mansions and riding in chauffeur-driven cars bow to them as masters of a new city. He thinks his girl should be the minister of the department of women's affairs while he himself could easily handle the job of minister of propaganda or minister of organization or even chairman of the Shanghai Soviet. As for the district party secretary Chung Hua, he is best suited to be a party representative in a factory. In Ma's view, Shanghai, with so many foreigners, is much too complicated a city for people like Chung Hua to manage. This opportunistic attitude finally makes Ma succumb to the cajolements and threats of a Kuomintang regimental commander, and betray his comrades.

Seeds of Flame is basically a tale of two worlds in Shanghai, the one of the foreign, prosperous and wealthy and the other of the wretched, impoverished and hopeless. Nevertheless, most of the workers believe that with their strength and skill they should have no difficulty in supporting their families. Almost without exception, they are apolitical, individualistic, and indifferent to organizational activities. They show an almost religious devotion to their crafts and have a profound sense of attachment to their factories. Thus Shanghai workers are not recruited by the Communists but driven Communist by nonchalant yet ruthless exploitation and their failure in the fight for survival. Although the author never suggests it, the story does allow the non-Communist interpretation that the year 1927 actually offered an opportunity for a system other than Communism in China. All the workers wanted was job security and a tolerable standard of living. But for the next two decades they continued to suffer the same hardships. The smouldering fire was never extinguished and burst into flame again towards the end of the 1940s.

Manchuria on the Eve of the Take-over

Workers do not reappear in Chinese novels covering the next two crucial decades until the Communist troops captured Liaoyang and Anshan in early 1948. *Dawn in Wind and Rain* depicts Anshan Iron and Steel Works under Communist control during the hectic five months from February to July. When the story ends the Anshan steel mill is evacuated for another brief period until its final liberation in November of the same year. Although the novel is highly commended, its unique candor in the treatment of cadres has been harshly criticised. The commentators contend that the party representative should not be portrayed as a pallid, pedantic intellectual with a propensity for philosophical theorizing. The portrayal of Lou K'un-hua and Tsang Ch'ung, two high-ranking cadres who show traces of departmentalism, is considered improper and unnecessary. A fourth cadre, Tai T'ien-hou, is regarded as a negative character, and his portrait a sarcastic, exaggerated sketch which has gone far beyond the scope of comradely exhortation.[10] The criticism is clearly ideological; from the artistic viewpoint the powerful characterization offers a revealing insight into the relations between cadres and workers and among the cadres themselves.

When the Communist troops drive out the Kuomintang army from Anshan they find the steel plant in a shambles.[11] During the two years of Kuomintang rule, from February 1946 to February 1948, the mill was a gold mine for corrupt and greedy officials. They stole everything they could lay hands on: instruments, machines, and even the white-gold boiler and diamond cutter in the laboratory. The Kuomintang officials were joined by professional thieves, hardware merchants, and street hooligans in turning a once bustling steel complex into a skeleton of metal ruins.

The workers of the steel plant have expected the Communists to enforce a different policy, so that they can return to work. But they discover to their acute pain that the Communist dismantling of the

---

[10] The critical views are summed up in Feng Mu, '*Feng-yü ti li-ming* ti ch'eng-chiu chi ch'i jo-tien' (The Merits and Shortcomings of *Dawn in Wind and Rain*), *Wen-i pao*, No. 14, July 1959, p. 37.
[11] Throughout the novel there is no hint of the dismantling and removal of machines by the Russians. The damage caused by the Soviet seizure of rolling stock and modern machinery in all the factories in Manchuria has been estimated at nearly $900 million according to the Pauley Commission report.

factory and removal of machines dwarfs what had been done by Kuomintang officials; by comparison, that was petty theft. Mountains of tools, parts, and equipment are loaded onto armed trucks, as though a battlefield were being cleared. One unit needs medical supplies, so its men ship off all the bottles containing chemicals from the chemistry laboratory. Transmission oil is mistaken for gasoline and taken away. Discipline is totally ignored, and even Yi Chiu-fan, the party secretary of Anshan, is unable to stop the removal by invoking the Party's urban policy.

Within a month, three different men have had the responsibility for supervising the Anshan Iron and Steel Works. Lou K'un-hua, deputy director of the bureau of resources in the department of military industry, is the third man in charge of the steel plant. Workers call him 'the chairman of wholesale removal', an apt title, for Lou has set up a removals committee. More than a hundred jobless workers are organized as carriers, while a whole platoon of soldiers is assigned the task of armed escort. He has built warehouses in Haich'eng for the storage of machines and instruments taken from the steel mill.

The man appointed as party representative to replace Lou K'un-hua is Sung Tse-chou. A college graduate, Sung used to work in the survey and research section of the Northwest Bureau of the Party Central in the Yenan days. His only property, apart from a bedding roll, is a precious Ming edition of poems by the T'ang poet Tu Fu. The description of this volume is not superfluous. It reflects Sung's life-style, his literary tastes, and his uncompromising character. On arrival, his first move is to request permission from the Liaotung branch bureau of the Party Central to retain all the representatives from various units sent to remove equipment. He buys back blueprints which have been sold as toilet tissue and wrapping paper in the second-hand market and recovers important production data, including a twenty-year history of the Showa Steel Works. Under his leadership, the dismantled steel plant is gradually restored to order.

Sung Tse-chou has been saddened by the dismal sight of the steel structures, forlorn and desolate, with foxes and rabbits inhabiting the ruins. He (or the author) shows no sympathy toward Lou K'un-hua's unplanned and undisciplined dismantling of the plant. The confrontation between Sung and Lou before the latter's departure for north Manchuria is a powerful scene. As old acquaintances in Yenan, Lou is excited to see Sung and immediately inquires about his arthritis and myopia. Sung has a habit of judging a man by his appearance. Lou still wears his faded military uniform with the sleeves casually rolled up; he has an old watch with Roman numbers, now almost unrecognizable, on his wrist. This gives Sung a good impression: the man still retains the Yenan style and has not been corrupted by city life. Nevertheless, Sung feels sorry for Lou, who has been so preoccupied with the interests of his own department that he has overlooked the larger problem of industrial reconstruction.

In the debate between the two cadres, the author spares no effort in exposing their differing views of the military situation as well as Lou's personal hostility toward the man who takes over his job. When Sung requests Lou to issue an order immediately halting the removal of machines, the latter raises the crucial question, 'What if the Kuomintang troops retake Anshan?' Unperturbed, Sung answers calmly that in that case they can have it.

'Oh!' Lou was irritated. 'You won't let your own people remove equipment. You want to save it for the Kuomintang! "They can have it"? How generous you are! Lucky you've been cleared during the Yenan rectification campaign. Otherwise, I'd question your ideology.'

Sung Tse-chou smiled.

Seeing anger all over Lou's face, Sung did not want their talk to reach deadlock. In order to convince him, he continued:

'Old Lou, how could I stop you from removing equipment! I'm merely doing things according to party instructions. As for the military situation, the leadership has said, "There's a possibility Anshan may fall again, but it will be quickly retaken." We'll let them have it tomorrow, but we'll recover it the day after. And then, it will be ours forever.'

'I know, "the final victory belongs to us," and "Communism will finally overcome capitalism." Brother, no need to tell me the old clichés. We can't stay at Anshan very long, the enemy at Mukden won't give up this city easily. It's still a see-saw situation. And so, leave nothing to the enemy, dismantle everything which can be dismantled, and remove everything which is removable.'[12]

The argument becomes heated. Sung contends that senseless removal amounts to destruction. Lou reminds him of the need for military production and military construction. Sung accuses Lou of departmentalism and of disregard for principle. Lou retorts with a personal attack, calling Sung an imperial envoy, and charges him of abusing his authority. He says he is not Sung's subordinate. When Sung explains that he is merely executing the order of the Liaotung Branch Bureau, Lou says that he only accepts orders from the Northeast Bureau and the Department of Military Industry. The debate leads nowhere; in his anger Lou K'un-hua marches out of his office, the handle of his automatic knocking against the door. Next moment, he jumps into a jeep and speeds off.

[12] *Dawn in Wind and Rain*, p. 161.

When Lou K'un-hua returns a few days later Sung Tse-chou is with a senior worker. Chieh Nien-k'uei, over fifty years old, has been a worker at the steel plant since its beginning. He had been fired by the Kuomintang manager the year before for his advanced age as though he were a worn-out machine. When he came to apply for re-employment, Sung Tse-chou was delighted, and treated him like a living reference book. The rich knowledge of the experienced worker, the respect and influence he enjoys among the other workers, and his deep attachment to the steel plant are regarded by Sung as crucial ingredients for the restoration of the factory. When Lou K'un-hua enters Sung's office Chieh Nien-k'uei is writing down, stroke by stroke, the names of reliable workers at the request of Sung Tse-chou.

Lou K'un-hua is portrayed as a soldier with a forthright character. He has been severely criticized at the Department of Military Industry in Harbin, so he openly concedes the loss of his case as soon as he sees Sung. Realizing that the two leaders have business to discuss, Chieh Nien-k'uei rises to leave. But he is stopped by Sung and asked to tell them more about reactions of the workers.

'As soon as we stopped dismantling and removing equipment, they felt secure, delighted. Their worries had gone, their complaints ceased.'

'What have they been worrying and complaining about?'

'They all said that the Communists would leave as soon as the steel plant was finished off and the Kuomintang would be back. The workers all complained and wouldn't listen, for they knew nothing of the military situation.'

'What did they actually say? It's good to know.' Sung Tse-chou said, smiling: 'No outsiders here, let's hear it.'

Chieh Nien-k'uei repeated everything he had heard. Lou K'un-hua was a restive man, not used to sitting still. He wanted to go, but refrained, since the talk had something to do with him. Leaning against Sung's bed, he listened, his broad forehead knitting deeper and deeper and his thick lips closed tightly as if he had swallowed a cup of bitter Chinese medicine. But he sat there motionless. In spite of himself, Sung Tse-chou's expression also turned grave, and he said in a low voice: 'Master Chieh, your information is truly a mirror.'

'You can't blame the workers, for they've no idea what it's all about. Of course, we're not at fault. We've battles to fight, need iron and steel, need machines to repair guns and rifles. The arsenal needs equipment. In the winter of 1945 when the Eighth Route Army was withdrawing I helped load trucks with lathes. Workers often exaggerate . . . Some said that one unit wanted to carry away every piece of iron. Since the plant is made of steel, they wanted to remove the whole steel mill as if it was a huge piece of pig iron. Others said that men from the Railway Bureau at Wafangtien were all bandits . . . Still others said, according to Shih Pao-shu, Director

Lou did not look like a Communist, more like a bandit chieftain . . .'[13]

Lou K'un-hua's reaction is immediate. He is shocked by this unexpected revelation. An old cadre, who has always been proud of his austere style, his ability to mingle with the masses, and his dedication to the interests of the Party, he is suddenly confronted with the workers' vision of himself, or more precisely with his real self. In his long career, he has never doubted his correct approach and his capacity for carrying out party instructions. Now he discovers what he has done is compared to robbery and his behavior equated to that of a bandit chieftain. It is clear to him that Chieh Nien-k'uei is an honest, kind-hearted senior workman who, though not a Communist, has regarded himself as one of them, and thoughtfully views the problem from both sides. Only at this point does he realize that removal of equipment is not just a matter of salvaging resources, nor whether a question of priority should be given to military production or economic reconstruction, but, more importantly, a political question. As long as they remove tools and machines from the steel plant, the workers regard the Communists as no better than the Kuomintang. They harbor a deep suspicion that the Communist control is not going to last, that the Communists have no interest in restoring Anshan Iron and Steel Works to normal production, and that the Communist Party shows no concern for the welfare and livelihood of the workers. With this understanding, Lou K'un-hua is totally reconciled with Sung Tse-chou and walks over to shake the old worker's hand in a gesture of heart-felt appreciation.

The author never treats cadre characters lightly, nor considers them immune to human weaknesses. On the contrary, he portrays cadres according to his observation and finds bureaucrats among them, as in any other large organization. While it takes a psychological shock to awaken Lou K'un-hua to his mistakes, a direct confrontation still fails to change the style and conduct of Tsang Ch'ung, deputy director of Shennan Railway Bureau. Whether there is a need or not, Tsang Ch'ung keeps ordering his men to remove steel plant property, from mountains of coal to freight cars.

Anshan Iron and Steel Works is now under the leadership of the manager Lo Ming-fang and the party representative Sung Tse-chou, assisted by Yi Chiu-fan, the secretary of the Anshan Municipal Party Committee. The three call a meeting in an attempt to halt Tsang Ch'ung's undisciplined looting of the steel factory. After wasting their precious time by keeping them waiting, Tsang Ch'ung finally arrives. He

[13] *Ibid.*, p. 175.

had actually arrived at Anshan railway station much earlier, but waited for a jeep to take him to the plant. Such an excuse further infuriates all three men, who are accustomed to austerity and simplicity. But Tsang Ch'ung, whose college degree was in transportation, shows no interest in their guerrilla style, and does not approve of their make-shift innovations. Lo Ming-fang, an uncompromising and hot-tempered man, starts off the meeting by reading a long list of items hauled away by Tsang Ch'ung's men. The latter simply denies all knowledge of removals. When he cannot reject all the evidence he simply shuffles off the responsibility onto his subordinates. Finally, the three have to remind Tsang Ch'ung of the Party discipline and at the same time appeal to his conscience. Tsang Ch'ung, who has made up his mind not to be engaged in a three-against-one debate, gives a perfunctory promise. He is relieved when the meeting is over and happily invites them to dine at Anshan railway restaurant as his guests. The invitation is declined; instead, he is asked as a favor to ship the grain expected to be delivered from Harbin as soon as it reaches Wafangtien.

Tsang Ch'ung never keeps his promise. Aware that Anshan steel workers need grain which cannot be locally supplied, the Finance Commission of the Party Central orders grain to be shipped from Harbin via Korea and Port Arthur to Wafangtien. But the grain is left unattended in freight cars on desolate tracks. It is discovered by accident by the deputy minister of heavy industry when he comes down to inspect the Anshan steel plant. Tsang Ch'ung's bureaucracy is severely reprimanded, but the story describes neither disciplinary action against him nor a change of heart.

The cadre drawn as a negative type is Tai T'ien-hou. There is an important difference between negative and villain types in the revolutionary ranks. A villain character is either a renegade or an impostor with whom the Party can disclaim any link. A negative type is still a cadre whose presence stains the purity of the revolutionary ranks. By portraying Tai T'ien-hou as a negative character, the author once more demonstrates his realistic rather than ideological approach to treating cadre characters.

Tai T'ien-hou had been a bureau chief, but was down-graded to chief clerk in the plant when a third criticism was added to his dossier. A carefree man who never takes anything seriously except his 220 lb. weight, he is often criticized by both the manager and the party representative. When a worker is crushed by a falling machine Sung Tse-chou blames himself for his failure to take precautionary measures. He sends for the dead man's son and wants to enter the orphan's name on the worker payroll. As the chief clerk brings in the boy, he jokingly calls the boy 'living treasure' and 'your third generation'. A serious, strict man, Sung is extremely displeased with Tai's frivolous attitude.

Later, when Sung discovers that Tai has bought a cheap, unpainted coffin, he insists that he must personally go and choose a good, painted coffin. As far as Tai is concerned, he could not care less in what kind of coffin a dead worker is buried; he resents Sung's fastidious approach toward such a trivial matter.

The chief clerk, who loves to enjoy life, used to have dishes of chicken, duck and fish on the dinner table at home. Now he has to content himself with cabbage and squash and takes it philosophically as the best way to reduce his weight. He smokes American-made Camel cigarettes and has an electric fan installed in his office. A fat man sweats easily, he explains, and it has never been his intention to gain weight in order to enjoy an electric fan. According to his reasoning, a man's weight is an objective reality; besides, the Party rule sets no limit as far as a member's weight goes. He resents Sung Tse-chou's rejection of his request to send for his young, pretty wife in Harbin. 'You people at the top have me to serve you,' he likes to think, 'but who will serve me if not my wife?'

The only person he is willing to respect is the manager Lo Ming-fang, who had been manager of an arsenal in the days of the Kiangsi Soviet, and took part in the Long March. The Party representative Sung Tse-chou, in Tai's eyes, is a junior Party man. Had it not been for the war against Japan, Sung would be teaching in high school at this time. The chief clerk has a particular distrust and instinctive dislike for intellectuals. When the engineer Fang Chin-fei asks him for wooden planks to make boxes for shipping instruments before the evacuation, he assumes an air of importance and dignity. He remembers that Fang, deputy manager of an electric plant during the Kuomintang occupation, had been sent to a training school at Antung, and had been assigned to the steel factory only a few months ago. He is furious that Fang should now dare to press him for wooden planks. He thinks to himself:

'Damn it! Only four months ago, you were our POW. It's not that easy to claim you are a revolutionary when you've had only a few meals in the revolutionary camp. Who knows if you're Red or white, with a brain still full of Japanese Heavenly Emperor, Manchukuo Emperor, and *China's Destiny*.[14] With two feet barely on the threshold of the Communist Party, still a good distance away from being a revolutionary, you've started to talk like a leader. This is outright insubordination! How dare you!'[15]

The serious symptoms of egoism, individualism, and bureaucracy in Tai T'ien-hou, painted in vivid and colorful strokes, must be an accurate reflection of the style and behavior of some cadres during the Civil War.

[14] A book by Chiang Kai-shek considered a blueprint for China's reconstruction.
[15] *Dawn in Wind and Rain*, p. 534.

The author cannot have invented such a character without a personal encounter with men like Tai. While critics regard this character as irrelevant to the story, their real concern is that the image of this cadre may tarnish the Party. If the Party ranks appear to have been filled with the likes of Tai, it can only show its liberal policy. Because of this policy of flexibility and tolerance toward people like Tsang Ch'ung and Tai T'ien-hou, the Communist Party was able to attract men of talent and imagination in its rivalry with the Kuomintang for political leadership of China.

Anshan Steel Workers

During this fluid situation, the primary task of the Communist leadership at Anshan Iron and Steel Works is to win the allegiance of workers. Most workers are basically suspicious of government officials, Kuomintang and Communist alike, and hostile to the attempts to dismantle and removed machines. The Party representative Sung Tse-chou understands the workers' reaction and also the importance of protecting the plant from further destruction. He knows that once the revolution is won on the battlefield and China under Communism embarks on industrial reconstruction, Anshan Iron and Steel Works will play a major role in the production of capital goods. At present, although he tries to stop the undisciplined and disorganized dismantling, he has to supply the arsenal with materials and parts and the army with equipment. Some of the shops, particularly the rolling mill, the bloomery, and the forge, must be quickly reopened. Both from the short-term and long-term view, in addition to ideological considerations, workers must be won over to serve the Communist cause.

The transformation of apolitical workers into committed supporters of the Communist revolution is depicted with remarkable success. The author describes in passing the familiar thesis of the interaction between the style of Communist leadership and reaction from the masses. When the dining hall staff want to prepare special meals for the Party representative and the factory manager, they reject the idea and eat with the others. The guard armed with an automatic stationed in front of the office by the order of the commander of two platoons of soldiers is immediately removed. Although the party representative knows that there are hidden snipers, he prefers to take the risk rather than turn the office into a yamen. Programs such as a two-week training course are obviously important for workers' orientation, but no attempt is made to elaborate on it. The author clearly treats the conversion of workers into the proletarian vanguard as a psychological process. The change in their mental attitude takes several stages; at each stage a dramatic incident is provided to bring about the change.

The first person converted is Chieh Nien-k'uei. He had drifted to Manchuria from Shantung at the age of eighteen, but always used to pay a visit to his mother in his native village every five years. During one visit in the early forties, he discovered life in the village under Communist guerrillas had visibly improved. So it seems quite natural that Chieh is willing and happy to work under the Communist leadership.

Furthermore, the life story of this old worker is told to reinforce the rationale for his loyalty toward the Communist Party. He started his apprenticeship at a Japanese factory two years after the Russo-Japanese War. Unable to memorize Japanese names of machines and tools, he suffered inhuman treatment from Japanese workers and foremen. At the age of twenty-one, he was transferred to the newly-formed steel plant at Anshan. He can tell the history of every blast furnace, open hearth furnace, machine shop, electrical repair shop, forge, bloomery, and smelter. Then after the Showa Steel Works, along with the whole of Manchuria, was returned to China and changed into the Anshan Iron and Steel Works, he suddenly found himself dismissed like useless slag, swept aside by his own countrymen. For this elderly workman, it is sufficient that he is not only rehired but also treated as an invaluable living encyclopaedia of the steel plant by the Party representative.

A close friend of Chieh Nien-k'uei, Wen Ch'ang-shan has heard stories about the Communists from the old worker. Even though he respects and trusts Chieh, Wen is not the kind of man to be easily convinced. This aloof, stubborn, uncompromising steelworker, known as 'Congealed Steel Ingot', is, nevertheless, willing to give Chieh's word the benefit of the doubt. During the brief period of the Communist occupation of Anshan in the winter of 1945, he witnessed Communist soldiers distribute food, oil, and other goods taken from Japanese warehouses among the workers. Comparing what the Eighth Route Army did to the theft of enemy property by Kuomintang generals and officials, Wen has made his choice. When Anshan is retaken by the Communists he actively participates in the workers' guard against looters of the steel mill. Although he aches to see machines and instruments shipped away by various Communist units, he tries to explain to other workers about the need of the Communist war effort. During the first hectic month of Communist control, Kuomintang agents are unknowingly appointed leaders of workers' guards and they fire Wen, but he refuses to turn in his armband and continues to patrol the plant on his own. He is the kind of man who never changes his mind once his opinion is formed.

The 100-ton-crane operator Shih Pao-shu, a friend of Chieh and Wen, is portrayed as an optimistic, humorous, comic figure. Nimble and restive, Shih always thinks of profitable ideas but always ends up with a loss. When the Kuomintang management failed to pay him he engaged in a retail business, only to lose all his savings. Later, when he is paid by the Communist management to guard against theft, he slips out to hunt rabbits and pheasants on the barren, deserted parts of the plant with his home-made gun. His excuse is that he is responding to the Communist call for improving the living standard of workers. Uncritical and credulous, he helps spread rumors, and exaggerates them considerably. Both Chieh Nien-k'uei and Wen Ch'ang-shan disapprove; but neither tries to interfere with his life-style.

In describing workers, the author shows no wish to content himself with ideological models. The influence of Chieh Nien-k'uei on Wen Ch'ang-shan and Shih Pao-shu plays a considerable part in converting their political allegiance, but it remains primarily the function of friendship. The author seems to be able to distinguish a working relationship from friendship and friendship from comradeship. Unless the process of transformation from working relationship to friendship and finally to comradeship is clearly demonstrated, the reader will remain unconvinced of the allegiance of workers to the Communist Party. This process is most effectively portrayed in the relations between Chieh Nien-k'uei, Wen Ch'ang-shan and Shih Pao-shu on the one hand and Hsu Ch'ing-ch'un on the other.

Hsu Ch'ing-ch'un, a lathe shop foreman, has left his job because he refused to collaborate with the Kuomintang manager in stealing factory property to sell. Once outside the plant, he experiences the overpowering effect of dissociating himself from his accustomed way of life and feels as if the ground is sinking beneath him. He stays with his parents-in-law in a nearby village and quickly takes part in the land reform as captain of the local militia. Although he receives six *mou* of land and one of the best house compounds expropriated from landlords, he suffers an acute sense of nostalgia. If the worker is the conqueror of the machine, in Hsu Ch'ing-ch'un's case the machine has also conquered him. He turns a spare room into a workshop with tools like files, pincers, and stainless steel rulers lined up the walls. These instruments are not exactly useful in repairing agricultural implements, but a mere look at them gives Hsu a certain psychological comfort and makes him feel as though he is living in the factory environment.

In other mediocre stories, the characterization of workers is so inapt that they might as well be peasants in workmen's garb. But the author of *Dawn in Wind and Rain* not only portrays workers with vigor and force but also draws a distinction between the mentalities of workers and peasants. When posters recruiting skilled workers appear in the village Hsu is one of the first to register. His wife's uncle, hearing Hsu will earn only three catties of *kaoliang* a day, tries to persaude him to stay, pointing out how in three to five years he will be a well-off peasant with grain filling his barn. Hsu laughingly dismisses the idea and says that if he endures village life any longer, his hair will soon turn grey. Using Old Sun's piece of log as an example, Hsu says:

'When Aunt Liu's stable was about to fall apart Old Sun let her have a piece of his log to prop it up. How much can a section of trunk cost? Well, it became a matter of great importance. Neighbors were invited, as it were in a conference, to discuss its worth. It's all right to haggle. Can't the matter be settled by having one side offer a price and the other the amount she's willing to pay? No, they don't do that. No one was willing to give an exact figure, but everyone made some comment. Those who tried to put in a word for Old Sun said: "It's a piece of red pine", "a piece of log like this is worth a fortune", "it can be used as a beam for a small house", "it must be six-foot long, straight and even", and "not a single rotten hole". Those who sided with Aunt Liu said: "This worn-out trunk won't last long", "not that good anyway", "rather lightweight, not tough stuff", "the bark is already mouldy", and "it shouldn't cost too much". Well, one side wanted to sell for more and the other to pay less, but both went at it in a roundabout way. Fuss for the better part of a day just over a piece of log.'[16]

Hsu Ch'ing-ch'un likes peasants, but he cannot stand the slow pace of village life. Villagers look at the sun to tell the time; their basic time unit is the season, spring for planting and autumn for harvest. When a peasant goes out to do business in town he will turn back simply because he has forgotten to close the pigsty. Then he will be on his way again, and again turn back, worried that a bamboo pole or a sickle left outside the door may be stolen. He may turn back a third time to bring with him a basket and hoe, so that he can pick up animal manure on the way. Hsu Ch'ing-ch'un is so excited about returning to factory life that he gets up before dawn. As his wife is fixing his lunch box for him, he asks her teasingly if her uncle will suggest that he carry a basket and pick up manure along the way.

Once he is put in charge of a workshop for making pickaxes and shovels for the army, he works day and night to fulfill the production quota. He shows no mercy to anybody who is unwilling to break his back to accelerate the pace of production. Although his responsibility is production, he also takes part in driving away burglars and thieves and rounding up hungry boys who make a living stealing from the steel plant. One day he catches a skinny little boy and threatens to beat him up. Frightened, the boy confesses that he has been hired to steal by a hardware-store owner. His boss has told him that if he is caught, Chieh Nien-k'uei will set him free. Hsu then discovers that Chieh's second

[16] *Dawn in Wind and Rain*, p. 293.

daughter is married to the son of the hardware merchant. Stunned and furious that Chieh, so trusted and commended by the plant leadership, should collaborate with a capitalist relative to rob the factory, he calls a workers' meeting to settle accounts with the treacherous hypocrite.

He consults no one, not even his deputy, Wen Ch'ang-shan, and smiles at his bright idea of giving the workers a great surprise. As the workers gather at the workshop, they recognize the little boy, who has been caught several times before, but are astonished to see a grave, sorrowful Chieh Nien-k'uei and his tearful and trembling daughter standing next to the little pilferer on the platform. They begin to work out the situation and clamour for an explanation. Wen Ch'ang-shan, who has known Chieh all his life, simply cannot associate this good honest man with anything improper and indecent. He walks up to the platform and, taking no notice of Hsu Ch'ing-ch'un's objection, takes Chieh to the seat next to his. When Chieh's daughter, even with Shih Pao-shu standing next to her like a fortress to shield her, can only weep, Wen bursts out that he wants to deal personally with that bully Hsu Ch'ing-ch'un. In this tense, explosive situation, someone calls out that the Party representative is coming.

Hsu Ch'ing-ch'un realizes that the situation is out of control and is relieved to see the arrival of Sung Tse-chou. He steps forward to welcome Sung and tries to brief him about the meeting. Cutting him short, the party representative tells Shih Pao-shu to lead the weeping young woman to sit next to her father. Then turning to Chieh Nien-k'uei, Sung holds the old workman's coarse hand and sincerely apologizes for not coming earlier. It turns out that the marriage was forced upon the Chieh family before the Communist take-over of Anshan, the woman has been treated like a slave in the hardware merchant's family, and Chieh has never collaborated with his capitalist kinsman. Hsu is criticized for his failure to listen to Chieh's explanations, to make an investigation into the matter, and to consult the factory leadership. Although Hsu has shown himself a man of principle, he has made a serious mistake by being subjective.

Though Sung Tse-chou sees both merits and shortcomings in Hsu's handling of the incident, Wen Ch'ang-shan never forgives Hsu for humiliating his best friend, which he sees as a personal insult. One rainy night, as Wen is patrolling the factory, he discovers that all the men he has placed at several spots to guard against burglars have disappeared. Someone tells him that Hsu has ordered them to join the workforce to speed up production. Wen can no longer stand the dictatorial style of Hsu, who has encroached upon his jurisdiction and has his men transferred without notifying him. Furious, he marches to Hsu's office, intending to teach him a lesson.

Hsu is not in his office but lying asleep, huddled beside a pile of new finished products, a marker still in his hand. Wen is going to question a workman, but is hushed up. Pulling Wen some distance away from the sleeping Hsu, the workman explains that the slightest noise will wake him, yet he has not had a chance to close his eyes for three days and nights. Walking away profoundly moved, Wen blames himself for not giving Hsu sufficient help and for never trying to find out what difficulties Hsu encounters in trying to keep to a very tight production schedule. That very night, some Kuomintang undercover agents, armed with weapons, come to dig up machines they have hidden in a remote corner of the factory. Trying to stop the removal of the machines single-handed, Wen receives a severe head wound.

This series of incidents lead to mutual respect and appreciation between Wen Ch'ang-shan and Hsu Ch'ing-ch'un. Hsu blames himself for Wen's wounds, but fortunately, under the intensive care of the hospital staff, Wen finally comes off the danger list. On the eve of the Communist evacuation from Anshan, Wen Ch'ang-shan receives a telephone call from Hsu.

> The voice in the receiver no longer belonged to the man who used to shout and yell, roar and bellow. Wen Ch'ang-shan was astonished. Almost unconsciously, there rose in Hsu Ch'ing-ch'un's mind a strange, dignified feeling, as if he had got rid of all worldly worries and earthly attachment and was entering a pure and serene realm. In a voice full of peace and tenderness incomprehensible to himself, he said:
> 'Comrade Wen Ch'ang-shan.'
> Calm and firm as usual, Wen answered:
> 'Comrade Hsu Ch'ing-ch'un.'
> . . . [17]

The word 'comrade' is so lavishly used in the post-1949 period as a form of address that it comes to mean no more than 'mister', simply a friendly greeting between fellow-workers, part of polite conversation. But in July 1948 in Anshan on the eve of the Kuomintang counter-offensive, the word, which for the first time slips out between the two workers, has a very rich meaning. It indicates the change of relationship from fellow workers and friends to comrades. It suggests an implicit commitment, a complete understanding between the two men of the aspirations and goals they share. Although the two men are still not Communists, they both spontaneously think Communist. This little incident provides the last link in the transformation of the workers into the proletarian vanguard.

[17] *Ibid.*, p. 588.

The Industrial Take-off and the New Status of Workers

Steel production, which was once used by economists as a measure of a nation's defense capability as well as industrial power, also receives the greatest attention in China as the basis of industrialization. In order to depict steelmaking as the symbol of China's struggle for industrialization, and steel workers as the representatives of the working class, Ai Wu spent considerable time in a factory, to familiarize himself with the industry's technology and experience the life of the workers. Such a serious attitude on the part of a veteran novelist[18] seems to promise a work of excellence. *Steeled and Tempered*, however, disappointingly turns out to be a hack work. The validity of the theory that intellectuals' participation in physical labor will change their outlook, concepts, and attitudes is difficult to evaluate. But the novel shows that Ai Wu remains an observer. He has failed to penetrate the minds of the workers, or even to see them as individuals. As a result, the main characters are surprisingly shallow; the conflicts between them are artificially contrived to create a certain amount of tension.

The story begins with a noisy scene of steelmaking on the eve of China's industrial take-off, as it embarks on the First Five-Year Plan. Some four years have elapsed since the dismantling and salvaging of machinery at the Anshan Iron and Steel Works in 1948. At that time Japanese engineers predicted that it would take over twenty years for the Chinese to restore steel plants to full-capacity production, and advised that better use could be made of the land by growing *kaoliang*.[19] But in the opening scene of *Steeled and Tempered*, as Liang Ching-chun, the newly-appointed party secretary to the steel plant, is riding in a car chauffered by a girl driver along a broad road, this is what he sees:

> The first thing Liang Ching-chun saw was the open yard where raw materials were kept. A train was just moving a load of ten-foot iron ladles, while another was carrying off a large quantity of black ore. The giant bridge-type crane overhead, lifting four iron tubs of ore, was pouring it out with a reverberating roar onto the platform of a huge building. Liang had never seen a building as big as this, made completely of iron and steel. High up, flames could be seen escaping

[18] Ai Wu's well-known novels published during the period 1938–49 include *The Fertile Plain (Feng-jao ti yüan-yeh)*, *On the River (Chiang-shang hsing)*, *My Native Village (Ku-hsiang)*, *Mountain Wilderness (Shan-yeh)*, and *A Woman's Tragedy (I-ko yü-jen ti Pei-chü)*. See C. T. Hsia, *A History of Modern Chinese Fiction, 1917–1957* (Yale University Press, 1961), pp. 633–4.

[19] *Steeled and Tempered*, p. 3. A similar prediction made by a Japanese engineer to the vice-minister of heavy industry then inspecting Anshan Iron and Steel Works is described in *Dawn in Wind and Rain*, p. 368.

from the gaping apertures of the fire doors of the open-hearth furnaces. Below, the row of kiln-like regenerative chambers, the slag chambers and the curved giant gas tubings loomed black and sombre. Golden-coloured liquid flowed down the furnaces. There was a smell of gas in the air. Beyond the yard, a row of tall chimneys shot up from the horizon, gently puffing out smoke of different colours: light red, pale green, light yellow, grey . . .[20]

The frenetic pace of steel production at the plant of the Liaonan Iron and Steel Company seems to be the single goal of all the employees, from the manager and the party secretary to furnace chiefs and workers. All eyes are confronted with slogans like 'Fight for the Motherland's Socialist Industrialization!' and 'Have you fulfilled your daily quota?' posted on the wooden palings and the bulletin board at the entrance to the factory building. But the battle for more and better steel creates strain and tension which in turn results in conflict between the workers. Since setting a new record in high-speed steel-making will not only put the furnace chief's name on a large blackboard or even in the national newspapers but also reward him with a bonus, keen competition arises among the chiefs of the three shifts. Competition quickly germinates distrust, jealousy and hostility. The production of record-breaking high-speed steel depends on constantly increasing the gas from the pipes of the coke oven and blast furnace. But when the silica bricks are white hot the furnace chief must reduce the heat to allow the furnace roof to turn from white to red, thus preventing it from melting. If a newly-overhauled furnace roof remains intact through thirty steel heatings, the chiefs of all three shifts will receive another bonus. The mutual distrust is thus compounded when a chief wants to set a record in high-speed steelmaking at the expense of melting the roof. Then he can collect a bonus for the new record, while the other two have to lose theirs because of the roof. In the end every chief suspects the other two of pursuing selfish aims at the cost of government property as well as his own income.

There are other problems. Yuan Ting-fa, A-shift chief of No. 9 furnace, has learned steelmaking the hard way as a worker under Japanese foremen. He still views the relationship between a furnace chief and his assistants and other workers as one between a master workman and his apprentices. He is unwilling to share his experience with other chiefs and workers because as an old-fashioned workman, he thinks that he should keep a little of his knowledge to himself. The publicity given to Chin Teh-kuei, C-shift chief, for setting a new record worries Yuan, who sees his prestige as the senior and most experienced workman threatened. He cannot help feeling a twinge of jealousy

---

[20] *Steeled and Tempered*, p. 3.

toward the young man and secretly suspects that the shop leaders prefer young workers to old-timers, though he is only thirty-two years old.

The conflict generated by competition between Chin Teh-kuei and the B-shift chief, Chang Fu-chuan, is further complicated by their interest in the same girl. Sun Yu-fen, a woman worker at a nearby Electric Repair Works, seems more interested in making relays than in getting married, but she is on friendly terms with both. The two men suffer sleepless nights; each begins to suspect the other of making things difficult for him. Their relationship rapidly deteriorates, with the help of a certain worker who keeps telling each of the other's progress with the girl.

The problem of disunity among the three chiefs of No. 9 furnace never gains the attention of the factory manager, who is preoccupied with production targets, quota fulfilment, and other statistics. His approach to the problem of high speed steelmaking is over-simplified. As long as workers have a chance to get their names published in newspapers and to receive a bonus, they will try to excel in production. But for the party secretary, the material incentive is insufficient, and increasing the political awareness of the workers is of primary importance. If they study current affairs and keep abreast of the progress of industrial reconstruction all over the country, he is convinced that they will devote themselves to improving steel production.

A good case can of course be made for showing material reward as a less effective incentive. But merely involving workers in discussing current affairs and keeping them informed of industrial progress elsewhere may not be a more effectual alternative. Another fundamental weakness of the Party secretary (or Ai Wu's conception of the function of Party secretary) is his simple-minded belief that political awareness means a worker's membership of the Communist Party. When he first arrived at the factory he witnessed a moving scene, when Chin Teh-kuei rushed to No. 7 furnace to help open the tap hole. In his efforts to break open the tap hole, Chin inserted two iron tubes deep into the furnace, paying no attention to the fire burning his gloves. At this split second, the operator in charge of the controls pushed the tipping gear button, and the furnace started slanting backward to pour out molten steel into the huge ladle hung under the 100-ton-crane. Chin's skill and nerve thus saved the molten steel from turning into waste product. Amazed and deeply moved, the Party secretary asked someone next to him if Chin was a Party member and received an affirmative answer. He nodded; that explained everything.

The Party secretary's approach to Yuan Ting-fa's haughty attitude as a master worker is to make him a Party member. The implication is that once a worker becomes a Party man, he will immediately place the interests of the Party and the country above his personal ambitions. This approach reflects the author's understanding (or misunderstanding) of the functioning of the Party. In all other novels, a person is initiated into the Communist Party only after he has proved his worth. This is the only case where the Party secretary wants to make a man a Party member because he is politically backward.

The theme of *Steeled and Tempered* is revealed in the counsel the Party secretary gives to Chin Teh-kuei:

> 'Steel is only made after it is tempered. We should study intensely, striving to make ourselves as hard as steel after it is tempered!'[21]

Yet, there is no evidence of Chin Teh-kuei or any other worker being tempered and steeled during the course of the story. The novel ends with Chin being severely wounded in his attempt to shut the valves to prevent the gas pipes from blowing up. As an emergency device, the gas pipes are linked to water pipes which can be turned on to fill the former with water to prevent any gas leakage. Though choked by hot smoke, Chin manages to push open the valves of the water pipes one after another, thus preventing the plant from being leveled to the ground. Just as he is finishing the job, something knocks him unconscious. The incident is designed to show Chin's valor, but it does not prove him a more courageous or dedicated man than before. Even without the benefit of the Party secretary's encouragement and advice, Chin would probably have done exactly the same, just as he had burnt his hands opening the tap hole at No. 7 furnace, when the Party secretary first arrived.

The accident at the furnace and Chin's wounds turn out to be the doing of a saboteur, a surprise as cheap as it is incredible. It is bad enough to attribute troubles to the work of a counter-revolutionary, but worse still when no explanations of the motives of such a saboteur are given. That undercover Kuomintang agents were trying to disrupt the operation of Anshan Iron and Steel Works in 1948, as described in *Dawn in Wind and Rain*, is perfectly credible. It is, however, quite improbable that in 1953 a lone saboteur should still be lurking in the dark to destroy a steel plant.

In *Steeled and Tempered* the workers have never been transformed; they simply joined in the socialist industrialization. There is perhaps no longer the need to show this process of transformation. Workers are different from peasants who have to give up a patch of land, an ox or an orchard, little enough, but nevertheless all they possess. The argument that peasants are better off now under the commune system does not obliterate the tensions, uncertainties, and anguish they suffered in the early stages of agricultural collectivization. Nor did the

---

[21] *Ibid.*, p. 203, English version, p. 257.

efforts of the government to persuade, enlighten, and promise peasants a bright future completely alleviate the agonies of villagers over the loss of their land before the arrival of better days. In this respect, workers are much more fortunate. They have never owned so much as a screw; hence, they are indifferent to the change from private to state ownership. From another point of view, they may well have been jubilant when factories were taken over from capitalists, mostly Japanese, British, French, or American.

Chinese workers never participated, except at the beginning and towards the end, in the bloody and painful revolution. They seem to have reaped the fruit without planting the seed. The failure of *Steeled and Tempered* is not so much due to the absence of intense conflict as to the portrayal of conflict and characters in ideological terms. Conflict is not necessarily reflected in violent action. Two fellow workers, who labor at the same furnace and live in the same dormitory, can have intense conflict without saying a word to each other. Ai Wu evades the real issues by inserting sabotage and rescue missions. It is of course a far more challenging task to portray the tempering and steeling of workers without the help of a saboteur.

That workers are happier people in Communist China today need not be questioned. *Steeled and Tempered*, though a failure as a work of art, does tell us about the new social status of workers. When a worker in his brand-new suit is on holiday in his native village, everyone notices him and talks about him. As a member of the vanguard, he becomes candidate for ideal husband in the dreams of most country girls, much to the envy of the young peasants. Workers are among the first privileged to own status symbols such as bicycles, watches, and radio sets. And urban life, with its stage shows and motion pictures, is so much more exciting than the slow pace of village life. In spite of the perennial exhortations to self-denial, material comfort is tacitly accepted as an important motive force.

Chinese workers, unlike their Western counterparts, have never known organization life in the form of the trade union movement and collective bargaining. In *Seeds of Flame* there is a description of the activities spontaneously organized by workers themselves to stop the take-over of the shipyard and to prevent a thousand workers being laid off. But this collective action is undermined by shrewd manipulation by the capitalists, with the result that most workers lose their jobs. In the absence of representative democracy and an independent press, workers have been the prey of predatory capitalists, domestic and foreign. It seems natural that they should look to the Communist Party for leadership, appreciate their newly-won social status, and be eager to contribute to the industrialization of China.

9

AGRICULTURAL COLLECTIVIZATION

I THE SOCIALIST MAN *VERSUS* THE RENEGADE

So far we have not discussed the literary trends as well as the doctrines guiding fiction-writing in Communist China. The reason is that the novels we have dealt with reflect the pre-1949 period and their themes cover various aspects of the armed struggle. Controversies did emerge from time to time, but they were basically academic, with no direct bearing on current policies. Novelists who chose to portray the socialist period, and the theme of agricultural collectivization in particular, faced a quite different problem. A description of what happened during the process of the socialist transformation of agriculture is not enough. They must perform the function of propagandists, to help persuade the peasants to accept official policies.

The socialist transformation of agriculture has been through three stages, from mutual-aid teams via elementary co-operatives to advanced co-operatives. The goals of the Party in agricultural socialization are multiple. First, mutual-aid teams will solve the shortage in manpower and farming tools. By 1953 a trend towards land reconcentration was already discernible. Peasant families who received land in the land reform but could not make efficient use of it due to the shortage of labor and tools were again in financial trouble. Some of these families had to borrow money at a high interest from rich peasants, and after two or three years had to pay their debts by selling their land.[1] If this trend were not stopped, it is conceivable that in a few more years a landlord class would re-emerge. Such an outcome would nullify all the efforts made during the land reform and result in a restoration of the old order. The Party could not stage another land reform without causing serious economic disruption and political disorder.

---

[1] These problems are pointed out in a survey of nine villages in Manchuria conducted in October–December 1953. See Chung-kung chung-yang tung-pei-ch'ü nung-ts'un kung-tso-pu (Department of Rural Works of the Northeast Bureau of the CCP), 'Sung-chiang Chi-lin ho Liao-tung chiu-ko ts'un ti t'iao-ch'a pao-kao' (Report of a Survey of Nine Villages in Sungkiang, Chilin and Liaotung), *Jen-min jih-pao*, February 15, 1954.

238   *Heroes and Villains in Communist China*

Then, socialism is the avowed goal of the Communist Party; communization of the means of production is the basis of a Communist society. In addition to the Party's ideological commitment, agricultural socialization is considered the only road to solving the poverty and backwardness which have plagued China for centuries. Only by this means can China undertake large-scale projects, such as the construction of dams and irrigation systems, the mechanization of agriculture, and the industrialization of the country.

During the early phase of agricultural socialization, a sense of optimism permeated the thinking of the leaders. They do not seem to have underestimated the tremendous difficulties likely to be encountered on the road to socialism, and were well aware that the objective conditions for socialization of agriculture had not been met, but felt that if the first step were not taken immediately, it might be too late. In the cautious initial stages, all coercive methods were ruled out, and the peasants were allowed to participate in mutual-aid teams on a voluntary basis. In view of the long tradition of private farming, they were not expected to form or join mutual-aid teams on their own initiative. But it was also argued that peasants were practical people: once the merits of mutual aid were demonstrated, they would be willing to participate in collective farming. So pilot projects were launched. The Party gave all possible support to ensure the success of pioneer mutual-aid teams, from interest-free loans to technical assistance for increasing productivity. On top of that, the local Party hierarchy provided political guidance as well as moral support to experimental mutual-aid teams. On the assumption that peasants would develop an interest and enthusiasm for collective farming once they saw the advantages of co-operation, the Party embarked on the program of agricultural socialization.

Neither Heroes nor Villains

The reliance on the awakening of the masses in developing socialism is the underlying thesis in Chao Shu-li's *Sanliwan Village*[2] and Chou Li-po's *Great Changes in a Mountain Village.*[3] Both novels describe the

[2] Chao Shu-li, *San-li-wan* (Peking: Popular Readers Publishing House, 1955), rev. ed. (Peking: People's Literature Publishing House, 1959); *Sanliwan Village*, trans. by Gladys Yang, (Peking: Foreign Languages Press, 1964).
[3] Chou Li-po, *Shan-hsiang chü-pien*, Vol. 1 (Peking: Writers' Publishing House, 1958); *Great Changes in a Mountain Village*, trans. by Derek Bryan, (Peking: Foreign Languages Press, 1961). 'Tsao ch'i – *Shan-hsiang chü-pien* hsü-p'ien chung ti liang chang' (Early Rise – Two Chapters from the Sequel to *Great Changes in a Mountain Village*), *Jen-min wen-hsüeh*, November 1959, pp. 4–15.

transition from elementary to advanced co-operatives. *Sanliwan Village* was first published in May 1955 and *Great Changes in a Mountain Village* completed in December 1957. The dates are significant from the viewpoint of theme, plot, and characterization. Up to this time, the governing literary theory has been socialist realism.

The theory of socialist realism as a guiding principle was expounded by Chou Yang at the Second Congress of Chinese writers and artists on September 24, 1953. After a broad assessment of socialist literature in the Soviet Union and China after the 'Yenan Forum Talks', Chou Yang singled out Ting Ling's *Sun over the Sungkan River*, Chou Li-po's *Hurricane*, and *The White-haired Girl (Pai-mao nü)* by Ho Ching-chih and Ting Yi as models for socialist realism.[4] These works are dull and unimaginative as literature, but at least they are enriched by wily and wicked villains.

When the program of agricultural collectivization was launched the landlord as villain had been removed permanently from China's countryside and fictional works. Even valiant and resourceful heroes, the dominant characters in novels portraying the armed struggle before 1949, had turned into dedicated and disciplined organization men. Thus, the characters who people *Sanliwan Village* and *Great Changes in a Mountain Village* are neither heroes nor villains, but positive and negative types.

Sanliwan Village reflects the early optimism of the leadership that the peasants' vision of the bright socialist future is more important than any other incentive. In the process of developing the elementary co-operative into the advanced type, model peasants were given opportunities to visit state collective farms and to witness the use of farming machines. There is a vivid description in the novel of a peasant telling others about a combine harvester he has seen working at the provincial state farm:

> ... It is true he had already given a talk on this, but as everyone was so eager to know more details, and kept asking him to describe just how many parts the combine harvester had and what was the function of each, he was reduced to acting out its movements. He told them the thing looked like a small, multi-storey building, and cut a swathe as wide as four or five harrows, stowing the grain it reaped into small rooms one above the other, threshing the wheat and winnowing it as clean as could be, then loading it on a truck ... He filled out his description with gestures.

[4] Chou Yang, 'Wei ch'uang-tsao keng-to-ti yu-hsiu-ti wen-hsüeh i-shu tso-p'in erh feng-tou' (Fight for the Creation of More and Better Literary and Artistic Works), *Wen-i pao*, No. 19, Oct. 15, pp. 7–16. For a discussion of Chou Yang's speech, see D. W. Fokkema, *Literary Doctrine in China and Soviet Influence, 1956–1960* (The Hague: Mouton & Co., 1965), pp. 37–42.

'How does it catch hold of so much wheat all at once?' demanded Chieh-hsi.

'It uses a very long wheel, as long as the wheel of our windmill. The flails scoop the wheat into a sort of trough . . .' He picked up two scythes and stepped into the millet field to illustrate what he meant, but took such a swipe that he knocked down two ears of millet.

'That machine needs repairing!' cried someone.[5]

The machine apparently fascinates the peasants and opens a new horizon in their rather conservative minds. The development of co-operatives is considered by the leadership to be an educational process. The peasants are made aware of the futility of the attempt to build private fortunes and are constantly reminded of how in the old days their hard-earned land was devoured by greedy landlords. Natural calamities, sickness, deaths, and other unforeseeable misfortunes can reduce a well-off peasant to the level of a pauper. They are urged to think in a different way, abandon the idea of pursuing their private interests, and think in terms of collective progress. Only by joining with others in strengthening co-operatives can their security be assured. They are encouraged to think in the long-term and develop a vision of the future. In *Sanliwan Village* this vision of an affluent community is presented in the form of a water-color painted by a professional artist who has come to experience life in the countryside:

The hills and Sandy Creek were thickly wooded now, and a little way up the hillside, not far from the flats, was a highway running north from the village. There were trucks on this road, and telegraph-poles beside it. Trees grew inside and all around the village, but nestling among them you could glimpse new roof tops. The farming now was on a much larger scale — on half the Lower Flats waved golden wheat, while the other half was divided into two parts, one for autumn crops, one for vegetables. The Upper Flats were given over to autumn crops. In the wheat fields on the Lower Flats combine harvesters were reaping the wheat, a cultivator was weeding the Upper Flats . . .[6]

The title of the picture is 'A Socialist Sanliwan,' a vision of the distant future no doubt. The peasants, the leadership reasons, after seeing some results of collective labor, will begin to entertain the notion that that day will finally come. This hope, this expectation, it is anticipated, will sustain their will to work hard, help them to forget immediate hardships, and enhance their confidence in the party policy.

The Communist Party's policy in the first half of the '50s, as shown

[5] *Sanliwan Village*, pp. 60–1, Yang, pp. 93–4.
[6] *Ibid.*, p. 128, Yang, pp. 194–5.

in *Sanliwan Village*, reflects a confidence that through competition between co-operative and private farming, the merits of socialism will be demonstrated. The co-operative, backed by the resources of the state, is bound to compare favorably with the archaic methods of individual farming. As a further incentive, each family's acreage and grade of land are appraised on entry as a basis for grain distribution at harvest time. Prices are also set for the livestock and tools turned over to the co-operative; their owners can draw interest. However that may be, the incorporation of land into the co-operative proves to be more difficult than anything so far encountered. Yuan Tien-cheng, a more or less typical peasant in *Sanliwan Village*, tries to hold back more land than he alone can farm. Others[7] simply refuse to join.

Fan Teng-kao, a local cadre, is typical of Party members who show no interest in the co-operative. He had been an activist during the land reform and served as the village Party secretary. Preoccupied with the idea of profit-making, he has hired a former horse-dealer as his mule-driver and has been peddling goods between town and village, in violation of the Party rules. He has refused to join the co-operative on the grounds that it should be a voluntary decision by each individual. Because of his profiteering, he has failed to be re-elected as the Party secretary. Instead of seeing this as a warning, Fan considers himself the victim of a power struggle. In his view, the new Party secretary Wang Chin-sheng's enthusiasm in starting the co-operative and opening a canal is a case of sheer exhibitionism. Wang has not only deprived him of power but is also scheming to get those two mules of his.

At a small-scale rectification meeting, Fan argues his case, not without eloquence. He says that when the Party told him to take office he complied. When it told him to settle accounts with landlords he did so. When no one dared to take the land expropriated from landlords and the Party urged him to give the lead, he again complied. Later, when people complained that he had received extra land, he returned it in accordance with party instructions. After the land reform, on the call of the Party to produce more grain, he increased his yield. He demands how anybody can accuse him of entertaining capitalist ideas.

Under a different system a man's drive for profit and gain would be regarded as honorable endeavor. But Sanliwan, or China, is moving toward socialism; moreover, Fan has benefited from the economic measures adopted by the Communist Party. His plausible claims are shattered by the arguments of Chang Lo-yi, the co-op chairman, who says:

---

[7] The strongest resistance comes from middle peasants. The portrayal of middle characters and the controversy surrounding it will be the subject of discussion in the next chapter.

'In the old society, you drove mules for Liu Lao-wu while I tilled his land for him. We were both his hired hands, and each knew just how many pecks of grain the other had. But compare yourself with the rest of our Party since then — didn't you do best of the lot? Yet you've the biggest grudge against the Party. Why? To my mind, it's just because you did too well. And all this at the expense of others, mind you, just like a capitalist. You drove mules for Liu Lao-wu, and now Wang is driving mules for you — you're trying to copy Liu. Since the Party won't stand for this, of course you bear the Party a grudge! Comrade! Brother! We've been friends for twenty years and, speaking both as your old comrade and old friend, I don't want to see you turn into a second Liu Lao-wu! That would be as bad as having Liu himself lording it over Sanliwan again. Think carefully now which road you ought to take!'[8]

Fan Teng-kao finally agrees to join the co-operative, not because he sees the light but because he has no choice. He has been under pressure from his own daughter, a Youth Leaguer, and has also received a stiff warning from the village Party committee. Although the Party policy makes it clear that it is up to each individual whether he joins the co-operative, Fan can no longer wear a Communist badge if he continues to behave like a backward peasant. So, partly by persuasion and partly by coercion, a member rejoins the Party rank.

By describing both normative and coercive methods, Chao Shu-li manages to tell a story of the peasants' conversion to the idea of an agricultural co-operative. Chou Li-po's *Great Changes in a Mountain Village*, dealing with the same theme, is much less convincing. The author has planned the story as a sequel to *The Hurricane*; the plot structure is strikingly similar to that of the earlier novel. While in *The Hurricane* a work team is dispatched to help carry out the land reform in a Manchurian village, in *Great Changes in a Mountain Village* a county-level cadre is sent to a backward village in Hunan to organize a co-operative. In *The Hurricane*, however, the author is able to reflect the acute class struggle and the brutal tactics adopted by the work team in destroying the landlord class. In developing the co-operative, tactics once used against class enemies cannot be employed against unwilling and rebellious peasants. Thus the unconvincing arguments made by cadres as described in the novel fail to justify the conversion of the peasants.

The leading cadre in *Great Changes in a Mountain Village* is Li Yueh-hui, Party secretary and chairman of the peasants' association. He loves to tell unfunny jokes and goes about things in a leisurely way. He is always so agreeable and good-tempered that he has earned the

---

[8] *Sanliwan Village*, pp. 119–20, Yang, p. 182.

nickname 'Granny'. The young woman sent by the county Party committee shows neither imagination nor skill in dealing with the problems of consolidating the co-operative. On the other hand, peasants, knowing that their land and livestock will have to go to the co-operative, show their opposition by cutting down bamboos and trees for sale in the market and slaughtering their most valued oxen. The author spends more than 250 pages in describing the restiveness of peasants and a bare fifteen pages on the formation of the advanced co-operative. He never attempts to describe the process of change from resistance to conversion; thus he reveals by default the intense opposition of peasants toward the policy of agricultural co-operation.

These two celebrated novels effectively make it clear that the agricultural policy of the Communist Party is less than popular. It appears to have generated opposition, apathy and pessimism, rather than the enthusiastic support anticipated. Since material incentives have failed, a normative incentive seems to be needed. In the view of the leadership, the pace of agricultural collectivization is slow because the masses have not been ideologically armed. The primary task is to create hero models who will lead the masses to socialism. The compilation *The Socialist High Tide in China's Countryside*[9] in 1956 was designed to meet this need. The data included in the three volumes of this document are primarily stories about successful co-operatives and socialist heroes who have helped to develop agricultural socialization. Mao Tse-tung, in his editorial note to one of the reports, 'Ch'en Hsüeh-meng, a Leader of the Co-operative Movement', says: 'In China heroes like him are counted in thousands and tens of thousands, but regretfully writers have not yet found them.'[10]

Hung-ch'i (Red Flag), the authoritative party journal, was inaugurated in June 1958 to cope with current problems on a theoretical level. The first issue, significantly, carries Mao Tse-tung's article 'Recommending a Co-operative'.[11] In the same issue a new literary theory, combining revolutionary realism with revolutionary romanticism, is presented to replace socialist realism in an article by Chou Yang.[12]

[9] Chung-kung chung-yang pan-kung-t'ing (The Staff Office of the Communist Party Central), ed., *Chung-kuo nung-ts'un ti she-hui-chu-i kao-ch'ao (The Socialist High Tide in China's Countryside)* (Peking: People's Publishing House, 1956).

[10] *Ibid.*, Vol. II, p. 544, quoted to repudiate Shao Ch'üan-lin's theory of portraying men in the middle in ' "Hsieh chung-chien jen-wu" shih tzu-ch'an-chieh-chi ti wen-hsüeh chu-chang' ('Portraying Men in the Middle' Is the Literary Proposition of the Bourgeoisie), *Wen-i pao*, Nos. 8/9, September 1964, p. 10.

[11] Mao Tse-tung, 'Chieh-shao i-ko ho-tso-she' (Recommending a Co-operative), *Hung-ch'i*, June 1958, pp. 3–4.

[12] Chou Yang, 'Hsin min-ko k'ai-t'o-liao shih-ko ti hsin tao-lu' (The New Folk Songs Cleared a New Road for Poetry), *Hung-ch'i*, June 1958, p. 35.

Attributing the theory to Mao Tse-tung, Chou Yang holds that Mao, in fact, has always applied the theory of combining revolutionary realism with revolutionary romanticism in his poems. The theory brings to a close the period of arid novels produced under the governing doctrine of socialist realism and opens a new era of imaginative literature.

Struggle sans *Villains*

The thrust of the theory of combining revolutionary realism with revolutionary romanticism lifts the quality of creative writing to a much higher level. The key word is romanticism, which allows some scope for the imagination. This more liberal theory nourished the publication of, among others, *The Builders*,[13] which is hailed as a landmark in the development of socialist literature; its hero, Liang Sheng-pao, is considered the embodiment of the 'socialist man.'[14] Superficially, the portrayal of individual heroes deviates from the principle of the mass line, but the importance of heroes as the moving force in developing socialism fits in perfectly with Mao Tse-tung's thesis that man is the prime factor in any form of struggle. Socialism is made by the socialist and Liang Sheng-pao, leader of a mutual-aid team, is the first 'socialist man' to appear in Chinese Communist Literature.

   Liang Sheng-pao has been brought in rags to Frog Flat at the age of three by his mother, among the teeming famine refugees from the upper country of Shensi. They were taken in by Liang the Third, a widower of forty, who had nothing but a narrow shack. He was an able-bodied man who stubbornly refused to give in, in spite of severe deprivation. No matter how hard he tried, he could only support mother and son at bare subsistence level. When Sheng-pao was thirteen he hired himself out as a half-pay farm hand. The boy swallowed insults from the landlord's son and worked even harder than his step-father in order to learn all about farm work. At eighteen he had mastered all the skills a peasant needed and earnestly began farming on his own. But

---

[13] Liu Ch'ing, *Ch'uang yeh shih*, Vol. I (Peking: Chinese Youth Publishing House, 1960); *The Builders*, trans. by Sidney Shapiro, (Peking: Foreign Languages Press, 1964). Two excerpts from the second of this four-volume project appeared: 'Ju tang' (Joining the Party), *Shanghai wen-hsüeh*, No. 12, December 5, 1960, pp. 3–13, and 'Liang Sheng-pao yü Hsu Kai-hsia', *Shuo-huo*, No. 1, 1964, pp. 16–29, 52.

[14] Chou Yang, 'Wo kuo she-hui-chu-i wen-hsüeh i-shu ti tao-lu' (The Path of Socialist Literature and Art in Our Country), *Wen-i pao*, Nos. 13/14, 1960, pp. 19–20; Li Hsi-fan, 'Ke-ming ying-hsiung tien-hsing ti hsün-li' (Review of Typical Revolutionary Heroes), *Wen-hsüeh p'ing-lun*, No. 1, Feb. 14, 1961, pp. 37–8; and Yao Wen-yuan, 'Chung-kuo nung-ts'un she-hui-chu-i ke-ming shih-Tu *Ch'uang yeh shih*' (Epic of Socialist Revolution in Rural China – After Reading *The Builders*), *Wen-i pao*, Nos. 18/19, September 26, 1960, p. 35.

despite a bumper harvest, grain had to be paid to the landlord as rent, and to repay a loan and interest to the money-lender, while the remainder was carted away by the tax collector. Worse still, Sheng-pao was conscripted by the Kuomintang army and had to be bought out with the money from selling the yellow ox. Deprived of all means of livelihood, the family survived until the liberation on wild vegetables, fallen wheat heads gathered from the harvested fields, and grain picked from the roadside.

All these events are described in the prelude. This background is important, for it provides all the essentials for the making of a hero in the new age of socialism. Liang, clearly of poor peasant denomination, has been exploited by the class enemies (landlord and money-lender) and oppressed by reactionary rule (the Kuomintang). He has been the witness and victim of famine and drought. Like so many other poor peasants, he has attempted to build his family fortunes by hard work, but without success. Herein lies the solid foundation for the party thesis that in a starkly poor country like China the only road to survival and progress is through the combined efforts of all the people. It is on men like Liang Sheng-pao that Chairman Mao counts to build a China free from starvation.

Why Liang Sheng-pao plunges into the drive to develop a mutual-aid team is best explained in a dialogue between father and son. The old man has been quarrelling lately with everyone in the family. He is furious to see Sheng-pao wasting time on meetings instead of concentrating on tilling the land like a good peasant should. He threatens to help squander money himself since no one is interested in building the family fortunes. Sheng-pao decides to enlighten his step-father by explaining the difference between collective prosperity and the spontaneous development of each for himself:

'Do you know what spontaneous development is, pa?' Sheng-pao asked. 'Let me give you an example and you'll see. Under the land reform we got ten *mou*, right? Let's say I didn't bother with the mutual-aid team. Let's say you and I worked as hard on these ten *mou* of ours as we did on the eighteen we rented from the landlord in the old days. Every year we'd use our surplus grain to buy more land. Isn't that what you want? But the Jen family doesn't have many people who can work, and they've got a lot of kids. They can't produce much without the help of the mutual-aid team. Every year they'd have to sell us a piece of their fields. That would be natural, wouldn't it? All right, in eight or ten years they'd be back to where they were before the land reform. All their land would be in our name. We'd be rich. They'd have to work for us. Right?'[15]

[15] *The Builders*, p. 114, Shapiro, p. 126.

Old Liang finds this very sensible talk, and he cannot conceal his delight. But he is a generous man, and says he is opposed to exploitation. They are not going to take on hired hands nor rent out grain at high interest, he maintains. But Sheng-pao cuts him short:

> 'You wouldn't be able to control it', said Sheng-pao. 'It's very strange. The more land and money a peasant gets, the less he feels like working. The carrying pole and hauling rope begin hurting his shoulder, they're uncomfortable. When you get to that stage, you want to let others do the work for you. Pa, what kind of mind can a man have who doesn't like to work? He's got nothing to do all day but think up schemes that are bad for other people and profitable to himself.'[16]

This little conversation suggests the reason for Liang Sheng-pao's determination to make a personal sacrifice for the sake of collective prosperity. Thus he is a hero with a new mission, indeed a more formidable one. In the heat of armed conflict a man can easily be aroused even to give his life. The making of a hero in a revolutionary war is the work, in no small part, of impulse, passion, and an urge to be identified with glory or martyrdom. Such heroism is the outcome of intense love and hate. Liang Sheng-pao's task is to lead a pioneer mutual-aid team, yet in this ordinary job he has to fight enemies as stubborn and relentless. His enemies are amorphous — poverty, ignorance, and obstinate thoughts of building family fortunes. They can be found in his step-father, in Kuo Chen-shan, the only other party member, and in most of his neighbors, who see what he is doing as stupid, laughable, and beyond their comprehension. The task has nothing extraordinary, glamorous, or heroic about it, but nevertheless demands extraordinary qualities — unqualified optimism, unwavering perseverance, undaunted fortitude.

Yet Liang Sheng-pao does not really possess these formidable qualities. The decision to form a mutual-aid team has not been made by him but by the Communist Party. He is not a hero fighting against overwhelming odds as it seemed at first. He is merely faithfully executing official policy and is perfectly well aware that the Party is behind him. This is made amply clear in a dialogue between Liang the Third and Lu, Party secretary of the township. Old Liang feels his step-son's efforts merely show the frivolity and recklessness of a young man. In his honest heart, he does not believe that a peasant should act like a hero, leading out an army of villagers, building a camp, setting up a cooking cauldron, spending a month cutting bamboo in the mountains. So he pours out his worries to Secretary Lu — if anything

[16] *Ibid.*, p. 115, Shapiro, p. 127.

happens, Sheng-pao may end up in jail. Hearing this, the secretary
bursts out laughing:

> 'What in the world are you talking about? Why should Sheng-pao
> have to go to jail? If anything goes wrong, the Communist Party will
> be responsible . . .'[17]

The difference between a hero and a socialist man is that between a
man who makes a decision on his own judgment at his own risk and a
Party member who sees himself merely as the agent of Party policy.
Liang Sheng-pao's treatment of Pai Chan-k'uei's application for
membership of his team illustrates his Party role clearly. Pai, formerly a
corporal in the Kuomintang army, received a few *mou* of paddy during
the land reform but has yet to learn how to work the land. His wife
Blue Moth had had affairs with different men before she finally married
the ex-corporal. The couple are despised by virtually everyone at Frog
Flat, so Pai's desire to join the mutual-aid team poses a challenge to
Sheng-pao. The team leader appears to be prepared to face the
challenge when he thinks to himself, 'You don't dare take on a fellow
like Pai, and you still want to change society!' But as soon as he raises
the issue with his teammates, he meets stiff opposition. Jen the Fourth
will leave rather than work with Pai, who does not even notice when his
ploughshare drops off. Kao Tseng-fu is even firmer; he states his
principle, 'the gold of the new society should not mingle with the
garbage of the old.' At home Sheng-pao is criticized not only by his
dubious father, but also by his gentle, helpful mother.

A struggle goes on in Sheng-pao's mind: should he side with the
opinion of the majority or stick to his own judgment? A decision to
take in Pai in the face of public opinion would make Liang Sheng-pao a
real hero. But heroes do not exist in the socialist society; Liang's own
judgment must be backed up by the party leadership. At the township
office he presents his arguments like a lawyer on behalf of a litigant to
Party secretary Lu. He seems to be so anxious not to lose his case that
the secretary smiles and says:

> 'Take Pai in, quick. If he didn't want to join, we couldn't force him
> to. We couldn't just assign him to one of the teams, could we? He
> wants to join? I only hope he means it. What's so dangerous about
> Pai? An assistant squad leader in a Kuomintang army horse-cart unit!
> What are we supposed to do with the old Kuomintang officers —
> there are a couple of thousand generals alone — kill them all? Accept
> them. Turn every one of them over to the people and let the people
> educate them . . .'[18]

[17] *Ibid.*, p. 258, Shapiro, p. 294.
[18] *Ibid.*, p. 480, Shapiro, p. 539.

Crisis makes the hero. In ordinary times, a hero is no different from the average. Only the most testing moment separates him from the crowd. The mutual-aid team has to face a crisis when two of the eight members pull out and others waver. The author has been skilfully building up a climax which should allow the hero an opportunity to prove his worth. Instead, the ensuing narrative damages the image of the hero irrevocably:

> 'I know you've got guts', Jen said quickly. 'You're very brave'.
> 'That's not it at all. The reason is I've got backing'.
> 'I know. Secretary Lu, Secretary Wang, they both support you —"
> 'That's not it either. Think now. Who have I got standing behind me?'
> 'I can't say. Just because you're doing a good thing, you shouldn't turn proud, young fellow'.
> 'The whole Communist Party and people's government are behind me . . .'[19]

It is not Liu Ch'ing the artist but Liu Ch'ing the propagandist who has made Liang Sheng-pao into a 'socialist man'. After all, the author tells a story to expound the Party policy. Liang Sheng-pao, the author explains, is merely a young Party member of simple peasant stock who has lived two different lives in the old and new society, personally feels the greatness of the Party, obediently listens to the word of the Party, and tries hard to carry out its directives. Liu Ch'ing admits that he has 'no intention of portraying Liang Sheng-pao as a dazzling hero'. Then he goes on to explain the type of hero Liang is:

> His behavior, first, must be conditioned by the objective historical circumstances, secondly, must respond to the need of the revolutionary development, and finally, must reflect the nature of his class, that is, the characteristics of the vanguard of the proletariat. In short, I wanted to portray Liang Sheng-pao as a loyal son of the Party. I feel this is the most fundamental, most typical trait of contemporary heroes. In this novel the socialist tide surges through the countryside, not because of Liang Sheng-pao, but because of the correct policy of the Party leadership.
>
> Liang Sheng-pao is being educated and is growing in the process of the socialist revolution. Between the lines of the narrative there walks a giant figure — the Party . . .[20]

[19] *Ibid.*, pp. 463–4, Shapiro, p. 521.
[20] Liu Ch'ing, 'T'i-ch'u chi-ko wen-t'i lai t'ao-lun' (Raise a Few Questions for Discussion), *Yen ho*, Aug. 1963, cited in Chao Yun, 'Tui "Kuan-yü Liang Sheng-pao hsing-hsiang" i-wen ti i-chien' (Commentaries on the Article 'Concerning the Image of Liang Sheng-pao), *Wen-hsüeh p'ing-lun*, No. 2, April 14, 1964, p. 90. The original article in *Yen ho* is not available.

What motivated the author to draw this image of a contemporary hero is thus made unequivocally clear. At this period in the socialist revolution, the Party no longer needs a hero like Chu Lao-chung of *Keep the Red Flag Flying*. Chu is dangerously individualistic; he sometimes even overshadows the Party. He is in the vein of Kuan Yü of *Romance of the Three Kingdoms*, Yüeh Fei of *The Life of Yüeh Fei*, or Wu Sung of *Water Margin*. Heroes of personal brilliance have no place in a collective society; as a matter of fact, they may be an obstacle on the road to socialism. As the people's hero, Liang Sheng-pao has to remain anonymous. This explains why, when the peasants of Frog Flat carry red banners in a long procession and beat drums and cymbals as they deliver the surplus grain to the state purchasing station, Liang Sheng-pao is not among the crowd. He has accomplished his mission and is preparing for the next task, forming a pioneer co-operative.

What makes *The Builders* more than a hack work is the portrayal of middle and negative characters. The theme of the novel is the justification of the Party policy of major change from the stage of 'new democracy' to the stage of socialist collectivism in 1953. Liu Ch'ing's great accomplishment is to show the subtle distinctions of attitude among those who oppose the Party policy of agricultural socialization.

Blind Wang is a man of deep-rooted habit, rather than a villain, a victim of injustice in feudal society. At seventy-eight he has become the tyrannical ruler, lording it over his wife, son, and daughter-in-law. He never forgets a lesson he learned in his youth. In the twenty-sixth year of the reign of Emperor Kuang Hsü, he stole crops from his landlord employer, got caught, and received eighty strokes in the county magistrate's yamen. Since then he vowed to be a loyal subject of the Emperor all his life and still talked about 'blessings from Heaven and officialdom' after the end of the Empire. During the land reform, he forbade anyone in his family to attend mass meetings and vociferously opposed the Communists. His unwavering belief is that property must be built up by an individual for himself and land reform is a subversion of the proper order. In the end he has to give in, for if he refuses to accept the land distributed to him, his son can no longer rent it from the landlord. Humiliated, he accepts the land and tries to justify his action by saying that it is still a blessing from Heaven and officialdom. He eventually forces his son to leave Liang Sheng-pao's mutual-aid team, since he has no confidence in the ability of a poor peasant to do anything right.

Kuo Shih-fu, the well-to-do peasant, is whole-heartedly devoted to the building of family wealth. The description of the construction of the roof frame of his new tiled house in the opening chapter is meant to symbolize the newly-gained economic status of middle peasants. Kuo may be selfish and lack compassion, but he is by no means a villain. His attempt to oppose Party policy is limited to the strenuous efforts he makes to increase the yield of his land in order to show that mutual-aid teams may not be a superior way of producing more grain. The conflict between his thinking and the Party policy is treated as a form of non-antagonistic contradiction among the people; the impression is given that he may still be won over by the Party and join the socialist road of collective farming.

The rich peasant Yao Shih-chieh is portrayed as the enemy of Liang Sheng-pao's mutual-aid team. This is the man, the author tells us, who has been reduced to the lowest level in the village after the land reform. 'All of Frog Flat was one family, but Yao was an outcast.' Such a man cannot be potentially dangerous. Even with his family fortune, which is by no means enormous – a square tiled house compound, a fine horse, and thirty-odd *mou* of paddies – he cannot do much harm.

The author registers all Yao's misdeeds which, in all fairness, may be an accurate reflection of actual events. During the spring shortage of food, he refuses to lend grain at low interest to the needy peasants and instead secretly carts it elsewhere at night for sale or for usury. When some spineless poor men crawl back to him begging to borrow a few measures of rice, Yao is deeply gratified. He feels he is getting his own back on the Communist Party. The cadres have repeatedly stressed the isolation of rich peasants, but the poor now come back to him with that familiar expression of desperation and expectation. Gradually, Yao gains courage and decides to defeat Liang Sheng-pao's mutual-aid efforts. He urges the well-off peasant Kuo Shih-fu to buy the same strain of fast-growing seed acquired by the team, spreads his fields thick with fertilizer, and even persuades one family to withdraw from Sheng-pao's team to join him. Since the Party counts on the success of the first mutual-aid team to prove the superiority of collectivism, Yao's activities amount to sabotaging the party policy. In addition, his method of 'mutual-aid' by trading animal power for manpower is presented as a subtle form of exploitation.

There is no direct confrontation[21] between the socialist and his opponent. This shows the author's artistic skill, for it would not have been very heroic of Liang to challenge the rich peasant Yao, spared by the leniency of the Party and now eking out a precarious living. Even if Yao is viewed as a villain, his influence is only indirect; he is an impotent rogue.

---

[21] The absence of face-to-face confrontation is pointed out as a weakness of the novel. See Yen Chia-yen, 'Kuan-yü Liang Sheng-pao hsing-hsiang' (Concerning the Image of Liang Sheng-pao), *Wen-hsüeh p'ing-lun*, No. 3, June 14, 1963, p. 20. But others contend that there is no lack of class struggle in the novel, but that it takes a more subtle, complex form. See Wu Chung-chieh and Kao Yun, 'T'an Liang Sheng-pao hsing-hsiang ti ch'uang-tsao' (Talks about the Creation of Liang Sheng-pao's Image), *Wen-hsüeh p'ing-lun*, No. 3, June 14, 1964, pp. 49–50.

The resistance to the Party policy of agricultural collectivization is not limited to ignorant poor peasants or crafty rich ones but also extends to cadres within the Party organization. The presence of this archetype of Party man who takes, or wants to take, the capitalist road, suggests the scale of opposition to the agricultural policy. While in *Great Changes in a Mountain Village* Li Yueh-hui, the village Party secretary, is merely a half-hearted promoter of the policy of co-operation, in *Sanliwan Village* Fan Teng-kao, who has been engaged in private farming and peddling goods on the side, finally joins the co-operative. The image of a selfish and profit-oriented cadre is more forcibly and unambiguously presented in *The Builders*.

Kuo Chen-shan, the only senior party member in Frog Flat (the other being Liang Sheng-pao, a candidate member), chairman of the village deputies, is determined to farm privately. Like most other peasants, Kuo's appetite for land has been whetted by the plot he was given during the land reform. He clearly sees that villagers work fervently to acquire more land and to build tiled houses, and he does not want to be left behind. Perfectly aware that the Party regulations forbid members to buy land and to engage in business dealings, he nevertheless has bought a two-*mou* peach orchard and has invested in a private brick and tile kiln. He always has good excuses. It would have been a terrible waste to leave that piece of land in the hands of that shoemaker; after all, the government policy is to increase production. As for his investment in the kiln business, that is a way of supporting national construction. Shrewd and discreet, every move he makes is unknown to anyone else. His little five-year plan for building family property is modest enough:

> He had started in 1951. The goal of his first five-year plan was to catch up with Shih-fu on average land ownership per family member. That was as far as he wanted to go, not a step further. He absolutely wouldn't permit his family holdings to approach the size of those of his enemy, the rich peasant Yao. That would be as incompatible with his 'political nature' as fire is to water.
> Rafter by rafter and beam by beam, he stealthily prepared the materials for his tile-roofed house, to be built during his second five-year plan – beginning in 1956. First, he would erect the main building. Then, in the third year of the plan, 1958, he would build the east and west wings. In the fifth year, 1960, he would put up the front building. He wouldn't move too fast. It wouldn't look right for a Communist.[22]

Kuo's activities and plans are presented as dangerous signs of capitalism. The goal of land reform is not to provide a basis for some peasants to build private properties, which inevitably would again

[22] *The Builders*, pp. 179–80, Shapiro, p. 201.

reduce others to the level of poverty, but to pave the way for socialism. The author, in his realistic description of Kuo's single-minded devotion to increasing his family's prosperity, nevertheless treats it as an anti-socialist pursuit.

Kuo Chen-shan, however, is not exactly a villain, but a cadre who has made mistakes. From time to time the author depicts Kuo as a good peasant, thrifty and hard-working. At one time he also had lofty socialist ideals, but gradually surrendered himself to the world of reality. For him the real world — the world of his wife and children, of a tiled house, and of an increasing land holding — is more pressing and important than the distant vision of affluent socialism. He is a fallen man, but his sins are still redeemable. In the epilogue we are told that Kuo has started his own mutual-aid team in the hope of vying with Liang Sheng-pao, but the latter has already organized a co-operative. When he protests to Secretary Lu that he is the proper man to lead the co-operative, the secretary tells him:

> 'The district committee has decided that you should be in charge of the mutual-aid team of Liberation Creek. I was just intending to talk to you. After you work with it for a year, you can take a number of teams and form a co-op. This will be good for you personally too . . .'[23]

Thus Kuo is actually put on probation and given a year to prove his worth. He never does, for Liu Ch'ing never had the opportunity to continue his multi-volume novel. His counter-part, Ma Chih-yueh of *Bright Sunny Days*.[24] becomes a renegade and impostor and is finally expelled from the Party.

The Intensification of the Struggle and Reappearance of Landlords

Liu Ch'ing's *Builders*, which initially received unanimous commendation for the creation of the socialist man Liang Sheng-pao, was soon involved in the controversy over middle characters. The lack of a face-to-face confrontation between the two opposing points of view was also criticized. This novel, like *Sanliwan Village* and *Great Changes in a Mountain Village*, reflects the confidence of the party leadership in

[23] *Ibid.*, p. 506, Shapiro, p. 567.
[24] Hao Jan, *Yen yang t'ien (Bright Sunny Days)*, Vol. I (Peking: Writers' Publishing House, September 1964); Vol. II (Peking: People's Literature Publishing House, March 1966); Vol. III, abridged version, *Shuo-huo*, No. 2, March 25, 1966, pp. 139–256.

the success of agricultural collectivization without antagonistic contradiction. When the Great Leap Forward policy of 1958 suffered setbacks and caused substantial damage to China's agricultural production, there arose a compelling need to find the reason for this failure. Any attempt to attribute the failure to mistaken policy ended with the fall of P'eng Teh-huai after the Lushan Conference of August 1959. The failure of the program can be conveniently attributed to sabotage by renegades and class enemies. Thus, in *Bright Sunny Days*, which describes the problems of a co-operative during the early summer of 1957, almost six years after the conclusion of land reform, we find the reappearance of the landlord along with the emergence of the impostor. In order to make this arrangement more credible, the author sets the story in a village near Peking, at the period of the Hundred Flowers Movement.[25]

Bright Sunny Days, in three volumes with more than a million words, was published rapidly between September 1964 and March 1966. The publication of this novel is contemporaneous with the criticism of Ou-yang Shan and Shao Ch'üan-lin and the early phase of the Cultural Revolution. The quickening and intensifying struggle between the socialist and anti-socialist forces portrayed in this novel reflects the deepening split within the party leadership. That the third volume is carried in *Harvest* (*Shuo-huo*) — a literary journal published in Shanghai, where the Cultural Revolution originated — suggests that the novel's theme agrees with the rationale for launching the Cultural Revolution.

In order to understand why the non-antagonistic contradiction between the two views of farming changes to become antagonistic, we must trace the intra-party dispute over literary policy. At the Tenth Plenary Session of the Eighth Central Committee of the Chinese Communist Party in 1962, Mao Tse-tung complained about the use of novels as an anti-Party platform. He made this statement:

> The use of the novel for anti-Party activities is quite an invention. To overthrow a political power, it is always necessary, first of all, to create public opinion, to do work in the ideological sphere. This is true for the revolutionary class as well as for the counter-revolutionary class.[26]

---

[25] In 1956–7 the Chinese Communist Party launched a movement called 'Let a Hundred Flowers Blossom, a Hundred Schools of Thought Contend', inviting intellectuals to discuss national affairs. Before long some outspoken intellectuals began to criticise Communist policies and demand the end of the Party's monolithic rule. By mid–1957 it turned into an 'anti-rightist' campaign against dissident intellectuals.

[26] Editorial, 'Wei-ta li chen-li, jui-li ti wu-ch'i,' *Hung-ch'i*, No. 9, 1967, p. 21; 'Great Truth, Sharp Weapon', *Chinese Literature*, No. 9, 1967, p. 13.

Mao made no specific charges against particular novelists, as far as we can determine from the available documents. It appears, however, that Mao's plea for novelists to reflect class struggle in fiction was allowed to pass unheeded by Chou Yang and his associates, who had the responsibility for art and literature.

In the summer of 1964 Mao Tse-tung became impatient and wrote in one of his instructions:

> In the last fifteen years these associations, most of their publications (it is said that a few are good) and *by and large* the people in them (that is not everybody) have not carried out the policies of the Party. They have acted as high and mighty bureaucrats, have not gone to the workers, peasants and soldiers and have not reflected the socialist revolution and socialist construction. *In recent years*, they have slid right down to the brink of revisionism. Unless they remold themselves in real earnest, at some future date they are bound to become groups like the Hungarian Petofi Club.[27]

The warning this time apparently struck home; in September a number of writers including Feng Ting, Yang Hsien-chen, Chou Ku-ch'eng, Shao Ch'üan-lin, and Ou-yang Shan were denounced.

In the army under the leadership of Lin Piao, however, a new literary theory has been applied since 1963 to supplement the theory of combining revolutionary realism with revolutionary romanticism. In Lin Piao's 'Instructions for Literary and Artistic Workers in the Army' issued in 1963, the theory of *san-ho-i* (three-in-one) was established to define the relationship between the leadership, the writer, and the masses.[28] According to this theory, the leadership is to set the theme, the writer to expound it by first experiencing life among the masses and then portraying it, and the masses to criticize the work and suggest changes.[29] This means simply that the leadership should have direct control over the theme of every novel. Ostensibly, the role of the masses as critics would liberalize the content of the novel; in reality, the

---

[27] 'I-chiu-liu-ssu nien liu-yüeh ch'i-jih ti p'i-shih', *Hung-ch'i*, No. 9, 1967, p. 9; 'Instruction of June 27, 1964', *Chinese Literature*, No. 9, 1967, p. 12. Original emphasis. The instruction was obviously made as a comment on some document which has not been made public. The Petofi Club, formed by liberal intellectuals, played a leading role in the Hungarian rising of 1956.

[28] Lin Yü, 'Tsai hsüeh-hsi ch'uang-tso chung "t'u-ch'u cheng-chih" ti t'i-hui' (My Comprehension of 'Politics in Control' in Learning about Writing), *Shuo-huo*, No. 1, Jan. 25, 1966, p. 21. For a detailed discussion of the application of this theory, see Chapter Eleven.

[29] The application of this theory to revolutionary Peking opera is illustrated by Chiang Ching in her appraisal of *The Great Wall Along the South China Sea* in July 1964. See Chiang Ching, 'T'an ching-ch'ü ke-ming', *Chieh-fang-chün wen-i*, No. 7, 1967, pp. 51–2; 'On the Revolution in Peking Opera', *Chinese Literature*, No. 8, 1967, p. 122.

masses, sensitive to fluctuations in the political climate, would readily express a more rigid view of the class struggle in time of crisis. After the publication of the first volume of *Bright Sunny Days* a meeting to discuss the novel was organized under the auspices of the editorial board of *Wen-i pao* and the cultural hall of Chaoyang district in Peking. After voicing their general approval of the novel, the participants, representatives of poor and lower middle peasants from nearby communes, pointed out that the socialist hero Hsiao Ch'ang-ch'un is too patient or lenient in treating bad elements and not aggressive enough in organizing the masses in the struggle against renegades and class enemies.[30] Artistic criteria play no part whatever in their evaluation.

Bright Sunny Days deals with the class struggle between the socialist camp led by the village Party secretary, Hsiao Ch'ang-ch'un, and the anti-socialist alliance, consisting of middle peasants, a rich peasant and a landlord, headed by a renegade. At Tungshanwu, a village not far from Peking, the demand for grain distribution on the basis of both labor and land in the early summer of 1957 suddenly becomes ominously like a counter-revolutionary conspiracy. Encouraged by the news of the Hundred Flowers Movement then in progress at Peking, the anti-socialist elements want to launch a similar movement in the village, to demand a democratic way of reaching a decision on the grain issue, and to return, eventually, to the system of private farming.

Hsiao Ch'ang-ch'un, the village Party secretary, is portrayed as a more resolute man than Liang Sheng-pao of *The Builders*. The characterization of a hero, even of the socialist type, depends less on his intellect or ideological sophistication than his conduct. A man's sterling character, in a truly Chinese sense, is best tested in his resistance to the temptation of woman. In *The Builders* Liu Ch'ing treats Su Fang's coquetry with Liang Sheng-pao as reprehensible; moreover, the hero has not gone through the real test.[31] In *Bright Sunny Days* Hsiao is trapped in the libertine Sun Kuei-ying's bedroom as a result of a plot by the renegade Ma Chih-yueh. A reader familiar with Communist novels of course will not expect a 'socialist man' to fall victim to the ploys of beauty. Hsiao Ch'ang-ch'ung, as anticipated, is irritated rather than aroused by the temptress. But he neither shows his temper nor tries to force his way out. Instead, he rolls a cigarette and unhurriedly gives her a political lecture.

[30] Tso P'ing, 'P'in hsia-chung nung hsi tu *Yen yang t'ien*' (Poor and Lower Middle Peasants Enjoy Reading *Bright Sunny Days*), *Wen-i pao*, No. 2, 1965, p. 11.
[31] For a discussion of the characterization of this woman, see Joe C. Huang, 'Villains, Victims and Morals in Contemporary Chinese Literature', *The China Quarterly*, No. 46, April/June 1971, pp. 346–8.

In a still more dramatic episode, the author describes the disappearance of Hsiao's six-year-old son. When all the villagers put aside their work of bringing in the wheat crop before the storm breaks to search for the lost boy, Hsiao is able to see the incident as a plot staged by anti-socialist elements to ruin the co-operative. He orders that the search be called off, and the task of salvaging the crop from bad weather be resumed immediately. Such a decision further demonstrates the dedication of the socialist, who is more concerned with the welfare of the masses than the safety of his son.

The man who leads the anti-socialist alliance is Ma Chih-yueh, vice-chairman of the co-operative and a senior Party member at Tungshanwu. Ma Chih-yueh's association with the Communist Party is traced to the time of the war against Japan. At that time he accidentally saved a Communist cadre and unwittingly became an instant hero. With this connection, he naturally became an important cadre at Tungshanwu during the land reform. He lost his post of Party secretary to Hsiao Ch'ang-ch'un when he invested a government loan and relief grain in a business venture and lost it all. In order to regain power, he incited well-off peasants to plead shortage of food and demand grain distribution on the basis of both land and labor. If the co-operative collapses under the attack and the private ownership system is restored, he will be the one to receive all the credit. Then Ma Chih-yueh can be undisputed boss of Tungshanwu once more. In this effort he is backed by the chairman of the *hsiang*[32] government, himself a cadre on probation because of his bureaucratic style and petty bourgeois subjectivism.

Under Ma Chih-yueh's leadership two types of men form the anti-socialist force; one motivated by economic gain alone and the other by the appetite for political power, as well as economic interest. Of the first type are the well-off middle peasants Crook Ma and Big Gun Ma. The root of their opposition, as the author concedes, is that 'from the peasant's viewpoint, taking possession of his land is as unbearable as taking possession of his woman.'[33] Both Mas have been unhappy and unwilling members of the co-operative, for they own more land than most. They want the co-operative to collapse, so that they can produce more than the others and eventually perhaps acquire more land. The justification for their action is best articulated by Big Gun Ma when he says:

---

[32] An administrative unit, usually a village consisting of ten or more *paos* – about a hundred households.
[33] Although the author makes the point in connection with a quarrel between two peasants straight after the land reform, the same can be said of the collectivization of land.

'I'm a middle peasant, one of the toiling masses! Wheat grows on my land, and I want an extra share. What's wrong with that, what law have I violated?'[34]

The same line of argument is used by Crook Ma in defending his selling of grain to merchants. He says:

'Why should I deny it? I'm prepared to accept the consequences of what I did. The grain was grown by me, not stolen from others. It's none of anybody's business, even if I threw it in river or in a sewer, much less sold it . . .'[35]

These utterances clearly challenge the Party policy, but instead of treating the two Mas as enemies, efforts are continually made to win their support for the co-operative.

Six-Finger Ma Chai and his son Li-pen fall into the second category. Ma Chai, a rich peasant isolated from the rest of the village community, naturally has a great stake in the destruction of the co-operative, the paradigm of the new system. His son, who has had a junior middle school education, is the bookkeeper of the co-operative. To show his political progressiveness, the young man has separated himself from his father. Although they still live under the same roof and their rooms face each other, a fence of corn stalks has been put up in the middle of the courtyard as a symbolic line of political division between father and son. But the young man lives under the shadow of his father and Ma Chih-yueh. He does everything Ma Chih-yueh tells him to do, including misusing army dependents' pension money that he is supposed to deliver. He counts on a Hundred Flowers Movement in Tungshanwu to seize political power. This is also the unconcealed wish of his father, who has been inciting middle peasants to demand the dissolution of the co-operative from the beginning.

The man unequivocally portrayed as a villain is the landlord Pigtail Ma who once virtually owned Tungshanwu. At the tender age of eighteen he purchased an official title and at twenty earned the respect of wealthy landlords, near and far, by refurbishing Buddhist temples. In the early years of the Republic he was a member of the editorial board in charge of revising and compiling the county annals. Although he appeared a devout Buddhist and kind-hearted humanitarian, he would rather have his grain rot in his barns than distribute it to starving peasants. But his life was spared during the land reform, and after serving a two-year prison term he was allowed to return to Tungshanwu and live quietly in a small house compound.

Pigtail Ma's thirst for revenge, however, never diminishes as time

[34] *Bright Sunny Days*, Vol. I, p. 117.
[35] *Ibid.*, Vol. II, p. 1104.

elapses. In the dead of night, he would go to the courtyard to perform a ritual. He would take out from a wooden box small human figures made of dough, with the names of village cadres written on them, and a needle stuck through the chest. Placing the dough figures on a table, he would pray to Jade Emperor in Heaven, the kings of Hell, Talagata in West Heaven, Generalissimo Chiang Kai-shek in Taiwan, and any wandering gods who happened to be passing by. He prays for the downfall of Communist rule, violent deaths to those goblins and devils who have ruined him and other good people, the restoration of Mr. Chiang, and his own salvation.

One night as he is performing the ritual, a gentle knock at the back door startles him. It turns out to be his relative Six-Finger Ma bringing him a letter. It comes from his second son, a university student in Peking. The letter contains good news about the Hundred Flowers Movement. It describes how he, his friends and professors are involved in an intense struggle against the rule of the Communist Party, and says he believes that the day of regaining political power is finally approaching. Pigtail Ma can no longer conceal his delight, and he cries out that the Communist regime will soon be overthrown. Without wasting a minute he ventures to step out of his house and pays a personal visit to Ma Chih-yueh. In the latter's house everyone is overjoyed to hear the good news, and some plans are worked out to bring down the co-operative at Tungshanwu.

The narrative is no doubt intended to establish the fact that anti-revolutionary and anti-Communist activities are gaining momentum and a loose alliance of anti-socialist forces is being formed. As one reads on, however, one cannot help feeling a certain sympathy and sorrow for the erratic and morbid behavior of Pigtail Ma, or even the more purposeful but nevertheless suicidal efforts of Ma Chih-yueh. One may be able to accept socialism as the only way of lifting China out of poverty and starvation, in cold reason, but it is hard to look on these little men as counter-revolutionaries. The eccentric conduct of Pigtail Ma and his macabre ritual is pathetic rather than sinister. His reliance on superstition, and his blind faith in a few lines in the letter of a youngster as a basis for challenging an enormous power structure, are clearly pathological.

A charge of sabotage based on such insubstantial evidence is clearly inadequate, so the author in the third volume arranges for more concrete acts of sabotage by both Pigtail Ma and Ma Chih-yueh. The landlord becomes a murderer who pushes Hsiao Ch'ang-ch'un's six-year-old son down a cliff. Murder is of course a criminal rather than a counter-revolutionary act. But the author manages to link the two by showing that the disappearance of the child causes the villagers to search for him, at the risk of losing the wheat crop in the stormy weather. Ma Chih-yueh pretends to show concern for the child's safety by encouraging them to continue the search while secretly hoping the neglect of the farm work will ruin the bumper harvest and thus the co-operative.

Even this frame-up proves less than convincing. Whatever the villains do, even murdering a cadre's child as a form of revenge, or trying to ruin the crop to create difficulties for the co-operative, their efforts do not amount to the sabotage of socialism. Even if this is their goal, the possibility of success never exists. They attempt the impossible. Man's inability to see his limits, and his blind pursuit of revenge while actually heading towards self-destruction, is the essence of tragedy in the making.

The Masses

Heroism, however, is also attempting the impossible, trying to conquer the seemingly unconquerable. The task of most people at Tungshanwu is to overcome selfish human motives. The endeavor has two dimensions: complete rejection of self-interest and helping others to abandon their own futile pursuit of selfish ends. In Chinese novels, as in real life, the true heroes are not the socialist men but the faceless masses. China's achievement in less than a quarter of a century must be attributed to the countless millions who have given up almost everything for a secure collective life. The artistic value of *Bright Sunny Days* rests in the portrayal of small men who are drawn from real life, not simply as ideological models.

Ma Lao-ssu, a cowherd of the co-operative, is well over sixty. Back in 1953 when poor peasants first formed a co-operative and managed to assemble two old cows and three bony mules, Ma Lao-ssu volunteered to herd the livestock. Han Po-chung, leader of the poor men's co-operative, would not allow it, for fear that the old man's poor health was not up to a job which demanded continual attention. But Ma Lao-ssu insisted, pleaded, and finally got the job. As the co-operative was too poor to build a stable, the old man tore down his *kang* and moved the animals into his own low shack. He used dry hay to make a bed and shared the same room with the beasts.

Now some middle peasants' complaints of food shortage call the attention of the Party secretary Hsaio to the problem. He realizes that there may indeed be a few families in need of state relief grain, and he immediately thinks of Ma Lao-ssu. When the young secretary walks into the thatched cottage, Ma Lao-ssu is in the middle of cooking. As soon as he sees Hsiao, the old man stops lifting the pot lid. Hsiao asks him with concern if he needs any relief grain, but Ma Lao-ssu says that he has no food problem and his supply is enough to last until harvest. He seems to be impatient with the conversation and in order to divert Hsiao's attention takes him to see a new-born calf, the pride of his herd. Although Hsiao thinks it strange that the old man is so unusually talkative, he is satisfied and takes his leave.

After walking some distance, Hsiao suddenly remembers that he has forgotten to tell the old man the site of a meeting scheduled for that evening. He returns to the shack and without knocking enters the room. Mao Lao-ssu is eating something from a large bowl. At the unexpected reappearance of Hsiao, he is completely at a loss. At this point, Hsaio realizes what the old man is doing.

> When Mao Lao-ssu saw the whole thing exposed he was both uneasy and regretful. As need breeds wisdom, he immediately assumed an air of indifference, held up the bowl and gulped a large mouthful. Chewing it with gusto, he said, smiling: 'Ch'ang-ch'un, don't worry, I'm trying this for a change.'
> Unable to contain his emotions, Hsiao Ch'ang-ch'un grabbed the bowl of wild herb and held it up under his nose. The dark, prickly wild vegetable mixed with a few grains of rice smelt acrid.
> For four or five years since agricultural co-operation began no family at Tungshanwu, not a single person, had ever eaten this stuff! No, the children had never even seen it![36]

There is another kind of sacrifice, another approach to meeting the food shortage crisis. In order to stop the complaints of certain middle peasants, so that there will be no tension before harvest, Han Po-chung, a production brigade captain, asks his wife Chiao Erh-chü to talk to her sister-in-law. Chiao Erh-chü considers herself a progressive woman and prides herself on her role as the wife of a cadre. She has been furious with Chiao Ch'ing's wife, who disgraced all the poor peasants and particularly herself by supporting those half-hearted middle peasants who complained of the food shortage. She promises her husband that she can change her selfish sister-in-law's mind, but he warns her that she must not use threats or lay down the law. Chiao Erh-chü readily agrees and is confident that she knows how to deal with her sister-in-law.

Mrs. Chiao Ch'ing is afraid of Erh-chü who has brought up her husband more like a mother than a sister. But she also knows that although Erh-chü is quick-tempered and brusque, she is actually a kind-hearted woman. When Erh-chü admonishes Mrs. Chiao Ch'ing, saying she should not have disgraced the poor peasants by supporting Crook Ma, she smiles, but complains that her child is hungry. She even threatens to go to the canal construction site to see her husband about their food shortage. Erh-chü warns her not to do this and forbids her to make a public scene. Mrs. Chiao Ch'ing says that Erh-chü's use of authority is a violation of the party rule. Erh-chü falls silent, remembering her husband's warning. She then promises that if Mrs. Chiao Ch'ing stops fooling around with those backward middle peasants, the child can go to eat at her house and she will give them two bushels of wheat after harvest. The matter is settled; Mrs. Chiao Ch'ing promises not to cry hunger again.

Erh-chü is so pleased with her success that she decides to persuade Han Po-an to be silent too. Po-an has been under strong pressure from his son and his son's girl-friend. He has planned his son's marriage for immediately after the harvest, but as things stand now the marriage has to be called off. Erh-chü tells Po-an that if he changes his backward attitude, there is still hope. She says that Ma Ts'ui-ch'ing is her adopted daughter, and if she gives the word, the girl will have no objection. Han is delighted and promises that he will not complain about the food shortage again even if he is starving to death. The negotiation is over in the time it takes to smoke a pipe.

After the accomplishment of her mission, Erh-chü hurries back to tell her husband and finds him with their adopted daughter Ma Ts'ui-ch'ing at the mill shed. Seeing joy written all over her face, Han Po-chung senses that things have gone smoothly. Erh-chü reports that the matter was settled when she promised Mrs. Chiao Ch'ing two bushels of wheat.

Before she could finish, Han-Po-chung became impatient. 'Heavens, what do you call this!'

Chiao Erh-chü said: 'You, why make such a fuss about a little thing. In order to help the smooth sailing of our co-operative, I will not cry even if a piece of my flesh has to be cut off. Ch'ang-ch'un put it well, when he said we ought to have the spirit of sacrifice!'

Han Po-chung leapt to his feet: 'Comrade, spirit of sacrifice, did you say? You give her grain for her false progress, money for selfishness!'[37]

Chiao Erh-chü is sheepish. As Po-chung departs angrily, she stops him and says that at least she has helped change Han Po-an's mind. This interests Ma Ts'ui-ch'ing, for with all her persistence and hard work she has not been able to do this. Seeing her husband is still angry, Erh-chü says that in this case she has not promised anything, not a single grain. She says that she has told him that if he abandons his backward thoughts, there will be no problem about the marriage between his son Tao-man and Ts'ui-ch'ing. This disclosure not only further enrages Po-chung but also infuriates Ts'ui-ch'ing, who charges Erh-chü of trading her for Po-an's sham progress.

[37] *Ibid.*, Vol. I, pp. 523–4.

Han Po-chung's criticism of his wife is aimed at her method, not her eagerness to see the success of the co-operative. He is, in effect, stressing a basic principle that a person's faith in the co-operative cannot be purchased. A personal relationship such as friendship or family ties may be used as a link in approaching a person, but it is belief in the co-operative that determines a person's true attitude. As a matter of fact, Erh-chü's sacrifice is considerable in view of her own family's bare sufficiency of grain. She is prepared to part with two bushels of wheat, not for her own sake but for the co-operative.

If socialism is to succeed in China, Ma Lao-ssu's self-denial and Chiao Erh-chü's enthusiasm are important factors. In the process of developing socialism, men like Blind Wang who has no faith in the mutual-aid team because it is headed by a poor peasant and Ma Lao-ssu who has complete faith in the co-operative because it is led by the Communist Party must both be viewed as real. One may disagree with the Communist Party's policy in developing agricultural collectivization, but one cannot question the intention of the Party in its search for a permanent solution to the root of China's poverty. Intention, for the Chinese, is always the overriding criterion in judging the policy of a government or the conduct of an individual. This popular attitude lends credibility to the appearance of people like Ma Lao-ssu and Chiao Erh-chü in works of fiction.

The Socialist Man versus *the Renegade*

The presence of characters like Blind Wang and Ma Lao-ssu in all the novels of agricultural collectivization suggests that they are drawn from real life. This consistency despite the change of governing doctrines suggests that the characters are typical rather than ideological. On the other hand, there is a significant change in the characterization of the 'socialist man' and the renegade. The change shows clearly that they are tailored to ideological needs rather than artistic criteria.

If the socialist man and the renegade do not reflect the reality of Chinese society during the socialist era, they nevertheless show the shift in ideology. The thematic change from *Sanliwan Village* and *Great Changes in a Mountain Village* to *The Builders*, and finally to *Bright Sunny Days* is clearly detectable. In the first two novels, there are neither heroes nor villains, only positive and negative characters. Conflict does exist between the two types; one is determined to carry out the Party policy of agricultural co-operation, while the other wants to pursue private interests. Nevertheless, the struggle is presented as a conflict between the socialist camp and unorganized individual peasants. The opponents of the co-operative are economically motivated, without a political goal; they only want to produce more and live better. In the end, the negative characters, those ignorant, backward peasants, are duly enlightened and, happily or reluctantly, join the co-operative.

In *The Builders* the conflict remains a contradiction between public and private interest. The opposition to the collective movement appears more pervasive, while the rich peasant acquires certain traits of a villain. Yao Shih-chieh, the *quasi*-villain, may have dark motives, but all he does to undermine socialism is lure one household from the mutual-aid team to be his farming partners and use more fertilizer to beat the team in production. No united front, however, is formed between the opponents of collective farming. Kuo Chen-shan, the party man who is just as eager to build his family fortunes, remains a deadly enemy of the rich peasant.

On the other hand, the emergence of the socialist man signifies a change in the leadership's assessment of the problem of agricultural collectivization. Liang Sheng-pao is born in response to the call of the leadership for people to lead the socialist movement. He is the prototype of the model peasant in the wake of the Great Leap Forward. He demonstrates the traits of the 'socialist man' through sacrifice, self-denial, and faith in the party policy. Although the author treats the conflict of interests between the socialist man and the rich peasant as 'antagonistic contradiction,' he avoids the portrayal of any direct confrontation between the two. The rich peasant is not condemned outright, for he must one day be transformed into a member of the new society.[38] More symbolic is the treatment of Pai, the ex-corporal in the Kuomintang army. That Liang has the courage to take in Pai as a member of his mutual-aid team shows his determination and optimism in transforming bad elements left over from the old society. Although the approval of the local party leadership reduces Liang's individual stature, it shows the attitude of the party toward educating and remolding former reactionaries.

The publication of the first volume of *Bright Sunny Days*, while Feng Ting, Yang Hsien-chen, Shao Ch'üan-lin, and others were being denounced during the Cultural Revolution, as well as the subsequent volumes, provides a clue to the changed theme of the story. The intra-Party split over the agricultural policy has not been bridged; on the contrary, the gap seems to have widened. Thus the conflict in *Bright Sunny Days* is more acute. If the socialist Hsiao Ch'ang-ch'un resembles Liang Sheng-pao in his resolve to pursue the collective path,

[38] Although according to Mao Tse-tung antagonistic contradiction cannot be reconciled *(On the Correct Handling of Contradictions Among the People)*, up to this time the regime has never adopted a policy of forcibly liquidating rich peasants as it did the landlord class during the land reform.

he differs from him in his ability to see the conflict from the class viewpoint and in ideological reasoning. The socialist must not only improve the methods of production and increase the yield of land but also understand the contradiction. The contradiction between the co-operative and backward middle peasants is a non-antagonistic one. In dealing with them, the Party secretary must attempt to change their attitude and thinking in order to win their co-operation. The delicate task of remolding a person's political thinking requires a sensitive and tactful approach to personal relations. On the other hand, the conflict between the co-operative and the rich peasant and landlord who want to restore the old system of private farming is fundamentally antagonistic. The Party secretary must try to strengthen the basis of his support among the masses, isolate the anti-socialist elements, gather evidence of their illegal activities, and expose their true motives.

In order to turn the opposition to the co-operative movement into a conspiracy of anti-revolutionaries, it becomes necessary to re-introduce the landlord. The landlord as a character in fiction had disappeared for a decade, since the land reform of 1947. The landlords as counter-revolutionaries, in Ting Ling's *Sun over the Sangkan River* and Chou Li-po's *Hurricane*, are lively and forceful characters, but in *Bright Sunny Days* the landlord Pigtail Ma seems an anachronistic presence. The author's endeavor to justify the presence of the landlord by describing his release after two years' imprisonment is clearly insufficient to explain his resurrection.

Since class struggle is to be substituted for 'non-antagonistic contradiction', a landlord is needed in Tungshanwu. Physically weakened and spiritually demoralized though he is, the landlord must pose a credible threat to the co-operative. The author meets this challenge by rekindling the smothered fire of hate in the landlord's mind, describing his hope for revenge through his student son, and by making him commit a murder.

Even a landlord such as this cannot act alone, without political backing. So, we find a traitor hidden in a revolutionary family. The deviant behavior of early examples of bad cadres is largely the result of selfish motives, a redeemable fault. But Ma Chih-yueh, vice-chairman of the co-operative and member of the party committee in Tungshanwu, belongs to a different category. He is not just a bad cadre, not even a renegade, but a saboteur. In order to prove that he is really a counter-revolutionary, his background is amended to show that he worked for the Japanese and the puppet regime during the war of resistance. He is after all not a cadre but an impostor who has wormed his way into the party organization. This background explains his motives for trying to destroy the co-operative; only by a change in the political system can he survive and regain power.

Ostensibly, this plot structure amounts to an admission of the impurity of the revolutionary ranks. The implications are far more serious. The book suggests that by 1957 (or indeed 1964–6, the time of its publication) the method used to consolidate a co-operative is still the same as during the land reform. The brutal tactics employed to overthrow the landlord, then truly the symbol of power, have to be used again to destroy an overthrown landlord and his old ally. This is an open testimony to the loss of confidence in agricultural collectivization and the necessity of using class struggle as a vehicle to reach the land of milk and honey.

10

AGRICULTURAL COLLECTIVIZATION

II MEN IN THE MIDDLE

The most intriguing as well as the most interesting character in the four novels discussed earlier is neither the socialist man nor the renegade but the middle-of-the-road peasant. While the characterization of the socialist man and the renegade is more or less ideologically oriented, the subtle and trenchant portrayal of the middle type reflects the behavior patterns of Chinese peasants more accurately. The successful characterization of men in the middle gave rise to a literary theory which in turn caused a prolonged debate whose repercussions are still being felt. A literary theory could not have provoked such intense and protracted controversy had it not been linked to a policy debate over the problem of agricultural collectivization. We shall therefore examine all these aspects in our analysis of the middle character and start with a review of the background of the theory of portraying men in the middle (*hsieh chung-chien jen-wu*).

The theory of portraying men in the middle was proposed by Shao Ch'üan-lin, a vice-chairman of the Chinese Writers' Association and secretary of the association's Party section. The debate over this theory, lasting from 1960 to 1962, rekindled in September 1964, and dragging on throughout the Cultural Revolution, can be viewed, first of all, as an offshoot of the controversy about the correct portrayal of the socialist hero and the definition of socialist realism. Since 1949 many writers have continuously advocated broadening the scope of socialist realism by depicting human weaknesses in heroes or at least the evolution from backwardness to progressiveness in the making of heroes.[1] During the

---

[1] Space does not allow a detailed account of the liberal views presented from 1949 to 1959 in a variety of arguments by Hu Feng, Ting Ling, Feng Hsüeh-feng, Ah Lung, Ch'in Chao-yang, T'ang Ta-ch'eng, Tu Li-chün, and Pa Jen. Discussions of these views and the repudiations may be found in D. W. Fokkema's *Literary Doctrine in China and Soviet Influence, 1956–1960* and Merle Goldman's *Literary Dissent in Communist China.* For a general denouncement of these views and Shao Ch'üan-lin's theory of portraying men in the middle, see 'Shih-wu nien lai tzu-ch'an-chieh-chi shih tsen-yang fan-tui ch'uang-tsao kung nung ping ying-hsiung jen-wu ti' (How the Bourgeoisie opposed the Creation of Worker, Peasant, and Soldier Heroes in the Past Fifteen Years), *Wen-i pao*, Nos. 11/12, December 30, 1964.

Great Leap Forward in 1958–9, the whole nation was in a state of frantic optimism, as if the millennium of Communist society were within reach. It was a season when the record-breaking achievements of labor and peasant heroes were continually being reported in the press, radio, and local wall newspapers. In the drive for record performance, everyone was a potential hero, and any question of making fictitious heroes less than perfect would have been completely out of tune with the mood of the people.

The setbacks in the commune movement resulting from inadequate preparation and poor management coupled with natural disasters caused the Party leadership to reconsider the pace of communization. The period from 1960 to 1962 is one of tactical retreat, reflecting the reappraisal of the general socio-economic-political situation in China. The need for a breathing space to allow economic recovery and consolidation ushered in a more relaxed political climate.

One factor believed to have contributed to the setbacks of the Great Leap Forward was that the psychological readiness of the great majority of Chinese peasants to join the communes had been over-estimated. In the top-level discussions inside the Party, many leaders, including Liu Shao-ch'i, Teng Hsiao-p'ing and P'eng Chen, contended that the establishment of people's communes was premature and over-optimistic. It was during this period that Shao Ch'üan-lin presented the theory of portraying men in the middle. It is, however, not clear whether Shao's proposal to shift the focus from heroes to men in the middle was urged by the Liu Shao-ch'i faction or whether he merely took advantage of the more relaxed climate to attempt to loosen the restrictive literary policy of the Party.

From the viewpoint of orthodox Party theoreticians, Shao's theory is clearly a heresy, but it was not openly repudiated until September 1964. *Wen-i pao*, the official organ of the Chinese Writers Association, which was to be published on August 11 (the regular publication date), did not reach the readers until September 30, 1964. In this combined issue of nos. 8–9, Shao's theory of portraying men in the middle is labelled a literary theory of the bourgeoisie, in the vein of the movie *The Life of Wu Hsün*, the theory of Hu Feng's counter-revolutionary clique, and other heretical views of the rightists. The denunciation of Shao's theory can be seen, in retrospect, as a prelude to the Cultural Revolution.

Although the term 'men in the middle' was coined by Shao Ch'üan-lin, novelists had already paid great attention to characters who could be classified neither as heroes nor as villains. Fully aware of the debates over the correct depiction of heroes and the repudiation of arguments for describing heroes' human weaknesses, they tried hard to present the personalities of their principal positive characters as flawless. At the same time, in order to reflect the complexity of life and to probe into the nuances of human feelings, they made great efforts to portray the inner lives of supporting characters. This explains why Liu Ch'ing spent more space on Liang the Third than on the 'socialist man' Liang Sheng-pao in *The Builders*. The result of this endeavor is highly rewarding. Authors are able to maintain ideological correctness by depicting heroes and villains in black and white and rely on other characters to avoid over-simplification. Creative writers in China would probably have a rich field to explore had Shao not attempted to construct a theory about men in the middle. Again, Shao's theory might not have aroused such intense debate had it not been tangled up with the disagreement among the leaders over the pace of agricultural collectivization.

The Theory of Portraying Men in the Middle

Shao Ch'üan-lin's theory of portraying men in the middle was first hinted at in 1960 when *Wen-i pao* and other journals published a number of commentaries on Liang Sheng-pao. In December 1960, at an editorial board meeting of *Wen-i pao*, Shao made the following observation:

> In *The Builders* Liang the Third is better portrayed than Liang Sheng-pao, for the former sums up the spiritual burdens of individual peasants through the centuries. But very few people have analysed Liang the Third, so that discussion of this work remains shallow.[2]

The theory of portraying men in the middle was formally proposed at an editorial meeting of *Wen-i pao* called to discuss the selection of important themes, on June 25, 1962. At this meeting Shao contended that novelists felt stifled under the restrictions of rules and taboos. They did not dare to touch on contradictions among the people, and expected critics to take the lead in discussing these problems. Shao attributed the superficiality of romanticism to the lack of a realistic foundation. He further argued that writers also felt inhibited in the creation of hero characters. Ch'en Ch'i-hsia's view[3] that characters should not be divided into positive and negative was certainly wrong, but by dividing characters into two opposite camps men in the middle

[2] The Editorial Board, 'Kuan-yü "hsieh chung-chien jen-wu" ti ts'ai-liao' (Materials Concerning 'Portraying Men in the Middle'), *Wen-i pao*, Nos. 8/9, September 30, 1964, p. 16.
[3] Ch'en Ch'i-hsia together with Ting Ling was denounced for attempts to split the literary ranks and to publish a journal to rival *Wen-i pao* during the anti-rightist campaign of 1957−8.

were neglected. This led to his contention that the middle type was the concentration of contradictions which should be properly reflected.

From August 8 to 16, 1962, a seminar on rural themes for short stories was held at Dairen under the auspices of the Chinese Writers Association. At the meeting Shao Ch'üan-lin had an opportunity to elaborate on his theory of portraying men in the middle. In his appraisal of creative writing in the previous years, he said, 'Our creative works, as a whole, have reflected the quality of the revolutionary fairly, but hardly at all the difficulty, length and complexity (of the revolutionary struggle). Characters are oversimplified, to show their heroism, their courage, thought and action, but the complexity of the struggle has not been adequately shown.'[4] He further pointed out that although characters with different vocations were depicted, their personalities remained similar. Readers would soon lose interest if every character were Red. If novelists focused only on hero characters, the path of creative writing would be very narrow. Novelists must write about men in the middle, whose personality traits could be drawn from the great majority of the people.

Shao Ch'üan-lin made it clear that he was opposed to the creation of a perfect hero image in the new era. He regarded this as 'one class, one type' dogmatism. He went on to elaborate on this point:

It is not that heroes must have defects, but rather they must be shown to have undergone a process of growth. If heroes are portrayed as perfect and flawless, the work then becomes (the embodiment of) the one class, one type theory. In *The Builders*, I feel, Liang Sheng-pao is not very successful. As a typical character, he can be found in many other works. Is Liang the Third a typical character? I think he is a highly typical character. Kuo Chen-shan is also a typical character. In *Keep the Red Flag Flying* Chu Lao-chung is of course typical, but so is Yen Chih-ho. Nowadays when critics discuss *The Builders* they only discuss Liang Sheng-pao but not the others; when they discuss *Keep the Red Flag Flying* they only discuss Chu Lao-chung but not Yen Chih-ho.[5]

Shao Ch'üan-lin considered the supporting characters, like Liang the Third and Kuo Chen-shan, whom he labelled 'men in the middle', more successful because they possess 'something of the past', the so-called 'spiritual burdens of individual peasants through the centuries'. Using this as a criterion, he suggested another character, Flour-Paste Ting of *Great Changes in a Mountain Village*. He was impressed by Flour-Paste Ting, for 'this character not only shows a capacity for progress but also

[4] The Editorial Board, 'Materials Concerning "Portraying Men in the Middle" ', *op. cit.*, p. 16.
[5] *Ibid.*, p. 17.

retains something of the past.' Sister Lan, the heroine of a short story,[6] was also cited as a middle character. Shao was not bothered by her selfish nature or her refusal to be converted to the cause of collectivism. For Shao Ch'üan-lin, contradictions such as those revealed in the attempt to change peasants' habitual way of thought could not be solved overnight.

Parallel with the theory 'men in the middle', is that of 'intensification of realism' (*hsieh-shih-chu-i shen-hua*). Focusing on the middle character would result in the intensification of realism. For Shao Ch'üan-lin, 'realism is the foundation of creative writing; without realism there can be no romanticism.' He urged writers to take real life as their subject, and reflect it truthfully: only thus could revolutionary romanticism be powerful and convincing.

After the Dairen meeting, other writers also published articles to support Shao Ch'üan-lin's argument. The list of typical middle characters was extended to include Shao Shun-pao,[7] Hsi Wang,[8] 'Muddlehead', 'Always Right',[9] Stubborn Ox Niu,[10] and 'I Knew All Along'.[11] The critics and writers who supported Shao Ch'üan-lin's theory were Mu Yang, Sh'en Ssu, Hou Mo, and Kang Cho,[12] all well-known and influential in literary circles.

As the Party secretary of the Chinese Writers Association, Shao must have been fully aware that his theory meant a major departure from the defined literary policy of the Party. He must have been sensitive enough to realize that his theory contained seeds of controversy or might even expose him to the charge of heresy. As it is important to maintain an ideological posture, the argument is presented as follows:

[6] Hsi Jung, 'Lan Ta-sao' (Sister Lan), *Jen-min wen-hsüeh*, July 1962.
[7] A character in T'ang K'e-hsin's short story 'Sha Kuei-ying,' *Shanghai wen-hsüeh*, February 1962.
[8] A character in Li Chun's title story in the collection *Li Shuang-shuang hsiao ch'uan* (*The Life of Li Shuang-shuang*) (Peking: Writers' Publishing House, 1955). For an English translation, see *Chinese Literature*, No. 6, 1960, pp. 3–26.
[9] Both are nicknames of characters in Chao Shu-li's *Sanliwan Village*.
[10] A character in Liu Shu-teh's 'Lao Niu Chin', *Pien-chiang wen-i* (*Frontier Literature*), October 1959; 'Stubborn Ox Niu', *Chinese Literature*, No. 7, 1959, pp. 6–24.
[11] The nickname of a character in Ma Feng's 'San-nien-tsao-chih-tao', *Huo-hua* (*Sparks*), January 1958; 'I Knew All Along', *Chinese Literature*, No. 7, 1959, pp. 67–85.
[12] Their views are expressed in the following articles: (1) Mu Yang, 'Ts'ung Shao Shun-pao, Liang San Lao-han so-hsiang-tao-ti' (Thoughts about Shao Shun-pao and Liang the Third), *Wen-i pao*, September 1962; (2) Sh'en Ssu, 'Wo tu "Lan Ta-sao" ' (My View of Sister Lan), *Huo-hua*, October 1962; (3) Hou Mo, 'Man t'an "Lan Ta-sao" ' (Some General Observations on Sister Lan), *Huo-hua*, October 1962; and Kang Cho, 'Shih-lun chin-nien-chien ti tuan-p'ien hsiao-shuo' (Preliminary Appraisal of Short Stories in Recent Years). The last article simultaneously appeared in *Hopei wen-hsüeh* and *Wen-hsüeh p'ing-lun*, October 1962.

1. Among the great masses of the people only a few are heroes and the majority are men in the middle; hence, novelists must create a large number of middle characters.

2. Since creative works must reflect the contradictions in society and contradictions are often concentrated in men in the middle, novelists must focus on the middle type.

3. The educational purpose of literary works is aimed at men in the middle; therefore, novelists must portray them in order to educate them.

4. Too much attention has been paid to hero characters and too little to men in the middle. When everyone writes about heroes the scope of creative writing becomes very limited; in order to broaden it, novelists must portray middle characters.[13]

The reasons offered to justify the theory seem plausible enough. Unfortunately, neither Shao Ch'üan-lin nor his supporters clearly defined the term 'men in the middle'. From Shao's lectures and other authors' articles, the conception of the middle type seems vague and confusing. Shao defines men in the middle as those people with the capacity for progress, as well as backward traits. Others suggest the backward people with shortcomings among the laboring masses as the middle type. Still others consider men in the middle as 'neither good nor bad, good as well as bad, mediocre, average people', or simply muddle-headed little men. The inclusion of all those between the two extremes of heroes and villains in the category of men in the middle defies any attempt at precise definition.

Apart from the vagueness of the concept, the idea itself is not Chinese. Traditionally, in the story-tellers' tales, legends, operas, songs, and classical novels, characters are always unequivocally divided into two opposite types, the loyal (*chung*) and the disloyal or treacherous (*chien*). The two concepts are originally used with reference to characters' relations with the emperor. The terms are later extended to those who are patriotic or dedicated to serving the people and those who betray the country or oppress the people. This polarization in Chinese fiction results in intense moral conflict. The notion that each individual has his own personality traits which straddle moral categories is Western and was introduced to China only in this century. In the novels of the May 4th vintage characters with both good and bad qualities are portrayed. But this tendency has never become popular with average readers, who are brought up in a society where human behavior has always been seen in terms of black and white.

---

[13] The Editorial Board, ' "Hsieh chung-chien jen-wu" shih tzu-ch'an-chieh-chi ti wen-hsüeh chu-chang' ('Portraying Men in the Middle' Is the Literary Proposition of the Bourgeoisie), *Wen-i pao*, Nos. 8/9, September 1964, pp. 3–4.

When the theory of portraying men in the middle is examined in the context of Communist ideology, it inevitably becomes a heresy. Literature and art are considered powerful weapons in the remolding of the Chinese temperament to fit in with the Communist conception of social order. If creative works stress the 'neither good nor bad' middle type and at the same time neglect the hero type, the result could be damaging to the revolutionary goals of the Party. Hero characters are the apostles of the revolution. Portraying the wavering attitude of the middle type will only encourage hesitation, doubts, and even resentment toward Party policies. This is the gist of the editorial of *Wen-i pao* pointing out the counter-revolutionary nature of Shao's theory:

> Should our literature and art focus on the portrayal of progressive characters among the workers, peasants, and soldiers or of the so-called 'neither good nor bad' men in the middle? Should the great achievements and meritorious deeds of the workers, peasants, and soldiers be praised, or should the so-called 'old things' in them be publicized or exposed? This is a fundamental question of the position of writers and artists as well as a fundamental question of division between the socialist literary line and the anti-socialist literary line. The promotion of 'portraying men in the middle' and 'intensification of realism' in effect encourages writers not to portray the progressive characters, not to praise the revolutionary spirit of the people, and not to inspire the people to progress, but to stress their backwardness and wavering attitude, to publicize or expose their shortcomings, and to lead the people to retreat.[14]

Wen-i pao further warns that the counter-revolutionary views of some people are very cleverly camouflaged. On the surface, they ceremoniously support the literary policy of the Party; actually, they promote anti-revolutionary or non-revolutionary ideas, in effect bourgeois and petit bourgeois ideas, to compete with the proletarian revolutionary ideas. They promote fallacies of the bourgeoisie bedecked with Marxist terminology, to appeal to the backward psychology of some people and to lure them to depart from the literary course of the proletariat, thereby making the progress of the revolution more difficult and complicated.

It is difficult to understand how Shao Ch'üan-lin's theory of portraying men in the middle reflects the literary views of the bourgeoisie or serves their interests. On the surface, Shao's theory seems unconventional or un-orthodox, but hardly counter-revolutionary. But if we relate the controversy to the policy dispute over agricultural collectivization within the Party, we shall see that the Shao Ch'üan-lin affair is not an isolated incident. The impact of Shao's

[14] *Ibid.*, p. 12.

theory will only be clear when we have examined the characters he singled out as examples of the middle type. The renegade Kuo Chen-shan of *The Builders* has been considered in the previous chapter. Yen Chih-ho, a historical figure in *Keep the Red Flag Flying*, discussed in Chapter 2, has no bearing on the debate over agricultural policy. Since Sister Lan is the principal character of a short story, she will not be considered either. To understand the Shao Ch'üan-lin affair, we shall discuss the other four characters on his original list, Liang the Third of *The Builders*, Muddlehead and Always Right of *Sanliwan Village*, and Flour-Paste Ting of *Great Changes in a Mountain Village*.

The Middle Characters

Before Shao Ch'üan-lin first formulated the theory of portraying men in the middle in December 1960, critics had already pointed out that the characterization of Liang the Third was a brilliant artistic achievement. Li Hsi-fan, a representative of the new breed of literary commentators, wrote an article in *Wen-i pao* in September 1960, evaluating Liang the Third as follows:

> It is true that portraits of old peasants with the dual, self-contradictory character of Liang the Third have appeared in many works reflecting life in our countryside. Still, without a doubt, in our contemporary literary works so far Liang the Third is the best drawn of these characters, able to sum up to a high degree the complex, conflicting life and spiritual outlook of such peasants: he presents an image which exposes the 'history of humiliation' in the life and spirit of an individual peasant who wants to build up his fortunes, showing how his character becomes full of contradictions which are generally related to private ownership through his trend toward spontaneous development. In this way, Liang the Third's portrait mirrors the entire history of peasants in the old days.[15]

After Shao's theory was formally proposed but perhaps still largely unknown outside the small circle of the Party's literary policy makers, the discussion of the figure of Liang the Third continued. An equally complimentary appraisal was offered by Yen Chia-yen, who observed:

> Liang Sheng-pao is no doubt the man with the most progressive ideas in the novel. But the most progressive figure in a work is not necessarily the most successful character artistically. In *The Builders*

[15] Li Hsi-fan, 'Man t'an *Ch'uang yeh shih* ti ssu-hsiang ho i-shu' (Some General Observations about the Theme and Artistry of *The Builders*), *Wen-i pao*, Nos. 17/18, September 26, 1960. The quotation is taken from an English version in *Chinese Literature*, No. 3, 1961, pp. 138−9.

this is none other than Liang the Third. . . . Although Liang the
Third does not belong to the genus of hero characters, he
nevertheless possesses great social significance and unique artistic
value. The success in exposing the breadth and depth of the class
struggle as well as life patterns in the countryside since the land
reform depends to a very large extent on this figure.[16]

The theme of *The Builders* is the conflict between two opposing
forces — those who attempt to increase their own family's prosperity
and those who are determined to develop mutual-aid teams. To use the
Communist parlance, it is a struggle between two paths — spontaneous
capitalism and revolutionary socialism. The hero Liang Sheng-pao
symbolizes the awakened peasants who are resolved to take the socialist
path and the rich peasant Yao Shih-chieh represents the opponents who
want to see the failure of agricultural collectivization. In between stands
Liang the Third. In him are concentrated all the contradictions. He has
no faith in mutual aid, yet he does not want to see the failure of the
first mutual-aid team. The role of Liang the Third therefore has great
significance, for upon his final attitude depends the success or failure of
the Party policy of agricultural collectivization.

Liu Ch'ing portrays Liang the Third with the imagination and power
of an austere realist. Like a sculptor using a chisel, he carves out the
image of Liang the Third in straight, sharp lines. Without any ambiguity
he describes the inherent traits of a typical Chinese peasant. Old Liang
cannot understand for the life of him why his step-son wants to waste
precious time on something called the mutual-aid team. The peasant
way of life that he learned from his father, grandfather, and ancestors is
to work hard and to take care of his own family — nothing more. He
has doubts, reservations, and objections to the whole business of
mutual aid. But as the father of the leader of a mutual-aid team, he has
no choice but to feel concern and even a secret hope for the success of
the team. The change in him goes slowly, step by step, but when he is
finally converted the reader too is convinced.

At the very beginning of the story, Liang the Third has already made
his daily round of gathering manure along the road at dawn. He is
irritated to see the door of his step-son's room still closed; he does not
know that the young man has already left to buy a new strain of rice
seed for the mutual-aid team. The subject of mutual aid has become a
bone of contention between father and son, for the old man has a
long-cherished plan to build his family fortunes. Although his life-long
fight for this goal has failed miserably and left its mark only in his

[16] Yen Chia-yen, 'T'an *Ch'uang yeh shih* chung Liang San Lao-han ti hsing hsiang'
(Comments on the Image of Liang the Third in *The Builders*), *Wen-hsüeh
p'ing-lun*, No. 3, June 14, 1961, pp. 63–4.

bowed back, the hope of prosperity never dies in him. When he was issued the land deed during the land reform, he knelt down and kowtowed in front of Chairman Mao's picture. The ten *mou* of rice paddies rekindled his ambition to become the head of a flourishing family in his old age. He dreams of living in a splendid house compound:

> He wore winter clothes with thick padding. A strong blue sash bound his waist. He was deliciously warm, so heavily upholstered in fact that he walked a bit clumsily ... He threw himself with great zeal into the endless tasks about the house. In the rear courtyard were pigs, chickens and ducks. Horses and oxen munched grass in the front courtyard. Taking care of all these domestic animals kept Liang very busy. But he enjoyed the work. It was a real pleasure. The grunting, clucking, quacking, neighing and mooing of the livestock, blended with the joyous shouts of children at play, are the most intoxicating kind of music to a peasant's ears. Liang positively revelled in them.[17]

But his dream is rudely shattered by Sheng-pao, who is determined to take a different road. The old man is at first puzzled that this intelligent young man should behave so strangely and fail to follow the peasant's only path to affluence. The news of Sheng-pao's joining the Communist Party is a blow so severe that he is unable to leave his bed for three days. When Sheng-pao wants to use the money earned from selling water chestnuts to help finance the mutual-aid team, the old man rebels. He asserts that he needs the money to get a new suit. When his wife reminds him that they can sell eggs, he declares that he is going to eat all the eggs laid by their five hens. 'I'll eat them coddled in the morning, scrambled at noon, and boiled at night.' He even threatens to go out to eat in a restaurant in the town. Why not join in the ruin of everything, he demands. The stubborn fight of Liang the Third is vividly described. Through him we can visualize the obstinate resistance of Chinese peasants to the political decision of agricultural collectivization.

There is another dimension to the conflict between father and son. It is not just that their visions are entirely different. The old man simply cannot stand the style of young Sheng-pao. With the habitual prudence common among Chinese peasants, old Liang is frightened by the unusually bold moves of Sheng-pao. His honest peasant philosophy is that 'people who do big things fall hard, while peasants who walk a road that's been trampled flat by thousands of generations, don't fall but live quiet, peaceful lives'.

In order to raise money for the mutual-aid team, Sheng-pao decides

[17] *The Builders*, p. 20, Shapiro, pp. 22–3.

to take a group of villagers to cut bamboos and to make brooms on Mount Chungnan. This makes old Liang extremely uneasy. A peasant would only spend a day or two there, earn whatever he could, and would assume responsibility only for his own safety. But here is his son, a man who can 'chew iron and spit nails' and is afraid of nothing. A subtle change gradually occurs in old Liang's state of mind. He always has an inferiority complex in front of his rich neighbors, but now he feels insignificant in Sheng-pao's presence.

His solicitude over the safety of the group for which Sheng-pao will be answerable leads the good-hearted old man to see Secretary Lu. He knows Lu not as a responsible cadre but as an honest, trustworthy peasant. After he pours out his worries and is assured that the responsibility for any accident will rest with the Party, he feels relieved. He is resigned. As long as he has food to eat and clothes to wear, Sheng-pao can do whatever he likes. He realizes that the world belongs to the young man. This is a crucial turning point for Liang. The change from obstinate opposition to passivity and resignation is the first sign of his conversion. We do not know how many peasants have been won over to support the policy of agricultural collectivization. Presumably, there are many. But no author has described their complicated, ambivalent feelings as successfully as Liu Ch'ing in the portrayal of Liang the Third.

There is another aspect of old Liang which must be explored. What is his real attitude, beneath that open, defiant opposition to his step-son's involvement in the mutual-aid team? While he never supports his son's efforts he watches the development of the mutual-aid team keenly. He notices that some of its members are not sincere in their support for mutual aid, and is concerned about its future. He is seen, alone, bending over the team's experimental seed-bed and secretly peering at the sprouts. He had shown the same anxiety when he first received the paddies during the land reform. There is something in him which gives the Party hope that peasants like Liang the Third can be won over. This is the honesty and practicality of the peasant's nature. The author describes Liang the Third's thoughts like this:

He knew he was close in spirit to Lu and Secretary Wang and Sheng-pao, even though he couldn't for the life of him understand why they were pushing mutual-aid and co-operation. 'When you can bring machines to till the land, then we can have a go at it,' he thought. 'We're scores of years away from socialism. What's the good of a lot of idle boasting?'[18]

When Blind Wang and another household withdraw from the mutual-aid team Liang the Third feels more resentment toward the two

[18] *Ibid.*, p. 255, Shapiro, p. 291.

families than distrust of the team's work. It is clear that he is not yet convinced about the policy of co-operation and his concern for the mutual-aid team is chiefly because of his affection for his son. In ideological terms, however, his secret hope for the success of Sheng-pao's team is considered a sign of his progressiveness.[19]

The strength of *The Builders* rests to a great degree on the portrayal of Liang the Third. There is no abrupt change in him from stubborn objector to zealous supporter, as often happens in other novels of a similar nature. Hard facts, rather than indoctrination, finally convince the old peasant. The superiority of the new brand of seed Sheng-pao boldly introduced, the successful experiment of the new seed-bed, the rewarding bamboo-cutting venture, the unshakeable confidence of Sheng-pao even after the withdrawal of two households, and finally the bumper crop reaped by the team all contribute towards the ultimate change in the attitude of Liang the Third.

In the epilogue, the author describes the eventual transformation of Liang the Third. While waiting to buy a bottle of oil in the queue at the supply and demand co-op, Liang the Third overhears others talk about Sheng-pao and the success of his mutual-aid team with great admiration. When people inquire about the father of this young team leader, someone says that the old man does not even have a name. Then they spot old Liang, his eyes full of tears. He is finally recognized as Sheng-pao's father and respectfully invited to move to the head of the queue to buy his bean oil. Warm and dignified in his brand new cotton padded clothes, the old man is overcome with emotion and lost in thought:

> When the autumn harvest ended, Sheng-pao told his ma he was going to have a new suit of cotton padded clothes made for pa before he did anything else, and fulfill the old man's dream.
>
> 'You're a good boy, son. You have a heart,' Liang the Third had said. 'It means more to me to hear you talk like that than whether I get those clothes or not. You go out and level the bumps in the world. Your grandpa told me it couldn't be done even if you used a shovel. I believed him and always accepted my fate. I passed his words on to you, but you didn't believe me. Go out and fight, then. I'll look after the household, sweep the courtyard and feed the pigs . . .'[20]

There is unusual unanimity among the commentators, whether they agree with Shao Ch'üan-lin's theory or not, that Liang the Third is probably the most successfully-drawn character in contemporary

[19] Yen Chia-yen, 'Comments on the Image of Liang the Third in *The Builders*', *op. cit.*, p. 68.
[20] *The Builders*, p. 510, Shapiro, p. 572.

Chinese fiction. The debate over whether Liang the Third is a typical 'backward' character is inconclusive, for in the end he is convinced of the merits of mutual aid and becomes a true supporter of agricultural collectivization. However, the other three characters singled out as typical men in the middle never really change their minds. They are Muddlehead and Always Right of *Sanliwan Village* and Flour-Paste Ting of *Great Changes in a Mountain Village*. These people would happily go back to private farming if they get the chance. As a result, the backward traits in Liang the Third are brought into focus while his progressive leanings and final conversion are eclipsed. Before we discuss the political implications of the debate over the middle type, we shall first review the characterization of these three unreformed middle characters.

Ma To-shou, nicknamed Muddlehead, and his wife, known as Always Right, have four sons. Their eldest son and daughter-in-law are faithful copies of the old couple and are aptly nicknamed Skinflint and Spitfire. Their second son is a county-level cadre and therefore does not live with them. Their third son is a soldier fighting in Korea, but the old couple do not consider it a family honor and have held the third daughter-in-law responsible for the young man's enlistment. The youngest son is Yu-yi, a junior middle school graduate, member of the Youth League and teacher in the village night school. Even with a cadre, a PLA soldier and a Youth Leaguer in the family, Muddlehead remains an old-fashioned peasant and refuses to join the co-operative. As a matter of fact, he does not want to have anything to do with his neighbors, and the front gate is always bolted as soon as dusk falls.

There is internal conflict within the family between Chu-ying the third daughter-in-law and a Youth Leaguer, and the rest of the family, except Yu-yi. The young woman has to do all the housework and still remains the target of a kind of family warfare. In order to clothe her little daughter and herself, she is given five catties of raw cotton, according to an old family rule, and is expected to do all the spinning, weaving and clothes-making. One day, after grinding flour at the mill all morning, she and her daughter are given only left-over noodle soup for their meal. The case is taken to the grievances committee, and after a hearing, the committee approves Chu-ying's plea to lead an independent life. Since this means that the family property has to be divided, Muddlehead unearths four deeds he prepared as an emergency measure in the heat of the rent reduction campaign years before. According to this division settlement, Chu-ying will get thirteen *mou* of land plus her share of rooms, furniture, and farm implements.

Now the leaders of the co-operative are planning to expand it and open a canal, but Muddlehead refuses to allow them to channel the waterway through a piece of land in Tilt Field he owns. Since the future of the co-operative depends on the canal, which will irrigate the entire area, the cadres have offered Muddlehead a number of options. He can pick any piece of land in exchange, he can demand rent, or he can be guaranteed the same amount of grain, but all offers have been rejected. As Muddlehead's family includes a county level cadre and a PLA soldier, the cadres are unwilling to use force, such as resorting to a compulsory purchase order. For his part, Muddlehead refuses to give up the piece of land precisely because he does not want to see the success of the co-operative. Chu-ying's separation from the family gives rise to the hope that she may receive the plot in Tilt Field. But it turns out that the land goes to Yu-fu, the county cadre. The leaders of the co-operative reason that whether the deed is genuine or not, they cannot object, as long as Chu-ying gets her fair share. They have already thought of another way to gaining access to that patch of land.

The second person in the family to revolt against the authority of Muddlehead and his wife Always Right is the youngest son, Yu-yi. Though the young man has been on good terms with two girls and finds it difficult to choose between them, Always Right decides to arrange a marriage between him and her sister's daughter, a recent divorcée. Usually a gentle, obliging son, Yu-yi is furious. Surprised at her son's disobedience, Always Right has him locked up. When he hears the news that one of the girls is getting engaged, good-natured Yu-yi rebels. Nothing can stop him now from getting his share of the property and living his own life.

At a meeting of the co-operative, it is announced that the cadres have written a letter to Muddlehead's second son, informing him of the planned canal. Since the waterway will run through the three *mou* in Tilt Field which, according to a separation settlement written ten years ago, is part of his property, they inquire if he will trade, sell or rent it to the co-operative. They promptly receive the brief reply that since as a government cadre he is unlikely to return to farm life, he gives all his land holding to the co-operative.

Muddlehead has been left with no choice but to join the co-operative. The old man has not changed his mind; the decision is forced on him by events beyond his control. Before coming to a final decision he calculates as follows:

> If they joined the co-op, the old couple's land and Yu-yi's share would come to twenty-nine *mou*, which, reckoning on an average of two bushels a *mou*, should bring them twenty-two bushels and four pecks in land shares. He and Yu-yi counted as one and a half workers, and if they put in three hundred workdays, they could earn forty-five bushels — sixty-seven bushels and four pecks altogether. If they stayed out of the co-op, they would only get fifty-eight bushels of grain — nine bushels and four pecks less . . .[21]

[21] *Sanliwan Village*, pp. 165–6, Yang, p. 247.

There is a fundamental difference between Liang the Third of *The Builders* and Muddlehead of *Sanliwan Village*. While old Liang takes pride in his step-son's achievement and sees that the collective road is good for the poor, Muddlehead remains reluctant. Only when it is clearly too late to stop family division and private farming is no longer to his advantage does he apply for admission to the co-operative. The goal of the Communist Party in the transformation of individual farming into agricultural co-operation is not only a change from private to collective ownership but also a reshaping of the peasants' attitude. The selfish way of thinking natural to Muddlehead may reassert itself at the first available opportunity. People like Muddlehead remain a potential threat to socialism.

The lack of large-scale support for the Party policy is also reflected in Chou Li-po's *Great Changes in a Mountain Village*. Like his earlier work *The Hurricane*, this novel has no hero. In the absence of a hero, the decision to form a co-operative comes from Party directives, and its success is made possible only by the supervision of cadres from elsewhere. The honesty of Chou Li-po is unquestioned. He describes in great detail different forms of peasant opposition to collectivization, such as felling trees and slaughtering livestock. As a creative work, however, the novel is a complete failure.

Without a hero, most of the characters who people the novel could qualify as men in the middle. 'Granny' Li Yueh-hui, chairman of the peasants' association, is never in a hurry to carry out Party policies. Chen Ta-chun, secretary of the Youth League, is short-tempered and often unable to see the essentials of co-operative policy. Li Yu-sheng, leader of a mutual-aid team and a determined Communist, does not know how to deal with his selfish wife and always worries about his family affairs. But Shao Ch'üan-lin only mentions Flour-Paste Ting as a typical man in the middle, so he deserves our special attention, to see the conceptual confusion of the theory.

Although Sheng Yu-ting is the first person to appear in the novel, he does not occupy much space nor the center of the stage. Nicknamed Flour-Paste Ting, he gives no thought to what he is doing. When he hears the rumor that bamboo groves are going to become public property he immediately cuts down a few bamboos to sell in the market. He prefers to sleep soundly at home than attend meetings, for his philosophy is that the Party can be relied on never to let poor peasants suffer losses. When he does attend a meeting he can walk out in the middle of a discussion and sleep innocently in the next room. Once he is entrusted with the task of persuading a middle peasant to join the co-operative, but accepts the man's invitation to have a drink without realizing that it is a trick, and completely forgets why he has come. He is one of the first to join the co-operative, for the simple reason that 'once we are in the co-operative, I shall never have to worry any more about where the next meal's coming from'.

The author never shows, as Shao Ch'üan-lin claims, what is of the past in Flour-Paste Ting and how his capacity for progress is evolved. No attempt is made to show the process of change in Ting, from the man who gets in first to sell his bamboos before collectivization to the one who voluntarily provides firewood to heat the meeting place. What distinguishes Flour-Paste Ting from other characters in the story is that he is more or less a comic figure that gives the novel a slightly humorous touch. It is this quality of buffoonery, rather than his attitude toward the co-operative, that invites Shao to choose him as an example of a typical middle character.

Individually considered, these characters are harmless enough. They do nothing to undermine the policy of co-operation; besides, they finally, though reluctantly, join the co-operative. In fact, before Shao Ch'üan-lin formulated the theory of portraying men in the middle, critics did not pay much attention to Muddlehead, Always Right, and Flour-Paste Ting, and their discussion of Liang the Third focused mainly on his transformation as a hopeful sign of the success of agricultural collectivization. But when these characters are grouped together and labelled as typical of men in the middle, attention is drawn to their common traits. If these four characters have anything in common, it is their opposition to the policy of agricultural co-operation. Suddenly, it is no longer merely a literary theory, but implicitly challenges Mao Tse-tung's view that the great majority of peasants are ready and eager to join agricultural co-operatives. It is the political message implicit in the theory of portraying men in the middle that we shall now consider.

The Policy Dispute Implied in the Shao Ch'üan-lin Affair

There appears to have been no disagreement among the leaders about the necessity for land collectivization if agriculture is to feed the nation's urgent program of industrialization as well as hundreds of millions of people. If land continues to be divided up in small patches, not only is it uneconomical, but any plan to introduce farming machines or develop commercial crops will be quite out of the question. Therefore the policy debate among the Party leaders has always focused not on *whether* but *when* the policy of agricultural collectivization should be carried out. One view held at various times and in various forms is that it must proceed at a deliberate pace, to avoid upsetting the economic order of the countryside, and to ensure normal grain production. Another view, somewhat over-optimistic but always consistent, is that if there is to be agricultural collectivization, it is better carried out immediately before some people again acquire large concentrations of land. It is much easier for peasants to accept collectivization before they develop a deep attachment to the land they now own.

The first policy decision on the development of agricultural co-operation by the Central Committee of the CCP was issued on December 15, 1951, and formally proclaimed on February 15, 1953. It outlines a three-stage process from temporary, seasonal mutual aid to year-round mutual aid and finally to an agricultural co-operative, with all land pooled. No target dates were given. The second policy decision, passed on December 16, 1953 at the Central Committee meeting, calls for the establishment of 800,000 agricultural co-operatives, embracing roughly 20 per cent of all the peasants, by the end of the First Five-Year Plan in 1957. But on July 31, 1955 Mao Tse-tung delivered an important policy speech 'Concerning the Problem of Agricultural Co-operation' at a meeting of members of provincial, municipal and regional Party committees. He compared the speed of agricultural co-operation to the pace of an old woman with bound feet. Although he encouraged the cadres to lead the agricultural co-operation campaign boldly, he still allowed eighteen years, through three consecutive Five-Year Plans, for the completion of agricultural collectivization. This set the target date for communization of land for 1968. From 1955 onwards, however, the pace of collectivization was greatly accelerated; by the end of 1958 most of the nation's land was communized. There is conclusive evidence to show that Mao is chiefly responsible for shortening the period of land collectivization.

The logic for the policy of speeding up agricultural collectivization may be sound, but its implementation has encountered enormous difficulties. The resistance of peasants to the collectivization policy reached proportions unknown in any of the previous programs. The peasants were fighting not only the loss of their land but also the change in their traditional way of life. The scope and intensity of the resistance as well as the complexity and subtlety of the forms in which it was expressed were not reported in the Party-controlled press, but are reflected in the novels we have been discussing.

In proposing his theory, Shao Ch'üan-lin not only singled out characters like Liang the Third, Muddlehead, and Flour-Paste Ting as typical middle characters but also stressed the broad center they represent. He put it like this:

> The center is large while the two extremes are small, for good and bad men are always small in number. Since various strata of people are situated at the broad center, it is very important to portray them and the contradictions concentrated in them.[22]

---

[22] The Editorial Board, 'Materials Concerning "Portraying Men in the Middle" ', *Ibid.*, p. 17.

This view places Shao in diametrical opposition to Mao Tse-tung's assertion in his speech 'Concerning the Problem of Agricultural Co-operation'. Chairman Mao says in this historic statement:

> With the exception of a small number (about 20–30 per cent of the rural population) of rich and relatively well-off middle peasants who have a wavering attitude toward co-operation, some of them are trying their best to take the road to capitalism, the great majority (about 60–70 per cent of the rural population) of poor and lower middle peasants have already realized that in order to get rid of poverty, to improve living standards, and to fight against natural calamities, they must join together and march on the road to socialism.[23]

When Shao Ch'üan-lin minimizes the importance of Liang Sheng-pao and considers both Kuo Chen-shan (who has been treated as a renegade) and Liang the Third as typical men in the middle, he implies that their behavior and thinking is typical of the majority of Chinese peasants. The debate over who is typical is by no means just a literary exercise. It is actually a policy debate clothed in the form of literary criticism. If we examine carefully policy disputes among Chinese leaders prior to the Cultural Revolution, we can detect a pattern of debate, couched in academic or theoretical terms, ostensibly over historical figures or literary characters. This is precisely the case in the controversy over whether Liang Sheng-pao or Liang the Third and Kuo Chen-shan typify Chinese peasants. If Liang Sheng-pao is typical, it means that Mao's assessment of the rural situation is correct and that the great majority of peasants are willing and eager to start mutual-aid teams. On the other hand, if Liang the Third and Kuo Chen-shan are typical, it then follows that Chinese peasants are not ready for socialism. This explains why most critics commenting on *The Builders*, instead of discussing the novel's artistic quality, earnestly quote from Chairman Mao's editorial notes in the documentary collection *The Socialist High Tide in China's Countryside*.[24]

The key word is 'typical'. It can be interpreted to mean 'representative'. When Shao Ch'üan-lin considers Liang the Third typical, Chu

---

[23] Mao Tse-tung, 'Kuan-yü nung-yeh ho-tso-hua wen-t'i' (Concerning the Problem of Agricultural Co-operation), quoted in Chu Chai, 'Ts'ung tui Liang San Lao-han ti p'ing-chia k'an "hsieh chung-chien jen-wu" chu-chang ti shih-chih' (From the Evaluation of Liang the Third to See the Essence of the Proposition of 'Portraying Men in the Middle'), *Wen-hsüeh p'ing-lun*, No. 6, Dec. 14, 1964.

[24] For instance, Li Hsi-fan quotes Mao's editorial comments on the article 'The Party Secretary Takes Part and the Entire Party Helps Run the Co-operative' in his 'Some General Observations about the Theme and Artistry of *The Builders*', *op. cit.*, Wu Chung-chieh and Kao Yun quote Mao's comments on 'Who Says a Chicken Feather Cannot Ascend to Heaven' in 'T'an Liang Sheng-pao hsing-hsiang ti ch'uang-tsao' (Talks about the Creation of the Image of Liang Sheng-pao), *Wen-hsüeh p'ing-lun*, No. 3, June 14, 1964, and Chu Chai's quotation, *op. cit.*

284 Heroes and Villains in Communist China

Chai, for instance, takes that to mean that the backward aspects of the character are general among the people.[25] Chu takes care to distinguish Shao's view that Liang the Third is typical (*tien-hsing-ti*) from Yen Chia-yen's view that the characterization of Liang the Third is successful (*ch'eng-kung-ti*). He agrees that the portrayal of old Liang is highly successful, but denies that the character is representative of the majority of peasants. Furthermore, he contends that Liang the Third is not really a middle character as defined by Shao. He equates Shao's men in the middle with backward people and points out old Liang's positive side as proof that the good peasant is by no means backward.

There is no conclusive evidence to show that Shao Ch'üan-lin served as the spokesman of the Liu Shao-ch'i faction in their dispute with Mao over the pace of agricultural collectivization.[26] On the other hand, he could not have been so bold as to challenge Mao's agricultural policy single-handed. Even as the secretary of the Party section of the Chinese Writers Association, Shao would not have the power to do so alone. One fact which suggests Shao Ch'üan-lin's political backing is that even after his theory of portraying men in the middle was labelled a bourgeois literary view and a distortion of Chairman Mao's 'Yenan Forum Talks', the debate was contained within the terms of literary discussion. It was not developed into a political campaign, as in the case of Hu Feng, until the wholesale rectification inside the Party during the Cultural Revolution.

The policy dispute implicit in the Shao Ch'üan-lin affair is further supported by the fact that the authors Liu Ch'ing, Chao Shu-li and Chou Li-po, who created Liang the Third, Muddlehead, Always Right, and Flour-Paste Ting, were not under attack at the same time as Shao Ch'üan-lin. It seems to suggest that from the artistic point of view the theory of portraying men in the middle is really irrelevant. A novel cannot just have two types of characters: heroes and villains. There must be supporting characters which play a variety of roles in the narration of human drama. A first-rate novelist will portray supporting characters with equal force and vigor. This explains why in the post-Shao Ch'üan-lin affair period, middle characters portrayed in depth still appear in novels.

Middle Characters after the Shao Ch'üan-lin Affair

In *Bright Sunny Days*, there are powerful descriptions of at least three men, Han Po-an, Ma Tzu-huai and Chiao Chen-mou, all middle peasants,

[25] Chu Chai, *op. cit.*, pp. 4–5.
[26] During the Cultural Revolution a mass of material was published to link Shao Ch'üan-lin's proposition of portraying men in the middle with the revisionist line of Liu Shao-ch'i and to accuse Shao as one of the spokesmen of the Liu Shao-ch'i faction, but I do not feel it can be used as conclusive evidence.

who qualify for Shao Ch'üan-lin's definition of men in the middle. They all show different degrees of selfishness and political awareness and maintain different attitudes toward the co-operative. As the contradiction between the pro- and anti-socialist forces deepens and the struggle gains momentum, their thinking, behavior patterns, and attitudes towards agricultural co-operation gradually change. In the end, their support for the co-operative still ranges from quiet passive involvement to intense and active participation.

Han Po-an, now over sixty, has been a widower for twenty years. He works harder than anyone else in the village; his thrift is unmatched. He never wastes a cent and uses only one bottle of oil in a whole year. When he makes a pot of soup he dips a chopstick into the oil bottle and then stirs it in the soup so that the soup will smell of oil. He is almost the best farmer in the entire village, second only to Chiao Chen-mou, and a good carpenter as well. Because he is a timid person who never dares quarrel with anyone, landlords like Pigtail Ma took pleasure in purloining land from him in the old days. Yet he is the last man to join the co-operative. He does so only when he realizes that if he continued to farm on his own, his son Tao-man would never be able to marry any girl. As a widower for so many years, he does not want his son to suffer his own fate and besides, the family badly needs a woman to see to the housework.

Once in the co-operative, he never feels at ease, because his land is now public property. When Ma Chih-yueh tells him that owners can receive half the yield from the land, this cautious peasant suddenly becomes active. He is to be seen everywhere, always pricking up his ears to catch the gist of other people's conversations. He is among the crowd of bystanders outside the meeting room where the discussion on grain distribution is going on. But as soon as a brawl seems imminent, he is frightened and slips away unnoticed.

Later in the day he is told by Crook Ma that village cadres will start a search for surplus grain and that if he has any, he had better get rid of it. Han Po-an denies it vigorously, but his whole body flinches. But when Crook Ma says that two 'comrades' from town are paying twenty cents for a catty of corn, Han asks in spite of himself about the price of millet. Terrified by the sound of his own voice, which seems quite unrecognizable, he mumbles an excuse and walks away without waiting for an answer.

The rumor that a search for grain will soon begin makes Han Po-an so unsettled that he immediately goes home. No sooner has he entered his compound than he bolts his front door and uses a piece of log as an additional prop. He takes out a key from his belt and opens a padlock on the door of the west room. Then he removes a cover from an unused *kang* and feels for his two sacks of millet. Yes, they are still there. These two sacks of millet are his insurance; as long as he has them, he feels secure. No one knows of the existence of the grain, not even his own son. Every day when he comes back from work in the field he likes to touch it and inhale its delicious aroma. No matter how frustrated, how miserable and how exhausted he feels, a mere touch of the grain makes him feel refreshed and free from worries.

After he has removed one sack to a safer place, a pit in a small storeroom at the backyard, he is startled by footsteps. It is his son, Tao-man, who looks at him with anger and disgust. As though caught stealing, Han Po-an shudders all over and cannot move. Actually, his son has not seen what he was doing. The young man is furious at his father's complaining of food shortage in public, with Crook Ma and Big Gun Ma. It has caused a rift between him and his girl Ts'ui-ch'ing. A quarrel ensues between the kind-hearted old peasant and his usually gentle son. Although there is no immediate reconciliation when the old man weeps, some form of peace is restored. The old man says with emotion that all he has done is for the young man and that as soon as Tao-man gets married after harvest he can do whatever he likes.

But Han Po-an has not a moment's peace of mind the whole afternoon. In the evening he decides to get rid of the millet. It is much safer to hold banknotes and besides, he can sell one sack and still keep the other. He smokes one pipe after another and waits impatiently for darkness to fall. Finally, the street becomes quiet, so he goes to see Ma Chih-yueh about the search. When Ma's ambiguous answer adds to his worries Han summons up all his strength to say that he wishes to sell some millet to the two merchants from town. He is destined to be disappointed once more, for he is told that they have gone. But Ma Chih-yueh wants to be helpful and assures Han that they will be back soon. Han is tremendously relieved to hear Ma say that if Han feels it unsafe to keep the grain at home, he can bring it over. Han Po-an walks home with nimble feet, but as soon as he touches the grain his heart sinks. After a considerable struggle, he hauls the sack of millet on his back and carries it to Ma's house. After unloading the sack inside Ma's house and hearing the door locked behind him, he has no more strength left and collapses on the steps.

The rumored search for surplus grain never materializes; on the other hand, the illegal selling of grain by Crook Ma and others is discovered. Although Han Po-an has not really been involved in the unlawful transaction and his intention remains a secret, he has somehow learned his lesson. But it proves too hard for Han to change; he has lived too long and suffered too much in the old society to adjust himself to the new way of life. He realizes that he must follow the example of other poor peasants who are completely dedicated to the co-operative. He finally comes to see that Crook Ma is interested only in his personal gain, at the expense of the co-operative, and discovers that Ma

Chih-yueh's real purpose is to destroy the co-operative. But he continues to feel secure only in his small private world. He has not changed into a man who sees the co-operative as a large family where people can share everything together, and perhaps never will.

Some twenty years younger than Han Po-an, Ma Tzu-huai is also a hard-working, prudent middle peasant. Though well-aware that the co-operative is in the hands of a capable, honest leader, he is still worried that Hsiao Ch'ang-ch'un is too young and inexperienced. When some people demand the landowners' share of grain, his uncertainty is further reinforced. No matter how grain is distributed, as a hard-working peasant who has earned more work points than most others, he cannot suffer losses anyway. But talk, rumors and all the fuss over grain distribution keep him so flustered that he cannot concentrate on his work.

When the question of grain distribution is being discussed among the cadres, Ma Tzu-huai also stands outside the meeting room, but hides behind a wall of people. At one point he grumbles, 'he is, too' without saying clearly that he too is short of grain. Besides, his voice is so low that no one actually hears him. Later, when Crook Ma comes to ask him if he wants to sell surplus grain, he reasons that this time he cannot blindly follow in the steps of others. He has always maintained the principle never to pursue improper gains and never to break the law. After listening to Secretary Hsiao's criticism of Crook Ma and others, he comes to realize that his demands for the land owners' share of grain and his complaints about the food shortage actually violated his own principle.

A few days later, he is invited to attend a meeting of poor and lower middle peasants. The moment he enters the meeting hall, he senses an unusual atmosphere. The hall is packed with people; an air of blitheness and congeniality prevails, as if members of a family were gathered for the New Year festival. He is warmly welcomed by the Party secretary Hsiao and seated among a group of elderly peasants. Listening to their chat and laughter and watching their faces full of confidence and faith, Ma Tzu-huai feels an irresistible pull of optimism. These are familiar faces, but they look strange and different, as if he were seeing them for the first time.

Ma Tzu-huai suddenly realized that there was a good distance between his own mind and those of the others. He had been thinking of quite different things. Although he had not opposed the co-operative, he had not whole-heartedly supported it as the others had. He had been worrying over everything, and his heart was never 'steeled'. Then which side did he belong to? The well-off middle peasant was suddenly confronted with this problem. Although it remained vague and indefinable and he had not yet had time to consider it carefully, he seemed to be giving it some thought. . . .[27]

Before he gets an opportunity to participate in the group discussion, his wife comes to fetch him. He is told that their son-in-law has just arrived to pay them a visit. This is the first time he has come since their daughter's marriage, and the news is a delightful surprise. As he hesitates, wondering whether it is proper for him to leave in the middle of the meeting, Hsiao Ch'ang-ch'un urges him to go. On their way home, the couple exchange impressions. Ma Tzu-huai says that he has seen the light and they must from now on give the co-operative their firm support. His wife tells him that their son-in-law said the same thing as soon as he arrived. This makes Ma Tzu-huai even more determined that he should never again let down his son-in-law, a Communist and production brigade leader, and make the young man ashamed of having married the daughter of a backward middle peasant.

The third character Chiao Chen-mou has a PLA officer for his son and the secretary of the village Communist Youth League for his daughter. He used to have an interesting hobby collecting imperial almanacs, and still keeps a set which is complete since the reign of Emperor Hsüan T'ung. Through a score of years he has developed an encyclopaedic knowledge of dates and festivals, dates auspicious for marriage, for ground-breaking, for travel, for dress-making, and for practically everything else, and piously followed the guidance of the almanac. Since the liberation his interest has shifted to the collection of Party policy statements and government proclamations. He has kept a good collection of resolutions of the Party Central, government decrees, statements by Premier Chou En-lai, and newspaper clippings of editorials, questions and answers, notices, and even advertisements.

This clever middle peasant was sceptical at first about the promises of the Communist Party, including *The Outline of Agrarian Law*. But as the new government kept doing things according to its publicly announced policies, he became totally convinced. Since then, he has developed an interest in collecting documents. One day as he and his cousin were driving back from making a delivery in Peking, he saw a new bulletin on the roadside. Though dead tired, he jumped down from the cart. His cousin told him that the bulletin was about the protection of forests and that since there was no forest in Tungshanwu, there was no need for him to be concerned. But Chiao Chen-mou insisted that it would be of use in the future and besides, documents were all related. His cousin thought it should not take him very long to read a bulletin, so he did not stop the cart. After travelling slowly for twenty *li*, his

---

[27] *Bright Sunny Days*, Vol. I, pp. 552–3.

cousin stopped at a village inn, had supper, and finished a pipe. Only then did Chiao Chen-mou arrive. The bulletin was too long, Chen-mou explained, and it took more time than he had realized to copy it down. He not only collects documents, but reads and memorizes every word. Whenever a cadre comes to Tungshanwu, he raises questions about one policy or another with the visitor. Not infrequently, visiting cadres think that the middle peasant wants to show off or to test their knowledge. He is of course absolutely serious and wants to understand the Communist Party and to do things according to its policies.

When he hears the talk about land receiving credit in grain distribution he takes down a bundle from the shelf. All the documents he has collected are wrapped in three layers of newspaper. He wants to find out if the matter is explained in Party policies, government proclamations, or Premier Chou's statements. He must do things in accordance with Party policy or the law. But even Chiao Chen-mou is shocked and alarmed to hear the rumor that cadres will start a search for surplus grain. As a practical peasant, he always keeps sufficient grain to last through even a lean year. No matter how good the co-operative is, it cannot guarantee that there will be no natural disaster. As an army dependent and the father of the secretary of the Youth League, he does not want to depend on government relief. But this thought is largely his rationalization, for in his heart he remains a peasant, and can rest in peace only with surplus grain at home.

Two events help change Chiao Chen-mou's attitude completely. The exposure of Crook Ma's secret selling of grain to black market merchants horrifies him, for the deal is a clear violation of the policy he remembers word for word. Then Hsiao's disclosure of Ma Lao-ssu's eating wild herb and his refusal to accept government relief grain makes an even stronger impact on Chiao. He goes to Hsiao Ch'ang-ch'un's house in great excitement without realizing that he is disrupting a discussion. After puffing at his pipe for a while, he finally knocks off the ashes and confides:

'Secretary, today is an unusual day. What Crook Ma and Ma Lao-ssu did has taught me a lesson. I've come to understand what is meant by a poor man's bones, a poor man's heart. I haven't got it, but I can be reborn, can change my bones. I reckon that with sufficient determination it's not difficult to become a Ma Lao-ssu. Secretary, to tell the truth, I've also retained a shameful tail . . .'[28]

Then, he goes on to say that he is resolved to cut off that tail. Raising four fingers, he declares that he has more than four sacks, half rice and half wheat. He explains that he has been keeping surplus grain

[28] *Ibid.*, Vol. I, p. 629.

for years. It never occurred to him to sell it on the black market, for he would never do anything against government policy. But the mere fact that he keeps the grain in order to have something to fall back on is a disgrace. The thought that he saves grain to feed worms while his good friends and neighbors are eating husks and wild herb makes him even more ashamed. One cannot just talk about policies, and not behave in accordance with them, like old Ma Lao-ssu. He announces that he has decided to cut off that tail completely and to share the same fate as everyone else. He wants to offer all his surplus grain to help solve the shortage of needy families.

The three men have gone through different processes of change and reached different stages of transformation. There can be no doubt that the Communist system has had a great impact on each individual, but everyone must respond in a very personal way. An individual's response, as shown in the cases discussed above, is determined by a number of variables, such as experience in the old society, personality, education, and age. These are personal factors. It is also affected by the family, neighbors, relatives, and friends. There are also the particular circumstances in which a man finds himself. There is a logical explanation for each person's behavior according to all these factors, which may be termed the sociological basis, in our academic parlance, or the material basis, in the Chinese Communist lexicon.

A theoretical structure may be given to explain the relationship between the hero model and the middle character. The argument presented in Chinese Communist ideology is twofold: human will determines material success, and the material basis in turn affects the human mind. The first part of the argument can be used to interpret the endeavor to create the hero model whose dedication and perseverance are two major factors in the success of rebuilding the physical and human environment. The second part ties in well as a justification for the portrayal of the middle character. As men with deeply-entrenched personality traits, developed in pre-Communist society, middle-of-the-road peasants are incapable of taking the initiative in seeking changes toward socialism. Their transformation is brought about by ecological factors in the process of social change.

The Shao Ch'üan-lin affair seems to have had little impact on the works of creative artists. In a few excellent novels published since then,[29] heroes, villains, and middle characters are given equal attention, and this accounts for their success. It is a heresy, from the ideological viewpoint, and a fallacy, from the artistic viewpoint, to stress the middle character at the expense of the hero model. There must be real

---

[29] In addition to *Bright Sunny Days*, we may cite *The Thundering Yangtse* as another example, see Chapter 5.

heroes in China; otherwise, it is impossible to explain the ground gained in developing socialism. The self-denial of heroes is the primary moving force in changing the physical and human environment, which in turn produces an effect on the thinking of the masses. The positive traits in heroes reflect the value system of the society of which they are a part. Novels dominated by middle characters will not only become boring but also unrealistic because they overlook ideology as a part of Chinese life as well as the changing reality itself.

11

THE P.L.A. IN TIME OF PEACE

The 1960s can be called the decade of Ou-yang Hai. The spirit of this period was first expressed in Lin Piao's call for the training of four-good companies and five-good soldiers in the autumn of 1960[1] and reached its zenith with the adoption of the new constitution of the Communist Party of China wherein Lin Piao was designated the successor to Chairman Mao in April 1969. The decade witnessed the emergence of soldier heroes – Lei Feng in 1963, Ou-yang Hai in 1965, Wang Chieh and Liu Ying-chun in 1966, Lu Hsiang-pi in 1967, and many more thereafter – all based on the same prototype. These model soldiers were meant to be emulated not only by other soldiers but also by the masses. Immediately after the appearance of the first five-good soldier Lei Feng, there was a nationwide 'Learning from the PLA' campaign, calling on everyone to look at the army as the cradle of a new revolutionary spirit.[2]

The Song of Ou-yang Hai[3] is the fictional version of the life of the soldier hero. The purpose of the author in drawing Ou-yang Hai, as in the stories of Lei Feng and other soldier heroes, is to prescribe a code of conduct, through the hero's activities. The author's normative construction of Ou-yang Hai's heroism apparently gained the approval of the leadership, since prominent literary figures and political leaders gave the novel overwhelming accolades. The novel was acclaimed by

---

[1] See John Gittings, *The Role of the Chinese Army*, pp. 245–6; also Hsiao Hua's report delivered at a military conference on February 2, 1963, *Jen-min jih-pao*, April 1, 1963. 'Four-good companies' are those distinguished in ideology, in political work, in the 'three-eight' working style (that is, in observing the Three Main Rules of Discipline and the Eight Points for Attention), and in arranging their everyday life. 'Five-good soldiers' are those who show good performance in political thinking, military training, working style, fulfilment of tasks and physical education.
[2] 'The Whole Country Must Learn from the PLA', *Jen-min jih-pao*, editorial, February 1, 1964.
[3] Chin Ching-mai, *Ou-yang Hai chih ko* (*The Song of Ou-yang Hai*) (Peking: People's Literature Publishing House, rev. ed., 1966). A condensed translation can be found in *Chinese Literature*, Nos. 7, 8, 9, 10, and 11, pp. 71–132, 30–96, 88–141, 75–103, and 61–104. The novel was first published by the PLA Literature Publishing House in 1965 and revised since the publication of this edition.

critics like Li Hsi-fan,[4] Yen Wen-ching,[5] and Liu Pai-yü, as a landmark
in the portrayal of contemporary heroes. The extravagant glorification
of the hero's conduct is best shown in a piece written by Liu Pai-yü:

The typical significance of Ou-yang Hai lies in the fact that he is a
new man with the most advanced revolutionary ideas of our age,
radiant with the light of Mao Tse-tung's thought; thus he represents
the finest essence of our age and is a contemporary hero, a model for
us to learn from.[6]

No less a celebrity than Kuo Mo-jo, whose calligraphy graces the
cover of the novel, says without a blush, 'We ought to receive education
from *The Song of Ou-yang Hai*, and we ought to emulate Ou-yang
Hai.'[7] On February 14, 1966, the author was received by Ch'en Yi, a
member of the politburo and a vice-premier, and Tao Chu, the first
secretary of the South China Bureau of the CCP. Ch'en Yi called the
novel an epoch-making work in the history of Chinese literature and the
fruit of joint endeavor through the leadership of the Party, the
enthusiastic co-operation of the masses, and the efforts of the author.[8]
Tao Chu urged all cadres who could read to study the novel in order to
learn about putting politics first and remolding themselves.[9]

In addition to the portrait of an ideal soldier hero, the novel can be
viewed as a document of norms, values, attitudes, and behavior in the
People's Liberation Army in the 1960s. It offers an unusual insight into
the internal structure and functioning of the army at company level. In
the novel we detect a fundamental change in the nature of the army, so
different from the one which fought brilliant battles like those in
Defense of Yenan and *Red Sun*. It is not that more than a decade of
peace has turned the army into a garrison force but rather that the
concept of soldiery has undergone a fundamental metamorphosis. The

[4] Li Hsi-fan, 'She-hui-chu-i shih-tai ching-shen ti tsui ch'iang-yin' (The Tenor of
the Spirit of the Socialist Epoch), *Wen-i pao*, No. 1, 1966.
[5] Yen Wen-ching, 'Mao Tse-tung ssu-hsiang tsai wen-hsüeh fang-mien ti sheng-li'
(The Triumph of Mao Tse-tung's Thought in Literature), *Wen-i pao*, No. 3, 1966.
[6] Liu Pai-yü, 'Ou-yang Hai chih ko shih kung-ch'an-chu-i ti chan-ko', *Wen-i pao*,
No. 4, 1966, p. 18; 'A Battle Song of Communism', *Chinese Literature*, No. 7,
1966, p. 143.
[7] Kuo Mo-jo, 'Mao Tse-tung shih-tai ti ying-hsiung shih-shih – Ch'iu *Ou-yang Hai
chih ko* ta *Wen-i pao* pien-che wen' (Epic of the Era of Mao Tse-tung – An
Interview by the Staff of *Wen-i pao* Concerning *The Song of Ou-yang Hai*), *Wen-i
pao*, No. 4, 1966, p. 14. Kuo is the president of the Chinese Academy of Sciences.
[8] 'Ch'en Yi, Tao Chu t'ung-chih tsai chieh-chien *Ou-yang Hai chih ko* tso-che shih
t'an she-hui-chu-i wen-hsüeh ch'uang-tso shang ti i-hsieh chung-yao wen-t'i'
(Comrades Ch'en Yi and Tao Chu Talked about Some Important Problems in
Socialist Literature When They Were Receiving the Author of *The Song of
Ou-yang Hai*), *Wen-i pao*, No. 3, 1966, p. 2.
[9] *Ibid.*, p. 3.

army has literally changed into a school for training in the socialist code of conduct, and its curriculum is learning self-denial through practice. Self-denial, of course, was a virtue cultivated and publicized from the beginning, but there were other virtues considered equally, if not more, important in a combat force. In other war stories, commanders, political commissars, and soldiers show qualities of bravery, resourcefulness, and imagination which contributed more to the revolutionary war than mere self-denial. Furthermore, in early war stories, self-denial is a personal virtue, and not necessarily an indispensable one. In *Defense of Yenan* the commander, Chou Ta-yung, and the squad leader, Wang the Tiger, of the Hero Company, are first of all fearless fighters and only secondarily men of unselfish dedication. In *Red Sun* the regimental commander Liu Sheng and the company commander Shih Tung-ken show no inclination toward self-denial. They want to distinguish themselves in battles and are very depressed when they feel that their fighting capacity has been underrated by the field commanders. In *The Song of Ou-yang Hai* the spirit of self-denial becomes the dominant virtue, without which a military man ceases to be a soldier of the people's army.

There is something more to the virtue of self-denial. The behavior of a soldier is no longer his own business. His military performance is not as important as the manner and style he displays in performing his professional duties. He must be constantly aware of the effect these may have on others, for he wants others to emulate him. With this preoccupation, he no longers behaves as a man but as a model. What is important is not how he behaves but how others will judge him, according to an established code of conduct. When other people's perception of him becomes the only gauge of merit and distinction, he becomes, inevitably, a poser rather than a real hero, socialist or otherwise. As a result, the army becomes, literally, a mutual admiration club. Since this quality of soldiery was conceived and promoted by Lin Paio, the fighting capacity of the army has never been tested. How efficient the new army is, it is hard to tell, but we gather from reading the novel a latent note of depression and pessimism, contrasting sharply with the sanguine and optimistic tone of early war stories.

Preparations for a Five-Good Soldier

The background of Ou-yang Hai is not unlike those of other Communist heroes; there is that same stress on deprivation in the social origins of the hero. The moment he is born, in an impoverished village called 'Ravens Nest' in northern Hunan, his home is visited by the village head. The man comes on official business to notify the family that their older boy has been chosen by the draft lottery. Since the boy is the only breadwinner other than the old man and a family's only son is exempt from conscription, Hai's father lies to the village head, saying the newborn is a girl. Although Hai's big brother is spared this time, his father has to pay a heavy conscription tax which forces the family to incur a heavy debt.

By the time Hai is seven, he still bears the girl's name of Ou-yang Yu-jung and wears his sister's worn-out tunic. With the intensification of the Civil War, the Kuomintang authorities speed up conscription; Hai's big brother is finally tied up and taken away. Deprived of this able-bodied laborer, the family can hardly survive. Little Hai has to go out in the piercing cold to beg for anything which may fill their empty stomachs. Landlord's children throw snowballs at him and call him fake girl. When he fights back they unleash a huge dog to bite him. Hunger and humiliation form the background of Hai's early childhood until the liberation.

This early experience seems to have hardened Ou-yang Hai's determination to be a revolutionary fighter when he reaches the age of eighteen. The story tells how Hai goes to four or five places to seek enlistment without success, and only his relentless efforts finally persuade the enlisting officer to make an exception and take him. What the author tries to show in his description of Hai's early life is the change of attitude toward military service. It is a long way from draft dodging to voluntary enlistment. There is an attempt, not altogether successful, to show the changed nature and image of the army, improved socio-economic conditions in the village, general political awareness among the villagers, the tendency of young men to see the army as a huge school, and their aspiration to broaden their knowledge and to seek opportunities in military service.

During the first few days of Ou-yang Hai's army life, he behaves like an unruly urchin. As soon as the train reaches the barracks in a village on the South China coast, he runs away from the group in the direction of the sound of an explosion. He has mistaken the dynamite charge set off by the construction detachment for a bombardment. The same thing happens the next day when his squad is holding a meeting. The squad leader has to rush after him, barefooted. When he brings Hai back to the barracks all he says is that Hai will be criticized if he runs wild again.

Chen Yung-lin, the squad leader, is Ou-yang Hai's first teacher in this large school. This is how the author describes the squad leader dealing with the new volunteers:

> As soon as the bugle blew the signal for lights out, Chen Yung-lin fixed the mosquito-nets one by one for every soldier and then blew out the lamp . . .

When Ou-yang Hai woke up the next morning Chen Yung-lin had already brought in washing water and had squeezed tooth-paste on everyone's toothbrush. Everybody felt happy, warm, and pleased to live this collective life . . .[10]

The responsibility of a squad leader in the Chinese army is comparable to that of a sergeant in the United States armed forces or that of a non-commissioned officer in the German and Japanese armies. In any army the man who leads the smallest unit forms perhaps the most important link in the military hierarchy, since he deals directly with soldiers. Whether an army is a fighting force or not depends to a large extent on the type of squad leader it has. He is usually a veteran of many battles, strict and tough, a fearless soldier and daunting trainer.

At first glance, the Communist squad leader seems rather like a kindergarten governess. He performs the role of the orderly who did the domestic work for warlords in the old days. The difference is that now he does it for the new volunteers. He is quite different from the squad leaders during the Civil War. It is true that Wang the Tiger of *Defense of Yenan* once mended clothes and repaired shoes for his men, but only after he and other Party members were criticized by the regimental political commissar for paying no attention to their soldiers. Another squad leader, Yang Chun of *Red Sun*, is considerate and solicitous in his treatment of the soldiers, but never did anything like that. Certainly it has been a tradition in the Red Army that squad and platoon leaders are always urged to treat their men as brothers in a large family, but Chen Yung-lin has gone much further, regarding the new soldiers as if they were his helpless children. The message is of course clear that by doing this the squad leader makes everyone feel a sense of warmth and satisfaction. Moreover, this approach, contrary to what one might expect, is intended to develop self-discipline and a sense of responsibility in the soldiers.

The Chinese seem to believe that soldiers cannot be transformed into a combat force by coercive discipline but only by gentleness and persuasion. The enormous patience of the squad leader is by no means atypical, for the company's political instructor behaves in precisely the same way. As soon as breakfast is over, the soldiers stand in formation to hear a talk by the political instructor. A man with dark stubble on his chin and cheeks introduces himself as Tseng Wu-chun. The way he pronounces his name 'Wu-chun' sounds like '*wu chin*', meaning 'five catties'. This provokes laughter from one of the soldiers. Instead of getting angry at the insolent and undisciplined reaction of the soldier, the political instructor admits freely that when he was little he was indeed called '*wu chin*'. His parents were so poor and illiterate that they

[10] *The Song of Ou-yang Hai*, p. 100.

did not know how to find a name for him. He was given to a landlord as payment for a debt. Later, a kind-hearted neighbor paid five catties of sorghum to buy him back. That was how he got the name of 'five catties'. After he joined the revolutionary army, a cultural instructor changed his name to '*Wu-chun*'. Although the sounds are nearly the same, this *wu* means 'military' and *chun* means 'army'. Then he goes on to say:

> 'He chose this name because he hoped I would carry a gun all my life and fight for the revolution. My guess is that among you comrades here,' he pointed along the ranks, 'some of you had no name before the liberation either, or at least no proper name. I'm sure I'm not the only one.'[11]

The political instructor could have scolded the rude soldier and lectured him on proper behavior in the army. Instead, he shows no pique, but gives a causal talk about his early life. The incident offers him an opportunity to close the distance between himself and the soldiers by confiding to them the miseries of his childhood. Mutual sharing of misfortunes is the first step towards the comradeship which the political instructor is trying to cultivate. He does so to win the hearts of the new soldiers who, since they are selected for their poor peasant background, are expected to be moved by hardships similar to their own and to emulate the candor and honesty of their officers.

These are the men who teach soldiers like Ou-yang Hai in the great school of the army. To transform a peasant boy into a dedicated revolutionary is a long process and requires strenuous effort. A good political instructor is expected to be able to tell the inner feelings of each soldier at any moment. He should spare no effort in learning about each soldier's family background, education, temperament, weaknesses, strengths, hobbies, and even eccentricities. Only when his brain becomes a living reference book about all the soldiers in his company can he boast of his success as a good political leader.

In the first few days of his army life, Ou-yang Hai experiences two disappointments. Immediately after the political commissar finishes his talk, Chen Yung-lin issues a weapon to each soldier. It is an axe for cutting timber to make props. Hai cannot believe his eyes: he expected to receive an automatic rifle or something of the sort. His hero is Tung Tsung-jui, a Korean war martyr, who threw his body loaded with sticks of dynamite into an enemy pillbox. As a matter of fact, he has brought *The Life of Tung Tsung-jui* with him. Hai has been hoping to throw himself into heroic battles as Tung did, two or three days after joining the army. When he is told that this is a construction detachment and the axe is their most important weapon, his heart sinks. The night before he had written a letter to his parents in which he proudly told them that he would be issued with a new kind of weapon manufactured in China itself. Now as he is walking dejectedly to the mountain he rips the letter in half, rolls it up into a ball, and tosses it over his shoulder. It lands squarely on the head of a man with stubble on his face, who is walking behind. The man is astonished, but after a moment's reflection, quietly picks up the letter and puts it in his kit-bag.

Ou-yang Shan cannot come to terms with the routine of felling timber. His military life is so terribly insignificant compared to the brilliant career of Tung Tsung-jui. One evening, the unit is shown a newsreel before the feature *The Battle of Sangkumryung.* Hai is profoundly shocked by the lamas' enslavement of peasants in the snow-locked mountainous region of Tibet. Without waiting to see the main feature, he dashes to the company headquarters and volunteers for the liberation of Tibet. He simply refuses to take 'no' for an answer and defiantly wants to leave that very night. His behavior suggests that of a spoiled child whose obstinacy hardens under the soothing coaxing of over-indulgent parents. In three days the company commander and the political instructor have received three petitions from Hai requesting transfer to the Tibetan front, but not once did it occur to them that this recalcitrant conduct deserved disciplinary action.

On the contrary, both the company commander and the political instructor take Hai's case seriously and have been discussing how the matter should be handled. Every night when everyone else is asleep, Tseng Wu-chun sits in front of an oil lamp, reading and re-reading Hai's petitions. He is completely preoccupied with a single thought, 'What a good piece of iron! How can it be tempered into steel?' The opportunity finally arrives one Sunday when Hai again dashes into the political instructor's office to inquire about a decision on his petitions. The political instructor takes Hai out for a walk; they climb over the mountain to face the roaring sea. A few paces away is a stone tablet with inscriptions already worn away by the weather. Instead of discussing Hai's request, the political instructor tells the story inscribed on the stone.

More than one hundred years ago, the political instructor begins, in the twenty-first year of the reign of Emperor Tao Kuang (1841) a British Imperial naval force invaded China's territorial waters. A military unit was sent from Hunan to defend the coast. Their crude home-made fire-arms proved no match for the cannons and guns of the five warships and two steam gunboats. The corrupt Ch'ing court had completely neglected defense fortifications, so the soldiers had to stand on rocks without cover. Before long they were cut off from the land by the rising tide. In order to block the enemy warships, the brave soldiers waded into the water to continue their fire. Finally, one warship, the

Modeste, was sunk, but all the soldiers, over a thousand men, were swallowed up by the sea. Tseng Wu-chun concludes his story by comparing what happened a century ago to the threat of invasion China faces at present. He tells Hai that they are there to garrison the southern gate of the motherland.

It is a remarkably crude story, but Ou-yang Hai appreciates its moral. The political instructor is not just telling him a story but explaining to him the importance of military construction. Heroism is not determined only by a brilliant record of killing the enemy. To become an anonymous hero, like those soldiers who refused to retreat under the British naval bombardment and the threat of the rising tide, should be the goal of every revolutionary fighter. The task of soldiers in a construction detachment is no less important than that of a fighting unit. At this moment, Hai makes up his mind; he no longer wants to be a combat hero like Tung Tsung-jui. He wants to withdraw his request for transfer to Tibet.

> Hai gave an embarrassed laugh.
> 'What's there to laugh about? You haven't fought in a battle or won any decorations so you don't write home. Is that how to behave? You ought to write. Your folks will be upset.'
> 'I . . . I did write.'
> 'So you did. But you didn't put it in the letter box, you heaved it up the mountain like a hand-grenade. I got a letter from your father this morning, asking me about you.' Tseng took the letter out of his pocket and gave it to Hai. 'Here. And you still claim you wrote.'
> 'Did you send my dad a letter, political instructor?'
> 'Since you didn't write, what else could I do? I sent it off according to this address.' Tseng produced Hai's crumpled missive. 'You hit me on the head with this the other day. I'm supposed to be your political instructor, but I had no idea what was going on in your mind. Now, the first thing you do when you get back today is write a letter home. Your mother is worried about you.'[12]

The conversation reveals a fundamental difference in the norm of conduct between Chinese society and societies of other cultures. The political instructor discloses without a moment's hesitation that he has carefully read Ou-yang Hai's personal letter. This would be considered an invasion of privacy by anyone brought up in a society where personal matters are jealously guarded against any form of encroachment. The political instructor would be charged with illegal surveillance of a soldier's private life and violation of his freedom. But such thoughts are totally alien to the Chinese. In the early days of the revolution it was not uncommon that leaders wrote family letters for

---

[12] *Ibid.*, p. 123, *Chinese Literature*, No. 7, 1966, p. 130.

their illiterate soldiers.[13] Ordinary peasants always had to ask somebody like a schoolteacher to write letters for them. Tseng Wu-chun not only read Hai's personal letter but had also taken the liberty to write to his parents about the young man's life in the army. 'What else could I do?' he asks. It seems to be the most natural thing in the world for him to do. He has done it not only as a political instructor but also as a friend or brother.

Ou-yang Hai feels precisely the same way; he shows no resentment at the political instructor's meddling with his private affairs. On the contrary, Hai would suffer an acute sense of estrangement in the large family of the army had the political instructor failed to give him love and care. Now he feels that he owes the political instructor genuine gratitude.

> Hai hastily snatched back the letter, blushing shame-facedly. 'This political instructor is really sharp', he thought. 'He's taken care of everything, and I never realised it. He can even tell what I'm thinking, just like Platoon Leader Chou. And I blamed him for playing chess and not caring about me. I'll be a thankless wretch if I don't go out and win a couple of merits after all he's done.'[14]

There is something more to the political instructor's efforts to ease a new soldier's psychological frustration. It is true that unless Hai's enthusiasm for battle is converted into a zeal for unsensational construction work, he will never be able to do his best in the construction detachment. Even more important at this early stage of the new soldiers' army life is the cultivation of an attitude of absolute openness among comrades. Once a man decides to dedicate himself to the revolution, he should have nothing to hide from the organization or other comrades. That is why Tseng Wu-chun freely talked about his own early childhood without worrying that the story might make him a laughing stock or detract from his dignity as the political leader of the company. Only by sharing with each other the glory and the setbacks, happiness and sorrow, excitement and distress, can a company behave and fight as one man.

By now Ou-yang Hai is fully conditioned for his new role in the army. He is determined to be a soldier of the people, like the political instructor, doing his best for others while taking no credit for himself. Only at this point does Tseng Wu-chun offer some adivce: 'A people's

---

[13] Mao Tse-tung himself frequently wrote family letters for his illiterate orderly during the Long March. See Chen Chang-feng, *On the Long March with Chairman Mao* (Peking: Foreign Languages Press, 1959).

[14] *The Song of Ou-yang Hai*, pp. 123–4, *Chinese Literature*, No. 7, 1966, p. 131.

soldier has to have a sense of consideration and discipline. He can't do whatever he pleases. Without an intelligent acceptance of discipline, no man can fight well on the battlefield.'[15]

Competition and Competitors

Since Ou-yang Hai first boarded the train with the other volunteers, he has faced a challenge from Liu Wei-cheng, in almost every aspect of his army life. Their first encounter is in the railway car on the Peking-Canton line. Liu Wei-cheng, a giant of a man, has won several hand wrestling matches and established an undefeated record. When no one else dares challenge the big fellow Ou-yang Hai steps forward. Little Huang, who serves as both referee and 'broadcaster' of the event, dismisses Hai as a lightweight, no match for the heavyweight Liu Wei-cheng. But Hai never gives up easily; he dares Liu to try him. In the first two rounds Liu effortlessly presses Hai's hand to the board. During the third round, Hai manages to hold his opponent's arm still. Knowing that he still has some strength in reserve for a final effort, Hai is confident that he can win. Just as he tries to adjust his position slightly, his hand is pressed against the board once more. It is now a three-nil victory for Liu Wei-cheng. Hai, however, refuses to concede defeat and declares that he can win the fourth time, as he has learned the trick of the game. In answer to his insistence, Little Huang urges Liu to give Hai another opportunity in a 'consolation match'. Big Liu seems rather generous; he promptly agrees to the suggestion. This time Hai exercises his hand, arm and joints, adjusts his sitting position, and firmly holds his rival's hand. To his great surprise, as soon as their hands touch, Big Liu simply lets his fall on the board. Before Hai realizes the situation, Liu Wei-cheng stands up and laughingly concedes defeat. The 'broadcaster' announces the birth of a new champion in a 'consolation match', amid laughter from the spectators.

It is a joke, Liu Wei-cheng harbors no malice when he tricks Hai into a victory everyone knows he has not won. But Hai is offended; he secretly vows that he will show the big fellow who the ultimate winner is. The episode is by implication a harmful prank which can turn fellow soldiers into rivals. In the army or in any other organized activity in China, competition is regarded as an important incentive to excel, and therefore greatly encouraged. But it is always so carefully arranged that the winner will take credit without becoming conceited, while the loser will feel no loss of face or self-confidence but try to do better in future.

[15] *Ibid.*

Ou-yang Hai is a born competitor. He always wants to do more than what is asked of him. Assigned to the timber-felling team, he wants to join the carriers and do heavier work. When Liu Wei-cheng tells Hai that his size is appropriate to felling timber, not carrying it, he is even more anxious to demonstrate his physical strength. Once in the carrier team, he races down the mountain with a 180-catty log on his shoulder. Then he takes the shortest and steepest paths to gain time for extra trips. He seems to have a compulsive need to distinguish himself among his peers.

At a demonstration of sledge-hammer technique, Hai wants to try his hand at the heavy tool, despite his lack of experience. He has to give up the idea, for no one is willing to risk his hand holding the spike for him. Again, among the new soldiers it is Liu Wei-cheng who exhibits his skill by ringing a few dozen steady blows on the spike. Hai feels frustrated, but does not give up. First, he observes the way others swing the hammer. Then he draws a white chalk mark on a tree stump, and practises swinging an eighteen-pound hammer against the mark in order to strengthen his arms and improve his accuracy. He practises so hard that his arms grow red and swollen.

At a hammer-swinging meeting, personally attended by the battalion commander, representatives from several companies demonstrate their skill. The representative from First Company, a veteran soldier, starts off by hitting the mark a hundred and fifty times. The Second Company's representative scores over a hundred and thirty. Third Company is represented by Liu Wei-cheng, who unhurriedly wields the sledge hammer and hits a record two hundred. Like an award-winning athlete, Liu retires amid applause, laughter, and cheers. As the battalion commander is about to summarize the merits and shortcomings of the three demonstrators, Ou-yang Hai stands up to volunteer for a try. But the man who holds the spike walks away as soon as he sees Hai. This leaves Hai flushing red, hammer in hand, alone in the center of the arena. At this moment, his company commander strides forward to hold the spike, and confidently invites Hai to proceed. Hai surpasses everyone, with two hundred and eighty blows.

Before the first year is over, Ou-yang Hai is promoted to be leader of the fourth squad. He has twice won the third-class distinction award; his squad has been chosen as the model for the best field exercises in the entire Division. The young soldier has successfully completed the first stage of his military career, and is now ready to embark on a new journey. He has filed an application for membership of the Communist Party. The Party representative, Tseng Wu-chun, decides it is time to use a different gauge — the Communist standard — to measure Hai's performance. So, when the battalion wants to send a good squad leader from Third Company to a provincial conference of activist militiamen as an observer, and also to demonstrate bayonet skill, Tseng suggests Liu Wei-cheng, now leader of First Squad, instead of Ou-yang Hai. The political instructor concedes that Hai has been good all along, but points out the young man's eagerness to win as a serious weakness. Consequently, the company Party branch decides on Liu. Ou-yang Hai's reaction to the decision becomes a test of his political maturity as a candidate for Party membership.

The company treats Liu's participation in the militia conference as a matter of great importance. Liu will represent not only the company but also the entire construction detachment or rather the People's Liberation Army. There are intense preparations to give Liu all possible support and assistance, so that he can do his best. The company commander gives Liu an opportunity to practice bayonet fighting with other soldiers, for he must show militia activists real skill with the weapon. Liu proves an excellent choice, as he beats all his opponents three-nil.

When it becomes clear that no one can take on the brawny Liu, somebody suggests the company commander Kuan. Noticing that Liu always leaves his left side open, Kuan thinks it a good idea to jab him there once or twice. In the first two rounds, each contestant scores once. The third round is a real match; after parrying, fencing, advancing, and retreating for some time, both are struck at the same instant. Unable to choose a winner, the referee declares the contest a draw. As Kuan removes his protective mask, he concedes defeat, giving credit to Liu's initiative in the last exchange. But he says that Liu has not learnt to overcome his weakness, and he will fetch somebody to give the big fellow a lesson.

Moments later, a soldier in full protective dress stands firmly at the centre of the arena. As Liu is looking for his opponent's weak spot, the short soldier lunges and hits Liu, abruptly and hard. The second round is a swift exchange of thrusts, and Liu is again hit on the left side of the chest. Liu is surprised at the opponent's clean smooth bayonet skill, but is determined to win the last round. As soon as the bayonets touch, Liu feels his gun so fiercely twisted that his palms go numb. Before he is able to regain his balance, his left side is stabbed again. Everyone is impressed by the stubby soldier's marvellous bayonet thrusts. As Kuan is about to give a short analysis of the superb bayonet contest, he discovers that the winner has already disappeared.

In the barracks the political instructor Tseng Wu-chun makes no effort to hide his displeasure at Ou-yang Hai's performance. Tseng tells Hai that Liu Wei-cheng is his comrade, and will represent the whole company at the forthcoming conference. If Liu has weaknesses, it is everyone's responsibility to point them out and help improve his bayonet skill. He continues:

> 'True, he isn't as good with the bayonet as you. But should we adopt
> your attitude in dealing with a comrade whose technique has flaws?
> He's going to that conference as the company's representative, as
> our army's representative, to work. Helping him is helping his work,
> is helping the conference of militia activists. Your annoyance at not
> being chosen is preventing you from realizing this. Maybe I'm
> treating the question too seriously, Hai, but it seems to me that your
> behavior today shows you don't really understand what 'representa-
> tive' means. You see it too much as an honor. That's why it didn't
> occur to you that you ought to help Liu correct his weaknesses in
> bayonet fighting. Suppose it is an honor? As revolutionaries, it isn't
> the sort of thing we should hanker after. We should compete with
> each other in being loyal to the Party, in whole-heartedly serving the
> people. We shouldn't compete with our comrades for honors.'[16]

Hai has never seen the political instructor in such an agitated state.
He senses that he has done something terribly wrong, but does not
understand what it is. Tseng Wu-chun continues with a story he has
never cared to tell. In the Kaiyuan campaign during the Civil War, the
company commander Kuan, then a new soldier, and another man
captured a heavy machine-gun from the enemy. This warranted a major
merit at a time when the Red Army was fighting with inferior weapons.
But neither of the two soldiers could tell, in the intensity and
confusion of the battle situation, who got hold of the gun first. Each
insisted that the other should get the credit; neither would accept the
citation. The political instructor then poses a question: why did the
two soldiers decline the glory? Ou-yang Hai's mind is left in turmoil; it
does not take him long to realize who the other soldier is.

That night Tseng Wu-chun cannot sleep. He has been repeatedly
asking himself if it is unreasonable to expect a boy of nineteen to show
the correct revolutionary attitude. Is it right for him, as political
instructor, to give a harsh reprimand to a soldier who has been in the
army only a year? Will the exhortation backfire, and so blunt his
enthusiasm? Will all this make Ou-yang Hai lose confidence? These
questions keep haunting him and give him no rest. Then he realizes it is
already dawn.

From the drill field came the sound of blows. The political
instructor looked up. In the pale morning light, two silhouettes were
fencing with bayonets. The smaller of the pair frequently stopped to
explain something, then the battle went on. Although Tseng
couldn't see them clearly, he recognized their familiar figures. The

---

[16] *Ibid.*, p. 177, *Chinese Literature*, No. 8, 1966, p. 62.

question that had been troubling him all night had, on the whole, already been settled.[17]

So Ou-yang Hai appears to have passed the test. During the first year of his army life, he has spared no efforts to excel. He has won several honors and citations, and does not cease to demand more of himself. All this is an impressive achievement, but it does not meet the criteria of a people's soldier. What distinguishes a revolutionary from a mere soldier is his motive. There is nothing extraordinary in a soldier's striving for distinction, if this is done to impress his officers and to work for his own promotion. A revolutionary who fights fearlessly in order to be decorated is only a pseudo-revolutionary. A genuine people's soldier will do everything to serve the people and at the same time will try to remain anonymous.

However, the incident of bayonet practice is not enough to show that Ou-yang Hai has become a fully-fledged revolutionary soldier. Admittedly, he has finally overcome his disappointment at not representing the company at the militia conference, and helped Liu Wei-cheng improve his bayonet skill, but only after receiving an admonition from the political instructor. He has yet to prove that he can take the initiative in shouldering a difficult task without claiming credit. The criterion for judging a revolutionary is his willingness to make a personal sacrifice in order to lighten the burden of his comrades. A revolution is never achieved by glory-seekers.

Shortly afterwards, the company receives an emergency call to build an embankment for a section of railway line. The soldiers are informed that the 'modern revisionists' have withdrawn all their technicians, as well as the blueprints, and have refused to supply China with key parts.[18] In order to show the modern revisionists that they cannot impose their will on China, the soldiers must make every effort to get the line open ahead of schedule so that machines of Chinese make can be shipped immediately to a certain defense factory. As the company settles down in a desolate area to start the construction project, they have to use makeshift tools. The only equipment each squad receives is two shovels. On his way back from the quartermaster's warehouse, Hai comes across Liu Wei-cheng. When Liu asks him where he has picked up the tools, Hai hands over the two shovels to Liu, knowing there are no more left. He says that he is going to deliver the shovels to Liu's squad.

Now Hai's men are left with only two pickaxes to work with. They have to use basins, tin cups, and bowls for scraping away the mud and loose soil. It is a difficult and trying task; Hai's hands become swollen.

---

[17] *Ibid.*, p. 180, *Chinese Literature*, No. 8, 1966, p. 65.
[18] This is the first time the modern revisionist appears as a shadow villain in a Chinese novel. This role has been so far reserved for the American imperialist.

At break, Liu comes over to Squad Four's section to pick up a few tips. Seeing Hai scooping mud with his bare hands, Liu realizes what he had done. Thrusting his shovel at Hai, Liu reminds him of the contest between their two squads. The competition would be unfair if Liu's squad were to win because of their better tools.

'That's no way to talk, big fellow.' Hai said hotly, pushing the shovel back at Liu. 'What's the difference? If we don't dig with our hands, your squad will have to. When you come down to it, there aren't enough tools. The quartermaster says a big batch is coming in a couple of days.'

'Right, right,' nodded Liu, extremely moved. He grasped Hai's hands in his and wouldn't let them go. Whether in hand-wrestling, carrying logs, wielding the sledge-hammer or in bayonet practice, never had those two pairs of hands met in such a tight, warm clasp. The situation helped both soldiers to see their past shortcomings, and gave them a deeper understanding of the purpose of contests, mutual aid, competitions and challenges. They realized why, even with an 'opponent', it was necessary to go into battle shoulder to shoulder and hand in hand . . . [19]

Only at this moment do the two soldiers understand the true meaning of competition, honor, and citation. These are simple devices to encourage ordinary soldiers to do their best. For those revolutionaries whose minds have transcended shortsighted egoism, there is no need for such artificial incentives. The desire to help others has become an instinct in a revolutionary. There is no greater reward than the satisfaction of making things easier for one's comrade through self-denial.

The Enemy Within

The Song of Ou-yang Hai is a novel of the People's Liberation Army, yet, strangely enough, it can be properly listed among the titles of pacifist literature. It contains no violence or hatred. And it is the only Chinese Communist novel totally free of villains, quasi-villains, and negative characters. To be sure, there are more shadow villains; in addition to the American imperialist and Chiang Kai-shek's reactionary regime, the modern revisionist has joined the anti-Chinese front. But such shadow villains have no substance; they exist only in the minds of the Chinese people. Commitment against conceptual villains is always ideological rather than personal; ideology, contrary to popular belief, is subject to adjustment under changing conditions. The conceptions of

[19] *The Song of Ou-yang Hai*, pp. 194–5, *Chinese Literature*, No. 8, 1966, pp. 76–7.

'capitalist imperialist', 'modern revisionist', and 'reactionary clique' are the products of ideology and will undergo change as ideology adapts itself to new reality.

During the decade of the 1960s the military spokesman was Lin Piao, whose treatise *Long Live the Victory of the People's War*, issued in 1965, shook the world, as a blueprint for China's ambition for conquest. In reality, the sensational thesis is no more than an elaboration and extension of Mao's theory of guerrilla warfare during the war against Japan and the Civil War. It was publicized more as an ideological offensive to break through the concept of containment. There has been no attempt, except for a few gestures, to put Lin Piao's thesis of world-wide revolution to the test. Had the Chinese actually considered the idea of world-wide guerrilla warfare against industrial states feasible, the treatise would have been written by Mao Tse-tung himself.

The document which really defines the role of the People's Liberation Army is not *Long Live the Victory of the People's War* but *The Song of Ou-yang Hai*. While in this novel the capitalist imperialist, the modern revisionist, and the reactionary regime constitute shadow villains in the background, there is a peculiar absence of hate. Their existence seems remote, amorphous and insubstantial. The Chinese always maintain a strong sense of nationalism under foreign aggression. In the novels of the war against Japan, the Japanese are real people with names, whose savagery in raping, killing, and burning is forcefully described. The Chinese of all walks of life — peasants, workers, students, artisans, merchants, and everyone else — show an intense desire for revenge against the Japanese. In *The Song of Ou-yang Hai* personal feelings against the shadow villains are virtually non-existent.

The training of Ou-yang Hai, or the new type of soldier, is thus for the defense of China against potential enemies. But what is more interesting in the training of Five-Good soldiers is the emphasis on the elimination of potential internal rather than external enemies. In a rhetorical sense, the soldiers are constantly reminded of the potential threat from without, but in the actual development of the story, the real effort is not to destroy reactionaries, subversive elements, or anti-revolutionaries, who do not exist in *The Song of Ou-yang Hai*, but the impure thoughts in a man's mind. The case of Hsueh Hsin-wen is an example of the potential danger in an otherwise hard-working, dedicated cadre and his eventual reform.

Hsueh Hsin-wen is an intellectual type who has come to the army from an administrative background. The political instructor Tseng, towards whom Hai developed genuine respect and affection, is no longer with the company. During construction work, Tseng had been wounded when he and the soldiers attempted to salvage the machinery in a storage shed from a deluge of rain and mountain torrents. Although his wounds had healed, his right arm was permanently disabled. Since he was no longer fit to work in the army, he went to join production in the countryside. In his place Hsueh Hsin-wen has temporarily taken over the responsibility for political work.

As the acting assistant political instructor, Hsueh shows a tendency to make subjective judgements. Once he enters Squad Seven barracks, and sees Liu Yen-sheng, a new soldier of only seventeen, with a stick of lighted incense in his hand, and hears him utter a Buddhist incantation. Without knowing that the incense is to be used for marking the course of the grenade in night practice, Hsueh gives the assistant squad leader a good telling-off for permitting practical jokes.

Now under the leadership of Ou-yang Hai, Squad Seven makes impressive progress. In one field exercise, attacking a hill position, Squad Seven is the first to reach the top. An incident occurs soon after the company commander has praised Squad Seven's outstanding performance. Liu Yen-sheng tosses a sweet potato to the assistant political instructor. He wants Hsueh to have a bite, as the southern sun is scorching in summer. Without bothering to ask or to wait for an explanation, Hsueh assumes that the boy soldier has violated military discipline by stealing sweet potatoes. Since Hsueh had earlier assured the battalion political instructor that there has been no damage to peasants' crops, he marches off to the battalion headquarters to offer self-criticism. What actually happened was quite different from what Hsueh assumes. The sweet potatoes had been given to little Liu by a peasant who saw him practising attacks with other soldiers under the burning sun though still quite a boy. Unable to decline the offer, Liu left twenty cents wrapped in a piece of paper, with a note expressing his gratitude.

That evening, in the assistant political instructor's office, a heated argument takes place between the innocent, uncompromising Yen-sheng and the complacent Hsueh Hsin-wen. Quoting Chairman Mao's famous dictum, 'no investigation, no right to speak', little Liu points out Hsueh's arrogance, as shown in his habitual expressions, 'I know without asking', and 'I guarantee it'. Hsueh, on the other hand, warns that Liu should not become conceited because of a little praise. When Liu uses Ou-yang Hai's approach of gentle persuasion as an example of the correct way of doing ideological work, Hsueh finds fault with the squad leader's coaxing and coddling, which has spoiled soldiers like Liu.

On learning of the quarrel between Liu and Hsueh, Hai examines his approach in dealing with Yen-sheng, but is unable to reach a conclusion. To his mind, Hsueh has been a good cadre, always eager to work hard and willing to help soldiers, though his style may not be tactful. In his usual candid manner, he advises little Liu not to answer back to a superior. But Liu has no intention of giving ground; instead, he urges Hai to stand up for his principles. The young soldier makes a distinction between 'answering back' and 'arguing a problem'. When Hai suggests that Liu should not pick flaws in the method of the leadership, Liu again disagrees and criticizes Hai for compromising on principle. If Hai knows the assistant political instructor is in the wrong but still will not criticize him, his attitude does not show consideration but 'liberalism'.

'Liberalism' (*Tzu-yu-chu-i*) is a serious charge, which deeply shocks Ou-yang Hai. The Chinese term, as defined in Mao Tse-tung's 'Combat Liberalism', refers to an attitude of unprincipled compromise, tolerance of mistakes for fear of creating hard feelings, and permisiveness in allowing incorrect views without rebutting them. Now Ou-yang Hai realizes that Yen-sheng has an uncorrupt, innocent mind which contrasts sharply with his own low ideological level:

'Yen-sheng is simple and honest, as you'd expect a boy raised in a revolutionary family to be. He's direct, practical. When he's wrong he corrects himself. He makes a clear distinction between right and wrong, and always acts according to his understanding of the situation. When he sees a shortcoming in the leadership he takes it very much to heart. He simply has to argue and struggle against it. That's really putting the interests of the revolution first. I have too many reservations about this sort of thing. It's a reflection of my low ideological level. It shows that I still haven't entirely got rid of my peasant mentality, my individualism — that's how I ought to see it.'[20]

The terms 'liberalism' and 'individualism' must be understood according to the Chinese definition and in the Chinese context. While 'liberalism' is equated to surrender of principle, 'individualism' here means a nice smooth attitude, which will please everyone and offend no one. These terms were originally borrowed from the West around the turn of the century, but their usages have been corrupted and their connotations have become extremely narrow. Yen-sheng is really fighting bureaucracy, epitomized in Hsueh's feigned acceptance of criticism and his actual exercise of authority and power. The description of little Liu's defiance in dealing with Hsueh's abuse of authority and his persistence in challenging the assistant political instructor's working style can be seen as a preview of the Red Guards' attacks on veteran leading cadres in the Cultural Revolution. The theoretical basis upon which young people justify their challenge to senior cadres is the same.

Since the differences between the assistant political instructor and

[20] *Ibid.*, p. 351, *Chinese Literature*, No. 10, 1966, p. 97.

soldiers in Squad Seven have not been resolved, more problems are bound to arise. One Sunday Yen-sheng goes to town to have his picture taken. Ou-yang Hai leaves for a village to buy bamboo. Since he has some twenty *li* to cover, Hai takes along his favorite novel *Red Crag* so he can go over parts of the story when he stops for a rest on the way. That evening, at roll call, the only two soldiers who have failed to return on time are Liu Yen-sheng and Ou-yang Hai. The assistant political instructor harshly criticizes Squad Seven for lax discipline. Later at the squad meeting, Liu explains that he has done twenty-two errands for other soldiers and in the end he did not even have time to see to his own business. When it is Hai's turn to explain why he was late back he realizes that if he explains what happened, the men would feel much more resentful for being unfairly and unjustly criticized. As a result, Hai stands up to defend the assistant political instructor. He tries to make a distinction between the good things Liu did and the regulations he violated. He manages to divert the soldiers' attention to the question of vigilance and the importance of a sense of discipline.

For his part, Hsueh has never been able to overcome his unconscious bias against Ou-yang Hai. When he is going over the preliminary report of the company's participation in helping the local people build the dam and repair roads, he finds Hai's name included in the list for citation. Hsueh is uncertain whether praising Hai in front of the whole company might not make the squad leader complacent again. At this point, an orderly from the battalion headquarters arrives to hand Hsueh a letter from a commune. The latter requests information about a soldier who has put out a fire, and rescued an old woman, leaving behind a half-burnt copy of *Red Crag*. Hsueh is truly impressed with the conduct of the soldier who simply called himself 'Lei Feng's battle companion' without revealing his real name. Seeing the name Chou Hu-shan still faintly visible on the cover of the book, Hsueh is convinced that the hero who saved the old woman's life does not belong to Third Company.

At a meeting of the entire company Hsueh summarizes the dam-building job and reads the list of men who receive citations for outstanding performances. The name of Ou-yang Hai is deliberately left out. The omission of Hai's name causes not only complaints from the rank and file but also criticism from the Party branch committee. Then Hsueh is informed by a soldier of Squad Seven that Hai has been working with burns on his hands for the past few days. The significance of this information strikes Hsueh; he races back to his office to take a second look at the letter inquiring about 'Lei Feng's battle companion'. Piecing together odd scraps of information, Hsueh slowly comes to see the whole picture. In order to verify whether the last piece fits the puzzle, the assistant political instructor asks Hai if he knows anyone by the name of Chou Hu-shan. Hai answers that that is the name of the Party secretary of his commune at home whom he saw during his recent furlough. There is no need for further questions, so Hsueh dismisses Hai. For the first time, Hsueh's complacency is severely shaken:

> Hsueh's head felt as if it was going to burst. He stared at the burned copy of *Red Crag*. With its red cover flapping in the night breeze, it looked as if it was on fire. Hsueh's heart, too, seemed to be in flames.[21]

It seems quite incomprehensible that Hsueh's heart should be in flames. There appears to be no need for Hsueh to experience this deep emotional disturbance. All that is involved is minor mistreatment of two soldiers, and the damage to the young men, if any, is by no means irreparable. Nevertheless, Hsueh's sense of guilt is real. It is caused not so much by his abuse of two ordinary soldiers as by the realization of his own inadequacy. Consciously or unconsciously, Hsueh has been trying hard to be a hero himself, a flawless revolutionary, a 'socialist man'. His conduct suggests that he ruthlessly demands more of himself towards the soldiers. Every night when he makes his rounds in the barracks he pays attention to little things in the hope that he will make everyone comfortable. When the company was helping the local people build the dam and roads, Hsueh carried loads so heavy that his new uniform was rubbed threadbare at the shoulders. He must have thought that he did all that could possibly be done by a dedicated cadre. Perhaps subconsciously he already considered himself a hero. Never has he doubted that he was serving the people every moment of the day.

The discovery that in spite of all he has done, he is still not up to the standard of a good cadre has thrown him into despair. He is no longer a cadre with a stainless record; he feels he is in disgrace. But Hsueh is not a villain. There are no doubt traits in his character which may be viewed as undesirable and which contribute to his mistakes. But the Chinese measure a person by his intention; Hsueh's good intentions are never in doubt. He seems to be the victim of his subjectivism, egoism, and individualism. If there is villainy in him, it can be overcome by his own efforts and the help of others. A more serious problem, however, is how to relieve his sense of guilt; otherwise, Hsueh will never be able to make peace with himself.

Confession in the Catholic culture is a means not only of receiving absolution but also of relieving the emotional burden of guilt. What follows in Hsueh's case is a public confession. The practice may be viewed as a therapeutic treatment of an individual's mental wounds. By continually mistreating Hai and Yen-sheng, despite criticisms from the Party branch committee, complaints from the rank and file, and

---

[21] *Ibid.*, p. 394, *Chinese Literature*, No. 11, 1966, p. 87.

warnings from the company commander, Hsueh has managed to isolate himself from the entire company. Now he finds himself in error, naked and alone outside the group. The sense of loneliness in a political culture where the norm is collective is overwhelming. Peace of mind can be restored only by public admission of guilt. It is also the only way for an individual to resume his place in the collective life.

An assembly is convened for the soldiers of Third Company, attended by battalion leaders. Pointing at a practice hand-grenade, a note Liu Yen-sheng left for commune members, and a burnt copy of *Red Crag* on the table before him, Hsueh relates the three incidents with profound emotion. In his self-analysis, he says that because he enjoys manual labor he feels self-righteous and even superior. His attitude toward criticism and self-criticism reveals a serious syndrome of individualism. His individualistic thinking fights stubbornly to protect itself. He publicly offers his apologies to Ou-yang Hai and regards his mistakes as shameful behavior. He expresses his pride in the Party for having nurtured soldiers like Ou-yang Hai. Finally, he promises to start his life all over again and pleads for help from all the comrades in Third Company.

The audience is at first shocked to learn about the assistant political instructor's irresponsible method of dealing with problems. They cannot believe that a cadre will reject ideas from the masses. But gradually they are moved by his sincere and merciless self-criticism. Finally, there is a feeling of admiration among the audience for a man who has changed from being an impetuous critic of others to a stern critic of himself. When Hsueh has finished his self-examination the battalion political instructor invites Ou-yang Hai to make comments. The squad leader praises Hsueh for being 'as merciless as a grenade towards his own mistakes and shortcomings'. Then Hai offers his own self-criticism:

'I felt put upon the day the assistant instructor criticized me, which shows I can't bear being misunderstood. Comrade Liu Shao-ch'i in *How to Be a Good Communist* says: "No one in this world can entirely avoid being misunderstood, but misunderstandings can always be cleared up sooner or later. We should be able to endure misunderstandings. . . " Feeling put upon was actually a sign that I lacked the political maturity a Communist ought to have. I hope the Party and the assistant instructor will educate us, make higher demands on us, supervise us more boldly, and help us meet the requirements of the Party as soon as possible. I promise to listen to the assistant instructor, and learn from his strict attitude towards ideological remoulding. Chairman Mao says: "If, in the interests of the people, we persist in doing what is right and correct what is wrong, our ranks will surely thrive." Our assistant instructor has followed Chairman Mao's instructions today. His spirit of serving the revolution is well worthy of our study.'

Thunderous applause rocked the club-room, manifesting the men's faith in Hsueh and their thanks to Hai for having expressed what was in their hearts.[22]

The narrative serves to define a new Chinese norm. The message is clear; a man after all is human, and liable to error. What matters is his attitude towards his own mistakes. If he can admit his mistakes and has the courage to correct them, he always has a chance to change his attitude. Public self-criticism does not denote humiliation; on the contrary, it is a demonstration of a person's courage in facing up to his shortcomings. Hsueh's public confession not only does not impair his dignity as a man, but in fact restores his prestige among the soldiers. When the confession is over he finds himself again surrounded by comrades who extend their hands in greeting. A soldier has rejoined the ranks.

The Song of Ou-yang Hai was the last full-length novel published in mainland China for several years. After it was published in 1965, the Cultural Revolution gained momentum. Since then, because of the disruption caused by the Red Guards, no novels of any length and weight were published, until Hao Jan's *The Golden Road* in 1972.[23] Therefore *The Song of Ou-yang Hai* can be seen to reflect the latest development in Chinese society; its normative prescriptions deserve our close attention. Of particular interest is the disappearance of villains for the first time in a story of political and ideological struggle. The absence of villains seems to suggest that the Chinese have gained great confidence in the ideological standard of the army. It appears to signal an important development from antagonistic contradiction between revolutionary and anti-revolutionary forces to non-antagonistic contradiction among the people. The conception of non-antagonistic contradiction implies that Chinese society is now free of villains; villainy exists only in one's own thoughts.

Reality, however, proves otherwise. 'The enemy within' can easily be explained as a philosophical construction, but as a social phenomenon it suggests gross over-simplification of highly complex reality. What has happened during and since the Cultural Revolution seems to reject the over-optimistic assessment of Chinese society as one totally free of antagonistic contradictions. The lack of villains and the absence of class

---

[22] *Ibid.*, p. 404, *Chinese Literature*, No. 11, 1966, p. 90.

[23] Hao Jan, *The Golden Road* (*Chin-kuang ta-tao*) (Peking: People's Literature Publishing House, 1972). This first volume of a multi-volume novel describes the beginning of mutual-aid teams in a village not far from Peking in the winter of 1950–1.

struggle contrasts sharply with the intensification of class struggle and
the re-introduction of the landlord as class enemy in *Bright Sunny
Days*, a work contemporary with *The Song of Ou-yang Hai*. This
contradiction in the themes of the two most recent novels is an
interesting phenomenon and will be discussed later when we consider
the process by which the story of Ou-yang Hai was written.

The Death of a Hero

In any novel, the reader has a right to expect that the death of the hero
of the title should constitute the climax of the story. The episode of the
death of Ou-yang Hai, who is crushed under a train, is by its nature
accidental, but the author has to portray the hero's plunging into death
as a conscious act. The theme of the novel is essentially the gradual
transformation in Ou-yang Hai, which prompts him to make a personal
sacrifice on every occasion, even to the point of sacrificing his life. In
effect, however, the hero seems so ready to die that he appears to be
looking for just such an opportunity.

Ou-yang Hai's death is caused by his attempt to push a horse, loaded
with a small cannon, out of the rail tracks. In doing this he saves the
passengers on the train, his comrades by the roadside, and valuable state
property, but he is crushed beneath the massive steel wheels. His
wounds are fatal; his life lingers only a short while. He dies on a
hospital bed with a calm smile, suggesting he feels that he has
completed an important task.

The description of the hero's death is extraordinarily over-simplified,
and the impression one gets is that the author rushes to his conclusion
without attempting to build up any momentum. What is interesting is
the author's description of Hai's mental state at the moment he dashes
toward the terror stricken horse. At that critical moment, Hai could have
been thinking of a tragedy which would involve many lives and costly
public property. The choice in his mind would be 'either the collective
interests or my own life'. He could have remembered the revolutionary
martyrs, real heroes as well as fictional characters, who have sacrificed
their lives for the revolution and the people. He could have heard the call
of these heroes, the political instructor Tseng, and above all Chairman
Mao. Or he could have repeated the pledges to serve his homeland and
the people that he made at the time of joining the army. After all this
speculation, the author then writes:

> Perhaps in that brief instant he said nothing, thought nothing.
> Perhaps he saw nothing, heard nothing. He had thought and seen
> and heard and said all of these things for more than ten years. It
> wasn't necessary for him to go over them again. In that moment of

crisis he had only one clear, compelling thought: 'I mustn't permit the destruction of people's lives and property. The time has come to die for the ideal of communism. A true Communist must plunge forward.'[24]

What the author tries to convey, in short, is that as a young man reared and educated in socialist thinking for more than ten years, Ou-yang Hai is able to sacrifice his own life to save other people and public property. The description of Hai's psychology is as superficial as it is unequivocally ideological. An ordinary man, not armed with Marxism, Leninism, and the thought of Mao Tse-tung, may also risk his life to save a passenger train from derailment. The act undertaken to prevent the destruction of lives and property seems to have little bearing on 'the ideal of communism'.

The death of Ou-yang Hai is at the centre of this more than 300,000-word novel, yet the death scene is sketchy, without color or force. Ou-yang Hai lacks the restless thrust of Liu Sheng of *Red Sun* and the defiant bravery of Hsu Yun-feng and Sister Chiang of *Red Crag*. Their deaths are the logical culminations of heroic struggles which have confronted either mental torture or physical danger, or both. But the unexpected ending of Ou-yang Hai's life comes about so much by accident that the author has to justify it by evoking the images of martyrs whom the young soldier has practically worshipped. Thus it becomes not the death of a hero but the imitation of heroes by a juvenile mind. Ou-yang Hai's urge to do good things, to make sacrifices for other people, and to risk his life if necessary, simply because he has been taught to behave that way, makes his death too much a posture. Even in death, he is more of a boy scout than a real hero.

What, one is forced to ask, makes this story, especially towards the end, a miserable failure? The answer seems to lie in the over-all preoccupation with ideological correctness rather than artistic excellence. Whether the author has the potential to write a good novel is a question to which there can be no answer at present. What can be ascertained are the causes for his failure. Unlike other Communist novelists who have the inner drive to create, Chin Ching-mai was commissioned to write the story of Ou-yang Hai. It is the fulfilment of an assignment – considered an important element in Chinese Communist literature – and the author's private vision has totally disappeared. This explains why, in a comparative sense, other characters, such as Hsueh Hsin-wen, are more alive than the hero of the title. The supporting characters apparently attracted less outside intervention than the hero, who is to be an ideological model. From the very start, the author has been painfully aware of the awesome responsibility of

[24] *Ibid.*, p. 440, *Chinese Literature*, No. 11, 1966, pp. 102–3.

portraying a hero who might be an example for nationwide emulation. He was too conscious of this to allow his imagination free rein. The death of Ou-yang Hai, ironically, symbolizes the close of an era of considerable success in Chinese literature; its renaissance is not yet in sight. It is important for us to examine the conditions under which *The Song of Ou-yang Hai* was written; conditions under which the most fertile imagination would be marred, creative talent stifled, and even genius crippled.

The Mass Line in Novel-Writing

The Resolution on the Strengthening of Political and Ideological Works in the Army passed at the Enlarged Meeting of the Military Commission in 1960 set up a program which was the brainchild of the Minister of Defense, Lin Piao. The catchwords are: 'Study the works of Chairman Mao, follow the teachings of Chairman Mao, act in accordance with the instructions of Chairman Mao, and be good soldiers of Chairman Mao.' Literary and artistic work in the army, according to the same resolution, 'must be closely linked with the troops' tasks and state of mind, to help uphold proletarian ideology, eradicate bourgeois ideology and consolidate and improve the army's fighting strength'.[25] Under these conditions, the author was transferred from an army drama troupe to a writing team. For his literary preparation, he was assigned to serve as a member of the rank and file in a company.

While Chin Ching-mai was living and experiencing the life of an ordinary soldier, he heard of the death of Ou-yang Hai in his attempt to save a train in the winter of 1963. He was ordered by the leadership of an army stationed in Canton to collect material about Ou-yang Hai's life and to write a novel about the hero's glorious martyrdom.[26] He was transferred to Ou-yang Hai's former company to experience the conditions of the hero's life as closely as possible. In writing the novel the author adopted about sixty of more than a hundred stories he heard about Ou-yang Hai. After each draft, he would read the story to the political commissar of Ou-yang Hai's corps and to the men of Hai's squad, to the Party committee of Hai's home county, to the cadres of the commune, and to Hai's relatives and friends. This attempt to follow the mass line meticulously sometimes leads to utter tedium. The author expresses his feeling like this:

> After revising each fresh draft of the novel, I would go down to verify my facts, and each time I entered again into the life of the

[25] Quoted in Chin Ching-mai, 'How I conceived and wrote *The Song of Ou-yang Hai*', *Chinese Literature*, No. 11, 1966, p. 106.
[26] Chin Ching-mai, 'Postscript', *The Song of Ou-yang Hai*, p. 443.

masses, I deepened my understanding of the hero. I made three major revisions in this way and checked up on the facts three times. This was rather hard work and I would not have been able to go through with it had I not studied Chairman Mao's *On Practice,* in which he writes' '. . . Practice, knowledge, again practice, and again knowledge. This form repeats itself in endless cycles, and with each cycle the content of practice and knowledge rises to a higher level'. After these various check-ups, those who knew Ou-yang Hai felt that the incidents were more or less accurate, basically reflecting Ou-yang Hai's true spirit. . .[27]

All these efforts are made merely to ensure the accuracy of the facts. Then there is the question of ideological correctness, far more serious than factual adherence. The main theme of the novel as the author originally conceived it is that 'Ou-yang Hai wanted to become a hero, and finally, when he realized what constituted a hero, became one without realizing it himself.'[28] Such an approach appears to be too individualistic, for the army leadership urged the author to focus on the Party and the times in portraying the hero, and to describe the growth of the hero as an outcome of the changes in the army. As a result, the author began to see the imprints of a specific age and a specific class as part of the concept of hero and heroism. In order to achieve this goal, the story of Ou-yang Hai must be related to historical events. A series of significant developments looms large in the background of the hero's life, including the Great Leap Forward of 1958, the suppression of the revolt in Tibet in 1959, the withdrawal of experts by the Soviet Revisionists and the drive for the study of Chairman Mao's works in 1960, the 'Two Recollections and Three Check-ups' campaign[29] in 1961, and the emergency preparations for war on the southeast coast in 1962. It should not be much of a problem to weave historical occurrences into a novel, as characters cannot exist in a vacuum. But to see the meaning of these political and ideological struggles clearly and to give them their correct interpretation is a staggering task. In the process of writing the author from time to time became completely desperate and finally had to report his problems to the political department and the cultural department of the army in Canton. Two problems he singled out as beyond his ability to reflect correctly were the struggle against Soviet revisionism and the proper handling of contradictions among the ranks of the people. He received assurances that as long as his basic orientation was right, he had no need to worry

---

[27] Chin Ching-mai, 'How I conceived and wrote *The Song of Ou-yang Hai*', *loc. cit.*, p. 118.
[28] *Ibid.*, p. 109.
[29] The campaign urged every soldier to remember class difficulties and national difficulties and to investigate his own viewpoint, fighting spirit, and work.

about committing errors, and the army leadership would assume the responsibility for any problems. At the same time, he was urged to make a more careful study of Chairman Mao's *On the Correct Handling of Contraditions among the People* and the nine commentaries on the open letter of the Central Committee of the CPSU.

Once the ideological issue was solved, the remaining problem was a technical one. When he was revising and polishing the several drafts, he sought and received help from professional writers, from members of his playwrights' team, from the writing group of the cultural department, and from the editors of the magazines *Liberation Army Literature* and *Harvest*. Thus, *The Song of Ou-yang Hai* can be viewed as the result of a collective effort, rather than the work of a single man.

The result of this writing process is a sterile work. The strict adherence to facts turns the story into a hybrid genre, something between a novel and a biography. It cannot be called biography because all the other characters are fictitious, but the search for factual accuracy has deprived the story of imaginative vigor. Chin Ching-mai's article about his experience in writing the novel ends with a note as depressing as it is fallacious:

> I have only just made a beginning in learning to understand the hero, follow his example and portray him. In future I must study Chairman Mao's works harder, do my best to go into the heat of the struggle and improve my writing technique. I must take Ou-yang Hai as my model, work tirelessly, advance steadily and propagate Mao Tse-tung's thought as long as I live.[30]

Nothing can be stranger than the notion that the author must emulate a model he has created himself. We cannot tell what the army would be like if every man in uniform became an Ou-yang Hai. But if every novelist has to write as Chin Ching-mai did, the paucity of Chinese literature is predictable. *The Song of Ou-yang Hai*, if nothing else, proves that Chinese literature has entered a dead end, misled by the theory of 'three in one' — the army leadership decides on the theme, the masses participate as critics, and the author only provides the writing skill.

One is therefore compelled to conclude that as art fails, ideology triumphs. Since, to ensure its ideological correctness, the story was written under the close supervision of the army leadership, the scrutiny of the masses, and the vigilance of the author, the work must be a perfect sample on that score. *The Song of Ou-yang Hai*, however, turns out to be one of the worst examples of revisionist literature.

When Ou-yang Hai is making his self-criticism he quotes a passage from Liu Shao-ch'i's *How to be a Good Communist*. This is the only

[30] *Ibid.*, p. 119.

time a quotation from Liu appears in fictional works. As we know, the ultimate goal of the Cultural Revolution was the overthrow of Liu Shao-ch'i, the leader who took the revisionist road. The author's ideological error in quoting Liu is of course easily mended. It can be revised out of the text; sure enough, it is replaced by a quotation from Chairman Mao's *Get Organized* in the English translation.[31] This deletion only corrects the most obvious example, but cannot eliminate the revisionist thesis underlying the novel. The call of Chairman Mao at the Tenth Plenary Session of the Eighth Central Committee in 1962 is 'never forget class struggle'. Since then those who defied his authority have expounded the theories of class reconciliation and of the end of class struggle. In the same issue of *Chinese Literature* appears both the fourth instalment of *The Song of Ou-yang Hai*, and an article repudiating Chou Yang's revisionist line for literature and art. Of the eight points documenting Chou's revisionist literary program, one is his thesis that class struggle has come to an end.[32]

The intensification of class struggle in the third volume of *Bright Sunny Days*, which appeared in the March 1966 issue of *Harvest*, is a rejection of Chou Yang's revisionist thesis, but *The Song of Ou-yang Hai*, which portrays neither class struggle nor villains, supports it. If Chou Yang may be labelled Liu Shao-ch'i's spokesman, peddling Liu's revisionist policy in literature and art, the same charge cannot be made against Chin Ching-mai. Born in 1930 and joining the army in 1949, Chin was merely an obscure actor in a drama troupe before he undertook to write the novel. There is no reason to suspect him of any connection with the Liu Shao-ch'i faction.

It appears that as part of his ideological training, Chin Ching-mai read Liu Shao-ch'i's *How to Be a Good Communist* many times, as well as articles about class conciliation and the end of the class struggle in Party-controlled journals. The quotation from Liu must have come spontaneously from his pen and the theory of the end of the class struggle automatically forms the basic thesis of his novel.[33] Thus, despite the strictest control, the novel fails to maintain ideological correctness. On the contrary, it shows how hopeless is the attempt to contain man's ideas within an ideological framework.

[31] For a detailed account of the several revisions of *The Song of Ou-yang Hai*, see D. W. Fokkema, 'Chinese Literature under the Cultural Revolution', *Literature East and West*, Vol. XIII, 3 and 4, December 1969, pp. 347–56.

[32] Wu Chi-yan, 'Repudiate Chou Yang's Revisionist Programme for Literature and Art', *Chinese Literature*, No. 10, 1966, pp. 131–5.

[33] Chin Ching-mai's lapse into oblivion came sooner than expected. By early 1968 his name was no longer mentioned in the press. He got into trouble, according to a Hongkong report, for his association with ultra-leftists Ch'i Pen-yü, Kuan Feng and Wang Li in July 1968. See *Hsing-tao jih-pao*, September 15, 1968.

12

POSTSCRIPT: LIFE, ART, IDEOLOGY

Of the novels published since 1949, a large number are of poor quality. One might attribute the failure of these works to ideological conformity. No doubt, the manufacturers of hack works are content to repeat the official line and to mouth clichés. But their failure owes perhaps as much to a lack of insight, sensitivity, and talent. The tendency to follow an established formula and avoid effort is also due to intellectual lethargy. Imaginative depiction of characters and events according to a writer's own observation is a far more challenging task. It requires a sense of artistic discipline.

On the other hand, prolific novelists of the pre-Communist era appear to have abandoned their creative life. Their main contributions to Chinese literature since 1949 have been limited primarily to editorial work and literary essays on the technical level. It is tempting again to suspect that their waning creative power is the result of ideological restrictions. The real reason seems to be somewhat different. Pre-publication control is exercised only on the selection of themes; stories of a purely private nature, unrelated to the larger problems of revolution and socialism, are precluded from socialist literature. Since veteran novelists like Mao Tun, Pa Chin, and Chang T'ien-yi did not take part in the armed struggle or in the socialist reconstruction, their imagination was never fired to write works of excellence in this field.

For writers to produce novels of substance in Communist China, they must be true believers. No unconvinced writer can tell stories of the period of armed struggle or of the era of socialism without fabricating pseudo-real incidents. Only true believers would risk their lives as undercover workers in the underground struggle, as organizers in the guerrilla war, or as men in uniform in the Civil War. When these people turned to writing, they also had faith in their creative work. They would portray their involvement in the revolution with a high degree of accuracy, for they never harbored any doubt about the rightness of their cause. Their struggle for authenticity owes as much to a pursuit of artistic truth as to a belief in their own dedication; they would not be put off by the shadow of a heresy charge. Their devotion

320

to the revolutionary struggle and to artistic validity are really two aspects of the same faith. The revolutionary and the writer must be one and the same in order to create a powerful drama.

If the novels we have studied truthfully reflect life in China, what then has happened in the last half-century under Communism? The first noticeable trend is the change of political order from chaos to stability, brought about by the organizational ability of the Communists. In the years of building a political base in the interior of China, tremendous efforts were made to stir up latent feelings of discontent and anger among peasants against the feudal society, in order to mobilize and organize them into a revolutionary force. This work was so thoroughly carried out that most peasants were intensely involved in the political struggle. The organizational talent of the Communists finally turned the masses into cadres and cadres into leaders. With the success of the revolution, Chinese society becomes very highly organized, and the Chinese people intensely politically-minded.

The increasing political awareness of the people is reflected in the changing behavior patterns of heroes and cadres. At the initial stage the revolution was led by Communist insurgents. The revolutionaries as portrayed in contemporary literature display traits characteristic of heroes in classical novels and popular tales, such as outstanding bravery, exceptional strength, and nobility of personality. The concept of heroism implicitly suggests individuality and personal willpower. Communist heroes, like their historical prototypes, largely act on their own judgment and rely on their own resourcefulness.

As China moves from a chaotic to an organized society, old-style heroes no longer perform useful functions. When society was unstable, fragmented, and disorderly, people longed for heroes of superhuman power to save them from their sufferings. Once rule and order are fully established, traditional heroes have to be replaced by 'socialist men'. The notion of heroes of personal distinction conflicts with ideology, with its principles of collective leadership and the mass line. Success must be attributed to the wisdom of the leadership and the co-operation of the masses. A 'socialist man' cannot claim the kind of glory due a traditional hero, for he is a part of the organization. He is anonymous; his behavior is controlled by the policy decisions made at the top of the political hierarchy.

A second trend is the change in the socio-economic basis of Chinese society. In the transition from revolutionary struggle to socialist reconstruction, the economic foundation changes from individual ownership to collective ownership of the means of production. This transformation causes a parallel shift in social relations. During the period of armed struggle, a hero's political conduct as a loyal Party man was found compatible with his social behavior as a loving son. In both instances, his behavior suggests normative values, but there is a fundamental difference. In the first instance, his conduct is ideologically oriented, for the Party has taught him to be a dedicated member. In the second, his conduct reflects moral values entrenched in Chinese society and tradition. The two normative values are remarkably congruous. Whether the hero's relationship with the Party on the one hand and with his parents on the other is interpreted as that between a man and the symbol of authority or as that between a man and the symbol of parentage, the fact is that there is no conflict between the two roles the hero plays. By the same token, a hero may be a loyal Party man and a faithful husband. There is a logical connection between the two roles; the former may be seen as an extension of the latter. This indicates that the behavior patterns of fictional models reflect Communist beliefs and norms intermingled with social *mores* and conventions. That the two aspects are complementary shows that certain aspects of Communist ideology are not entirely alien to the traditional culture.

Under the socialist system, however, conventional social norms governing relations between old and young, husband and wife, relatives and friends are reduced to a secondary place. A man's first allegiance is to the collective; only within the collective framework does he play a secondary role as son, husband, or relative. This implies a fundamental change from a family-oriented to a community-oriented code of social conduct.

At the same time, the concept of villainy has also changed from socially-condemned behavior to conspiracy measured in political terms. In pre-Communist society villains were tyrannical landlords, predatory capitalists, or corrupt officials. The political dimension of the villains' conduct as exploiters also conforms to its social dimension as an offence against *mores* and conventions. A landlord's rape of his tenant's daughter for instance, shows him both as oppressor and sinner.

Once the revolution succeeds, the people, liberated and under the protection of the government, will no longer be victimized. As a result, it is no longer oppressors and exploiters but counter-revolutionaries who play the role of villains. Their schemes are not directed against helpless people but against socialism. That villains can no longer ruin innocent people protected by the system but can turn against the system itself is of course only ideologically valid. The notion does reveal, however, the shift in the role of villain; it is no longer one individual against another but one against the group.

The accuracy of the novelists' depiction of life in China is best manifested in the response of Chinese readers. Since they have lived through the same turmoil and upheavals themselves, they can verify the authenticity of stories against their own experiences. It is a general misconception that since Chinese writers are notoriously free with propaganda pieces, the Chinese people have been thoroughly brainwashed. This is clearly not the case. The Chinese people, sensitive to fluctuations in the political climate, know how to retain a corner in their minds as a private store for their feelings, ideas and opinions. They will reveal their feelings only when they believe them to be innocuous.

One indication of the existence of a private world in each individual is the diversity of interests revealed in their choice of novels, which is made according to individual taste rather than the instructions of the Party. Although statistical data are scanty and incomplete, we have some information from a few small-scale surveys.

In December 1962, the creative work research section of the Chinese Writers Association did a survey of reading habits in Tinghsing, Wangtu, and T'anghsien, and conducted a number of interviews in Fup'ing, Laiyuan, Yungch'eng, and Tinghsien.[1] Their study of the reading habits of commune members, village cadres, amateur writers, and young schoolteachers in the seven-county area of Hopei province discloses some very interesting information.

The first significant finding is the sophistication of rural readers. Only novels of artistic quality or with sophisticated plots gain any popularity; not a single novel of a purely propagandist nature is mentioned. Of contemporary novels reflecting the armed struggle and socialist reconstruction, the most widely read are *Tracks in the Snowy Forest, Keep the Red Flag Flying, The Song of Youth,* and *Sanliwan Village.* Classical novels such as *Water Margin, Romance of the Three Kingdoms, Romance of the Warring States (Lieh kuo), Pilgrimage to the West* (or *Monkey*), and *Tales from Liao Chai* remain their favorite reading. The interest in popular tales of lesser artistic merit, but full of battle action, like *Generals of the Yang Family (Yang chia chiang)* and *Generals of the Hu Family (Hu chia chiang)* has never waned among rural readers. Even *Cases of Magistrate Shih (Shih kung an), Eight Heroes (Ta pa yi),* and *Eight Young Heroes (Hsiao pa yi),* which have been repudiated for their feudal and reactionary themes, are still in wide circulation and available in second-hand book markets.

The habit of listening to stories is preserved as a part of village life, particularly in the slow seasons. One commune member gives this graphic account of the activities in his village:

When the autumn crop had been brought in, story-tellers became

[1] Chung-kuo tso-chia hsieh-hui ch'uang-tso yen-chiu-shih cheng-li, (The Creative Work Research Section of the Chinese Writers Association, ed.), 'Chi i-tz'u kuan-yü hsiao-shuo tsai nung-ts'un ti t'iao-ch'a' (A survey of the Novel in the Villages), *Wen-i pao*, No. 2, 1963, pp. 11–14.

busy in the evenings. Older people loved to hear *Tales from Liao Chai*, *Water Margin*, and *Three Swordsmen* (*San hsieh chien*); young people, however, were interested in contemporary stories such as the episode of 'Defeating the Tinker in a Verbal Battle' in *Tracks in the Snowy Forest*. Sometimes people were still unwilling to disperse well after 11.30 at night.[2]

Another peasant said that with the coming of electricity, there were forty or fifty radio sets in his village. When the program of *Red Crag* was on the air, people crowded into a room to listen to the broadcast.

Whether in reading or in listening to stories, the tastes of rural people vary according to their age, education, and habits. While young people prefer novels of revolutionary themes, older people still retain their interest in old popular tales. The study shows that the contemporary novels which have a great appeal to a rural audience contain three common characteristics: (1) intense conflict, complicated plot, and suspense, (2) a popular form and vernacular expression, and (3) vivid and vigorous characterization. In short, if a novel's style is close to that of the classical novel and popular tale, it has great appeal.

Similar taste in the selection of novels is reported in a study of production brigade members in a commune near Peking.[3] The peasants' favorite novels are *Red Crag*, *Keep the Red Flag Flying*, *Tracks in the Snowy Forest*, *The Builders*, and *Bright Sunny Days*. Most of them remember vividly episodes such as the pig-tax resistance campaign in *Keep the Red Flag Flying*, the seizure of Tiger Mountain by strategy in *Tracks in the Snowy Forest*, and Liang Sheng-pao's endeavor to buy a new strain of fast-growing seed in *The Builders*. They have great admiration for Hsu Yun-feng and Sister Chiang of *Red Crag* for their unflinching character, Yang Tzu-yung of *Tracks in the Snowy Forest* for his stratagem, Liang Sheng-pao of *The Builders* for his determination to lead the mutual-aid team, and Chu Lao-chung of *Keep the Red Flag Flying* for his bravery. They like these novels because the stories reflect what actually happened during the armed struggle or in daily life as they have heard or witnessed it themselves.

A team organized by the literature research section of the Chinese Academy of Sciences also made a survey among villagers of four production brigades at Chiuli commune, Shouhsien, Anhwei province,

---

Ibid., p. 11.

[3] Pei-ching T'ung-hsien Hsü-hsin-chuang kung-she Hsiao-ying ta-tui tu-shu hsiao-tsu (The Study Group of Hsiaoying Brigade, Hsühsinchuang Commune, T'ung-hsien, Peking), 'Ying-hsiung hsing-hsiang ku-wu ho chiao-yü wo-men' (Hero Characters Encourage and Educate Us), *Wen-hsüeh p'ing-lun*, No. 1, 1966, pp. 44–5.

from October 13 to 30, 1965.[4] They held fourteen discussion meetings involving seventy-seven people[5] and sent a written questionnaire to seventeen who had more than elementary school education. The frequency count of novels mentioned in the written interviews shows:

Tracks in the Snowy Forest 11
The Song of Youth 10
Bitter Herb 8
Red Crag 7
In an Old City 6
The Railway Guerrillas 6
Keep the Red Flag Flying 5
Red Sun 5
and
Behind the Enemy Line 4.

Classical novels appear to have become less popular:

Water Margin 4
Pilgrimage to the West 3
Romance of the Three Kingdoms 3
and
The Life of Yüeh Fei 2.

Mao Tun's *Midnight* and Pa Chin's *Mist, Rain, and Lightning*, both products of the 1930s, and *Seven Swordsmen and Five Good Fellows*, a popular tale, are each mentioned once. This does not fully reflect the

[4] Chung-kuo k'o-hsüeh-yüan wen-hsüeh yen-chiu-so Anhwei Shou-hsien Chiu-li kung-she lao-tung shih-hsi tui (The Team of Physical Labor Participants of the Literature Research Institute of the Chinese Academy of Sciences), 'Anhwei Shou-hsien Chiu-li kung-she she-yüan yüeh-tu ho p'ing-lun wen-hsüeh tso-p'in ti t'iao-ch'a' (A Survey of Reading Habits and Judgment of Literary Works Among Members of Chiuli Commune, Shouhsien, Anhwei Province), *Wen-hsüeh p'ing-lun*, No. 1, 1966, pp. 36–43.

[5] Socio-political breakdown of the participants:

Village cadres	5	Poor peasants	39
Militiamen	17	Lower mid. peasants	14
Elem. ag. schoolteachers	18	Middle peasants	19
Reading room activists	7	Upper mid. peasants	19
Commune members	30	Small rentiers	2
		Landlord's offspring	1
Total	77		
		Total	77

High sch. education	7	Party members	10
Junior high sch. education	14	League members	18
Elem. sch. education	19	non-members	49
Old style private sch. ed.	3		
Illiterate	34	Total	77
Total	77		

popularity of the novels; it also suggests what is available in the brigade reading room. It is pointed out, for instance, that the waiting list for *Keep the Red Flag Flying* and *The Builders* is so long that most people have not yet had a chance to read them.

A number of significant comments emerged from the discussion meetings which reflect the attitude, taste, and increasing sophistication of rural readers. First of all, they would like to see hero characters withstand ordeals, overcome difficulties, and defeat enemies in clearly-defined class struggle or in the battlefield. The natural tendency to identify with the hero is as strong as ever among rural readers.

Secondly, they prefer characters divided without ambiguity into black or white. The conflict between heroes and villains must be tense, and the plot complex. They like to read a story with a beginning and an end. This explains the lack of interest in short stories, that are often slices of dramatic events, and poems, that usually have no development. The moralistic attitude toward fictional models and the interest in the traditional types of story remain the same among rural readers now as in pre-Communist days.

Thirdly, their interest is beginning to shift from classical to contemporary novels, Fewer people now read purely imaginary stories such as *Canonization of Gods* (*Feng sheng pang*). The reason, as given, is that old tales, though full of action, are clearly unreal, while new novels have an educational value. They want to learn about the new society from novels.

Fourthly, they are interested in stories where characters are divided clearly along class lines. They begin to examine themes of fictional works from the class viewpoint and develop a strong sense of love or hate toward a character's class stand. They always look for the party leadership in stories and are critical of works where cadres fail to follow Party instructions. In this respect, Communist political education in the last few decades appears to have taken root.

Finally, they always compare characters and incidents portrayed in novels to people and events in real life, especially to their own personal experiences. They often raise the question whether fictional characters resemble real people and whether incidents actually happened or could have happened. They contend that only stories which truthfully reflect life are good. This is a remarkably sophisticated approach and the beginning of literary criticism. When a peasant judges a novel by asking himself whether it is real, he is using the fundamental criterion of literary critics. It is an independent judgment.

With the intensive rural education campaigns waged since the establishment of the regime, the majority of peasants have become educated, and only older people remain illiterate. If education makes it easier for the regime to reach rural people through the media of mass communication, it also equips them with the ability to make an independent judgment. As the peasants' intellectual horizon is widened, their need for intellectual nourishment is proportionately enhanced. This does not mean that Chinese peasants have developed an immunity to propaganda or that ideology can no longer influence their way of life. There is, however, a clear limitation to how far political control can be extended. As the surveys show, the peasants have learned to examine plots from the class viewpoint, a major development in their attitude. On the other hand, they also judge stories according to the likelihood of their actual occurrence.

During the Yenan days, literature and art were regarded as an important vehicle for shaping the political ideas of the Chinese peasants. It was a crucial medium for reaching the masses, in order to win their support for the Communist Party. Since the success of the revolution, especially in the post-Great Leap period, debates took place within the top leadership over whether the acceleration of agricultural collectivization was a mistake, whether in socialist China class struggle still existed, and whether ideological or military training should be given priority in the army. In their stories novelists reflected one view or another. Some deliberately took sides to promote the line of one faction or another. Works of art and literature were thus suspected of being used as a platform for intra-party dispute, and sometimes actually were. The ultimate outcome of the quandary was the tightening of political control over creative works. Only slogan-loaded propaganda pieces have been published since the Cultural Revolution.

Life in China, however, is not as simple as the propaganda would suggest. Oversimplification of complex and complicated human and social phenomena will hamper the development of sound policies towards solving problems. Propaganda can be self-deceiving, in the sense that it may mislead the propagandists rather than the people. It is likely that rural people may become so fed up with propaganda that they will lose interest in it completely. A Party-led campaign to promote pure propaganda material can of course press peasants to buy it or read it, but they may simply read it without enjoyment and, furthermore, without believing in it.

China today has not yet fully recovered from the trauma of the Cultural Revolution. Serious research work has not been resumed, advanced education remains at the initial stage of recovery, and professional journals, with a few exceptions, have not reappeared. But this state of affairs is not likely to last long; a cultural renaissance may bloom sooner than expected. Novels of artistic merit will have to replace works of pure propaganda. This prediction is based on the simple promise that if the cultural vacuum remains unfilled, sooner or later peasants will seek escape in old popular tales. The market of ideas will be taken over by stories such as *Generals of the Yang Family, Cases of Magistrate Shih*, and *Eight Heroes*, which preach feudal values and norms.

Ideology, properly considered, forms an important part of every political culture. It is a set of normative values sustained by popular faith. People accept ideology, because it has become, through a process of socialization, an integral part of their system of belief. If this is to happen, ideology must come to terms with the reality of life and address itself to the needs of the people. In that case, ideology reflects life as much as it defines it.

China under Communism has never been a static society. Many changes occurred in the last quarter of a century as a result of the cross-pressure of political and social forces. The fluidity of the situation is typical of a revolutionary political order. As this revolutionary political order mellows into a mature political order, diversity of ideas will become more tolerable and acceptable. At the same time, the unfortunate entanglement of artists and writers in political debates over policies will be avoided. The season for the blossom of a hundred flowers can be ushered in by a recognition of the respective autonomy of art and ideology.

SELECT BIBLIOGRAPHY

Sources other than Chinese are not listed; the Chinese source is also highly selective. If an English version of a Chinese reference is available, it is listed side by side with the Chinese title.

I. Novels

Ai Hsuan, *Ta chiang feng lei* (*The Thundering Yangtse*) (Peking: People's Literature Publishing House, 1965).

Ai Ming-chih, *Huo chung* (Peking: Writers' Publishing House, 1963); 'Seeds of Flame', *Chinese Literature*, Nos. 4 & 5, 1964.

Ai Wu, *Pai lien ch'eng kang* (Peking: Writers' Publishing House, 2nd ed., 1962); *Steeled and Tempered* (Peking: Foreign Languages Press, 1961).

Chao Shu-li, *San-li-wan* (Peking: People's Literature Publishing House, rev. ed., 1959); *Sanliwan Village* (Peking: Foreign Languages Press, 1964).

Chih Hsia, *T'ieh-tao yu-chi-tui* (Peking: Writers' Publishing House, rev. ed., 1965); *The Railway Guerrillas* (Peking: Foreign Languages Press, 1966).

Chin Ching-mai, *Ou-yang Hai chih ko* (Peking: People's Literature Publishing House, rev. ed., 1966); 'The Song of Ou-yang Hai', *Chinese Literature*, Nos. 7, 8, 9, 10, and 11, 1966.

Chou Li-po, *Pao-feng chou-yü* (Tientsin: New China Book Co., 1949); *The Hurricane* (Peking: Foreign Languages Press, 1955).

————, *Shan hsiang chü-pien*, Vol. I (Peking: Writers' Publishing House, 1958); *Great Changes in a Mountain Village* (Peking: Foreign Languages Press, 1961).

————, 'Tsao-ch'i − *Shan hsiang chü-pien* chung ti liang chang' ('Early Rise' − two chapters from the sequel to *Great Changes in a Mountain Village*), *Jen-min wen-hsüeh*, November 1959.

Ch'ü Po, *Lin hai hsüeh yüan* (Peking: People's Literature Publishing House, 2nd ed., 1959); *Tracks in the Snowy Forest* (Peking: Foreign Languages Press, 1962).

Hao Jan, *Yen yang t'ien* (*Bright Sunny Days*), Vol. I (Peking: Writers' Publishing House, 1964).

————, *Yen yang t'ien*, Vol. II (Peking: People's Literature Publishing House, 1966).

————, 'Yen yang t'ien, Vol. III', *Shuo-huo*, No. 2, March 1966.

Kao Yun-lan, *Hsiao-ch'eng ch'un-ch'iu* (Peking: Writers' Publishing House, 1956); *Annals of a Provincial Town* (Peking: Foreign Languages Press, 1959).

Li Ying-ju, *Yeh-huo ch'un-feng tou ku-ch'eng* (Peking: Writers' Publishing House, rev. ed., 1961); 'In an Old City', *Chinese Literature*, Nos. 11 and 12, 1965.

Liang Pin, *Hung-ch'i p'u* (Peking: Chinese Youth Publishing House, 1958); *Keep the Red Flag Flying* (Peking: Foreign Languages Press, 1963).

————, *Po huo chi* (*Sowing the Flames*) (Peking: Writers' Publishing House, 1963); 'A Tale of the Green Woods', *Chinese Literature*, No. 3, 1961.

Liu Ch'ing, *Ch'uang yeh shih*, Vol. I (Peking: Chinese Youth Publishing House, 1960); *The Builders* (Peking: Foreign Languages Press, 1964).

————, 'Ju tang' (Joining the Party), *Shanghai wen-hsüeh*, No. 12, December 1960.

————, 'Liang Sheng-pao yü Hsu Kai-hsia', *Shou-huo*, No. 1, 1964.

Lo Kuang-pin and Yang Yi-yen, *Hung yen* (Peking: Chinese Youth Publishing House, 1962); 'Red Crag', *Chinese Literature*, Nos. 5, 6, and 7, 1962.

Lo Tan, *Feng yü ti li-ming* (*Dawn in Wind and Rain*), Vol. I (Peking: Chinese Youth Publishing House, 2nd ed., 1963).

————, *Feng yü ti li-ming*, Vol. II (Peking: Chinese Youth Publishing House, 1964).

Ou-yang Shan, *San chia hsiang* (Peking: Writers' Publishing House, rev. ed., 1960); 'Three Family Lane', *Chinese Literature*, Nos. 5 and 6, 1961.

————, *K'u tou* (*Bitter Struggle*) (Canton: People Publishing House, 1962).

Szu-ma wen-sheng, *Feng-yü T'ung chiang* (*Storm over the T'ung River*) (Peking: Writers' Publishing House, 1964).

Ting Ling, *T'ai-yang chao tsai Sang-kan ho shang* (Peking: New China Book Co., 1949); *Sun over the Sangkan River* (Peking: Foreign Languages Press, 1954).

Tu Peng-cheng, *Pao-wei Yen-an* (*Defense of Yenan*) (Peking: People's Literature Publishing House, 1954); 'At the Great Wall', *Chinese Literature*, No. 1, 1956.

Wu Chiang, *Hung jih* (Peking: Chinese Youth Publishing House, rev. ed., 1964); *Red Sun* (Peking: Foreign Languages Press, 1961).

Yang Mo, *Ch'ing-ch'un chih ko* (Peking: People's Literature Publishing House, rev. ed., 1960); 'The Song of Youth', *Chinese Literature*, Nos. 3, 4, 5, and 6, 1960.

II. Essays, Commentaries and Reviews

Chang Kang, 'Chin Teh-kuei ho wo-men sheng-huo tsai i-ch'i — Kang-t'ieh kung-jen tso-t'an *Pai lien ch'eng kang*' (Chin Teh-kuei Is One of Us — Steelmakers Discuss *Steeled and Tempered*), *Wen-i pao*, No. 8, April 1958.

Chang Li and Yi Shui, 'Mei chung pu tsu ti hsia-tz'u – Lioh t'an *San chia hsiang* ts'un-tsai ti chi-ko ch'üeh-tien' (Flaws in Perfection – A Brief Discussion of Some Defects in *Three Family Lane*), *Tso-p'in*, January 1960.

Chang Pei, 'Tu *Shan hsiang chü-pien*' (On *Great Changes in a Mountain Village*), *Wen-i pao*, No. 18, 1958.

Chang Pi-ying and Ch'en Ch'in-p'ing, 'Fang *Ch'ing-ch'un chih ko* tso-che Yang Mo' (An Interview with Yang Mo, Author of *The Song of Youth*), *Chung-kuo ch'ing-nien pao*, August 9, 1959.

Chao Ling, 'A Novel about the Liberation War', *Chinese Literature*, No. 7, 1960.

Chao Shu-li, '*San-li-wan* hsieh-tso chien hou' (Before and after writing *Sanliwan Village*), *Wen-i pao*, October 1955.

———, 'Yü tu-che t'an *San-li-wan*' (A Response to Readers about *Sanliwan Village*), *Wen-i pao*, No. 10, 1962.

Chao Yang, '*Red Crag*, a Modern Epic', *Chinese Literature*, No. 5, 1965.

Chao Yen (Huang Ch'iu-yün), 'Ke-ming ch'un-ch'iu ti hsü-ch'ü – Hsi tu *San chia hsiang*' (Prelude to a Revolutionary Epic – after happily reading *Three Family Lane*), *Wen-i pao*, No. 2, 1960.

Chao Yun, ' "Kuan-yü Liang Sheng-pao hsing-hsiang" i-wen ti i-chien' (Opinions on the Article 'Concerning the Image of Liang Sheng-pao'), *Wen-hsüeh p'ing-lun*, No. 2, 1964.

Ch'en Fei-ch'in, 'Jang *Hung jih* ku-wu wo-men chi-hsü ch'ien-chin' (Let *Red Sun* Encourage Us to March Forward), *Peking wen-i*, August 1958.

Ch'en Kang-feng, '*Lin hai hsüeh yüan* ti i-shu chieh-kou' (On the Artistic Framework of *Tracks in the Snowy Forest*), *Chieh-fang-chün wen-i*, June 1958.

'Ch'en Yi, Tao Chu t'ung-chih tsai chieh-chien *Ou-yang Hai chih ko* tso-che shih t'an she-hui-chu-i wen-hsüeh ch'uang-tso shang ti i-hsieh chung-yao wen-t'i' (Comrades Ch'en Yi and Tao Chu Talked about Some Important Problems in Socialist Literature When They Were Receiving the Author of *The Song of Ou-yang Hai*), *Wen-i pao*, No. 3, 1966.

Ch'en Yung, 'Kuan-yü i-shu ho cheng-chih' (Art and Politics), *Chung-kuo ch'ing-nien*, July 1957.

———, '*Pao-feng chou-yü*' (On *The Hurricane*), *Wen-i pao*, No. 11/12, 1952.

Cheng Po-ch'i, '*Ch'uang yeh shih* tu-hou sui-kan' (Thoughts after Reading *The Builders*), *Yen-ho*, January 1960.

Chia Wen-chao, 'Ch'uang-tsao kuang-hui ts'an-lan ti sihn ying-hsiung hsing-hsiang – Po Shao Ch'üan-lin t'ung-chih ti "Hsieh chung-chien jen-wu" li-lun' (Creating Shining New Hero Images – Repudiating Comrade Shao Ch'üan-lin's Theory of 'Portraying Men in the Middle'), *Wen-hsüeh p'ing-lun*, No. 2, 1965.

'Chiang-chia wang-p'ai chün ti chüeh-mu-jen tso-t'an *Hung jih*' (Grave Diggers of Chiang's Crack Army Discuss *Red Sun*), *Wen-i pao*, November 1958.

Ch'ih Liao-chou 'I-ko yu-hsiu kung-jen ying-hsiung hsing-hsiang — P'ing *Pai lien ch'eng kang* chung ti jen-wu Chin Teh-kuei' (The Heroic Image of an Outstanding Worker — Comments on Chin Teh-kuei of *Steeled and Tempered*), *Jen-min jih-pao*, December 26, 1957.

Chin Ching-mai, *'Ou-yang Hai chih ko* ti yün-niang ho ch'uang-tso', *Wen-i pao*, No. 3, 1966; 'How I Conceived and Wrote *The Song of Ou-yang Hai,'*, *Chinese Literature*, No. 11, 1966.

Chou-Li-po, 'Kuan-yü *Shan hsiang chü-pien* ta tu-che wen' (Answers to Readers' Questions on *Great Changes in a Mountain Village*), *Jen-min wen-hsüeh*, July 1958.

Chou Yang, 'Building a Socialist Literature — A Speech Delivered at the Second Session [Enlarged] of the Chinese Writers Association on February 27, 1956', *Chinese Literature*, No. 4, 1956.

————— 'Hsin min-ko k'ai-t'o-liao shih-ko ti hsin tao-lu' (The New Folk Songs cleared a New Road for Poetry), *Hung-ch'i*, June 1958.

—————, 'Wo kuo she-hui-chu-i wen-hsüeh i-shu ti tao-lu', *Wen-i pao*, No. 13/14, 1960; 'The Path of Socialist Literature and Art in our Country', *Chinese Literature*, No. 10, 1960.

Chu Chai, 'Shih-tai ke-ming ching-shen ti kuang-hui — Tu *Hung yen*' (The Glory of Epoch-making Revolutionary Spirit — after reading *Red Crag*), *Wen-hsüeh p'ing-lun*, No. 6, 1963.

—————, 'T'an *Shan hsiang chü-pien* chi ch'i-t'a' (On *Great Changes in a Mountain Village* and Related Matters), *Wen-hsüeh p'ing-lun*, No. 4, 1959.

—————, 'Ts'ung tui Liang san lao-han ti p'ing-chia k'an "hsieh chung-chien jen-wu" chu-chang ti shih-chih' (From the Evaluation of Liang the Third to see the Essence of the Proposition of 'Portraying Men in the Middle'), *Wen-hsüeh p'ing-lun*, No. 6, 1964.

—————, 'Tu *Ch'uang yeh shih*' (On *The Builders*), *Yen-ho*, April 1960.

Chu K'o-yu, 'Lun *T'ai-yang chao tsai Sang-kan ho shang*' (Comments on *Sun over the Sangkan River*), *Jen-min wen-hsüeh*, October 1957.

Ch'ü Po, 'Kuan-yü *Lin hai hsüeh yüan*' (About *Tracks in the Snowy Forest*), *Peking jih-pao*, November 9, 1957.

Chung-kuo k'o-hsüeh-yüan wen-hsüeh yen-chiu-so Anhwei Shou-hsien Chiu-li kung-she lao-tung-shih-hsi-tui (The Team of Physical Labor Participants, the Institute of Literature Research, the Chinese Academy of Sciences), 'Anhwei Shou-hsien Chiu-li kung-she she-yüan yüeh-tu ho p'ing-lun wen-hsüeh tso-p'in ti t'iao-ch'a' (A Survey of Reading Habits and Judgment Ability of Literary Works among Members of Chiuli Commune, Shouhsien, Anhwei Province), *Wen-hsüeh p'ing-lun*, No. 1, 1966.

Chung-kuo tso-chia hsieh-hui ch'uang-tso yen-chiu-shih cheng-li (The Creative Work Research Section of the Chinese Writers Association, ed.), 'Chi i-tz'u kuan-yü hsiao-shuo tsai nung-ts'un ti t'iao-ch'a' (A Survey of the Novel in the Villages), *Wen-i pao*, No. 2, 1963.

'Defense of Yenan', *Chinese Literature*, No. 2, 1955.

Editorial, 'Kuan-yü *San chia hsiang, K'u tou* ti p'ing-chia wen-t'i' (On the Question of Evaluating *Three Family Lane* and *Bitter Struggle*), *Wen-hsüeh p'ing-lun*, No. 6, 1964.

Editorial Board, ' "Hsieh chung-chien jen-wu" shih tzu-ch'an-chieh-chi ti wen-hsüeh chu-chang' ('Portraying Men in the Middle' Is the Literary Proposition of the Bourgeoisie), *Wen-i pao*, September 1964.

――――, 'Kuan-yü "Hsieh chung-chien jen-wu" ti ts'ai-liao' (Materials concerning 'Portraying Men in the Middle'), *Wen-i pao*, September 1964.

Fan Tzu-lin, 'Shih t'an *Yen yang t'ien* ti ssu-hsiang i-shu t'eh-seh' (Preliminary Comments on the Ideological and Artistic Qualities of *Bright Sunny Days*), *Wen-hsüeh p'ing-lun*, No. 4, 1965.

Fang Ming, 'How Liang Pin Came to Write *Keep the Red Flag Flying,*' *Chinese Literature*, No. 7, 1960.

――――, 'Yeh huo shao pu chin, ch'un-feng ts'ui yu sheng – Tu *Yeh-huo ch'un-feng tou ku-ch'eng*' (Even Brushfire will not burn it up, for the Spring Breeze will blow it to Life again – after reading *In an Old City*), *Wen-i pao*, No. 1, 1959.

Feng Chien-nan, 'T'an Chu Lao-chung' (Comments on Chu Lao-chung), *Wen-hsüeh p'ing-lun*, No. 1, 1961.

Feng Hsüeh-feng, 'Lun *Pao-wei Yen-an* ti ch'eng-chiu chi ch'i chung-yao-hsing' (On the Achievement and Importance of *Defense of Yenan*), *Wen-i pao*, No. 14, 1954.

――――, '*T'ai-yang chao tsai Sang-kan ho shang* tsai wo-men wen-hsüeh fa-chan shang ti i-i' (The Significance of *Sun over the Sangkan River* in our Literary Development), *Wen-i pao*, No. 10, 1952.

Feng Mu, 'Ch'u tu *Ch'uang yeh shih*' (Preliminary Thoughts after reading *The Builders*), *Wen-i pao*, No. 1, 1960.

――――, '*Feng yü ti li-ming* ti ch'eng-chiu chi ch'i jo-tien' (The Merits and Shortcomings in *Dawn in Wind and Rain*), *Wen-i pao*, No. 14, 1959.

――――, 'Ke-ming ti chan-ko, ying-hsiung ti sung-ko – Lioh lun *Hung jih* ti ch'eng-chiu chi ch'i jo-tien' (A Revolutionary Battle Song, a Heroes' Panegyric – a Brief Discussion on the Merits and Short-comings in *Red Sun*), *Wen-i pao*, No. 21, 1958.

――――, 'Lioh t'an wen-hsüeh shang ti "fan-mien chiao-yüan"' (On the Negative Characters in Literature), *Wen-i pao*, No. 7, 1962.

Feng Mu and Huang Chao-yen, 'Hsin shih-tai sheng-huo ti hua-ch'üan – Lioh t'an shih-nien-lai ch'ang-p'ien-hsiao-shuo ti feng-shou', *Wen-i pao*, No. 19/10, October 1959; 'Novel Writing in Recent Years', *Chinese Literature*, No. 3, 1960.

Fan Tzu-pao, Chao Chin-liang and Wang Hsien-p'ei, 'Tsen-yang p'ing-lun Liang san lao-han, T'ing Mien-hu, Yen Chih-ho' (How to Evaluate Liang the Third, Flour-Paste Ting and Yen Chih-ho), *Wen-i pao*, No. 3, 1965.

Hao Jan, 'Je-je ti ku-li, yu-li ti pien-t'se – Tsai *Yen yang t'ien* nung-min tu-che tso-t'an-hui shang ti fa-yen' (Warm Encouragement, Forcible Stimulation – Talks at a Peasant Readers' Discussion Meeting on *Bright Sunny Days*), *Wen-i pao*, No. 2, 1965.

Ho Ch'i-fang, '*Ch'ing-ch'un chih ko* pu-k'o fou-ting' (*The Song of Youth* Should Not Be Denounced), *Chung-kuo ch'ing-nien*, No. 5, 1959.

Ho Chih (Ch'in Chao-yang), 'Hsieh-shih-chu-i kuang-k'uo-ti tao-lu' (Realism – the Broad Road), *Jen-min wen-hsüeh*, September 1956.

Ho Hsiao, 'Fang *Lin hai hsüeh yüan* ti tso-che' (An Interview with the

Author of *Tracks in the Snowy Forest*), *Wen-hui pao*, September 26, 1959.

Hou Chin-ching, 'Ts'ung *Tsai lieh-huo chung yung-sheng* tao *Hung yen'* (From *Immortality in Blazing Fire* to *Red Crag*), *Wen-i pao*, No. 3, 1962.

Hsia Shun, 'Kuan-yü *Lin hai hsüeh yüan* ti kai-pien' (Conversion of *Tracks in the Snowy Forest* into Peking Opera), *Chü-pen*, No. 7, 1958.

Hsiao Chung, ed., 'Meng-liang-ku chan-yü ti ts'an-chia-che t'an *Hung jih – Hung jih* tso-t'an-hui chi-lu che-yao' (Participants of the Mengliangku Campaign discuss *Red Sun* – a Summary Report of the *Red Sun* Discussion Meeting), *Chieh-fang-chün wen-i*, July 1958.

Hsieh Kuang-ning, 'Fang "Liu Hung" – *T'ieh-tao yu-chi-tui* chung ti liang-wei ling-tao-jen ti hua-shen, Lin Chin-shan t'ung-chih pien-shih ch'i-chung-chih-i' (An Interview with 'Liu Hung' – Comrade Liu Chin-shan, one of the leaders in *The Railway Guerrillas*), *Chieh-fang-chün jih-pao*, April 8, 1957.

Hsiao Tung and Ch'i Ngo, 'Ying-hsiung ti jen-min, wei-ta ti tang – Tu hsiao-shuo *Hung-ch'i p'u*' (Heroic People, Great Party – after reading the novel *Keep the Red Flag Flying*), *Peking wen-i*, September 1958.

Hsiung Pai-shih, 'Wo-men ts'ung *Sang-kan ho shang* yü *Pao-feng chou-yü* li hsüeh-hsi shih-mo' (What can we learn from *The Sangkan River* and *The Hurricane*?) *Chung-kuo ch'ing-nien*, December 8, 1951.

Hu So, 'Ke-ming ying-hsiung ti p'u-hsi – *Hung-ch'i p'u* tu-hou chi' (The Lineage of Revolutionary Heroes – Reflections after reading *Keep the Red Flag Flying*), *Wen-i pao*, No. 9, 1958.

Huang Chao-yen (Huang Ch'iu-yün), 'On *The Song of Youth*', *Chinese Literature*, No. 6, 1960.

Huang Ch'iu-yün, 'Ch'u tu *K'u tou*' (Preliminary Thoughts after reading *Bitter Struggle*), *Wen-i pao*, No. 2, 1963.

'Huo chung tsai ch'ing-nien ti hsin-chung jan-shao – Ho-pei Pao-ting shih-fan hsüeh-hsiao hsüeh-sheng tso-t'an *Hung-ch'i p'u*' (Flames kindle in the Minds of the Young – Students at Paoting Normal School in Hopei discuss *Keep the Red Flag Flying*), *Wen-i pao*, No. 9, 1958.

Jen Wen, 'Chung-kuo nung-ts'un ho-tso-hua ch'u-ch'i ti shih-shih – P'ing *Ch'uang yeh shih*' (Epic of the Early Phase of Agricultural Co-operation in Rural China – on *The Builders*), *Jen-min wen-hsüeh*, June 1960.

Kuo Cheng-yüan, 'Kuan-yü *San chia hsiang* p'ing-chia ti chi-ko wen-t'i – Yü Wang ch'i t'ung-chih shang-chioh' (Some Problems in Evaluating *Three Family Lane* – to consult with Comrade Wang Ch'i), *Tso-p'in*, January 1960.

Kuo K'ai, 'Chiu *Ch'ing-ch'un chih ko* t'an wen-i ch'uang-tso ho p'i-p'ing chung ti chi-ko yüan-tse wen-t'i – Tsai p'ing Yang Mo t'ung-chih ti hsiao-shuo *Ch'ing-ch'un chih ko* (Comments on Matters of Principle in Literary Creation and Criticism in the Discussion of *The Song of*

Youth — a second Review of Comrade Yang Mo's Novel *The Song of Youth*), *Wen-i pao*, February 1959.

————, 'Lioh t'an Lin Tao-ching ti miao-hsieh chung ti ch'üeh-tien — P'ing Yang Mo ti hsiao-shuo *Ch'ing-ch'un chih ko*' (Brief Commentaries on the Shortcomings in the Characterization of Lin Tao-ching — A Review of Yang Mo's Novel *The Song of Youth*), *Chung-kuo ch'ing-nien*, No. 2, 1959.

Kuo Mo-jo, 'Mao Tse-tung shih-tai ti ying-hsiung shih-shih — Chiu *Ou-yang Hai chih ko* ta *Wen-i pao* pien-che wen' (Epic of the Era of Mao Tse-tung — an interview by the staff of *Wen-i pao* concerning *The Song of Ou-yang Hai*), *Wen-i pao*, No. 4, 1966.

'Lao chan-shih hua tang-nien — Pen-k'an chü-hsing *Hung-ch'i p'u* tso-t'an-hui chi-lu che-yao' (Recollections of the Old Warriors — a summary Report of Talks at the Discussion Meeting on *Keep the Red Flag Flying* called by this Journal), *Wen-i pao*, No. 5, 1958.

Li Hsi-fan, 'I-pu ch'ung-chi ti-tang ling-huen ti hao tso-p'in (A Soul-Stirring Novel), *Wen-i pao*, No. 3, 1962.

————, 'Ke-ming ying-hsiung tien-hsing ti hsün-li' (Review of Typical Revolutionary Heroes), *Wen-hsüeh p'ing-lun*, No. 1, 1961.

————, 'Man-t'an *Ch'uang yeh shih* ti ssu-hsiang ho i-shu', *Wen-i pao*, No. 17/18, 1960; 'Comments on *The Builders*', *Chinese Literature*, No. 3, 1961.

————, 'She-hui-chu-i shih-tai ching-shen ti tsui-ch'iang-yin' (The Tenor of the Spirit of the Socialist Era), *Wen-i pao*, No. 1, 1966.

————, 'T'an *Hung-ch'i p'u* chung Chu Lao-chung ti hsing-hsiang ti ch'uang-tsao' (On the Image of Chu Lao-chung of *Keep the Red Flag Flying*', *Jen-min jih-pao*, August 18, 1959.

Li Shih-wen, '*Ch'uang yeh shih* tsen-yang miao-hsieh nung-ts'un chieh-chi tou-cheng' (How Rural Class Struggle is reflected in *The Builders*), *Shuo-huo*, No. 4, 1964.

Li Ying-ju, 'Kuan-yü *Yeh-huo ch'un-feng tou ku-ch'eng*' (On *In an Old City*), *Jen-min wen-hsüeh*, No. 7, 1960.

Liang Pin, 'Man-t'an *Hung-ch'i p'u* ti ch'uang-tsao' (Some General Observations on the Creation of *Keep the Red Flag Flying*), *Jen-min wen-hsüeh*, June, 1959.

————, 'Wo tsen-yang ch'uang-tso-liao *Hung-ch'i p'u*' (How I Wrote *Keep the Red Flag Flying*), *Wen-i yüeh-pao*, May 1958.

Liang Ping, 'T'an *Hung jih* ti chi-ko jen-wu' (Talks on some Characters in *Red Sun*), *Wen-i yüeh-pao*, February 1958.

Liu Pai-yü, '*Ou-yang Hai chih ko* shih kung-ch'an-chu-i ti chan-ko', *Wen-i pao*, No. 4, 1966; 'A Battle Song of Communism', *Chinese Literature*, No. 7, 1966.

Liu Shao-t'ang, 'Wo tui tang-ch'ien wen-i wen-t'i i-hsieh i-chien' (My Opinions on the Current Problems in Literature), *Wen-i hsüeh-hsi*, No. 5, 1957.

Lo Kuang-pin, Lin Teh-pin, and Yang Yi-yen, 'Tsai lieh-huo chung teh-tao yung-sheng' (Immortality in Blazing Fire), *Hung-ch'i p'iao-p'iao*, No. 6, 1958.

—————, *Tsai lieh-huo chung teh-tao yung-sheng* (*Immortality in Blazing Fire*) (Peking: Chinese Youth Publishing House, 1959).

Lo Sun, 'Tsui Sheng-tung ti kung-ch'an-chu-i chiao-k'o-shu' (Most Lively Textbook of Communism), *Wen-i pao*, No. 3, 1962.

Lou Hsi, 'I-tai feng-liu ti k'ai-tuan — P'ing *San chia hsiang*' (Prelude to a Generation of Noble Spirits — Comments on *Three Family Lane*), *Tso-p'in*, May 1960.

Lu Chien, 'Chao Shu-li and His Writing', *Chinese Literature*, No. 9, 1964.

Lu I-fan, '*San chia hsiang* ho *K'u tou* ti ts'o-wu ssu-hsiang ch'ing-hsiang — Chien yü Miu Chün-chieh, Lu Tsu-p'in, Chou Hsiu-ch'iang san t'ung-chih shang-chioh' (The Erroneous Thought Tendency in *Three Family Lane* and *Bitter Struggle* — to consult with Comrades Miu Chün-chieh, Lu Tsu-p'in and Chou Hsiu-ch'iang), *Wen-hsüeh p'ing-lun*, No. 5, 1964.

Lung Shih-hui, '*Lin Hai hsüeh yüan* ti jen-wu k'e-hua chi ch'i-t'a' (Characterization and Related Matters in *Tracks in the Snowy Forest*), *Jen-min wen-hsüeh*, No. 1, 1958.

Ma Ching-po, 'Tu *Lin hai hsüeh yüan* hou so-hsiang-ch'i-ti' (Thoughts after Reading *Tracks in the Snowy Forest*), *Jen-min wen-hsüeh*, No. 1, 1958.

Ma Han-ping, 'Tu *Pao-wei Yen-an* ti chi-chang' (After Reading the Serialized Chapters of *Defense of Yenan*), *Chieh-fang-chün wen-i*, May 1954.

Ma Shih-t'u, 'Ch'ieh shuo *Hung yen*' (Speaking of *Red Crag*), *Chung-kuo ch'ing-nien*, No. 11, 1962.

Ma T'ieh-ting, 'Lun *Ch'ing-ch'un chih ko* chi ch'i lun-cheng' (On the Controversy over *The Song of Youth*), *Wen-i pao*, No. 9, 1959.

Mao Hsing, 'Tui shih-nien-lai hsin Chung-kuo wen-hsüeh fa-chan ti i-hsieh li-chieh' (Some Insight into the Development of Literature in New China in the last ten years), *Wen-hsüeh p'ing-lun*, No. 5, 1959.

Mao Tse-tung, 'Kuan-yü cheng-ch'ioh ch'u-li jen-min nei-pu mao-tun ti wen-t'i' (On the Correct Handling of Contradictions among the People), *Mao Tse-tung chu-tso hsüan-tu* (Peking: People Publishing House, 1966).

—————, 'Tsai Yen-an wen-i tso-t'an-hui shang ti chiang-hua' (Talks at the Yenan Forum on Art and Literature', *Mao Tse-tung hsüan-chi*, Vol. III (Peking: People Publishing House, 1953).

Mao Tun, 'Fan-ying she-hui-chu-i yo-chin ti shih-tai, t'ui-tung she-hui-chu-i ti yo-chin', *Jen-min wen-hsüeh*, August 1960; 'Reflect the Age of the Socialist Leap Forward, Promote the Leap Forward of the Socialist Age! — a Report delivered to the Third Congress of Chinese Literary and Art Workers on July 24, 1960', *Chinese Literature*, Nos. 11 and 12, 1960.

—————, 'Tsen-yang p'ing-chia *Ch'ing-ch'un chih ko* (How to Evaluate *The Song of Youth*), *Chung-kuo ch'ing-nien*, No. 4, 1959.

—————, 'Tu liao *Huo chung* i-hou ti tien-ti kan-hsiang' (Thoughts after reading *Seeds of Flame*), *Shuo-huo*, No. 2, 1964.

Miu Chün-chieh, Lu Tsu-p'in, Chou Hsiu-ch'iang, 'Kuan-yii Chou Ping hsing-hsiang ti p'ing-chia wen-t'i – Yü Ts'ai K'uei t'ung-chih shang-chioh' (Concerning the Evaluation of the Image of Chou Ping – to Consult with Comrade Ts'ai K'uei), *Wen-hsüeh p'ing-lun*, No. 4, 1964.

Mu Yang, 'Ts'ung Shao Shun-pao, Liang san lao-han so-hsiang-tao-ti' (Thoughts about Shao Shun-pao and Liang the Third), *Wen-i pao*, September 1962.

Pa Jen, 'Lioh lun ying-hsiung jen-wu' (A Brief Discussion on Hero Character', *Jen-min wen-hsüeh*, No. 2, 1958.

––––––, 'Man-t'an *Pai lien ch'eng kang* (Some General Observations on *Steeled and Tempered*), *Wen-i pao*, No. 7, 1958.

––––––, 'Tien-hsing wen-t'i sui-kan' (Random Thoughts on the Question of Typical Characters), *Wen-i pao*, May 1956.

Pei-ching-ta-hsüeh chung-wen-hsi ssu-nien-chi 'Chung-hua-jen-min kung-ho-kuo wen-hsüeh-shih' pien-wei-hui hsiao-shuo-tsu (The Novel Section of the Committee on the Compilation of 'History of Literature of the People's Republic of China' of the Senior Class, Department of Chinese Literature, Peking University), *'Pao-wei Yen-an* – Chieh-fang chan-cheng ti shih-shih' (*Defense of Yenan* – Epic of the War of Liberation), *Wen-hsüeh chih-shih*, January 1959.

Pei-ching-ta-hsüeh chung-wen-hsi ssu-nien-chi tang-tai wen-hsüeh p'ing-lun-tsu (The Contemporary Literature Review Section of the Senior Class, Department of Chinese Literature, Peking University), 'Kung-ch'an-tang-yüan ti kuang-hui hsing-hsiang – *Yeh-huo ch'un-feng tou ku-ch'eng* tu hou' (Shining Images of Communists – On *In an Old City*), *Kuang-ming jih-pao*, January 30, 1959.

Pei-ching T'ung-hsien Hsü-hsin-chuang kung-she Hsiao-ying ta-tui tu-shu hsiao-tsu (The Study Group of Hsiaoying Production Brigade, Hsühsinchuang Commune, T'unghsien, Peking), 'Ying-hsiung hsing hsiang ku-wu ho chiao-yu wo-men' (Hero Characters encourage and educate us), *Wen-hsüeh p'ing-lun*, No. 1, 1966.

'Sanliwan Village', *Chinese Literature*, No. 4, 1955.

Shanghai Revolutionary Mass Criticism Group, 'A Reactionary Novel Which Commemorated an Erroneous Line – Comments on Ou-yang Shan's "A Generation of Noble Spirits",' *Chinese Literature*, No. 3, 1970.

Shao Ch'üan-lin, 'Wen-hsüeh shih-nien li-ch'eng', *Wen-i pao*, No. 18, 1959; 'The Writing of the Last Ten Years', *Chinese Literature*, No. 12, 1959.

'Shih-wu-nien-lai tzu-ch'an-chieh-chi shih tsen-yang fan-tui ch'uang-tsao kung nung ping ying-hsiung jen-wu ti' (How the Bourgeoisie Opposed the Creation of Worker, Peasant, and Soldier Heroes in the Last Fifteen Years), *Wen-i pao*, No. 11/12, 1964.

Shih Yen, '*Hung jih* ti jen-wu' (Some Characters in *Red Sun*), *Chieh-fang-chün wen-i*, July 1958.

Staff Reporter, 'I-chiu-liu-erh nien ch'ang-p'ien chung-p'ien hsün-li' (A

Review of Novels and Novelettes published in 1962), *Wen-i pao*, No. 1, 1963.

————, 'I-chiu-liu-i nien ch'ang-p'ien hsiao-shuo yin-hsiang chi' (Impressions of Novels published in 1961), *Wen-i pao*, No. 2, 1962.

Ssu Niao, 'Lun *Lin hai hsüeh yüan* ti ch'uang-tso fang-fa' (On the Writing Skills of *Tracks in the Snowy Forest*), *Ch'ang-chiang wen-i*, April 1959.

'Su-lien ta-shih-kuan tai-piao Ssu-ta-lin chiang-chin wei-yüan-hui shou-yü Ting Ling teng Ssu-ta-lin chiang-chin' (The Soviet Embassy representing the Stalin Award Committee confers Stalin Prizes on Ting Ling and others), *Wen-i pao*, No. 11/12, 1952.

T'ang Chih (T'ang Ta-ch'eng), 'Fan-suo kung-shih k'o-i chih-tao ch'uang-tso ma? – Yü Chou Yang t'ung-chih shang-chioh chi-ko kuan-yü ch'uang-tsao ying-hsiung jen-wu ti lun-tien' (Can a Scholastic Formula guide Creative Writing – discussing some Views concerning the Creation of Hero Characters with Comrade Chou Yang), *Wen-i pao*, No. 10, 1957.

Ti T'ung-t'ai, 'T'an Chou Ta-yung ho t'a-ti lien-tui' (Chou Ta-yung and His Company), *Yü-wen chiao-hsüeh*, No. 15, 1957.

Ting Ling, 'Life and Creative Writing', *Chinese Literature*, No. 3, 1954.

Ts'ai K'uei, 'Chou Ping hsing-hsiang chi ch'i-t'a – Kuan-yü *San chia hsiang* ho *K'u tou* ti p'ing-chia wen-t'i' (The Image of Chou Ping and Other Problems – Concerning the Evaluation of *Three Family Lane* and *Bitter Struggle*), *Wen-hsüeh p'ing-lun*, No. 2, 1964.

Tso P'ing, 'Hsiao tzu-ch'an-chieh-chi ti tzu-wo piao-hsien – Kuan-yü *San chia hsiang*, *K'u tou* ti t'ao-lun tsung-shu' (Self-Expression of the Petty Bourgeois – a Summary Report of Discussions concerning *Three Family Lane* and *Bitter Struggle*), *Wen-i pao*, No. 10, 1964.

————, 'P'in hsia-chung nung hsi tu *Yen yang t'ien*' (Poor and lower middle Peasants enjoy reading *Bright Sunny Days*), *Wen-i pao*, No. 2, 1965.

Tu Li-chün, 'T'an fan-mien jen-wu ti hsing-ke miao-hsieh' (On the Portrayal of Negative Characters), *Jen-min wen-hsüeh*, November 1956.

Tu Peng-cheng, 'What Makes Me Write', *Chinese Literature*, No. 1, 1960.

Wang Chao-wen, 'Chan-tou-hsing ti hsin-li miao-hsieh' (Psychological Description of Heroic Struggle), *Wen-i pao*, No. 3, 1962.

Wang Chung-ch'ing, 'T'an Chao Shu-li ti *San-li-wan*' (Comments on Chao Shu-li's *Sanliwan Village*), *Jen-min wen-hsüeh*, November 1958.

Wang Hsi-yen, 'Shih lun *Pai lien ch'eng kang*' (Preliminary Comments on *Steeled and Tempered*), *Wen-hsüeh p'ing-lun*, No. 4, 1959.

————, 'Tu *Shan hsiang chü-pien*' (On *Great Changes in a Mountain Village*), *Jen-min wen-hsüeh*, July 1958.

Wang Jo-yü, 'Kuan-yü wen-hsüeh ch'uang-tso chung tang ti ling-tao kan-pu hsing-hsiang' (On the Image of Party Cadre in Literary Works), *Jen-min wen-hsüeh*, August 1956.

Wang Liao-ying, '*T'ai-yang chao tsai Sang-kan ho shang* chiu-ching shih shih-mo-yang ti tso-p'in?' (What Kind of Work is *Sun over the Sangkan River?*), *Wen-hsüeh p'ing-lun*, No. 1, 1959.

Wang Shih-teh, 'P'ing-chieh *Hsiao-ch'eng ch'un-ch'iu*' (On *Annals of a Provincial Town*), *Wen-i pao*, No. 3, 1958.

Wang Yü, 'T'an *San-li wan* chung ti jen-wu miao-hsieh' (Characterization in *Sanliwan Village*), *Wen-i yüeh-pao*, September 1955.

————, 'Tu *Hung jih*' (On *Red Sun*), *Yen-ho*, June 1957.

Wen Chieh-jo, '*Hung yen* tsai Jih-pen' (*Red Crag* in Japan), *Wen-i pao*, No. 3, 1964.

Wu Chiang, 'Hsieh-tso *Hung jih* ti chi-tien kan-shou' (Thoughts after writing *Red Sun*), *Wen-i pao*, No. 19, 1958.

————, 'Hsieh-tso *Hung jih* ti ch'ing-k'uang ho i-hsieh t'i-hui' (The Conditions under which I wrote *Red Sun* and some of my Comprehensions), *Jen-min wen-hsüeh*, January 1960.

————, 'Man-t'an hsieh hsiao-shuo' (Some General Observations on Novel Writing), *Wen-i yüeh-pao*, December 1958.

Wu Chung-chieh and Kao Yun, 'T'an Liang Sheng-pao hsing-hsiang ti ch'uang-tsao' (On the Image of Liang Sheng-pao), *Wen-hsüeh p'ing-lun*, No. 3, 1964.

Wu Yang, 'Yang Mo and her Novel *The Song of Youth*', *Chinese Literature*, No. 9, 1962.

Yang Mo, '*Ch'ing-ch'un chih ko* tsai-pan hou-chi' (Postscript to the Second Edition of *The Song of Youth*), *Kuang-ming jih pao*, January 19, 1960,

————, 'Shih-mo li-liang ku-wu wo hsieh *Ch'ing-ch'un chih ko*' (Forces that encouraged me to write *The Song of Youth*), *Chung-kuo ch'ing-nien pao*, May 3, 1958.

————, T'an Lin Tao-ching ti hsing-hsiang' (About the Image of Lin Tao-ching), *Jen-min wen-hsüeh*, No. 7, 1959.

Yao Pen, 'P'ing *Yeh-huo ch'un-feng tou ku-ch'eng*' (On *In an Old City*), *Wen-i yüeh-pao*, January 1959.

Yao Wen-yuan, 'I-pu shan-yao-choh kung-ch'an-chu-i ssu-hsiang kuang-hui ti hsiao-shuo — Lun *Ch'ing-ch'un chih ko* tsai ssu-hsiang shang ho i-shu shang ti t'eh-seh" (A Novel radiating the Light of Communism — Comments on the Ideology and Art of *The Song of Youth*), *Yü-wen chiao-hsüeh*, October 1958.

————, 'Chung-kuo nung-ts'un she-hui-chu-i ke-ming shih — Tu *Ch'uang yeh shih*' (Epic of the Socialist Revolution in Rural China), *Wen-i pao*, No. 17/18, 1960.

————, *Tsai ch'ien-chin ti tao-lu shang* (*On the Road to Progress*) (Shanghai: People's Literature House, 1965).

Yen Chia-yen, 'Kuan-yü Liang Sheng-pao hsing-hsiang' (Concerning the Image of Liang Sheng-pao), *Wen-hsüeh p'ing-lun*, No. 3, 1963.

————, 'Liang Sheng-pao ho hsin ying-hsiung jen-wu ch'uang-tsao wen-t'i' (Liang Sheng-pao and the Problem of Creating New Hero Characters), *Wen-hsüeh p'ing-lun*, No. 4, 1964.

————, 'T'an *Ch'uang yeh shih* chung Liang san lao-han ti hsing-hsiang' (Comments on the Image of Liang the Third of *The Builders*), *Wen-hsüeh p'ing-lun*, No. 3, 1961.

Yen Li, 'I-chiu-liu-san nien ti ch'ang-pien chung-p'ien hsiao-shuo' (Novels and Novelettes of 1963), *Wen-i pao*, No. 1, 1964.

Yen Kang, '*Po huo chi*' (On *Sowing the Flames*), *Wen-i pao*, No. 1, 1964.

Yen Wen-ching, 'Mao Tse-tung ssu-hsiang tsai wen-hsüeh fang-mien ti sheng-li' (The Triumph of Mao Tse-tung's Thought in Literature), *Wen-i pao*, No. 3, 1966.

Ying Ch'i-hou, '*Pai lien ch'eng kang* ti chi-ko jen-wu hsing-hsiang' (Some Characters in *Steeled and Tempered*), *Wen-i yüeh-pao*, April 1958.

Yü Tzu, 'Ou-yang Shan teng jen ti li-tzu cheng-ming-liao shih-mo' (What Have the Examples of Ou-yang Shan et al. Shown?) *Wen-i pao*, No. 4, 1952.

INDEX

INDEX